Open Wide the Doors to Christ

Discovering Catholicism

Open Wide the Doors to Christ

Discovering Catholicism

Lucas R. Pollice, MTS

Foreword by Bishop Kevin W. Vann of Fort Worth

Emmaus Road Publishing
Steubenville, Ohio
www.emmausroad.org

Emmaus Road Publishing
1468 Parkview Circle
Steubenville, Ohio 43952

 Published 2013
Printed in the United States of America.
Fifth printing 2023

Library of Congress Control Number: 2013950305
ISBN: 978-1-937155-16-2

Cover design and layout by: Theresa Westling
Image credit: Archway into the Sun / iStockphoto

Imprimatur: Most Rev. Kevin W. Vann, JCD, DD
Bishop of Fort Worth
October 21, 2008

The Imprimatur is an official declaration
that a book is free from doctrinal or moral error.
No implication is contained therein that those who
grant the imprimatur agree with the contents,
opinions, or statements expressed.

Acknowledgements

To Pope John Paul II

The Church is forever indebted and grateful to you for your example, your teachings, and your great love for Christ.

"Well done, my good and faithful servant. . . . Come, share your master's joy." (Mt. 25:21)

Pope John Paul II, pray for us.

Many people made this book possible in a variety of ways, to all of whom I am truly grateful. I am deeply indebted to my mother-in-law, Marynell Konderla, for all of her countless hours spent in tedious editing and layout. Without her unselfish dedication, this book would not have been possible. I am also very grateful to my father-in-law, John Konderla, for believing in the vision of this book and for providing the financial support necessary for making this a reality.

Thanks also to my sister Jennifer Darrow, Matt and Lauren Warner, Christi Morrow, Shannon Morrow, and John and Mandy Cox, for their help in the cover design, editing, and for their many great ideas and insights.

I also thank those who have supported me in my ministry over the years. I especially thank Bishop Kevin Vann for his confidence in me and for his enthusiastic support for this book. I also thank Fr. Jim Gigliotti, T.O.R., and Fr. Mike Ciski, T.O.R., for their friendship, guidance, and pastoral wisdom. Thanks also to the many members of the RCIA team at Saint Maria Goretti Church for their dedication, support, and encouragement in the writing of this book.

I also thank the Konderla family for the great kitchen table theological discussions and insights, much of which are in this work.

I certainly am very indebted to the many professors who were so influential in my theological education at both Franciscan University of Steubenville and the Institute for Pastoral Theology at Ave Maria University. I especially thank Professor Douglas Bushman for his inspiration and love for the Church.

I am deeply grateful to my parents, John and Kathy Pollice, for their love, prayers, and constant encouragement, and especially for giving me the gift of my Catholic faith.

Finally, to my beloved wife, Mary, and to my children, Cecilia, Nick, Tim, Christian, and Julia: thank you for your inspiration, for your daily witness to me of Christ's love, and for the many sacrifices you have made to make this book possible. To you all, I am forever grateful!

Contents

Part One
THE CREED: THE PROFESSION OF FAITH

Section I: I believe in God the Father Almighty, Creator of Heaven and Earth

Section II: I believe in Jesus Christ, the Only Son of God

Section III: I believe in the Holy Spirit, the Holy Catholic Church, the Communion of Saints, and Life Everlasting

Part Two
THE SACRAMENTS: THE CELEBRATION OF THE CHRISTIAN MYSTERY

Part Three
LIVING AND WITNESSING THE CHRISTIAN LIFE

Abbreviations

Gen.	Genesis	Ob.	Obadiah
Ex.	Exodus	Jon.	Jonah
Lev.	Leviticus	Mic.	Micah
Num.	Numbers	Na.	Nahum
Deut.	Deuteronomy	Hb.	Habakkuk
Josh.	Joshua	Zeph.	Zephaniah
Judg.	Judges	Hg.	Haggai
Ruth	Ruth	Zech.	Zechariah
1 Sam.	1 Samuel	Mal.	Malachi
2 Sam.	2 Samuel	Mt.	Matthew
1 Kings	1 Kings	Mk.	Mark
2 Kings	2 Kings	Lk.	Luke
1 Chr.	1 Chronicles	Jn.	John
2 Chr.	2 Chronicles	Acts	Acts of the Apostles
Ezra	Ezra	Rom.	Romans
Neh.	Nehemiah	1 Cor.	1 Corinthians
Tob.	Tobit	2 Cor.	2 Corinthians
Jdt.	Judith	Gal.	Galatians
Esth.	Esther	Eph.	Ephesians
1 Macc.	1 Maccabees	Phil.	Philippians
2 Macc.	2 Maccabees	Col.	Colossians
Job	Job	1 Thess.	1 Thessalonians
Ps.	Psalms	2 Thess.	2 Thessalonians
Prov.	Proverbs	1 Tim.	1 Timothy
Eccl.	Ecclesiastes	2 Tim.	2 Timothy
Song	Song of Songs	Titus	Titus
Wis.	Wisdom	Philem.	Philemon
Sir.	Sirach	Heb.	Hebrews
Is.	Isaiah	Jas.	James
Jer.	Jeremiah	1 Pet.	1 Peter
Lam.	Lamentations	2 Pet.	2 Peter
Bar.	Baruch	1 Jn.	1 John
Ezek.	Ezekiel	2 Jn.	2 John
Dan.	Daniel	3 Jn.	3 John
Hos.	Hosea	Jude	Jude
Joel	Joel	Rev.	Revelation
Am.	Amos		

Note to the Reader

- All quotes have been presented exactly as they were in the original source; therefore, pronouns and adjectives relating to God may differ in style with the text of this book. This also creates differences in the capitalization of some words, as well as punctuation differences.
- **Bold Words**—At the end of each chapter is a list of "Key Words to Know" from the Catechism (also referred to as "CCC"). A bolded word within a chapter indicates that the word is included on this list.
- *Italicized words*—Within the text are italicized words that indicate that they are of special importance and meaning to the issue being addressed.

Foreword

Dear Brothers and Sisters in Christ,

When we recently observed the thirtieth anniversary of the election of Pope John Paul II, I thought back to the time when I was watching this momentous event on a television set at Kenrick Seminary in St. Louis, Missouri. We were just finishing lunch in the seminary refectory when one of the professors came into the dining hall to announce that, "The smoke is white!" We all rushed to the various television sets in the seminary. Somehow we knew that we were making history that day, and then again some days later when during the Mass to inaugurate the beginning of this pontificate he challenged each one of us to "Do not be afraid. . . . Open wide the doors to Christ."

We are only beginning just now, I believe, to appreciate the impact of his pontificate on the Body of Christ, the Church. Therefore, I believe that the title for this new important work of catechesis, *Open Wide the Doors to Christ: Discovering Catholicism*, by Lucas Pollice, of the Diocese of Fort Worth, is not only an apt title but a very fitting one for the age in which the Lord's providential care has brought us all.

To this work Mr. Pollice not only brings his academic background and training in theology, but also his experience as a catechist and Director of Religious Education at a large parish in the Diocese of Fort Worth, and now Director of Catechesis for the Diocese of Fort Worth. Most importantly, he brings to this work his own faith and commitment as a disciple of the Lord in his life as husband and father.

Just a glance at the table of contents will reveal that it is a sound and thorough resource for those seeking Baptism and entrance into the Catholic Church, and also for those seeking to be admitted to full communion through the process of the Rite of Christian Initiation for Adults. I have found this work to be easy to read, thorough and concise. The RCIA Teacher's edition should be a real help to catechists and teachers in all areas of the life of the Church. As pastor of parishes large and small, I was concerned at times if those enrolled in the RCIA process were being exposed to the fullness of the beauty and truth of our Faith, so they could make a free and informed decision. I believe that this work of Lucas Pollice certainly answers those concerns that I had as a parish priest. In addition to the RCIA, I believe this is also a great resource for adult education and catechesis in general. It is well indexed to the *Catechism of the Catholic Church*!

Most importantly, I believe it is important to see what begins and ends this work. It opens with what draws all people to our various programs and endeavors: Our search for God and our response to His promptings—"*Faith is our response to this gift of revelation that God freely offers to us through Christ*" (p. 5); and it ends with prayer—"*Prayer is essential to faith and a natural extension of our faith*" (p. 375). Thus, all of the content is seen in the context of faith and prayer, and our response to the call of God the Father, Son, and Holy Spirit in our lives, and how this is known and lived in the *communio* of Faith, the Church.

In this time which certainly reflects the ministry of John Paul II as Bishop of Rome and Universal Pastor, Mr. Pollice has done a great service for us in this book, which will help all of us to be better disciples and followers of Christ, so that we can ever more open the doors of our hearts to Him and *be not afraid!*

† Kevin W. Vann
Bishop of Fort Worth
October 21, 2008

Introduction

The title *Open Wide the Doors to Christ* was chosen for this book because it speaks so directly and powerfully to what it means to be a Christian in our modern world today. In fact, it was with these simple yet profound words, "Open wide the doors to Christ," that *both* Pope John Paul II and Pope Benedict XVI began their ministries, which would lead the Church into the third millennium. What does it mean to open wide the doors to Christ? How does this invite us to live our calling as His followers?

I would like to begin with the words of Pope Benedict XVI as he concluded his homily during his first Mass as pope. This homily serves as a mission statement, not only for the ministry on which he was embarking, but also as the mission for the entire Church. Let us start by reflecting on these powerful words of Benedict XVI:

> At this point, my thoughts return to 22 October 1978, when Pope John Paul II began his ministry here in Saint Peter's Square. His words on that occasion constantly echo in my ears: "Do not be afraid! Open wide the doors to Christ!"
>
> The Pope was addressing the mighty, the powerful of this world, who feared that Christ might take away something of their power if they were to let him in, if they were to allow the faith to be free. . . . The Pope was also speaking to everyone, especially the young. Are we not perhaps all afraid in some way? If we let Christ enter fully into our lives, if we open ourselves totally to him, are we not afraid that he might take something away from us? Are we not perhaps afraid to give up something significant, something unique, something that makes life so beautiful? Do we not then risk ending up diminished and deprived of our freedom?
>
> And once again the Pope said: No! If we let Christ into our lives, we lose nothing, nothing, absolutely nothing of what makes life free, beautiful and great. No! Only in this friendship are the doors of life opened wide. Only in this friendship is the great potential of human existence truly revealed. Only in this friendship do we experience beauty and liberation.
>
> And so, today, with great strength and great conviction, on the basis of long personal experience of life, I say to you, dear

> young people: Do not be afraid of Christ! He takes nothing away, and he gives you everything. When we give ourselves to him, we receive a hundredfold in return. Yes, open, open wide the doors to Christ—and you will find true life. Amen. (Papal Installation Mass, April 24, 2005)

Pope Benedict XVI's words so beautifully call us to completely open ourselves to Christ, who is the Way, the Truth, and the Life.

Our modern culture presents for us a strange dualism. On the one hand it seeks to understand and solve questions of the deepest meaning of the universe, the world around us, the purpose and meaning of life, and our existence as human beings. But at the same time it often presents a culture of fear, hopelessness, and death.

As Pope John Paul II so powerfully expressed in his first encyclical letter in 1979, "The Redeemer of Man" *(Redemptor hominis):* Christ is the answer! He is the One who comes to reveal to us the fullness of truth, the truth about God, and the truth about ourselves. He is the answer only if we open ourselves fully to Him.

Pope John Paul II not only taught this, he *lived* it. He showed us that there is nothing to fear in embracing Christ, no matter what life throws at us. His life witnessed to us that only in Christ is it possible for a humble man from Poland to take the world by storm. His life was evidence that one could face the fears and tragedies of life, even an assassin's bullet, and still experience and express the love of God. He proved that through Christ, love and peace could conquer the seemingly invincible evil of communism. And finally, in his last days, he witnessed to the world that only in Christ is death the beautiful sleep through which we awaken into eternal life.

Following his example, *what is there to be afraid of? What do we have to lose?* We must open wide the doors to Christ and to the beauty and power of His truth, so that we may truly find the meaning of life. This is the message and mission that we must all take to our modern culture: in Christ there is only life and truth. Coming into contact with the truth of Christ, and believing it, is like breathing pure oxygen, and once you get a breath of it, you do not forget it.

Many people have given in to the temptation of watering down the truth through fear of proclaiming it in its fullness. They have abandoned, or forgotten, the richness of the two-thousand-plus years of Christian Tradition handed down through the Church. Many adult Catholics do not know their faith, and are missing out on the beauty and true freedom that is Catholicism because they fear to embrace the truth and embrace Christ. In many catechetical circles, Catholicism has lost its radiant beauty and power and has become quite benign, and it has often taken the form of a purely cultural phenomenon. The time has come at the dawn of the new evangelization, envisioned by Pope John Paul II, to reclaim this beauty and power of the Catholic faith, especially in the areas of catechesis and evangelization. The time has truly come: *"Do not be afraid! Open wide the doors to Christ!"*

In light of this calling of the Church I present this book as a very thorough and detailed presentation of the faith. It will enable its readers, whether they are in the process of becoming Catholic, or are already Catholic, to experience the transforming power of the truth of Christ. While it is not an exhaustive presentation of the teachings of the Church, this book is written to present the foundational truths of Catholicism, the "meat and potatoes" of the faith, so that its readers can be truly grounded and immersed in what it means to be Catholic. It is intended to be an introduction to, and a presentation of, the Church's teachings on the creed, the sacraments, the moral life, and prayer. I've written it with those who are learning and seeking to become Catholic in mind.

Included with each chapter are the sections of the *Catechism of the Catholic Church* (also referred to as "Catechism" or "CCC") that address the material covered, so that readers can continue their learning. This book also presents the Catholic faith in a way that adults can understand, while at the same time challenging its readers to dig deeper and hopefully to continue to grow in understanding of their faith.

The material, as one will see, does not shy away from even the most difficult and countercultural teachings of Christ and His Church. For what do we have to be afraid of? The truth sets us free. Catholics and those who are seeking to be Catholic should be inspired by the teachings of the Church. They are not just rules and regulations, nor a set of laws that limit our freedom and potential. One cannot approach the faith as simply a set of rigid teachings and moral rules. It is so much more than that. *The teachings of Christ and the Church are the very answers to the deepest longings of the human heart.* They are not a no to this or a no to that, but rather a *yes to life and goodness and freedom.* This is what Jesus Himself was telling us when He said, "I came so that they might have life and have it more abundantly" (Jn. 10:10). To open wide the doors to Christ is to open ourselves to the fullness of life and what it means to be human.

This book is also a presentation of the faith in light of the teachings of the Second Vatican Council and the writings of Pope John Paul II. Vatican II and John Paul II do not present new teachings, or doctrines, but instead they present the Catholic faith in a *new and dynamic way* that answers the many facets and dimensions of the pressing questions our modern society so often asks. They both present a powerful exposition of faith that reaches out to the modern world and invites a response. Their presentation of the truths of Christ enables people to truly open wide the doors of their hearts and minds without fear. I hope this book will further a dialogue, a dialogue of love and truth that Christ desires to have with each one of us, if only we open our hearts and minds to Him.

This book was especially written in light of the *Rite of Christian Initiation of Adults* (RCIA), which is the process established by the Church through which she brings in new members. It is so important for those who come to the Church and join her faithful to be well formed in the faith. RCIA presents a unique moment of evangelization, not only to those who are seeking to become Catholic, but also to their spouses, families, sponsors, and the parish community. Often the new converts to Catholicism remind all, especially cradle Catholics, of the power and richness of the faith. Converts come to the Church seeking to know Christ and the fullness of the faith. It is the *serious responsibility* of the Church, and those to whom this ministry of evangelization and catechesis has been entrusted, to form the candidates and catechumens in the faith, so that they are able to embrace and live Catholicism to its fullness.

This book is given as a powerful tool to catechize and evangelize converts to Catholicism, and to form them and encourage them to truly open wide the doors to Christ and His Church. It will help those who are becoming Catholics to learn the sources and roots of their faith, and also help them to discover new ways of knowing and experiencing the Tradition of the Church, especially in the light of Vatican II and the dynamic papacy and teachings of Pope John Paul II. My sincere hope is that this book will help them along the journey of *faith seeking understanding* that accompanies daily ongoing conversion to which we are all called.

I conclude with the unforgettable and encouraging words of Saint Paul.

> For I am convinced that neither death, nor life, nor angels, nor principalities, nor present things, nor future things, nor powers, nor height, nor depth, nor any other creature will be able to separate us from the love of God in Christ Jesus our Lord. (Rom. 8:38–39)

Do not be afraid! Open wide the doors to Christ!

PART ONE

THE CREED: THE PROFESSION OF FAITH

Chapter 1

What Is Faith?

Reading the Catechism: Paragraphs 26–49; 142–197

> Faith and reason are like two wings on which the human spirit rises to the contemplation of truth; and God has placed in the human heart a desire to know the truth—in a word, to know himself—so that, by knowing and loving God, men and women may also come to the fullness of truth about themselves.
>
> —Pope John Paul II, Encyclical Letter on Faith and Reason *Fides et ratio* (September 14, 1998), no. 1.

We begin our discussion of Catholic belief by addressing the basic question of faith. What exactly is faith, and what does it mean to have it?

Faith is our response to what God reveals. It is not merely the intellectual assent to a revealed truth, which we cannot fully understand; it is the full submission and surrender of our whole self, our intellect *and* will, to all that He reveals to us.

This surrendering allows God to penetrate our life, our entire being, so that we may be transformed and become holy, allowing Christ to work in and through us so that we may share in His very life. "[Y]et I live, no longer I, but Christ lives in me" (Gal. 2:20).

Faith is at the very foundation of the Christian life because it is our response to the invitation of our Creator to have communion with Him. It is through faith that we completely open ourselves to Him and come into relationship with Him.

Man's Search for God

God created man to be in His presence and be filled with His life. When He created Adam, He "blew into his nostrils the breath of life" (Gen. 2:7). This breath of life is divine life, an intimate union and sharing in the life of God.

It is our very nature as human beings to desire God and to be in communion with Him. This is what is meant when the Catechism states, *man is by nature a religious being* (see 28). We all have a "God-sized" hole in our hearts that only He can fill. We long to answer the questions of life, to fill our emptiness with truth, to have fullness of life. Saint Augustine realized this profound truth about human nature when he beautifully wrote, "You have made us for yourself, O Lord, and our hearts are restless until they rest in you" (*Confessions of St. Augustine*).

Throughout history, in every culture and place, evidence is found of man seeking the divine; seeking the communion and relationship with God for which he was made. Numerous examples of religious expression are found in the traditions of the Greeks and Romans, the Egyptians and Babylonians, the Vikings and Native Americans, and the various expressions of Eastern spirituality. These cultures had very little in common and little, or no, contact with each other, yet each had its own way of reaching out to know the divine. Even the great ancient philosophers like Plato and Aristotle, through reason alone, came to the conclusion that there must be a transcendent supreme being.

Because man's reason is darkened by sin, and because we are finite physical creatures, we can come to know God only in a very limited sense and only through what He has created. This is why so many expressions of religious belief were the worship of nature.

However, because God loved us so much and desired to once again have communion with us, He unfolded His loving plan of salvation in which He chose to reveal Himself to man. He first did this through His gradual **revelation** of Himself to His chosen people as seen in the Old Testament, and then, in the fullness of time, He completely revealed Himself to us through His Son, Jesus Christ. Jesus, fully divine and fully human, came to make known not only who God our loving Father is, but to show us what it means to be fully human. His life demonstrated what it means to live with the Father in total communion and obedience, and through that relationship to enjoy the fullness of life with Him. The Son of man (Mt. 8:20) is the perfect man who completely reveals man to Himself. Jesus offers to all people the possibility of union with God for which all men have been searching throughout history. That union with the transcendent, the divine, is what fulfills man's nature and gives life its ultimate meaning. "I came so that they might have life and have it more abundantly" (Jn. 10:10).

Faith: Our Response to God

Faith is our response to this gift of revelation that God freely offers to us through Christ. It is not just mere intellectual activity, or the simple acceptance of something as true that cannot be "proven." Rather, it is the *complete submission of our intellect and will* to God who reveals Himself and offers salvation to us. It is an offering up to our Creator, a rending open of our hearts and minds to Him so that we may fully receive all that He desires to give us. Our response of complete submission to Him is called the "obedience of faith." We hear and see what He has spoken to us, done for us, and asks of us; we accept it with our whole minds and hearts so that God's salvation may be accomplished in us.

> The obedience of faith (Rom. 16:26; see 1:5; 2 Cor. 10:5–6) is to be given to God who reveals, an obedience by which man commits his whole self freely to God, offering the full submission of intellect and will to God who reveals [First Vatican Council, Dogmatic Constitution on the Catholic Faith, Chap. 3], and freely assenting to the truth revealed by Him. (Second Vatican Council, Dogmatic Constitution on Divine Revelation *Dei Verbum* [November 18, 1965], no. 5)

Responding to faith does involve our intellect. It is the assent of our minds to revealed truths that we cannot yet fully comprehend in this life. But God does not simply want us to know Him intellectually; He wants us to live in Him and experience Him intimately. Therefore, a complete response of faith also involves the submission of our wills, a surrendering of all that we are and all that we do. Through our obedience of faith, God can transform us, heal us, and use us as His instruments so that we can fully experience and participate in His life.

Have you ever heard the expression "Actions speak louder than words"? This is true because *action follows from being*—our actions express the true disposition of our heart and mind. If we truly believe in God, all that we are and all that we do will flow from that core belief and our desire to be in union with Him. Our faith in Him will affect every aspect of our life, not only what we think, but even more profoundly, what we do.

For example, is it enough to simply know that I love my wife, but do nothing to show my love? Shouldn't my actions and the entire way I approach life be a reflection of this love? As a matter of fact, aren't my actions the most profound statement of my heart? In the same way, a husband can believe that he loves his wife and even state it for the world to hear, while gravely betraying that love through his actions.

The same holds true with our faith in God. If we truly desire to know and love Him, and become a true follower of Christ, is it enough to merely know Him or simply tell Him we love Him without it being reflected in our lives? No. If we truly love Him, then our whole lives, everything that we say and do, will reflect that love and show in our actions. This is exactly what Saint James teaches us in his epistle.

> What good is it, my brothers, if someone says that he has faith but does not have works? Can that faith save him? If a brother or sister has nothing to wear and has no food for the day, and one of you says to them, "Go in peace, keep warm, and eat well," but you do not give them the necessities of the body, what good is it? So also faith of itself, if it does not have works, is dead. (Jas. 2:14–17)

It is vital for us to remember that faith is the full submission of ourselves to what we believe. It goes beyond mere intellectual belief. It is an act of intellect *and* will, requiring a total response of heart, thought, and action.

Abraham and Mary: Examples of "The Obedience of Faith"

To further understand faith as a complete submission of intellect and will, let us look at two exceptional examples.

First, in the Old Testament of Scripture we see the example of Abraham who was asked by God to sacrifice his own beloved son. Although he did not understand God's purpose he was willing to be completely obedient. Abraham was ready to sacrifice his precious child with a faith that strengthened him to follow God's will. Not only does this foreshadow God's own sacrifice of His Son, it shows the faith of a man that extends far beyond mere belief to the very core of his being. It shows the obedience of a father who is willing to sacrifice the child of his heart to the will of God in whom he had put his trust (see Gen. 22:1–18).

Then in the New Testament, we see the example of Jesus' mother Mary. Her faith was truly tested when she was a young girl, around thirteen years of age. She had lived her faith daily throughout her life, but this test of faith was one that would change the course of history. She was asked by a messenger from God to bear the Incarnation of God, the Messiah, whom she and her people had been awaiting for several thousand years. She was asked to play a pivotal role in God's plan for the salvation of the world, and she did not turn away from the responsibility that was being placed before her. In complete trust she accepted that her virgin body would bear God's Son, although she did not completely understand how it could be. She stepped into the unknown of God's plan humbly pledging to be the "handmaid of the Lord." In words anticipating those of her own Son years later (see Lk. 22:42), she said, "Be it done unto me according to your word" (Lk. 1:26–38).

In both of these examples we see the profound faith with which we are called to act in our own lives. Abraham and Mary, like us, were mere humans called into relationship with the divine Creator of all things. A simple belief or acknowledgement of God was not enough. This communion with Him required the complete gift of self, body and soul, intellect and will. We are called to step forward with that same spirit into the unknown of God's plan for us, with a complete obedience of faith.

Essential Characteristics of Faith

Faith Is a Grace

Faith is both a gift and a grace of God. This is its first and most important characteristic. No one can have faith except through the grace of God and the power of the Holy Spirit. This is why we say that grace precedes faith.

The reason that you are reading this book right now, the whole reason that you desire a deeper understanding and relationship with God, is because He has called you to this moment and has given you the grace to respond in faith to His invitation.

We must always recognize that our own faith is a gift from God and is totally dependent upon His grace. It is very humbling to realize that we cannot take one step closer toward Him without His help. However, this reveals to us God's great love for us and that He is constantly drawing us closer to Himself. He desires union with us and has reached down to give us a gift that would allow us to know Him intimately despite our human limitations. As

Christians, we must always thank God for the gift of faith and always pray for the grace to sustain our faith in this life, whatever may come our way.

Faith, by Its Nature, Must Be Free

Since faith is a human act, by its nature it must be a free act. No one can force another to have faith. Although it is true that God bestows this gift on us, we have the capability to respond to it and accept it, or to turn away and reject it. Even God, in His omnipotence, cannot force us to believe in Him. He desires our union with Him, yet He respects our free will, and it is we who must choose to embrace His gift in order to receive it.

Moreover, faith in God and His revelation is the *realization of true freedom.* We can only experience true human freedom when we respond to the fullness of what it means to be human, when we find the truth for which we have been searching (see CCC, 160).

Faith Is a LifeLong Journey

Faith is an ongoing process, not just a one-time event of "coming to faith." Our hearts and minds must be open to God and His salvation each and every day so that He will be able to accomplish His work within us. Faith is the beginning of eternal life that will be fulfilled when we one day enjoy the fullness of God's presence in heaven. This openness, this "obedience of faith" to all that God has revealed to us through Christ, is the disposition we ought to have throughout our lives. Life, for man, is a journey of faith and ongoing **conversion** in which we turn away from sin and toward God. We come to know that transcendent God who draws us into relationship with Himself through a continuous opening of our hearts and minds to Him, and all that He desires for us and desires to give us.

Through the obedience of faith—the complete submission of our hearts and minds to God—we completely surrender and open ourselves to His revelation so that we may become holy and pleasing in His sight and accomplish His works. We give ourselves wholly and entirely to Him. *It is a total submission; it is holding nothing back.* We give Him our reason, our intellect, our will, who we are and what we do. We allow Him to guide us and to help us live the way that He wants us to live. This surrendering of ourselves to God through faith is the complete gift of ourselves to Him who has already pledged to us a total gift of Himself through Christ Jesus.

Are Faith and Reason Compatible?

Faith Seeking Understanding

One of the great Church Fathers, Saint Anselm, defined theology (the study or science of God) as "faith seeking understanding." Faith prompts us to seek a deeper knowledge of God and what His plan and will is for us.

Mary's example at the Annunciation shows great faith, but a faith that was seeking understanding. When the angel told her that she was going to conceive a child, she accepted with faith what God was telling her through the angel. She clung to His words; she believed them because they came from God, even though she did not fully understand them. But Mary's faith did not stop there. She sought to more deeply understand the meaning of God's word so that she could more deeply know, love, and serve Him better. She pondered His word in her heart and mind and asked questions. "How can this be, since I have no relations with a man?" (Lk. 1:34). *Asking questions is not doubting.* Mary's question does not show doubt, but rather shows that she believes God's revelation and desires to know His will even more profoundly so that she will be able to more perfectly cooperate with His plan.

Our relationship with God is like any relationship. Whether with a spouse or a friend, we seek to know ever more deeply who they are, and the more we come to truly know them, the more we can grow in love and friendship with them. The same applies to our faith in God and our relationship with Him. We certainly do not know everything about Him, but that does not mean we stop seeking.

God's revelation may be at times difficult to understand, or difficult to live, or very countercultural, but this does not mean we just reject it or give up. In those times, like Mary, we cling with faith to what God has revealed to us; we surrender our intellect and will to what He has made known. But then we ponder it, we ask questions, we read the Scriptures, we pray about it. What if Mary thought the angel's words were just too hard to accept and live out? What if she did not ponder God's word in her heart and ask questions? What if she did not pray for the grace to live faithfully according to His will?

Our faith in God requires that we always seek to more deeply understand His revelation so that we may more deeply love and serve Him.

Faith and Reason

One of the most common charges against faith in our modern culture is that it contradicts reason, or that beliefs we hold are unreasonable. Nothing could be further from the truth. Faith does not contradict reason, it builds upon and perfects it. It takes what we can know through our limited human reason and enables us to understand the truths about God and ourselves on a completely new level.

We see this with Mary during the Annunciation. It seems "unreasonable" that she could be with child since she had never had relations with a man. However, because of her faith and desire to understand, Mary continues to seek understanding of God's revelation and plan, and God reveals to her that her child is not conceived through a man but rather through the power of the Holy Spirit. There is no way that Mary could have come to know this through her reason alone. But through her faith in God's revelation she comes to know that her Son will be conceived through the Holy Spirit.

Is this unreasonable, or is God's plan simply *beyond Mary's natural reason?* This is the crucial point. We use the term "mysteries" to describe the truths about God that we do not understand because they are beyond the capacity of our reason currently bound by space and time and darkened by sin. This does not make them unreasonable or any less true.

For example, if I ask my four-year-old what eight times eight is, he might recite the answer, as if "eight times eight equals sixty-four" were a line in one of his nursery rhymes. Yet the concept of multiplication is simply beyond his reason at this point in his human existence. Does that mean that the proposition "eight times eight equals sixty-four" is not true? Of course not. It just means that this truth is beyond his reason, not contrary to it or non-existent.

How many complex truths are out there that many of us are unable to understand at this moment? That does not mean they are false, or non-existent, or contrary to reason. The same applies to the mysteries of God. We know they are true because He has revealed them to us, but many of them are beyond our reason, which is limited in many ways while we are in this world. We can come to a limited and imperfect understanding of them through our reason alone. However, through God's revelation and our faith-seeking-understanding, we can continue to ponder these truths and apprehend them more deeply until the fullness of time, when we shall see God face to face.

By adhering to God's revelation and seeking to more deeply understand it, our faith builds upon our reason and makes it more perfect. It allows us to know and understand things that we would not have been able to know through our reason alone. This dual and inseparable relationship of faith and reason are the two irreplaceable and indispensable means through which we come to know God. It allows us to enter into the profound depths of His mystery as well as to discover who we are as children of God created in His image and likeness.

From the Catechism: Key Words to Know

REVELATION: God's communication of Himself, by which He makes known the mystery of His divine plan, a gift of self-communication that is realized by deeds and words over time, and most fully by sending us His own divine Son, Jesus Christ (50).

FAITH: Both a gift of God and a human act by which the believer gives personal adherence to God who invites his response, and freely assents to the whole truth that God has revealed. It is this revelation of God that the Church proposes for our belief, and that we profess in the creed, celebrate in the sacraments, live by right conduct that fulfills the twofold commandment of charity (as specified in the Ten Commandments), and respond to in our prayer of faith. Faith is both a theological virtue given by God as grace, and an obligation that flows from the first commandment of God (26, 142, 150, 1814, 2087).

CONVERSION: A radical reorientation of the whole life away from sin and evil and toward God. This change of heart is a central element of Christ's preaching, of the Church's ministry of evangelization, and of the Sacrament of Penance and Reconciliation (1427, 1431, 1423; cf. 821).

Chapter 2

Divine Revelation: How Does God Reveal Himself to Us?

Reading the Catechism: Paragraphs 50–100

> It is clear, therefore, that sacred tradition, Sacred Scripture and the teaching authority of the Church, in accord with God's most wise design, are so linked and joined together that one cannot stand without the others, and that all together and each in its own way under the action of the one Holy Spirit contributes effectively to the salvation of souls.
>
> —Second Vatican Council, Dogmatic Constitution on Divine Revelation *Dei Verbum* (November 18, 1965), no. 10

The question of how we can come to know God has been one of the most challenging questions posed to man throughout the centuries. How can human beings, who are finite and limited by space and time, possibly come to know the transcendent and eternal God?

As we addressed in the last chapter, there are two ways in which we can come to know God. We can come to imperfect and partial knowledge of Him through our *reason* alone. But it is through our faith in what He reveals to us about Himself, which we call *divine Revelation,* that we come to a true and more complete knowledge of Him, and thus enter into a personal and intimate relationship with Him. It is not an either/or; the two are indeed the "wings" upon which our spirit rises to the knowledge of the living and true God.

In this chapter we will look more closely at the means by which God reveals Himself to His people, how Christ's Church has handed on that revelation through the centuries, and where we find the fullness of God's revelation today.

God Reveals Himself through Divine Revelation

God does not desire that we have an imperfect and limited knowledge of Him. Rather, because He loves us, He wants us to truly know Him and the greatness of His love and mercy. He desires us to understand His plan of life for us.

Even when mankind lost communion and intimate knowledge of Him through the first sin, God did not condemn us, but rather out of love and mercy for us chose to reveal Himself so that we could once again know Him and love Him in a very intimate and personal way. Therefore, we come to a full and complete knowledge of God through faith in His revelation, which surpasses the capacities of our human reason. Divine Revelation does not contradict reason, but rather builds upon it and perfects it so that we can come to know truths about God that were lost to our reason after the first sin. In fact, through divine Revelation, our human reason is being healed and restored to its original state in which we enjoy living in the knowledge and contemplation of God, for which our reason and intellect were made. Man no longer needs to search for the knowledge of the divine for which He thirsts, for God has fully revealed Himself to us through Jesus Christ.

God First Reveals Himself Gradually

In the course of human history, God did not fully reveal Himself to man immediately, but He did so gradually over time. He slowly and patiently prepared humanity for His ultimate gift of revelation and salvation in Jesus Christ. For God the Father knew that the human family would not be able to handle a full and immediate revelation of Himself. So He initiated what we call salvation history, or the **economy of salvation.** Throughout the centuries He gradually revealed His divine plan of salvation until in the fullness of time He fully revealed Himself to us through His only Son, Jesus Christ.

Why did God reveal Himself in this way? Because our loving Father and Creator knows us better than we know ourselves. He knows that our wounded human nature needed to be gradually brought back into His light.

Have you ever been in total darkness and had someone turn on a very bright light? It hurts your eyes and you cannot see, even in the light. However, if you gradually brighten the light, you can see more and more clearly without your eyes being hurt.

An even better example is the nature of how we learn. If I want to teach someone who knows nothing about algebra, I cannot start with a very difficult equation and expect them to understand or solve the problem. I have to start with numbers and counting, then simple addition and subtraction, then multiplication and division, and so forth. There is a certain progression of steps and procedures—a "pedagogy," or gradual teaching and revealing—that one must go through that builds a foundation of understanding. Greater understanding must be built upon each previous step before we can get to that equation. I cannot simply put down an algebra book in front of someone and expect him to learn and understand.

This principle is true with God's revelation to the human family. If God came down in all His glory, majesty, and power, and fully revealed Himself, man would not have been able to understand, or grasp, all that He is. So He came to us in what we call a "divine pedagogy," in which He patiently and gradually revealed to the human family who He is and what His divine plan is. He gradually taught us through both words and deeds His identity and His plan of salvation so that in the fullness of time, when He sent His Son Jesus into the world to both fully reveal God to man and man to Himself, we would be ready and prepared to accept Him.

The Old Testament

It is in the Old Testament of the Bible where we read about and come into contact with God's gradual revelation. The Old Testament is the dramatic story through which God reveals to us the truths about creation, the human person, His plan for marriage and family, the first sin and the Fall of humanity, and then His merciful response and the unfolding of His plan of salvation.

God's gradual revelation has a twofold purpose: (1) To slowly reveal to the human family who He is and what His plan of salvation to be accomplished through His Son, Jesus Christ is, and (2) to gather together His chosen people, Israel, as the "emerging Church" so that in the fullness of time, Christ will bring about the unity of the entire human race in the universal, or Catholic Church.

Therefore, throughout the Old Testament we see God offering a series of covenants through which He reveals Himself, and also gathers and prepares His chosen people for the coming of Christ. A covenant is established when God solemnly promises certain things to His people and they, in turn, promise to be faithful to Him in their words and actions. Although the people of the Old Testament are consistently unfaithful to His covenants, God continually offers new and more profound covenants to His people until at last, Jesus Christ seals the New and Everlasting Covenant between God and man in His Blood.

Since the plan of salvation that was gradually revealed in the Old Testament is for the dual purpose of preparing God's people for the coming of Christ and the establishment of His Church, we see Christ and the Church as much in the Old Testament as in the New Testament. However, we do not see Christ explicitly, but foreshadowed in different events, characters, and prophesies. Here are a few examples:

- Moses is a type or foreshadowing of Christ. Moses delivered the chosen people from slavery to the Egyptians, which is a foreshadowing of Christ who came to save all of humanity from slavery to sin. (Ex. 12:31–36)
- Christ is prophesized in many of the writings of the great prophets, especially Isaiah, who tells us:
    - The Messiah is coming and will be born of a virgin (Isa. 7:14);
    - He will rule Israel with justice, and the spirit of the Lord will be upon Him (Is. 11:1–9);
    - The Messiah will be a suffering servant who will bear our sins and be crushed for our infirmities (Is. 53).

In many other remarkable ways the Old Testament gradually reveals and foreshadows God's plan of salvation that in the fullness of time will be fulfilled in Christ. We will be taking an even closer look at the Old Testament in the next chapter on the Bible.

Jesus Christ: The Fullness of God's Revelation

"In times past, God spoke in partial and various ways to our ancestors through the prophets; in these last days, he spoke to us through a son, whom he made heir of all things and through whom he created the universe" (Heb. 1:1–2). God has revealed all things through His Son, Jesus Christ, for He is the fullness of God's revelation. It was the revelation of Christ for which God gradually prepared His chosen people in the Old Testament, and it is in the revelation of Jesus Christ that God communicates to us all that He is, all that He desires for us, and all that He pledges to us in the New and Everlasting Covenant. Jesus is the climax and fullness of God's revelation; all things are revealed in Him. Jesus, who is both human and divine, is the definitive revelation of God.

> Jesus Christ, therefore, the Word made flesh, was sent as "a man to men." He "speaks the words of God" (Jn. 3:34), and completes the work of salvation which His Father gave Him to

> do (see Jn. 5:36; 17:4). To see Jesus is to see His Father (Jn. 14:9). For this reason Jesus perfected revelation by fulfilling it through his whole work of making Himself present and manifesting Himself: through His words and deeds, His signs and wonders, but especially through His death and glorious resurrection from the dead and final sending of the Spirit of truth. Moreover He confirmed with divine testimony what revelation proclaimed, that God is with us to free us from the darkness of sin and death, and to raise us up to life eternal. (*Dei Verbum,* no. 4)

Since Christ is the fullness of God's revelation, there is no new revelation to come. Everything that God wishes to communicate to the human family is communicated in Christ's life and ministry. *Divine Revelation is fully manifested and completed in the Person of Jesus Christ.*

However, Christ entrusted to the Church a sacred **deposit of faith** that is to be handed down and applied to each generation throughout history until the end of time. This deposit of faith contains the fullness of revelation manifested in Christ. As a result, the Church, from the time of the Apostles and throughout the centuries, has faithfully preserved, handed on, and prayerfully and lovingly pondered Christ's words, deeds, teachings, and commands in order to bring the entire human race to the light and freedom of Christ.

The Transmission of Divine Revelation

Let us look to exactly how God chose to preserve, hand on, and interpret to each generation the fullness of His revelation throughout history until the end of time.

Currently there are over thirty thousand different Christian denominations in the United States alone. They all have, in one way or another, different beliefs concerning exactly what Christ has revealed to us. So, where can we find the fullness of God's revelation and where can we find the authoritative teaching of Christ? This is one of the fundamental issues that divide Christians today.

Many Christians claim that the fullness of Christ's revelation and His authoritative teaching is in the Bible alone, and all that Christ desired to communicate to us is contained within its pages. However, as we will explore, Christ first established a Church with a teaching authority founded upon the Apostles and their successors. These men, entrusted with the teaching authority of Christ, hand on faithfully the entire deposit of faith that is contained in both Sacred Tradition (the oral and living teaching of the Apostles) and Sacred Scripture (that part of Tradition that has been written under the inspiration of the Holy Spirit). Therefore, it is the teaching authority of the Church, Sacred Tradition, and Sacred Scripture that fully contain and faithfully hand on the entire deposit of faith entrusted by Christ to His Church.

Jesus Chose to Institute an Apostolic Church

When we examine the life and ministry of Christ, it becomes very clear that He willed to establish an apostolic Church in which He entrusted to the Twelve Apostles all that He is: His life, ministry, teachings, and mission.

Jesus chooses and prepares the Twelve Apostles

What is the first thing that Jesus did at the beginning of His public ministry after being baptized in the Jordan? Did He write the Bible? Did He teach the multitudes? No. He chose His Apostles. He chose them at the beginning of His ministry because He wanted them to be the unique and privileged witnesses of His life, ministry, and teachings in order to prepare them to hand on the Gospel to the world. He chose them because it was His plan to establish a Church and guide it by the Apostles, who would be His teachers and witnesses to the entire world. "Come after me and I will make you fishers of men" (Mt. 4:19). He chose the Apostles as the ones who would go out into the world to gather men and women for Christ. But He first needed to teach and train them. They accompanied Him for three years in order to know Him intimately, learn to follow His example, and be strengthened by His presence—all to prepare them to be the ones who would hand on all that He entrusted to them.

Jesus prepared the Apostles for the mission of transmitting the Gospel by revealing to them privileged teachings and allowing them to witness crucial events during His ministry. Imagine all of the conversations and teachings He must have had with the Apostles during those three years. Imagine all that He must have been able to tell them and teach them concerning His mission, His identity, and His plan. We see in Scripture that the Apostles had many privileged moments and teachings.

- When the Apostles asked Jesus why He taught in parables, Jesus replied that to them it has been given to know the secrets of the kingdom of heaven, but to others it has not been given. (Mt. 13:10–11; Lk. 8:9–11; Mk. 4:10–11)

- Jesus took the Apostles aside and predicted to them that the Son of Man will be delivered to the chief priests and the scribes, suffer and die under the Gentiles, and rise again on the third day. (Mt. 20:17–19; Lk. 9:22)
- On the Mount of Olives, the Apostles came to Jesus privately and asked Him what will be the signs of His coming and of the close of the age, and Jesus revealed the signs to them. (Mt. 24 and 25; Mk. 13)
- Jesus took Peter, James, and John up the mountain with Him where He was transfigured before their eyes. (Mt. 17:1–8; Mk. 9:2–8; Lk. 9:28–36)

Other examples are numerous in which the Apostles received privileged teachings and are the sole and unique witnesses to important and paradigmatic events in the life of Jesus.

Jesus gives the Apostles His authority

All throughout His life and ministry, both before and after His death and Resurrection, Jesus is seen giving His authority directly to the Apostles. No one else in the New Testament is given this unique and powerful mission to act in the name of the Son of God. *Jesus bestowed authority specifically upon the Apostles to share in His mission in building the Church through teaching, governing, and ministering in His name.*

Teaching

Many times the Apostles were instructed by Christ Himself to go into the world and to teach in His name. The Apostles are the sole authoritative teachers who have received their teaching authority from the very words and actions of Christ. Let's look at three examples from the Gospels.

- Jesus told the Apostles, "Whoever listens to you listens to me. Whoever rejects you rejects me. And whoever rejects me rejects the one who sent me." (Lk. 10:16)
- Before the Ascension, Jesus commanded the Apostles to go and make disciples of all the nations, teaching them to observe all that He has commanded, and He promised to be with them always until the close of the age. (Mt. 28:19–20)
- Jesus appeared to the Apostles and commanded them to go into the entire world and preach the Gospel to all creation, and they went forth and preached everywhere while the Lord worked with them through many signs. (Mk. 16:15–20)

Thus, Christ is knowingly and willingly granting the Apostles His own teaching authority so that they will be the authoritative and convincing teachers who will transmit to all generations the Gospel of Christ.

Governing

Jesus also gave the Apostles the authority to guide and govern the Church. Not only are the Apostles appointed by Christ to be the authoritative teachers in the Church, but they are also given the mandate by Christ to govern the Church in all matters: doctrine, worship, and discipline.

- Jesus called Peter the rock upon which He will build His Church, giving him the keys of the kingdom and announcing that whatever he binds on earth will be bound in heaven, and whatever he loosed on earth will be loosed in heaven. (Mt. 16:15–20)
- Jesus told the Apostles that they would sit on thrones, judging the twelve tribes of Israel in His kingdom. (Lk. 22:28–30)
- Paul, writing to the Corinthians, explained that it is God Himself who has established and commissioned the Apostles and given them the Holy Spirit in their hearts as a guarantee of His guidance of them and His authority working through them. (2 Cor. 1:21–22)

Thus, the governing authority of the Apostles is not established by man, but by God Himself.

Ministering

The Apostles were given the authority by Christ to minister in His name. Through this authority, they came to share in a unique way the mission of Christ as the instruments through which He administers His graces and gifts. He willed that the Apostles would fully participate with Him in His ministry of sanctification, forgiveness of sins, and spiritual and physical healing.

- Before the Ascension, Jesus commanded the Apostles to go and make disciples of all the nations, baptizing them in the name of the Father, and of the Son, and of the Holy Spirit. (Mt. 28:19)
- At the Last Supper, Jesus granted the Apostles the authority to make present the Eucharist when He commanded, "Do this in memory of me." (Lk. 22:19)
- Jesus appeared to the Apostles and breathed the Holy Spirit on them, giving them the power to forgive and retain sins. (Jn. 20:22–23)

- Jesus summoned His Twelve Apostles and gave them authority over unclean spirits, telling them to cast the spirits out and to heal every disease and infirmity; then He sent them forth to the lost sheep of the house of Israel. (Mt. 10:1–15; Mk. 6:7–13)

Christ gives Peter authority over the Church

While all the Apostles were given the authority and the mission by Christ to teach, govern, and minister in His name, Peter was set apart and given a unique role by Christ that emphasized His teaching and governing authority over all the Apostles and other disciples. This is seen most profoundly in Matthew 16:

> When Jesus went into the region of Caesarea Philippi, he asked his disciples, "Who do people say that the Son of Man is?" They replied, "Some say John the Baptist, others Elijah, still others Jeremiah or one of the prophets." He said to them, "But who do you say that I am?" Simon Peter said in reply, "You are the Messiah, the Son of the living God." Jesus said to him in reply, "Blessed are you, Simon son of Jonah. For flesh and blood has not revealed this to you, but my heavenly Father. And so I say to you, you are Peter, and upon this rock I will build my church, and the gates of the netherworld shall not prevail against it. I will give you the keys to the kingdom of heaven. Whatever you bind on earth shall be bound in heaven; and whatever you loose on earth shall be loosed in heaven." Then he strictly ordered his disciples to tell no one that he was the Messiah. (Mt. 16:13–20)

In this very powerful scene, Jesus is asking the Apostles who others think He is, but in reality, He is asking *them* who *they* think He is. While the other Apostles give many different answers, Peter is the one who sees the real identity of Christ as the Messiah and responds, "You are the Messiah, the Son of the living God." Jesus replies, "Blessed are you Simon, son of Jonah, for flesh and blood has not revealed this to you, but my heavenly Father." Jesus is revealing a profound truth. Peter has been given a unique gift, or charism, by the Father to know and teach the truth, and his knowledge of Jesus' identity is a result of this special gift. *Jesus recognizes this gift and special role of Peter and bestows on him a unique teaching and governing authority over all the Apostles and the entire Church.*

Jesus changes Peter's name from Simon to Peter, which means "rock" (in Greek *petros*). The changing of one's name in the Scriptures means a new identity, mission, and calling. For example, God changed Abram's name to Abraham when he responded to God's invitation of faith and became the father of all of God's people. In the same way Jesus changes Simon's name to Peter to show his new identity and mission as the "rock" and head of the Church.

Jesus calls Peter "rock" and it is upon "this rock" that Jesus will build His Church. Why does Jesus build His Church upon Peter? *It is fundamentally in response to Peter already exercising his teaching authority given to him by the Father.* He has received a gift of wisdom to know the truth about Christ, and also a teaching charism to proclaim it with clarity and without error.

No mere human revealed to Peter that Jesus was the Messiah. He had not yet told Peter that He was the Messiah, and many were still seriously grappling with exactly who Jesus was. But Peter was given the gift to know the truth, and he faithfully proclaimed it to the Apostles. He will be the one who will lead, teach, and strengthen the Apostles and the other followers after the Resurrection and Ascension of Jesus.

It will be this Church, founded upon the teaching and governing authority of Peter, against which even the gates of hell will not prevail. Thus, another fundamental point: If Peter has been given a special teaching charism to know and proclaim the truth, then the Father, through the working of the Holy Spirit, will also give that same teaching charism to Peter's successors as well. The Church has remained intact and faithful to Christ's teaching for over two thousand years because of this unique teaching authority given to the successors of Peter, the popes in communion with the bishops.

Recognizing Peter's gift of teaching the truth, Jesus grants him a unique and profound authority: "I will give you the keys to the kingdom of heaven. Whatever you bind on earth shall be bound in heaven, and whatever you loose on earth will be loosed in heaven." Jesus entrusts to Peter the keys to the Church. What does this mean? In Jesus' time, when the master was going to leave his estate for a time he would entrust to his head servant the keys to the estate. This servant was entrusted with the full authority of his master while he was away. The servant does not replace the master, but possesses his authority in his absence. Peter becomes the "Vicar" of Christ; that is, he has been given the full authority of the Master over His Church until He comes again. With this authority comes great responsibility. The servant who is given the keys of the master is expected to take care of and run the estate in the way the master desires. *In the same way, Peter's authority is one of service and obedience to the will and teachings of Christ. It is the sole responsibility of Peter and his successors to authoritatively and faithfully teach and hand on what Christ has taught and willed.*

Bestowal of the teaching and governing authority of the Church upon Peter is also seen in John's Gospel. After His Resurrection, Jesus and Peter have a profound and personal encounter on the shores of the Sea of Galilee:

> When they had finished breakfast, Jesus said to Simon Peter, "Simon, son of John, do you love me more than these?" He said to him, "Yes, Lord, you know that I love you." He said to him, "Feed my lambs." He then said to him a second time, "Simon, son of John, do you love me?" He said to him, "Yes, Lord, you know that I love you." He said to him, "Tend my sheep." He said to him the third time, "Simon, son of John, do you love me?" Peter was distressed that he had said to him a third time, "Do you love me?" and he said to him, "Lord, you know everything; you know that I love you." (Jesus) said to him, "Feed my sheep." (Jn. 21:15–17)

In this powerful passage, three times Jesus exhorts Peter to "feed and tend my sheep." This is a very deliberate and meaningful action by Christ. He restores Peter and forgives him for his threefold denial during Jesus' Passion. But even more importantly, Jesus commissions Peter as the head and shepherd of the Church, for in the Scriptures three always means divine and complete. Just before Jesus' departure when He ascends into heaven, we see the divine commissioning of Peter as the head of the Church, responsible for feeding (teaching and ministering) and tending (governing) the Church.

In addition, Peter is seen throughout the entire New Testament as the leader of the Apostles and the head of the Church. (See "Tradition and Teaching Office of the Church in the New Testament" at the end of this chapter for numerous examples.)

The Apostles and their successors are the authoritative teachers in the early Church

After the Ascension of Christ, the Apostles and their successors became the authoritative teachers of the Gospel, handing on and protecting the traditions entrusted to them by Christ. Not only did they begin their apostolic ministry of preaching and handing on the Gospel of Jesus Christ, but as the early Church began to grow and emerge, they began to choose successors to continue the ministry.

The Apostles knew the importance of choosing successors to continue their apostolic ministry. This is no more clearly seen than in the choosing of a successor of Judas Iscariot, who had betrayed Christ and then killed himself.

> During those days Peter stood up in the midst of the brothers (there was a group of about one hundred and twenty persons in the one place). He said, "My brothers, the Scripture had to be fulfilled which the Holy Spirit spoke beforehand through the mouth of David, concerning Judas, who was the guide for those who arrested Jesus. He was numbered among us and was allotted a share in this ministry. He bought a parcel of land with the wages of his iniquity, and falling headlong, he burst open in the middle, and all his insides spilled out. . . .
> Therefore, it is necessary that one of the men who accompanied us the whole time the Lord Jesus came and went among us, beginning from the baptism of John until the day on which he was taken up from us, become with us a witness to his resurrection." So they proposed two, Joseph called Barsabbas, who was also known as Justus, and Matthias. Then they prayed, "You, Lord, who know the hearts of all, show which one of these two you have chosen to take the place in this apostolic ministry from which Judas turned away to go to his own place." Then they gave lots to them, and the lot fell upon Matthias, and he was counted with the eleven Apostles. (Acts 1:15–26)

Here we see, even before Pentecost, the importance that the Apostles placed on choosing successors to carry on the apostolic ministry.

We also see other examples of choosing successors to the apostolic ministry.

- The Twelve chose seven men from among the disciples to assist in the preaching of the Word of God, and they prayed and laid hands upon them. (Acts 6:3–6)
- After the council held at Jerusalem, the Apostles and elders immediately appointed men to go out to the new churches and proclaim the definitive teaching in order to settle disputes about circumcision. (Acts 15:22–28)

- Paul was appointed a preacher and an Apostle to teach the Gentiles in faith and truth. (1 Tim. 2:7)
- Paul commanded Timothy to take what he had heard from him and entrust those teachings to faithful men who would then be able to teach others. (2 Tim. 2:2)
- Paul left Titus in Crete to appoint elders in each town in order to clarify the teachings handed down to them. (Titus 1:5)
- After preaching the Gospel to a city, Paul and Barnabas appointed elders for the new Christians in each church. (Acts 14:21–23)

The chosen successors of the Apostles were entrusted with the Gospel and were to hand on the traditions given to them to those who came later. Thus, their successors fully shared in the apostolic ministry given to the Apostles by Christ Himself. They were the unique and authoritative teachers of the New Testament Church who taught, preserved, and defended Gospel Tradition. (See "Tradition and Teaching Office of the Church in the New Testament" at the end of this chapter.)

As the early Church continued to grow and spread across the ancient world in the second and third centuries, the writings of the early Church fathers clearly show that the bishops, as the successors of the Apostles, continued to be the ones who had the authority to teach, govern, and minister in the name of Christ. The fact that the teaching authority of the pope and bishops was preserving the true teaching of Christ and the unity of the Church is one of the most common themes in these early writings. Here are just a few examples:

> The Apostles received the Gospel for us from the Lord Jesus Christ; Jesus, the Christ, was sent from God. Thus Christ is from God and the Apostles from Christ. In both instances the orderly procedure depends on God's will. And so the Apostles, after receiving their orders and being fully convinced by the Resurrection of our Lord Jesus Christ and assured by God's word, went out in the confidence of the Holy Spirit to preach the good news that God's kingdom was about to come. They preached in country and city, and appointed their first converts, after testing them by the Holy Spirit, to be bishops and deacons of future believers.
>
> **Saint Clement, *Letter to the Corinthians*, AD 80**

Those indeed who belong to God and to Jesus Christ—they are with the bishop. And those who repent and come to the unity of the Church—they too shall be of God, and will live according to Jesus Christ. Do not err, my brethren: if any one follows a schismatic, he will not inherit the kingdom of God. If any man walks about with strange doctrine, he cannot lie down with the passion. Take care, then, to use one Eucharist, so that whatever you do, you do according to God: for there is one Flesh of our Lord Jesus Christ, and one cup in the union of His Blood; one altar, as there is one bishop, with the presbytery, and my fellow servants, the deacons.
Saint Ignatius of Antioch, *Letter to the Philadelphians*, AD 110

I hasten to urge you to harmonize your actions with God's mind. For Jesus Christ—that life from which we can't be torn—is the Father's mind, as the bishops too, appointed the world over, reflect the mind of Jesus Christ.
Saint Ignatius of Antioch, *Letter to the Ephesians*, AD 110

And the Church of the Corinthians has continued in the correct doctrine to the time of Primus, who has become Bishop in Corinth, and with whom I conversed at length on my way to Rome, when I spent some days with the Corinthians, during which time we were mutually refreshed in the correct doctrine. When I had come to Rome, I made a succession up to Anicetus, whose deacon was Eleutherius. And after Anicetus, Soter succeeded; and after him, Eleutherus. In each succession and in each city there is a continuance of that which is proclaimed by the Law, the Prophets, and the Lord.

At that time there flourished in the Church Hegesippus, whom we know from what has gone before, and Dionysius, bishop of Corinth, and another bishop, Pinytus of Crete, and besides these, Phillip, and Apollinarius, and Melito, and Musanus, and finally, Irenaeus. From them has come down to us in writing, the sound and orthodox faith received from tradition.
Eusebius of Caesarea, *History of the Church*, AD 150

> Although there are many who believe that they themselves hold to the teachings of Christ, there are yet some among them who think differently from their predecessors. The teaching of the Church has indeed been handed down through an order of succession from the Apostles and remains in the churches even to the present time. That alone is to be believed as the truth which is in no way at variance with ecclesiastical and apostolic tradition.
>
> **Origen, *The Fundamental Doctrines,* AD 225**

> The Church is one, and as she is one, cannot be both within and without. For if she is with Novatian, she was not with [Pope] Cornelius. But if she was with Cornelius, who succeeded the bishop Fabian by lawful ordination, and whom, beside the honor of the priesthood the Lord glorified also with martyrdom, Novatian is not in the Church; nor can he be reckoned as a bishop, who, succeeding to no one, and despising the evangelical and apostolic tradition, sprang from himself. For he who has not been ordained can neither have nor hold to the Church in any way.
>
> **Cyprian of Carthage, *Letters* 75:3, AD 253**

Christ's Revelation Is Transmitted through Sacred Tradition and Sacred Scripture

We have clearly seen (1) that Jesus intended to establish an apostolic Church founded on the teaching and authority of the Apostles, and (2) how the Apostles and their successors began to preach and hand on all that Christ had entrusted to them. But exactly how has all that Christ revealed to us been handed down throughout the centuries? We will now explore how Christ's revelation, the sacred deposit of faith, is transmitted through Sacred Tradition, Sacred Scripture, and the authority of the Apostles and their successors so that the fullness of what Christ has revealed to us is faithfully handed down until the end of time.

As the New Testament Church began to emerge and grow, the teaching of the Apostles was handed on in two ways: (1) "Orally by the apostles who handed on, by the spoken word of their preaching, by the example they gave, by the institutions they established, and what they had received [from Christ]" (CCC 76). We call this Sacred Tradition. (2) "In writing by those apostles and other men associated with the apostles who, under the inspiration of the Holy Spirit, committed the message of salvation to writing" (CCC 76). We call this Sacred Scripture or the New Testament of the Bible.

Saint Paul also explains how the revelation of Christ is handed on, "Therefore, brothers, stand firm and hold fast to the traditions that you were taught, either by an oral statement or by a letter of ours"

(2 Thess. 2:15). Here we clearly see the means through which the sacred deposit of faith entrusted to the Apostles and their successors is transmitted to each generation: a teaching office ("that you were taught"), Sacred Tradition ("by oral statement"), and Sacred Scripture ("or by a letter of ours").

> But in order to keep the Gospel forever whole and alive within the Church, the Apostles left bishops as their successors, "handing over" to them "the authority to teach in their own place." This sacred tradition, therefore, and Sacred Scripture of both the Old and New Testaments are like a mirror in which the pilgrim Church on earth looks at God, from whom she has received everything, until she is brought finally to see Him as He is, face to face (see 1 Jn. 3:2). (*Dei Verbum,* no. 7)

Sacred Tradition

Sacred Tradition is the living witness and presence of Christ, which was entrusted to the Apostles and their successors through their authoritative teaching, their example, and the institutions they established. Sacred Tradition is none other than Christ Himself as handed on throughout history (tradition means "to carry across"). This oral Tradition continues to be passed on primarily through apostolic succession, that is, through the teachings of the popes and the bishops united to them. Tradition is also handed on in other ways through the life and ministry of the Church.

Tradition is handed on through apostolic succession

Tradition is passed on through the teaching and governing of the successors of Peter and the Apostles (i.e., the **pope** and the **bishops**), who through

apostolic succession have been given the authority to teach and govern by Christ. As we saw, this was seen so clearly in both the New Testament and in the writings of the early Church Fathers. This teaching office has continued in an unbroken line of authority even to this day. The pope and the bishops, as the present day successors of the Apostles, are called the **magisterium**, or teaching office, of the Church (*magistra* in Latin means teacher). They have the responsibility to see that the sacred deposit of faith left to us by Christ and handed on through Tradition and Scripture is preserved, defended, and handed on in its fullness to all generations until the end of time.

> And so the apostolic preaching, which is expressed in a special way in the inspired books, was to be preserved by an unending succession of preachers until the end of time. Therefore the Apostles, handing on what they themselves had received, warn the faithful to hold fast to the traditions which they have learned either by word of mouth or by letter (see 2 Thess. 2:15), and to fight in defense of the faith handed on once and for all (see Jude 1:3). Now what was handed on by the Apostles includes everything which contributes toward the holiness of life and increase in faith of the peoples of God; and so the Church, in her teaching, life and worship, perpetuates and hands on to all generations all that she herself is, all that she believes. (*Dei Verbum,* no. 8)

Thus, the pope and the bishops do not have the authority to invent new doctrine or to delete or change what has been entrusted to them. Their authority comes from Christ Himself, who commands them to faithfully hand on, untarnished and complete, all that He taught them and commanded them.

Tradition is also passed on in the very life of the Church

Sacred Tradition is also passed on through the lives and faith of all the faithful who are in alignment with the teachings of the Church. This is called the *sensus fidelium*, or the sense of the faithful. Tradition lies within the life of faith lived out in each member of the Church as we continue to ponder and embrace all that Christ has given to us and commanded of us. Thus, the richness of the Tradition of the Church can be found in the simple prayer and faith of the common man.

Tradition is also passed on through the liturgical life of the Church

Lex orandi, lex credendi: "The law of prayer is the law of faith." The liturgy is an important element of Sacred Tradition, because the Church is continuously pondering and meditating upon the mysteries of Christ and celebrating the mighty works of God accomplished in Christ. It is similar to families gathering together for feasts and holidays to celebrate, ponder, and hand on family traditions and memories. Since the Church is the family of Christ, when we come together in the liturgy to celebrate God's salvation in Christ, we also encounter and hand on the Tradition of the Church through our prayers and worship.

Sacred Tradition is a living Tradition

Sacred Tradition is a living Tradition, not one that is stagnant. While the fundamental truths of Sacred Tradition revealed by Christ and entrusted to the Church do not change, they do unfold over time as the Church continues to ponder and live out its mysteries. This is a crucial point. While doctrine does not change, it does develop as the Church better grasps its meaning. The Magisterium, under the guidance of the Holy Spirit, guides, defends, protects, interprets, and applies the deposit of faith to each generation. Through this handing down, the Church comes to have a better grasp of what Christ revealed.

> This tradition which comes from the Apostles develops in the Church with the help of the Holy Spirit. For there is a growth in the understanding of the realities and the words which have been handed down. This happens through the contemplation and study made by believers, who treasure these things in their hearts (see Lk. 2:19, 51) through a penetrating understanding of the spiritual realities which they experience, and through the preaching of those who have received through Episcopal succession the sure gift of truth. For as the centuries succeed one another, the Church constantly moves forward toward the fullness of divine truth until the words of God reach their complete fulfillment in her. (*Dei Verbum,* no. 8)

Sacred Scripture

Sacred Scripture is a part, or an aspect, of the sacred deposit of faith that has been "crystallized" in written form under the inspiration of the Holy Spirit. This was done by some of the Apostles or those closely associated with the

Apostles who, for various reasons, put down into writing what was already being handed down through Sacred Tradition.

For example, Luke, a close companion of Paul, wrote his Gospel and the Acts of the Apostles as a legal defense for Paul at his trial in Rome. Many of Paul's letters were written to teach and encourage the Christian communities that he had already established in places like Corinth, Ephesus, Galatia, and Philippi. Paul also wrote to individuals, Timothy and Titus, to whom he had handed on the apostolic ministry and left to oversee local churches, to teach and exhort them in their ministry. As the Church read and pondered these and other writings, she chose certain ones and proclaimed them to be inspired by God in a unique way. These writings were declared the "canon" of the New Testament.

Up until about the fourth century there was no definitive list of the books that comprised the Old and New Testament. The Church established the canon of Scripture by several local synods (gatherings of bishops), especially the Synod of Hippo in AD 393 and the Synod of Carthage in AD 397. This list was accepted until the Protestant Reformation questioned the integrity of the canon. Some of the Protestant reformers removed certain books that did not support their reformed theology, such as 1 and 2 Maccabees and much of the Wisdom Literature. The Council of Trent officially responded to these errors and authoritatively defined the canon of Scripture in AD 1546. (This will be discussed in more detail in the following chapter on the Bible.)

Sacred Scripture, Sacred Tradition, and the Magisterium together hand on the fullness of Christ's Revelation

Since Sacred Scripture is the earliest crystallization of the sacred deposit of faith and the inspired Word of God, it along with Sacred Tradition is a twin source of divine Revelation. Scripture, although very important, is only the part of the sacred deposit of faith that has been committed to writing. Sacred Tradition and Sacred Scripture are uniquely and intrinsically interwoven. Scripture can never be interpreted apart from Tradition, and all truths of Tradition are latent within Scripture. Thus, it is both Sacred Scripture and Sacred Tradition handed on and interpreted by the Magisterium of the Church that constitutes the fullness of divine Revelation:

> Hence there exists a close connection and communication between sacred tradition and Sacred Scripture. For both of them, flowing from the same divine wellspring, in a certain way

> merge into a unity and tend toward the same end. For Sacred Scripture is the word of God inasmuch as it is consigned to writing under the inspiration of the divine Spirit, while sacred tradition takes the word of God entrusted by Christ the Lord and the Holy Spirit to the Apostles, and hands it on to their successors in its full purity, so that led by the light of the Spirit of truth, they may in proclaiming it preserve this word of God faithfully, explain it, and make it more widely known. Consequently it is not from Sacred Scripture alone that the Church draws her certainty about everything which has been revealed. Therefore both sacred tradition and Sacred Scripture are to be accepted and venerated with the same sense of loyalty and reverence. (*Dei Verbum,* no. 10)

Therefore, Scripture does not contain in itself all that Christ revealed. The Apostle John testifies to this point at the end of his Gospel, "There are also many other things that Jesus did, but if these were to be described individually, I do not think the whole world would contain the books that would be written" (Jn. 21:25).

In addition, Scripture can only be properly interpreted and fully understood in light of the Tradition from which it comes. While Scripture provides the material part, or the "crystallization" of Tradition, it is Tradition that sheds its light on and pulls together the full meaning of the Scriptures. The Scriptures are like bricks, they hold within themselves those important and foundational aspects of Tradition that has been committed to writing by the inspiration of the Holy Spirit. Tradition is the mortar; it pulls together the full meaning of the Scriptures, keeps them in the proper context, and brings out their significance. If you only had bricks, you would just have an unorganized pile of bricks. But Scripture and Tradition together make a building, the Church, with the fullness of all that Christ desires to reveal and hand on to us.

The Scriptures do not contradict the Tradition from which they come. In the same way, Sacred Tradition is latent throughout the Scriptures, whether explicitly or implicitly. Scripture and Tradition do not contradict each other, but rather together contain the entire sacred deposit of faith entrusted to the Church by Christ.

Finally, it is the Magisterium of the Church, the pope and the bishops, who as successors of the Apostles, have been given the authority by Christ to teach, pass on, interpret, apply, and defend the deposit of faith to each generation. Thus, the Magisterium is the authentic interpreter and guarantor of the Word of God, as expressed in both Sacred Tradition and Sacred Scripture. The Magisterium is like a referee; it determines what is truly in accordance with Sacred Tradition and Sacred Scripture, and assures that Sacred Scripture is interpreted faithfully in light of Sacred Tradition. Again we look to *Dei Verbum* from Vatican II:

> But the task of authentically interpreting the word of God, whether written or handed on, has been entrusted exclusively to the living teaching office of the Church, whose authority is exercised in the name of Jesus Christ. This teaching office is not above the word of God, but serves it, teaching only what has been handed on, listening to it devoutly, guarding it scrupulously and explaining it faithfully in accord with a divine commission and with the help of the Holy Spirit, it draws from this one deposit of faith everything which it presents for belief as divinely revealed. (no. 10)

The Catholic Church Contains the Fullness of Truth

Thus, Sacred Scripture, Sacred Tradition, and the Magisterium together are intimately joined in faithfully transmitting to all generations the full and entire deposit of faith revealed by Christ and entrusted to the Church. They are like a three-legged stool. If all three legs are intact, the stool is on a sound foundation. However, if you remove one or two legs, the stool collapses into disunity and chaos. This has been seen throughout the history of Protestantism, which has reduced God's revelation to the Bible alone. Without Sacred Tradition and the Magisterium, interpreting the Bible has led to numerous divisions and debate. The "Bible alone" theory certainly has not brought continuity and unity throughout Christianity, but rather continues to cause divisions and disunity.

It is, in fact, the Catholic Church that has remained the one true Church that dates back to Christ Himself. This is a hard truth for many, but only the **Catholic Church** contains the fullness of Christ's revelation that has been handed down throughout the centuries. No other Church can claim this. There is an unbroken history, Tradition, and line of authority. Other Christian churches, by abandoning Sacred Tradition and the Magisterium, have a fragment of the Church, a piece of it. But their root is the Catholic Church; it is ultimately their true home. The Catholic Church by preserving the fullness of Christ's teaching and way of life for over two thousand years, contains within herself the fullness of truth and the Christian life as "the church of the living God, the pillar and foundation of truth" (1 Tim. 3:15).

Tradition and Teaching Office of the Church in the New Testament

I. The Twelve Apostles were chosen by Christ to be the unique witnesses of His life and mission, preparing them to hand on the Gospel to the world.
   A. Christ chose the Twelve Apostles at the beginning of His public ministry to train them to be fishers of men.
      1. Jesus first called Simon Peter and Andrew, and they immediately dropped their nets and followed Him. (Mt. 4:18–20; Mk. 1:16–19)
      2. Jesus called James and John, the sons of Zebedee, and immediately they left their boat and their father and followed Him. (Mt. 4:21–22; Mk. 1:19–20)
      3. After the miracle of the wondrous catch of fish, Jesus told Peter, James, and John that they would soon be fishers of men. (Lk. 5:1–11)
      4. After praying all night to God, Jesus called His disciples together and chose from them Twelve whom He called Apostles. (Lk. 6:12–16)
      5. After meeting Jesus, Andrew brought his brother Simon to Him, and Jesus renamed him Peter. (Jn. 1:40–42)
   B. Christ prepared the Apostles for the mission of transmitting the Gospel by revealing to them privileged teachings and allowing them to witness crucial events during His ministry.
      1. The Apostles were given privileged teachings by Christ.
         a. Jesus instructed the Apostles to utter in the light what He told them in the dark; and what was whispered to them, proclaim on the housetops. (Mt. 10:27)
         b. When the Apostles asked Jesus why He taught in parables, Jesus said that to them it has been given to know the secrets of the kingdom of heaven, but to others it has not been given. (Mt. 13:10–11; Lk. 8:9–11; Mk. 4:10–11)
         c. Jesus did not speak to the crowds without a parable, but privately to His Apostles He explained everything. (Mk. 4:34)
         d. Jesus took the Apostles aside and predicted to them that the Son of man would be delivered to the chief priests and the scribes, suffer, and die under the Gentiles, and rise again on the third day. (Mt. 20:17–19; Lk. 9:21–22)
         e. On the Mount of Olives, the Apostles came to Jesus privately and asked Him what will be the signs of His coming and of

the close of the age, and Jesus revealed the signs to them. (Mt. 24–25; Mk. 13)

f. Jesus told the Apostles privately that they are blessed, and that many prophets and kings desired to see what they see and hear what they hear, but did not see or hear. (Lk. 10:23–24)

2. The Apostles were the sole witnesses to important events during Christ's ministry.
   a. Jesus took Peter, James, and John up the mountain with Him where He was transfigured before their eyes. (Mt. 17:1–8; Mk. 9:2–8; Lk. 9:28–36)
   b. Jesus took Peter and the two sons of Zebedee with Him to the garden where He experienced His agony and commanded them to remain there and watch with Him. (Mt. 26:37–38; Mk. 14:33–34)
   c. Jesus only took with Him Peter, James, and John when He raised Jarius' daughter from the dead. (Mk. 5:37)

II. Jesus bestowed authority specifically upon His Apostles to uniquely share in His mission in the building of the Church through teaching, governing, and ministering in His name.

A. Jesus gave the Apostles the authority to teach in His name and govern and guide the Church.

1. The teaching authority of the Apostles comes from Christ Himself.
   a. Jesus told the Apostles, "He who hears you hears me, and he who rejects you rejects me." (Lk. 10:16)
   b. Before the Ascension, Jesus commanded the Apostles to go and make disciples of all the nations, teaching them to observe all that He has commanded, and promised to be with them always until the close of the age. (Mt. 28:19–20)
   c. Jesus appeared to the Apostles and commanded them to go into the entire world and preach the Gospel to all creation, and they went forth and preached everywhere while the Lord worked through them with many signs. (Mk. 16:15, 20)
   d. Jesus foretold that the Apostles would receive power from on high when the Holy Spirit comes and that they would be His witnesses in Jerusalem, in all Judea, Samaria, and to the ends of the earth. (Acts 1:8)
   e. The Gospel preached by Paul is not man's gospel, nor was He taught it, but it is the revelation of Jesus Christ. (Gal. 1:11–12)

f. Paul was thankful that the Thessalonians received the Word of God not as coming from mere men but as truly from God Himself. (1 Thess. 2:13)
g. All who believed devoted themselves to the teaching of the Apostles and the breaking of the bread. (Acts 2:42)

2. Jesus gave the Apostles the authority to guide and govern the Church.
   a. Jesus called Peter the rock upon which He would build His Church, giving him the keys of the kingdom and announcing that whatever he binds on earth will be bound in heaven, and whatever he looses on earth will be loosed in heaven. (Mt. 16:15–20)
   b. Jesus told the Apostles that they would sit on thrones in His kingdom, judging the Twelve Tribes of Israel. (Lk. 22:28–30)
   c. Paul explained that it is God Himself who has established and commissioned the Apostles and given the Holy Spirit to them as a guarantee of their guidance and authority. (2 Cor. 1:21–22)
   d. The Apostles were commissioned by God, set apart from those whom Paul labeled as merely "peddlers of God's word." (2 Cor. 2:17)
   e. Paul explained that their confidence comes from the authority God has given them to be His ministers of the New Covenant. (2 Cor. 3:4–6)
   f. Paul told the Corinthians that they themselves are the "letter of recommendation" showing that the Apostles' authority comes from Christ Himself. (2 Cor. 3:2–3)

B. Jesus gave the Apostles the authority and power to administer the sacraments.
   1. Before the Ascension, Jesus commanded the Apostles to go and make disciples of all the nations, baptizing them in the name of the Father and of the Son and of the Holy Spirit. (Mt. 28:19)
   2. At the Last Supper, Jesus granted to the Apostles the authority to make present the Eucharist when He commanded them to "Do this in remembrance of me." (Lk. 22:19)
   3. Jesus appeared to the Apostles, breathed the Holy Spirit on them, and gave them the power to forgive and retain sins. (Jn. 20:22–23)

C. Jesus gave authority to the Apostles to rebuke evil spirits and heal the sick.

1. Jesus called to Him His Twelve Apostles and gave them authority to cast out unclean spirits and to heal every disease and infirmity. He sent them forth to the lost sheep of the house of Israel. (Mt. 10:1–15; Mk. 6:7–13)
2. Jesus gave the Apostles authority over the full force of the enemy as well as the ability to tread upon serpents and scorpions. He said that their names are written in heaven. (Lk. 10:19–20)

III. Peter was set apart and given a unique role by Christ that emphasized his teaching position and governing authority over the Apostles and the other disciples.

A. Peter was the first Apostle called by Christ in all four Gospels. (Mt. 4:18–20; Mk. 1:16–19, Jn. 1:42; Lk. 5:1–11)

B. Peter was given a special grace of the Father to recognize Christ as the Messiah.

1. Peter confessed at Caesarea Philippi that Jesus is the Christ, the Son of the living God. Jesus said that flesh and blood had not revealed this, but His Father in heaven. (Mt. 16:13–17)
2. While they were alone, Jesus asked the Apostles who they thought He was, and Peter responded, "The Christ of God." (Lk. 9:18–20)
3. After the Bread of Life discourse, Peter confessed that Jesus has the words of eternal life and is the Holy One of God. (Jn. 6:68–69)

C. Jesus commissioned Peter to be the head of the Apostles and the head of the Church.

1. Jesus called Peter the rock upon which He would build His Church, giving him the keys of the kingdom and announcing that whatever he binds on earth will be bound in heaven, and whatever he looses on earth will be loosed in heaven. (Mt. 16:18–19)
2. Jesus foretold Peter's denial, yet He commanded Peter to strengthen His brethren after he repents. (Lk. 22:32)
3. On the shore of the Sea of Tiberias, Jesus commissioned Peter three times to feed and tend His sheep. (Jn. 21:15–17)

D. Jesus took Peter with Him to witness important events during His ministry.

1. Jesus took Peter, James, and John up the mountain with Him where He was transfigured before their eyes. (Mt. 17:1–8; Mk. 9:2–8; Lk. 9:28–36)

2. Jesus only took with Him Peter, James, and John when He raised Jarius' daughter from the dead. (Mk. 5:37)
3. Jesus took with Him Peter and the two sons of Zebedee to His agony in the garden and commanded them to remain there and watch with Him. (Mt. 26:37–38; Mk. 14:33–34)

E. At crucial times, Jesus called on Peter to lead the Apostles.
   1. Jesus called Peter to be an example of faith by coming to Him by walking on the water. (Mt. 14:28–33)
   2. When Jesus found the disciples sleeping in the garden, He rebuked Peter for not staying awake and praying. (Mt. 26:40; Mk. 14:37)

F. After the Resurrection, Peter acted as the head of the Apostles and the Church.
   1. Peter was the first of the Apostles to witness evidence of the Resurrection.
      a. When the women told the Apostles what they had seen at the tomb, they thought it was just an idle tale, but Peter rose and ran to the tomb. He looked in and saw the linen cloths by themselves and went home wondering what had happened. (Lk. 24:10–12)
      b. Peter and John both ran to the tomb, but Peter was the first to go in and investigate. (Jn. 20:3–10)
   2. The disciples of Jesus recognized Peter's authority as the head of the Apostles.
      a. After discovering that the stone had been rolled away from the tomb, Mary Magdalene went to Simon Peter and told him what she had seen. (Jn. 20:1–2)
      b. When Peter and John ran to the tomb, even though John reached the tomb first, he did not go in but let Peter enter first to see what had happened. (Jn. 20:3–10)
   3. Peter exercised his unique ministry as the head of the emerging Christian Church.
      a. Peter, filled with the Holy Spirit, preached at Pentecost, and three thousand souls were added to their number. (Acts 2:14–41)
      b. Peter was the one who stood and announced that a successor to Judas must be chosen to take his place among the Twelve. (Acts 1:15–25)
      c. Peter was guided by the Holy Spirit to allow Gentiles to be members of the Church. (Acts 11:3–18)

d. Upon hearing Peter's Spirit-guided pronouncement, the circumcision party accepted Gentiles becoming Christians. (Acts 11:18)
e. During the debate with regard to circumcision of the new Christians, it was Peter who finally rose and spoke to the other Apostles and elders with authority as the assembly listened in silence. (Acts 15:6–12)

IV. After the Ascension of Christ, the Apostles and their successors became the authoritative teachers of the Gospel, handing on and protecting the traditions entrusted to them by Christ.

A. The Apostles realized the importance of choosing successors to continue their apostolic ministry.

1. Peter stood and announced that one must be chosen to take the place of Judas among the Twelve and chose Matthias, who had accompanied them during the time that Jesus was with them. (Acts 1:15–25)
2. The Twelve chose seven men from among the disciples to assist with duties of charitable works and daily distribution so the Apostles could devote themselves to prayer and the ministry of the word, and they prayed and laid hands upon them. (Acts 6:3–6)
3. After the council held at Jerusalem, the Apostles and elders immediately appointed men to go out to the new churches and proclaim the definitive teaching in order to settle the disputes about circumcision. (Acts 15:22–29)
4. James, Peter, and John were reputed to be pillars of the Church, and they gave Paul and Barnabas the "right hand of fellowship." (Gal. 2:7–9)
5. Paul was appointed a preacher and an Apostle to teach the Gentiles in faith and truth. (1 Tim. 2:7)
6. Paul commanded Timothy to take what he had heard from him and before many witnesses entrust those teachings to faithful men who would be able to teach others. (2 Tim. 2:2)
7. Paul left Titus in Crete to appoint elders in each town in order to clarify the teachings. (Titus 1:5)
8. After preaching the Gospel to a city, Paul and Barnabas appointed elders for the new Christians in each church. (Acts 14:21–23)

B. The Apostles and their successors were entrusted with the Gospel and were to hand on the traditions given to them by Christ.

1. The Apostles and their successors were entrusted with the Gospel of Christ.
   a. Speaking to the appointed elders of the churches of Ephesus, Paul told them that they must guard the churches, with which they had been entrusted, from false teachings. (Acts 20:28)
   b. Paul explained that whatever was contrary to sound doctrine and the Gospel of God, which were entrusted to him, belonged to the lawless and the disobedient. (1 Tim. 1:8–11)
   c. Paul urged Timothy to follow the pattern of the sound teaching that he heard from him and to guard the truth that had been entrusted to him by the Holy Spirit who dwelled in them. (2 Tim. 1:12–14)
   d. Paul commanded Timothy to entrust the teaching of the Apostles to faithful men who would be able to teach others. (2 Tim. 2:2)
   e. Paul was entrusted with preaching God's Word by the command of Christ. (Titus 1:3)
   f. Paul was entrusted with bringing the Gospel to the uncircumcised, and Peter was entrusted with bringing the Gospel to the circumcised. (Gal. 2:7)
2. The Apostles and their successors handed on the traditions given to them by Christ.
   a. At the beginning of his Gospel, Luke explained that he was compiling a narrative of the things that were accomplished among them and were delivered to them by those who were eyewitnesses and ministers of the Word. (Lk. 1:2)
   b. Paul and Timothy traveled from city to city to pass on the teaching given by the Apostles and elders for the churches to observe, and the churches were strengthened in the faith. (Acts 16:4–5)
   c. Paul commended the Corinthians for remembering him and maintaining the traditions as he had delivered them. (1 Cor. 11:2)
   d. Paul received the institution of the Eucharist from the Lord, and he also delivered it to the Corinthians. (1 Cor. 11:23–26)
   e. Paul handed on to the Corinthians the Gospel, which he himself received, and in which they would have salvation if they "held fast" to it. (1 Cor. 15:1–2)
   f. Paul told the Philippians to do all the things that they learned, received, and heard from him. (Phil. 4:9)

g. The author of the letter to the Hebrews told them to imitate the men who brought the Word of God to them, but not be led astray by false teachings. (Heb. 13:7–9)
h. Paul instructed Timothy to continue in what he learned from him and what he firmly believed, and also to hold to what he learned from the sacred writings, which were inspired by God and profitable for teaching. (2 Tim. 3:14–16)
i. Paul instructed Timothy to command and teach the things he handed to him and to read the Scriptures to the public along with teaching and preaching. (1 Tim. 4:11–14)

C. The Apostles and their successors preserved and defended the Gospel Tradition handed to them from Christ.
1. The Apostles and their successors emphasized the importance of preserving and teaching the sound doctrine they had received from Christ.
a. A bishop was instructed to hold firm to the true Word as taught, so that he would be able to give instruction in sound doctrine and refute those who contradicted it. (Titus 1:9)
b. Deacons were called to be serious and to hold the mystery of faith with a clear conscience. (1 Tim. 3:8)
c. Titus was to teach only what befits sound doctrine. (Titus 2:1)
d. Paul told the Romans that their obedience to the "standard of teaching" given by the Apostles leads to righteousness. (Rom. 6:17–18)
e. Saul and Barnabas spent a year in Antioch to ensure the new Christians were taught well with sound doctrine. (Acts 11:26; 15:35)
f. Paul and Barnabas were sent to Jerusalem to go before the Apostles and elders to clarify the Apostles' teaching regarding circumcision because it was causing much dissension and debate. (Acts 15:2)
g. After the council held at Jerusalem, the Apostles and elders immediately appointed men to go out to the new churches and proclaim the definitive teaching in order to settle these disputes about circumcision. (Acts 15:22–28)
2. The Apostles and their successors rebuked false teachings and teachers.

a. Paul wrote of Hymenae and Philetus, who swerved from the truth by holding that the Resurrection was past already. (2 Tim. 2:17–18)
b. Those insubordinate men who taught without authority and confused and upset entire families were to be silenced because they had no right to teach. (Titus 1:11)
c. Titus was to admonish a factious man once or twice, and after doing so have nothing more to do with him. (Titus 3:11)
d. Paul urged the Romans to avoid those who create difficulties and dissensions in regard to the "doctrine" they had been taught by the Apostles. (Rom. 16:17)
e. Paul admonished the Galatians for so quickly deserting the true Gospel for a false gospel, and he said that anyone preaching a gospel different from the one received from him should be accursed. (Gal. 1:6–9)
f. Paul warned the Corinthians not to follow any false Apostles, even if they were eloquent speakers. (2 Cor. 11:4–6)
g. Paul commanded the brethren to keep away from anyone who was not in union with the "tradition" that they had received from the Apostles. (2 Thess. 3:6)
h. Paul and Titus did not yield to false teachers, even for a moment, in order to preserve the truth of the Gospel. (Gal. 2:5)
i. Even the demons recognized only the authority of Paul and did not recognize the authority of false teachers. (Acts 19:13–16)

From the Catechism: Key Words to Know

ECONOMY OF SALVATION (DIVINE ECONOMY): From a Greek word (*oikonomia*, literally "management of a household" or "stewardship") that refers to God's revelation and communication of Himself to the world in time for the sake of the salvation of all humanity; hence, the economy of salvation (258, 1066). The Fathers of the Church distinguished *oikonomia* from *theologia*; the latter term refers to the mystery of the internal life of the Trinity (236). The economy of salvation, on the other hand, refers to God's activity in creating and governing the world, particularly with regard to His plan for the salvation of the world in the Person and work of Jesus Christ, a plan that is being accomplished through His Body the Church, in its life and sacraments; hence, the "sacramental economy" (1076, 1093).

DEPOSIT OF FAITH: The heritage of faith contained in Sacred Scripture and Sacred Tradition, handed on in the Church from the time of the Apostles, from which the Magisterium draws all that it proposes for belief as being divinely revealed (84; cf. 1202).

POPE: The successor of Saint Peter as Bishop of Rome and Supreme Pontiff of the universal Catholic Church. The pope exercises a primacy of authority as Vicar of Christ and shepherd of the whole Church; he receives the divine assistance promised by Christ to the Church when he defines infallibly a doctrine of faith or morals (880–882).

BISHOP: One who has received the fullness of the Sacrament of Holy Orders, which makes him a member of the episcopal college and a successor of the Apostles. He is the shepherd of a particular church entrusted to him (1557; cf. 861, 886).

APOSTOLIC SUCCESSION: The handing on of apostolic preaching and authority from the Apostles to their successors the bishops through the laying on of hands, as a permanent office in the Church (77, 861).

MAGISTERIUM: The living, teaching office of the Church, whose task it is to give an authentic interpretation of the Word of God, whether in its written form (Scripture) or in the form of Tradition. The Magisterium ensures the

Church's fidelity to the teaching of the Apostles in matters of faith and morals (85, 890, 2033).

CATHOLIC CHURCH: The Church established by Christ on the foundation of the Apostles, possessing the fullness of the means of salvation that He has willed: correct and complete confession of faith, full sacramental life, and ordained ministry in apostolic succession (830).

Chapter 3

The Bible

Reading the Catechism: Paragraphs 101–141

Ignorance of Scripture is ignorance of Christ.
—Saint Jerome, from the prologue
of his commentary on Isaiah

As we saw in the last chapter, the **Bible** is that part of the sacred deposit of faith that has been "crystallized" in writing under the inspiration of the Holy Spirit. This crystallization of Tradition became known as Sacred Scripture. These holy writings serve as the core, or heart, of the sacred deposit of faith, which has been faithfully handed down to each generation through the teaching office of the Catholic Church.

We will discuss how the Bible was never meant to stand alone as the only source of God's revelation, or to be interpreted alone apart from the Tradition from whence it came. The history of Protestantism is a living witness of the consequences of interpreting and reading the Bible apart from Sacred Tradition. Far from bringing about unity and clarity in faith, it has resulted in the continuing fragmentation of Christianity.

This chapter will show the proper place of Sacred Scripture as a vital part of the whole of Sacred Tradition, interpreted and handed on by Christ's Church as He established. It will also address the proper ways to interpret Scripture, examine the history of the Bible as it was compiled in the early Church, and finally, provide an overview and outline of both the Old and New Testaments—how the two work together to reveal and prepare us for God's salvation fulfilled in Jesus Christ.

The Development of the Canon of Scripture

Throughout the first four centuries after Christ's death, the Magisterium of the Church gradually collected the books of the Bible into what is called the **canon** (meaning measure, or rule) **of Scripture**. The Church was given the responsibility and authority to discern which writings were "measured" to be inspired by the Holy Spirit and worthy to belong to the sacred canon of Scripture. Let us take a closer look at how the Bible came to be.

The Old Testament was already intact at the time of Christ in a collection called the Septuagint, which was the Greek translation of the Hebrew, or Jewish, Scriptures. The Jewish faith already held these writings as inspired, and the early Fathers of the Church almost universally accepted the Septuagint as the inspired Old Testament, which prepared for the coming of Christ and which Christ fulfilled. They used the Old Testament as proof that Jesus Christ was indeed the Messiah.

While the Old Testament was already written and intact at the time of Christ, the New Testament did not begin to be written until about AD 50, almost twenty years after the Resurrection of Christ, Pentecost, and the birth of the Church. After the Apostles, their associates, and successors began to preach the Gospel. As the Church grew, some of the Apostles and those closely associated with them wrote letters of instruction, guidance, and encouragement to certain communities. For example, Paul wrote letters to several Church communities that he had established to correct false teachings or admonish sinful behaviors, and also to continue to teach and clarify certain doctrines. These letters of Paul to the various Church communities, such as the Corinthians, the Ephesians, and the Philippians, comprise about 25 percent of the New Testament. Other Apostles, such as Peter, James, and John, also wrote letters of instruction, which the early Christians treated as holy writings.

Meanwhile, some of the Apostles and their associates wrote down the story of Christ's life. The exact dates that the Gospels were written are not certain; however, scholars believe they were written between AD 65 and AD 95. Matthew's Gospel was written for Jewish converts. Mark's short Gospel was written as catechesis for the new Gentile converts. Luke's Gospel and the Acts of the Apostles were written as a legal defense for Paul, who was to be tried in Antioch. These three Gospels we call the "synoptic" Gospels because they are very similar in style, structure, and chronology, and they seem to borrow stories and sources from each other. John's Gospel was written last—about AD 90–95. His Gospel gives events and teachings of Jesus not found in the synoptics, and its focus is a much deeper theological understanding of Christ's life, death, and Resurrection. Because these Gospels were the earliest depictions of the life and teaching of Jesus and were written by Christ's own Apostles or their close associates, they were quickly identified in the early Church as inspired writings containing the witness of Jesus.

Other so-called "gospels," such as the "gospel of Thomas," were in circulation, but these were heavily influenced by the Gnostic heresy popular at that time, even among some Christians. Because these so-called gospels, various other letters, and writings contradicted the teaching of the Apostles, they were rejected as not being truly inspired writings.

The official canon of the New Testament was declared only after much time, prayer, and debate. Some of the Apostle's successors thought that certain books were not inspired, such as the Letters of Jude and the Letter to the Hebrews. Others claimed that the writings of Clement, an early successor to Peter, were inspired. But slowly there emerged a consensus within the Church's Magisterium on what was truly inspired, and what was not. The criteria generally used as the standard to measure the canonicity of writings were as follows:

1. The text had to have been written in the apostolic age, between AD 33–95.
2. The text had to have been written by an Apostle or a direct associate of the Apostles.
3. The content had to be in keeping with apostolic teaching and Tradition.

In AD 382, Pope Damasus I convened a council of bishops in Rome to settle the matter of the canon of Scripture. At the council, he issued a decree that codified the canon of Scripture to include the books of the Old Testament contained in the Septuagint as well as the twenty-seven books of the New Testament. The canon was also affirmed at the Synod of Bishops in Hippo in AD 393, and later at the Synod in Carthage in AD 397. Both synods were heavily influenced by Saint Augustine, and by the late third century the Church finally had her official canon, which is upheld and honored in the Catholic Church to this day.

The Deuterocanonical Books (or the "Apocrypha")

This same canon was unquestioned throughout the history of the Church up until the time of the Protestant Reformation over a thousand years later in the sixteenth century. The Protestant Reformers challenged the canonicity of several books, which became known by Protestants as the "apocrypha." In 1545 the pope convened the Council of Trent to respond to the Reformers rejection of Catholic doctrine. One act of the Council reaffirmed what had been taught from the early Church and officially defined the canon of Scripture.

The apocrypha (also called the deuterocanonical books) includes Tobit, Judith, 1 and 2 Maccabees, Wisdom, Sirach, and Baruch. The Reformers also rejected six chapters in Esther and three chapters in Daniel. Those books were rejected for several reasons, but primarily they were discarded because they conflicted with the new theology the Reformers were proposing. They did not believe in prayer for the dead (Tob. 12:12; 2 Macc. 12:39–45), nor did they believe that the saints and angels were interceding for those on earth (2 Macc. 15:14; Tob. 12:12, 15). We know this from Luther's own words indicating that he wanted to toss Esther and Maccabees into the Elbe River.

Protestants also justified their decision by saying that the deuterocanonical books were found only in the Greek canon of the Old Testament (the Septuagint) and not in the Hebrew canon extant (still existing) at the time. At the time of the Apostles, however, the Septuagint had been the accepted translation of Scripture for three hundred years. In fact, the Septuagint was the Scriptures that Jesus and the Apostles themselves used! The Church had continuously regarded these seven books as an indistinguishable part of the Canon of the Old Testament for fifteen hundred years.

It must also be mentioned that Luther wanted to remove, or at least regard as non-apostolic, parts of the New Testament. Hebrews, James, Jude, and Revelation appeared at the end of his translation of the Bible and were called the New Testament "apocrypha." This lack of respect for such a vital part of the foundation of Christianity clearly illustrates the need for the Church's guidance, authority, and teaching office to safeguard both Sacred Scripture and Sacred Tradition.

The Old Testament

Now that we have seen how the canon of Scripture was compiled within the Church, let us explore in more detail exactly what the Old and New Testaments reveal concerning the Father's loving plan of salvation accomplished by Christ.

The Old Testament reveals creation, the Fall of humanity into sin, God's plan of salvation, and the gradual revelation of Himself to the chosen people of Israel. In the Old Testament we see that God did not abandon humanity after the Fall, rather out of the chaos of sin He slowly and lovingly gathered a chosen people and prepared them for redemption in Christ.

The Old Testament Reveals a Series of Covenants between God and His People

The Old Testament reveals a series of covenants established by God between Himself and His chosen people. A **covenant** is much more than simply a contract, or an agreement. It is a very solemn promise in which God and His people enter into a pledge of love and fidelity. God offered covenant after covenant to humanity, even though time after time God's chosen people were disobedient and failed to be faithful to the covenants.

Here are some of the people with whom God made covenants.

- Adam and Eve, husband and wife, the first parents of the human family.
- Noah and his family, the faithful remnant of a humanity consumed by sin.
- Abraham, our father in faith, the progenitor of the Twelve Tribes of Israel, and the foundation of God's chosen people.
- Moses, who gained his people's freedom from slavery to the Egyptians and brought them to the Promised Land.
- David, who became the king of the nation of Israel, one of the great kingdoms of the ancient world.

Each covenant in the Old Testament not only reveals more about God and His plan of salvation, but also brings about the gradual gathering and preparation of His people. The covenants prepare for and are fulfilled in the coming of Christ, who established the New and Everlasting Covenant with all of humanity, extending it to the very ends of the earth through the Catholic Church.

The Old Testament Foreshadows and Prepares God's People for Christ

Since the Old Testament is the gradual unfolding of God's plan of salvation, it can be said that it is ultimately all about Christ. That is why the Church in her wisdom did not discard it but kept it as the first part of the canon—because it reveals Christ.

However, Christ's revelation in the Old Testament is not explicit, but can be seen through analogies and what is also called **typology**. In typology, characters or events foreshadow or point to events and people who come in the future. These individuals and events foreshadow Christ and His fulfillment of the law and prophecies. There are many examples throughout the Old Testament. In retrospect, with all that we now know of Christ, the sacraments, and the Church, we see how perfectly God was preparing His chosen people for His plan of salvation in Christ.

A prime example of typology in the Old Testament can be seen in the story of Adam, the first man God created. He is actually called an anti-type because he is the symbol of the exact opposite of all that Christ is. Paul writes using this form of typology in his letter to the Romans:

> Therefore, just as through one person sin entered the world, and through sin, death, and thus death came to all . . . [and] by that one person's transgression the many died, how much more did the grace of God and the gracious gift of the one person Jesus Christ overflow for the many. . . . For if, by the transgression of one person, death came to reign through that one, how much more will those who receive the abundance of grace and of the gift of justification come to reign in life through the one person Jesus Christ. (Rom. 5:12–17)

Typology has been used abundantly in the study of Scripture from before the time of Christ. In this text we too, using typology, will study many examples from the Old and New Testaments which help us to better understand Christ, Mary, the Church, the sacraments, and so on. Through this method we will come to a deeper understanding of God's plan of salvation in Christ.

Three Parts of the Old Testament

Historical Narrative: Genesis–2 Maccabees

The historical books including Genesis through 2 Maccabees give the theological history of the Hebrew people. It covers about forty-five hundred years of history, from the early recorded Hebrew accounts of creation to the era of the Maccabean revolt, about one hundred years before Christ. This part of the Old Testament reveals the series of covenants that God made with mankind and how His people continued to be both faithful and unfaithful to them. It also reveals the consequences of their infidelity as well as God's merciful response in offering new and more profound covenants. The first five books are called the Pentateuch, or the Torah, and contain the heart of the Mosaic Law. They are considered the most sacred of all the Old Testament writings.

The Wisdom Literature: Job–Sirach

The Wisdom Literature including Job through Sirach was derived from Hebrew prayer and spiritual life. They give deep insight into the spirituality of God's chosen people. These writings are very poetic. They penetrate to the heart of the people's relationship with God and of His love for them. The Book of Psalms contains one hundred fifty Hebrew prayers of an amazing variety of topics. Several of the books of the Wisdom Literature were written by David and his son Solomon, while others were written at various times throughout the history of Israel.

The Prophetic Books: Isaiah–Malachi

The prophetic books including Isaiah through Malachi were written in the later part of the history of Israel, primarily during the time of the divided kingdom and during the period preceding, during, and after Israel's exile into Babylon. The prophets had a twofold purpose. At first, the prophets came to warn Israel about their unfaithfulness to the covenant and the looming consequences. However, the prophets also brought the good news of God's coming salvation in the Messiah. These books contain numerous prophecies concerning this Savior—prophecies that would be fulfilled by Christ. Certainly, Isaiah was the most explicit prophet concerning Christ's coming, so much so that his book is often called the Fifth Gospel, or the Gospel of the Old Testament. Not only does Isaiah accurately predict Christ's birth, he also has explicit predictions concerning Christ's Passion and death (see Is. 53:1–12).

The New Testament

The New Testament records the life and ministry of Jesus, and the activity and teachings of the Apostles and the early Church. The New Testament was written through the inspiration of the Holy Spirit by some of the Apostles, or by men closely associated to their ministry. All the books of the New Testament were written between about AD 50 and AD 95.

Four Parts of the New Testament

The Gospels

The **Gospels** of Matthew, Mark, Luke, and John are the inspired stories of the life and ministry of Jesus. Matthew, Mark, and Luke are very similar, while John is an elaboration of the first three. We hold a special reverence for the four Gospels because they record the life and ministry of Christ.

The Acts of the Apostles

The Acts of the Apostles, written by Luke, records the activity of the Apostles and the growth of the early Church.

The Epistles

The epistles are a collection of letters written by the Apostles or their associates to the early Church communities throughout the ancient world. These letters are important because they clearly show the apostolic teachings and the developing theology of the early Church. Most of the letters are written by the Apostle Paul, but others are written by Apostles like Peter and John.

Revelation

Written by the Apostle John, the book of Revelation is a highly symbolic book concerning the final victory of Christ, and it is largely liturgical in nature. It reveals that we in the earthly liturgy participate in the heavenly liturgy and already participate in the victory over sin won by Christ, the Lamb of God. Revelation also speaks of the end times when Christ will come again and restore in its fullness the kingdom of God.

The Interpretation of Scripture

It is very important to establish the appropriate ways in which the Scriptures are to be interpreted in light of Sacred Tradition and their place within the whole of God's revelation. There are three important criteria that must be observed when interpreting the Bible faithfully.

Three Criteria for Interpretation

Within the context of Sacred Tradition

Sacred Scripture must be interpreted in the context of the Sacred Tradition from which it came. Our interpretation of Scripture cannot contradict the living Tradition of the Church. Since Scripture is that part of Tradition committed to writing under the inspiration of the Holy Spirit, it can only be accurately interpreted within that same Tradition. Unity exists between Scripture and Tradition, whereby together, under the guidance of the Holy Spirit and authority of the Magisterium, they transmit in its fullness the entire revealed Word of God.

Content and unity of the whole of Sacred Scripture

The content and unity of the whole of Scripture must be given special attention. Even though there are many different books written by different authors, the Bible must be seen as a unified whole. One should interpret any passage in the context in which it was written, taking into account the author's intention, literary style, culture, and world view of the time. However, we must also interpret the passage in light of the unity of the Scriptures. While it is important to understand the meaning and purpose of an individual passage, it cannot be interpreted in isolation. This is a frequent error of fundamentalist Protestants and other movements within Christianity. Wee cannot build a theology around isolated passages. The Bible was intended to be seen as a unified whole, with all the books working together to form one message of salvation in Jesus Christ. Any interpretation of the Scriptures must be understood within the content of the whole, and any individual passages cannot truly contradict any other part. The Bible is ultimately a work of the Holy Spirit and God cannot contradict Himself.

Analogy of faith

It is also important to pay attention to the **analogy of faith.** The Bible was not written as a history book or a story book, it was written under the **inspiration** of the Holy Spirit to communicate to mankind certain theological truths necessary for salvation. The analogy of faith indicates a rule, or guide, for the exegesis or study of Scripture. Any correct explanation or interpretation of a biblical passage or book will not contradict other truths inherent in the entire body of faith taught by the Church. Biblical scholars adhering to the analogy of faith would never interpret a passage of Scripture in a way that it would oppose any part of revelation. They would never set the sacred writers against each other, as, for example, Martin Luther did with regard to Paul and James. Not paying attention to the analogy of faith led Luther to a contrived contradiction between the sacred writers on the relationship of "faith and works," to an incorrect interpretation of the text, and to the incorrect teaching of sola fide. There must be a coherence of the truths of the faith.

In conclusion, we must keep in mind that through Sacred Scripture, God our heavenly Father comes "lovingly to meet his children, and talks with them" (*Dei Verbum,* no. 21). He, who desired to reveal Himself to us, inspired the writing of the Scriptures and sent the Holy Spirit to guide the Church whom He entrusted with the great responsibility of protecting, interpreting, and handing on the revelation of His Son and the plan of salvation fulfilled in Christ.

The Outline of the Bible

THE OLD TESTAMENT

I. Creation

A. First Story of Creation (Gen. 1–2:3)
B. The Second Story of Creation (Gen. 2:4–25)
C. The Creation of Man and Woman in the Image and Likeness of God (Gen. 1:26–28)
D. The First Covenant (Gen. 1:29–30; 2:15–17)

II. Original Sin: The Fall of Adam and Eve

A. The Temptation (Gen. 3:1–5)
B. The Fall (Gen. 3:6)
C. The Consequence (Gen. 3:7–24)
D. The Proliferation of Sin
   1. Cain and Abel: The world's first murder (Gen. 4:1–16)
   2. The wickedness of man was great on the earth (Gen. 6:5)

III. Noah and the Flood (FAMILY)

A. The Call of Noah (Gen. 6:11–22)
B. The Flood (Gen. 7–8)
C. The New Covenant with Noah (Gen. 9:1–18)
D. The Tower of Babel: The Chaos of Sin (Gen. 11:1–9)

IV. Abraham: The Father of God's People (TRIBE)

A. The Covenant with Abraham (Gen. 12:1–9)
B. The Test of Abraham (Gen. 22:1–19)
C. The Patriarchs: Isaac, Jacob, Joseph (Gen. 23–38)
D. Joseph goes to Egypt (Gen. 39–50)

V. Moses: Redemption and Revelation (PEOPLE)

A. The Israelites are taken into slavery in Egypt (Ex. 1)
B. The Salvation of Moses (Ex. 2:1–10)
C. Moses Flees Egypt (Ex. 2:11–25)
D. The Call of Moses (Ex. 3–4)
E. The Confrontation with Pharaoh and the Nine Plagues (Ex. 5–10)
F. The Tenth Plague: The Passover (Ex. 11–13)

G. The Escape from Egypt and Crossing of the Red Sea (Ex. 14–15)
H. Israel in the Desert: The Unfaithful People and the Mercy of God (Ex. 16–18)
I. The Covenant with Moses: The Ten Commandments (Ex. 19–20)
J. The Laws and Sacrifices of the Mosaic Law (Deuteronomy and Leviticus)
K. The Conquering of the Promised Land (Joshua)
L. The Cycle of Judges: Disobedience, Judgment, Deliverance, Obedience, Disobedience, etc. (Judges)

VI. David: The Kingdom of Israel (NATION)
The Wisdom Books written

A. The Desire for a King (1 Sam. 8:1–9)
B. The Reign and Failure of King Saul (1 Sam. 13–15:9)
C. The Anointing of David (1 Sam. 16)
D. The Davidic Covenant (2 Sam. 7:1–29)
E. The Sin of David (2 Sam. 11:1–27)
F. King Solomon (1 Kings 1–11)

VII. Period of Division and Turmoil
The Prophetic Books written (2 Kings–2 Maccabees)

A. The Kingdom Divides: Israel and Judah
B. The Judgment of the Northern Kingdom of Israel
C. Exile and Restoration of Judah

THE NEW TESTAMENT

I. The Life and Ministry of Christ: The Gospels

A. The Synoptic Gospels
    1. The Gospel of Matthew
    2. The Gospel of Mark
    3. The Gospel of Luke
B. The Gospel of John

II. The Acts of the Apostles: The Growth and Ministry of the Catholic and Apostolic Church (UNIVERSAL CHURCH)

III. The Epistles of Paul and Other Apostles

A. The Letters of Paul or the New Testament Letters

1. Letter to the Romans
2. First Letter to the Corinthians
3. Second Letter to the Corinthians
4. Letter to the Galatians
5. Letter to the Ephesians
6. Letter to the Philippians
7. Letter to the Colossians
8. First Letter to the Thessalonians
9. Second Letter to the Thessalonians
10. First Letter to Timothy
11. Second Letter to Timothy
12. Letter to Titus
13. Letter to Philemon
14. Letter to the Hebrews

B. The Letters of the Apostles or Catholic Letters

1. The Letter of James
2. The First Letter of Peter
3. The Second Letter of Peter
4. The First Letter of John
5. The Second Letter of John
6. The Third Letter of John
7. The Letter of Jude

IV. The Revelation of John: The Heavenly Banquet of the Lamb of God and the Second Coming of Christ

From the Catechism: Key Words to Know

BIBLE/SACRED SCRIPTURE: The books that contain the truth of God's revelation and were composed by human authors inspired by the Holy Spirit (105). The Bible contains both the forty-six books of the Old Testament and the twenty-seven books of the New Testament (120).

CANON OF SCRIPTURE: The Church's complete list of sacred books of the Bible (120).

COVENANT: A solemn agreement between human beings or between God and a human being involving mutual commitments, or guarantees. The Bible refers to God's covenants with Noah, Abraham, and Moses as leaders of the chosen people, Israel. In the Old Testament, or Covenant, God revealed His law through Moses and prepared His people for salvation through the prophets. In the New Testament, or Covenant, Christ established a new and eternal covenant through His own sacrificial death and Resurrection. The Christian economy is the new and definitive Covenant that will never pass away, and no new public revelation is to be expected before the glorious manifestation of our Lord Jesus Christ (56, 62, 66).

TYPOLOGY: The discernment of persons, events, or things in the Old Testament which prefigured, and thus served as a "type" (or prototype) of the fulfillment of God's plan in the Person of Christ. The typology of the Old Testament, which is made clear in the New Testament, demonstrates the dynamic unity of the divine plan of salvation (128).

GOSPEL: The four Gospels are the books written by the evangelists Matthew, Mark, Luke, and John which have for their central object Jesus Christ, God's Incarnate Son: His life, teachings, Passion and glorification, and His Church's beginnings under the Spirit's guidance (124, 514).

ANALOGY OF FAITH: The coherence of the truths of the faith among themselves and within the whole plan of revelation (114).

BIBLICAL INSPIRATION: The gift of the Holy Spirit that assisted a human author to write a biblical book so that it has God as its author and teaches faithfully, without error, the saving truth that God has willed to be consigned to us (105).

Chapter 4

Creation and the Fall of Adam and Eve

Reading the Catechism: Paragraphs 279–421

> Whoever eats my flesh and drinks my blood has eternal life, and I will raise him on the last day.
>
> —John 6:54

With an overview of Sacred Scripture and with an understanding of the tools to interpret it, we can now explore specifics. We will first look at creation. The Book of Genesis shows us that God created a material and spiritual world. This first book in the Bible gives us insight into God's intentions in creation. It discloses important theological truths about the nature of angels and human beings and their relationship with each other and with God. It also has plenty of drama. We see angels who rebel against God. Then our first parents, Adam and Eve, tempted by the leader of the fallen angels, also disobeyed God. Their rebellion—the first sin of mankind—has dire consequences. Yet there is hope; God is merciful. He announces and inaugurates His plan of salvation and redemption that He will ultimately accomplish in Jesus Christ.

The Creation Stories

In the Book of Genesis (which means "beginning"), God reveals His definitive plan and purpose for creation and the human family. Genesis actually begins with two different creation stories. The first tells us how God gradually created the world over a series of six days with the creation of man and woman in the "image and likeness" of God as the pinnacle and ultimate purpose of His creation. God commands them to "be fertile and multiply; fill the earth and subdue it" (Gen. 1:28). On the seventh day God rests and ponders the goodness of His creation.

In the second story of creation, the man **Adam** is first created "out of the dust of the ground," and God "blew into his nostrils the breath of life" (Gen. 2:7). Thus, man's life is a sharing in the very life of God in His "image and likeness." God then creates the rest of creation for and at the service of the man, but the man still finds himself unfulfilled. So God casts Adam into a deep sleep and takes one of his ribs and fashions out of it a woman named **Eve**. The man rejoices at the sight of Eve and exclaims, "This one, at last, is bone of my bones and flesh of my flesh; this one shall be called 'woman,' for out of 'man' this one has been taken" (Gen. 2:23). This second creation story ends with Adam and Eve becoming "one flesh," and they were naked, yet felt no shame.

Purpose of the Creation Stories

Why are there two creation stories? The book of Genesis is actually a compilation of stories that had been handed down orally over a very long period of time in the ancient Hebrew tradition, before they were committed to writing in what became the Book of Genesis. These stories come from two principle traditions, the Yahwist and the Priestly. While the stories differ, they nonetheless each contain the same theological truths about God, creation, the human person, and God's plan for humanity. They are not meant to be records, or logs, of exact history or science. The Hebrew people who told them and eventually committed them to writing knew little of science, and their history was handed down to them in "mythological" tales. A mythological tale uses stories, analogies, and symbols to reveal and transmit specific theological and moral truths, not necessarily those of history and science. Thus, these creation stories do not tell us literally and scientifically how God created the universe; rather, they reveal foundational and fundamental theological truths for all times and cultures to understand. Therefore, we can see that both stories are true.

The Foundational Truths Contained in the Creation Stories

These two creation accounts reveal to us the following fundamental theological truths.

God is the creator of all things

Both creation stories reveal that God is the creator of all things. He created the heavens and the earth, and all things upon the earth and in the sea. There is nothing that exists that God did not create.

God created all things good

The first story of creation repeatedly emphasizes that all things are created good. Since God is all-good and, in fact, is Goodness itself, He is incapable of creating evil. Many people throughout history, even to this day, have believed that various parts of creation are evil in themselves. For example, the Gnostic and some New Age religions believe that what is material is evil and only what is spiritual is good. Genesis clearly teaches that all that God has made is good. When He was finished, He proclaimed it to be "very good" and pondered its goodness on the seventh day.

Man and woman are created in the "image and likeness" of God

Also made clear in both creation accounts is that man and woman are the pinnacle and purpose of God's creation, and are created to enjoy communion with Him and to participate in His life. In the first creation story, man and woman are the final act of His creation. God creates man and woman "in our image, after our likeness" (Gen. 1:26). They are the only creatures that are created like God because they share in His life.

In the second story, God breathes His life into Adam's nostrils; thus Adam receives and shares in God's very life, and an intimate communion is established between Adam and God. Eve is created from Adam, so she too shares in divine life and enjoys communion with God.

Man and woman are called to intimate communion with one another

Two other fundamental truths are revealed in these stories. First, man is not created to be alone but to be in communion with another. God by His very nature is communal—the intimate communion of three divine Persons. Man, who is created like God, is also called to communion. We are all called to communion with God. It was for this that man was made. But we are also created to have communion with each other, to be in relationship with other human beings. This is especially evident in the second creation story. Despite all of the other things God had created, man was still lonely and unfulfilled. *Adam did not fully recognize his identity and experience the fullness of his humanity until he was in communion with another person like himself.*

Second, God willed that man and woman come together in a unique and special union where the two give a complete and total gift of self to the other. God created the human family as man and woman to complement and complete the other. "That is why a man leaves his father and mother and clings to his wife, and the two of them become one flesh" (Gen. 2:24). Here we see the divine institution of marriage, where a man and a woman are called to come together in total and lifelong love. This total gift of self is so profound that they become "one flesh."

The communion of man and woman is for the creation of new human life

In this intimate communion man and woman become co-creators with God in bringing forth new life. God commands man and woman to "be fertile and multiply; fill the earth and subdue it" (Gen. 1:28). Thus, man and woman become "one flesh" not only to unite in intimate communion and love with one another, but to create with God new human life by their love expressed sexually. From the very beginning God desired that in marriage and sexuality, we would both experience love and be created out of love, sharing in the life and love of the Trinity.

The creation stories were not written and inspired by the Holy Spirit to reveal exact history or science, but rather to reveal something far more profound—the fundamental theological truths about God and humanity. Remember, while the Bible does contain within itself a lot of history, it is not meant to be a history or science book. Rather it reveals to us those truths necessary for salvation that God wanted to be crystallized into writing for all time through the inspiration of the Holy Spirit.

Metaphysics: The Study of God's Creation

Now that we have established the theological truths revealed to us in Sacred Scripture about creation and God's plan for the human family, it is very important to take a closer look at what God has created, things both visible and invisible, and to ask: Where does man fit into the big picture? What is our relationship with God and with other creatures that God has created? These questions are as old as mankind, and the search for the answers are the subject of the philosophy called metaphysics—"the study of being."

The Spiritual Realm

All of creation can be distinguished according to the spiritual realm and the material realm. The spiritual realm consists of those realities that are pure spirit. The spiritual is invisible to the human eye, but is very real. Microwaves and radio waves are helpful comparisons. They are constantly passing by us and through us. Does that mean that they are not real? No, otherwise we would not have television or radio. It is just that our sense of sight cannot perceive them. The same is true with the spiritual realm of creation. Our sense of sight is not programmed to see invisible realities while we are here on earth. So just because we cannot see something does not mean that it is not real.

God is pure spirit

God is not bound by space and time. He is what we call *transcendent*. From the Latin meaning "surpassing," transcendence is God's existence apart from and outside of creation and the finite world. While God is at the same time present everywhere, "omnipresent," His existence is beyond the finite world and is in no way confined to it. God is also eternal, which means He had no beginning and has no end. Nothing created God; He always was. He is the First Cause, the First Mover, and the Creator: He is Being Itself. Everything else that exists was created by Him and is held in being by Him. In addition, since God has no end, He will always be, and nothing can destroy Him or cause Him to end or cease to exist. This reality may be hard for us to imagine and grasp because everything we experience has a beginning and an end. But it is reality nonetheless.

The Angels were created by God and are also pure spirit

Angels were created by God to be His heavenly court, to glorify Him always and in all things, and to enjoy His presence. They serve Him in various ways, but especially as the messengers of His plan of salvation. Like God, they are not bound by space or time, and while they can be present in the finite world they are in no way confined to it. Angels also share in the life of God. They are in close communion with Him and are created in the likeness of God in that they have intellect and free will. Thus, they are able to reason and, because of free will, can freely love God and serve Him. Angels are not eternal, for they were created by God. But they are immortal; that is, they will live forever and can never be destroyed.

Angels have various functions and duties as servants of God, as can be seen throughout the unfolding of God's plan of salvation. Some have been messengers, some serve to protect human beings, others have led the people of God. The Cherubim with a fiery revolving sword closed paradise after the first sin. Angels are also divided into choirs, or groups, which form a hierarchy (from highest to lowest): Seraphim, Cherubim, Thrones, Dominions, Powers, Virtues, Principalities, Archangels, and Angels.

The Material Realm

The material realm is that part of creation that consists of the physical world. Human senses can perceive most of the physical world, and therefore it is visible, although there are aspects of it that humans cannot see or hear under ordinary circumstances. The material world is finite. God created all of it, and thus it has a beginning. It will pass away and is progressing toward its end. All things in the material world are bound by space and time. It encompasses all of material creation from basic things such as rocks and minerals, to higher life forms such as plants and animals. All things in the material world will eventually come to an end, with one exception—us. Man is the only thing in the material world that is immortal.

Human Beings: Body/Soul Composite

Man is the most unique creature in all of creation, because only we exist in both the material and spiritual world at the same time. We are made up of a spiritual **soul** and a material body.

We were created in the image and likeness of God. We are like God in that we possess a soul, which is a sharing in the very nature and life of God. Although we lost the likeness of God through original sin, it can be regained in Baptism. Man is endowed with both an intellect and a free will. Through our intellect we can reason, and through our free will we can choose to love God and others. He created us with free will so that we may both accept His love and love Him in return. Love by its very nature must be chosen and given; it must be a free act of the will. We can use our free will to choose to love God for which we were made, or as we will see, we can choose to abuse our free will to disobey and offend God through sin.

We were created with a material body that is intimately joined to our souls. God did not create our bodies as a mere "shell" or "dwelling place" for our souls.

There is no "dualism" that pits the body against the soul, seeing the physical as holding a person back from experiencing true spirituality. Rather, our body and soul together make us human. Through our bodies, our souls sense and experience the material world, and in the same way our soul is expressed through the body and our actions. Thus, we must always treat our bodies with the same utmost respect as our souls because they are intimately and inseparably joined. Only when sin entered the world did a struggle, or conflict, arise between our body and soul, because sin distorts and disorders our human nature. However, through the Resurrection, Christ restores the unity of body and soul.

Because man is the only creature in the material world that is created with a spiritual soul in the image and likeness of God, we are fundamentally different and set apart from all other creation. No other material creatures have a spiritual soul that possesses an intellect and a will that enables them to freely choose to love or to hate. As we saw clearly in the creation accounts, man is the pinnacle and the purpose of God's creation.

The whole reason that God created the universe was for us, so we could experience His life and love and love our Creator in return. *Human beings have a dignity that far surpasses all of creation.* Angels, being a higher order of being than humans, enjoy a greater dignity in the *order of being* (see Thomas Aquinas, *Summa Theologica*, Question 59, Article 3). But as the Son of God united Himself to a human nature and not an angelic nature, we can speak of a greater dignity of the human person in light of the Incarnation elevating our dignity in the *order of grace*. The modern scientific, biological, and environmentalist attempts to bring human beings on par in dignity and nature to other animals is a serious error that degrades the true nature of human beings and distorts their relationship with nature. God gave humanity dominion and stewardship over all of creation. Indeed, this stewardship involves great responsibility to care for and respect nature. However, to bring the dignity of nature and the environment to the same level as the dignity of the human person is an indication of the general lowering of human dignity throughout our culture. In fact, the dignity of each and every human being is so great in the eyes of God that He even commanded the angels to serve, protect, and guide us, and to be His messengers to us.

The Fall of the Angels

This very plan of God—to have the angels serve man—ultimately led to the rebellion and fall of the angels. As we discussed, angels are pure spirit, and they, like man, are created with an intellect and free will. The angels were given the opportunity to choose to love and serve God, or to rebel and turn away from Him. Lucifer (means "light-bringing") was one of the Seraphim, the highest order of angels. He was the most powerful angel, and thus he was the leader and head of the heavenly host. When Lucifer heard God's plan to create man in His image and likeness and to command the angels to be man's servant, Lucifer's pride swelled up. He could not imagine that he, the most powerful and glorious angel in heaven, would have to serve a mere human being. So he rebelled against God and His plan, and incited other angels to rebel with him. There was a great civil war in heaven. Armed with the power of God, Michael the Archangel, along with the other good angels, drove Lucifer and his evil angels out of heaven and into hell, the eternal state of separation between God and those creatures—angels and humans—who have permanantly chosen to reject God. Lucifer then became Satan, the prince of darkness, and the other evil angels became **devils/demons**. Thus, **evil** entered God's creation through the free will of His creatures. God did not create evil, for He is all-good; rather, evil is the result of creatures with free will choosing against good.

Satan and the other devils retain their intelligence and power, although infinitely inferior to the divine power of God. They spend eternity cursing their Creator and seeking ways to offend and hurt Him, but they know that they cannot destroy Him. If they cannot destroy God, what would be the best way that they could hurt or offend Him? By destroying His children created in His image and likeness. Remember, man was the motive for the angels' rebellion, and if Satan and his devils can eternally separate man from God, they can destroy God's own likeness in which we are made. In their sin-twisted intellects, they hope to gravely hurt God by eternally separating man from Him. So Satan inaugurates his own plan, to "prowl about the world seeking the ruin of souls" (see 1 Pet. 5:8)

Satan and his devils are very real, and we are the objects in an ongoing spiritual battle. We can cooperate with Satan's plan of **temptation**, sin, and separation from God, or we can cooperate with God and His kingdom of love, justice, and peace. In this battle we need God's grace, power, and Word to "quench all [the] flaming arrows of the evil one" (Eph. 6:16). Pope Paul VI (1964–1978) was once asked what was the greatest threat to the Church in the modern world. His response was not atheistic communism. It was not nuclear war. His response was that too many people no longer believe in the existence of Satan. Why is this such a threat? If we are not even aware that we have an enemy and know who he is, then we are easy prey for his influence and temptations. But if we know that we are in a battle and we are properly equipped to fight and withstand the enemy, then we will be victorious through the power of Jesus Christ! As Christians, we are in a spiritual battle, a battle that has eternal consequences. We can shrug off the existence of the devil as a scare tactic of medieval Christianity, or we can take the advice and instruction of Saint Paul who exhorts us to be ready to fight *the* good fight:

> Finally, draw your strength from the Lord and from his mighty power. Put on the armor of God so that you may be able to stand firm against the tactics of the devil. For our struggle is not with flesh and blood but with the principalities, with the powers, with the world rulers of this present darkness, with the evil spirits in the heavens. Therefore, put on the armor of God, that you may be able to resist on the evil day and, having done everything, to hold your ground. So stand fast with your loins girded in truth, clothed with righteousness as a breastplate, and your feet shod in readiness for the gospel of peace. In all circumstances, hold faith as a shield, to quench all (the) flaming arrows of the evil one. And take the helmet of salvation and the sword of the Spirit, which is the word of God. With all prayer and supplication, pray at every opportunity in the Spirit. (Eph. 6:10–18)

The Fall of Adam and Eve

In Genesis chapter 3 we see the unfolding of Satan's clever plan to seek out and spiritually destroy man and separate us from God. This powerful story tells us that we are created with free will and have the responsibility to use that free will to choose what is good according to the plan of God our Father and Creator. It also demonstrates that we can choose to abuse our free will and choose against God's plan of goodness for us and ultimately reject the life and love that God offers. Satan enters human history and by deception and temptation influences Adam and Eve, our first parents, to rebel against God and fall into the first sin. However, God does not abandon them, but inaugurates His own plan of salvation that will restore humanity to communion with Him and crush the head of Satan and his rebellion.

The Tree of Life vs. the Tree of Knowledge of Good and Evil

We see in the second creation story that God planted a beautiful garden in Eden and within this garden were two important trees.

> The Lord God planted a garden in Eden, in the east, and placed there the man whom he had formed. Out of the ground the Lord God made every tree grow that was delightful to look at and good for food, with the tree of life in the middle of the garden and the tree of the knowledge of good and evil.
>
> The Lord God then took the man and settled him in the garden of Eden, to cultivate and care for it. The Lord God gave the man this order: "You are free to eat from any of the trees of the garden except the tree of knowledge of good and evil. From that tree you shall not eat; when you eat from it you shall die." (Gen. 2:8–9; 15–17)

The tree in the middle of the garden is the tree of life, and this tree represents eternal life and union with God. Eating of the tree of life is symbolic of sharing in the very life of God and having intimate communion with Him. It is in the very center of the garden because it speaks to God's plan for us in creation—filled with God's life and in intimate union with Him.

The second important tree is the tree of the knowledge of good and evil. God forbids Adam to eat from this tree, for if he eats of it, he will be doomed to die.

Why does God forbid Adam to eat of this tree? And if Adam is not to eat of this tree, why did God put it there in the first place? Many people see this as God testing Adam, but God is not testing Adam. He rather is revealing to him that he has free will. Adam has absolute freedom; he can eat from any tree in the garden. *But he will only be truly and authentically free if he chooses to eat from the tree of life, because the fullness of the meaning of his life and of his nature as a human being can only by found in union with God.* Pope John Paul II beautifully articulates this point:

> With this imagery, Revelation teaches that *the power to decide what is good and what is evil does not belong to man, but to God alone.* The man is certainly free, inasmuch as he can understand

> and accept God's commands. And he possesses an extremely far-reaching freedom, since he can eat "of every tree of the garden." But his freedom is not unlimited: it must halt before the "tree of the knowledge of good and evil," for it is called to accept the moral law given by God. In fact, human freedom finds its authentic and complete fulfillment precisely in the acceptance of that law. God, who alone is good, knows perfectly what is good for man, and by virtue of his very love proposes this good to man in the commandments. (Encyclical Letter on The Splender of Truth *Veritatis splendor* [August 6, 1993], no. 35)

Consequently, Adam can also choose to abuse his freedom, and instead of looking to God his Creator and Father to determine what is truly good for him, Adam can turn away from God's goodness and determine for himself what is good and evil—an action to Adam's detriment. This is why God forbids him to eat from the tree of the knowledge of good and evil. As we will see, when man takes it upon himself to determine what is good or evil, he no longer sees himself as a creature dependent on the will and plan of his Creator, but views himself instead as a god, a rival of the true God. This is a fundamental rejection of God and of man's true nature.

The First Sin

God established His first covenant with Adam. He created Adam full of His life and love, and Adam remained in relationship with God as long as he chose to love God and obey His commands. As long as Adam ate of the fruit of the tree of life and remained in union with God, he enjoyed eternal life. However, Adam could and did break his covenant with God by rejecting God's will for his life as he ate of the tree of the knowledge of good and evil.

At the beginning of Genesis 3, a new creature enters the scene, a snake or serpent. This serpent is an image of Satan, who will now inaugurate his own plan for the destruction of God's children by influencing and tempting Adam and Eve to break their covenant with God.

> Now the snake was the most cunning of all the wild animals that the LORD God had made. He asked the woman, "Did God really say, 'You shall not eat from any of the trees in the garden?'" The woman answered the snake: "We may eat of the

> fruit of the trees in the garden; it is only about the fruit of the tree in the middle of the garden that God said, 'You shall not eat it or even touch it, or else you will die.'" (Gen. 3:1–5)

What we see here is the paradigm temptation. The serpent deceives Eve by first questioning God's command, "Did God really tell you not to eat of any of the trees in the garden?" Satan, the prince of lies, begins to bring doubt into Eve's mind about what God had commanded. Then the serpent begins to deceive her about who God really is. He does not want Eve to see God as her Creator and loving Father who knows what is best for her and will eternally care for her and love her. Rather, through his deception Satan distorts the truth about who God is: "No, God knows well that the moment you eat of it your eyes will be opened and you will be like gods who know what is good and what is bad." Eve is confused. Her knowledge of God has been shaken. She may have been thinking that maybe God is not who we thought He is. Maybe He doesn't want us to eat the fruit of that tree because He knows we can be like Him. Maybe He really does not love us, but just wants to keep us from being all that we can be. Maybe we will really know what it means to live if we forget this God and His laws that hold us back and, instead, do things the way we want and when we want. Through his deception and cunningness, Satan has tempted Eve to rebel against God. It takes a twisting of the truth, a lie, to get Eve to want to turn away from God.

As the temptation increases, the fruit of the tree of the knowledge of good and evil looks more and more appealing. Eve contemplates how nice it would be to be like God, to know what is good and bad, to have total and all-encompassing freedom. She falls into the temptation and sins against God. "The woman saw that the tree was good for food and pleasing to the eyes, and the tree was desirable for gaining wisdom. So she took some of its fruit and ate it; and she also gave some to her husband, who was with her, and he ate it" (Gen. 3:6). Adam and Eve have broken their covenant with God. They have rejected God as the only One who knows what is good for them and, instead, have exalted themselves to be like gods. No longer are they in the likeness of God, but rather they have completely distorted who they are and have separated themselves from God who is their very life. Adam and Eve have committed the **original sin**.

Through Adam and Eve's original sin, all of humanity has fallen away from God. In fact, all of creation is thrown into chaos through the first sin. As a consequence, everyone is now born into the world in a fallen state—the state of original sin. We come into this world spiritually dead. It is only through Christ's redemption that we are able to once again have communion with God and share in His divine life. That gift is given to us through the Sacrament of Baptism, where God's grace and life are infused into us, and we become a new creation in Christ.

The Consequences of the First Sin

> Then the eyes of both of them were opened, and they knew that they were naked; so they sewed fig leaves together and made loincloths for themselves. When they heard the sound of the Lord God walking about in the garden at the breezy time of the day, the man and his wife hid themselves from the Lord God among the trees of the garden. (Gen. 3:7–8)

The consequences of the first sin are immediate and devastating. We see in the creation stories that God transformed chaos into the unity and perfection of the cosmos. Now sin enters the world and takes that unity, perfection, and goodness, and brings about chaos and disunity. Adam and Eve were created to be "one flesh" in complete, total unity and unconditional love. Now that their eyes have been opened, they experience the evil consequences of their choice, and they realize that they are naked. They feel shame and hide themselves from the presence of God. Thus, disunity between the man and the woman enters the world because they have separated themselves from God and His plan for them. The image and likeness of God in them is distorted. They are no longer filled with His life and love. Their human nature is gravely disordered. They have literally forgotten who they are.

When they hear the sound of the Lord moving about in the garden, they hide themselves from Him. They now fear Him. Their perception of God has completely changed. No longer do they experience Him as their loving Father whom they can completely trust and with whom they can live in His goodness. God is now a rival, someone they cannot trust. Not only have they separated themselves from God's life and love, but also they go so far as to hide themselves from Him. This is the nature of sin. We choose to separate ourselves from God. We choose to hide ourselves from Him. We choose to reject His life and His love. It is not God who hides His face from us, but we who turn away from Him.

God's Response to the First Sin

What is God's response to all this? It would seem logical for God to say, "I cannot believe you did this! I went out of my way to create the whole universe for you, to set you in this beautiful garden, and I gave you all you needed, including a share in my own divine life. And what did you do? You did the one thing I told you not to do! You dwell in your own misery that you created for yourself!" But that is not God's response. *God's first response is to seek out and find His children that are now lost.* "The LORD God then called to the man and asked him, 'Where are you?'" (Gen. 3:9). God does not abandon Adam and Eve after the first sin, but comes searching for them. His response is *mercy.* Even though Adam and Eve completely rejected Him and made themselves His rivals, God still searches for them and reaches out to them in love. However, Adam and Eve's response reveals the chaos, disunity, and mistrust that have entered the world through the first sin.

> The LORD God then called to the man and asked him: Where are you? He answered, "I heard you in the garden; but I was afraid, because I was naked, so I hid." Then God asked: Who told you that you were naked? Have you eaten from the tree of which I had forbidden you to eat? The man replied, "The woman whom you put here with me—she gave me fruit from the tree, so I ate it." The LORD God then asked the woman: What is this you have done? The woman answered, "The snake tricked me, so I ate it." (Gen. 3:9–13)

I wonder what would have happened if at that moment when God came to him, Adam had dropped to his knees before God and said, "Have mercy on me, for I have sinned against my Lord and God." Instead, Adam blames God for giving him the woman who gave him the fruit. Eve blames the serpent for tricking her. Adam and Eve, now separated from God's grace, see God as their enemy, their rival, and one whom they fear and mistrust. Sin has brought chaos, disunity, and distortion between Adam and Eve and between them and God.

The First Announcement of God's Plan of Salvation

What happens next in this dramatic story is absolutely stunning. God, after witnessing the lack of repentance of Adam and Eve, reveals to them the natural consequences of their sin and the true identity of the serpent. This is not God punishing Adam and Eve. He is rather showing them the horrible consequences that have occurred because of their sinful choice.

> The LORD God said to the serpent,
> "Because you have done this,
>   cursed are you above all cattle,
>   and above all wild animals;
> upon your belly you shall go,
>   and dust you shall eat
>   all the days of your life.
> I will put enmity between you and the woman,
>   and between your seed and her seed;
> he shall bruise your head,
>   and you shall bruise his heel."
> To the woman he said,
> "I will greatly multiply your pain in childbearing;
>   in pain you shall bring forth children.
> yet your desire shall be for your husband,
>   and he shall rule over you."
> And to Adam he said,
> "Because you have listened to the voice of your wife,
>   and have eaten of the tree
> of which I command you,
>   'You shall not eat of it,'
> cursed is the ground because of you;
>   in toil you shall eat of it all the days of your life;
> thorns and thistles it shall bring forth to you;
>   and you shall eat the plants of the field.
> In the sweat of your face
>   you shall eat bread
> til you return to the ground,
>   for out of it were you taken;
> you are dust,
>   and to dust you shall return."
> The man called his wife's name Eve, because she was the mother of all the living. (Gen. 3:14-20, RSVCE)

However, in the midst of God's pronouncement of the consequences of sin, God reveals something remarkable. When addressing the serpent God says, "I will put enmity between you and the woman, and between your seed and her seed; he shall bruise your head, and you shall bruise his heel." (Gen. 3:15, RSVCE). What is God revealing here? He is revealing His plan of salvation. In the fullness of time, there will be the offspring of a woman, who will come and strike at the head of Satan. The woman is Mary and her offspring is Jesus. It is Jesus who will strike at the head of Satan, crush him, and overturn his sinful work. Even though Adam and Eve rejected God and His covenant, and remained unrepentant after He called them to Himself, God immediately revealed and set into motion His plan of salvation. This is called the *protoevangelion*, or the "first announcement of the good news."

Banishment from the Tree of Life

> Then the Lord God said: See! The man has become like one of us, knowing good and evil! Now, what if he also reaches out his hand to take fruit from the tree of life, and eats of it and lives forever? The Lord God therefore banished him from the garden of Eden, to till the ground from which he had been taken. He expelled the man, stationing the cherubim and the fiery revolving sword east of the garden of Eden, to guard the way to the tree of life. (Gen. 3:22–24)

God banished Adam and Eve from the garden and forbid the eating of the fruit from the tree of life. However, God did not do this to punish Adam and Eve, but rather to keep them from living forever in their sin. God created man to live forever in His life and love, not in sin. So, out of mercy God banned them from the tree of life. Adam and Eve were unable to undo the effects of their sin without God's help. So God will send a Savior and once again offer access to the tree of life and eternal life in communion with Him.

Jesus Is the New Adam

It was through one man, Adam, that sin and death came into the world, and it is through one man, Jesus Christ, that all of humanity is restored to justification and life. This is why Jesus is called the new Adam. Through perfect obedience to His Father and acceptance of the Cross, Jesus redeems and atones for the disobedience of Adam. God's plan of salvation that was announced to Adam and Eve is completely fulfilled and culminated in the death and Resurrection of Jesus. Saint Paul teaches this eloquently in his Letter to the Romans:

> Therefore, just as through one person sin entered the world, and through sin, death, and thus death came to all, inasmuch as all sinned—for up to the time of the law, sin was in the world, though sin is not accounted when there is no law. But death reigned from Adam to Moses, even over those who did not sin after the pattern of the trespass of Adam, who is the type of the one who was to come. But the gift is not like the transgression. For if by that one person's transgression the many died, how much more did the grace of God and the gracious gift of the one person Jesus Christ overflow for the many. And the gift is not like the result of the one person's sinning. For after one sin there was the judgment that brought condemnation; but the gift, after many transgressions, brought acquittal. For if, by the transgression of one person, death came to reign through that one, how much more will those who receive the abundance of grace and of the gift of justification come to reign in life through the one person Jesus Christ. (Rom. 5:12–19)

There is a remarkable parallel between the disobedience of Adam and the results of his sin in the Old Testament, and the perfect obedience of Jesus and the results of His righteousness in the New Testament. It might be called "The Tale of Two Gardens." Here we so clearly see how Jesus entirely atones for and reverses Adam's sin of disobedience. Through His sacrifice on the Cross, Jesus restores our communion with God and grants us eternal life once again.

Adam in the Garden of Eden

Let us return for a moment and recap what happened in Genesis 3. Adam was in the Garden of Eden and faced a fundamental choice as a result of his free will. Adam could eat of the tree of life, which is intimate communion with God through obedience to His plan and commands. Or Adam could choose to reject God, His life and plan, and view himself as a god who could determine for himself what is good and evil. With Eve's participation Adam ate of the fruit from the tree of the knowledge of good and evil. Through their disobedience, Adam and Eve were *banned from eating of the fruit of the tree of life, which would give them eternal life and union with God.* They now suffered death, separation from God, and the natural consequences of sin. Through Adam, sin and disobedience entered the world. Consequently, all of us are born disfigured by sin. No longer do men and women know God as Father. Rather than follow God, we are inclined to do our own will. We have literally lost our identity and forgotten the dignity and destiny to which we are called.

Jesus in the Garden of Gethsemane

Now let us go to Matthew 26. We find Jesus in the Garden of Gethsemane on the night before His Crucifixion.

> Then Jesus came with them to a place called Gethsemane, and he said to his disciples, "Sit here while I go over there and pray." He took along Peter and the two sons of Zebedee, and began to feel sorrow and distress. Then he said to them, "My soul is sorrowful even to death. Remain here and keep watch with me." He advanced a little and fell prostrate in prayer, saying, "My Father, if it is possible, let this cup pass from me; yet, not as I will, but as you will." When he returned to his disciples he found them asleep. He said to Peter, "So you could not keep watch with me for one hour? Watch and pray that you may not undergo the test. The spirit is willing, but the flesh is weak." Withdrawing a second time, he prayed again, "My Father, if it is not possible that this cup pass without my drinking it, your will be done!" Then he returned once more and found them asleep, for they could not keep their eyes open. He left them and withdrew again and prayed a third time, saying the same thing again. Then he returned to his disciples and said to them, "Are you still sleeping and taking your rest? Behold, the hour is at hand when the Son of Man is to be handed over to sinners. Get up, let us go. Look, my betrayer is at hand." (Mt. 26:36–46)

In the garden Jesus, like Adam, faced a fundamental choice. Jesus could obey the Father's plan of salvation, and the next day be beaten, scourged, spat upon, nailed naked to a cross, and left hanging for three agonizing hours, thereby making reparation for all of the sins committed against God for all time. Or Jesus could preserve His life, disobey the Father, and follow His own will and desires. Not only did Jesus obey the Father, but He also completely surrendered to the will of the Father three times, which in Scripture always means perfection. He perfectly obeyed the Father's plan, embracing the Cross to save us from our sins.

This obedience of Jesus has remarkable consequences. He who hung upon the Cross is no mere man. He is God Himself. Through His obedience, He atones for the disobedience of Adam. The wood of the Cross recalls the wood of the tree of life in the Garden of Eden. *The crucified Jesus becomes the new tree of life from which Adam and all his descendants had been banned since the first sin.* But from what exactly were they banned? They were banned from *eating of the fruit* of the tree of life. If Jesus hung upon the Cross is the new tree of life, then what is its fruit?

> Jesus said to them, "Amen, amen, I say to you, unless you eat the flesh of the Son of Man and drink his blood, you do not have life within you. Whoever eats my flesh and drinks my blood has eternal life, and I will raise him on the last day. For my flesh is true food, and my blood is true drink. Whoever eats my flesh and drinks my blood remains in me and I in him. Just as the living Father sent me and I have life because of the Father, so also the one who feeds on me will have life because of me. This is the bread that came down from heaven. Unlike your ancestors who ate and still died, whoever eats this bread will live forever." (Jn. 6:53–58)

The fruit of the new tree of life is the Eucharist, Jesus' own Body and Blood, that He gives us to eat and drink so that we can once again have intimate communion with God and eternal life with Him, which was lost through the disobedience of Adam.

Consequently, through His perfect obedience, Jesus embraced the tree of the Cross, which became the new tree of life, destroying sin and death. Jesus is the new Adam who reverses the sin of the original Adam and brings salvation to all humanity.

We see in these two passages why the Father's plan required Jesus to be fully God and fully human. Jesus truly becomes God's mercy and reconciliation to man, and at the same time He becomes man's obedience and reconciliation to

God. Because Jesus is truly human, His perfect obedience to the Father atones for the disobedience of the first man, Adam. But also because Jesus is God, He has the power to become in Himself the new tree of life that restores humanity's communion with God that was lost through original sin. All of salvation history culminates at this moment, giving profound meaning to Christ's last words as He hung upon the tree, "It is finished."

From the Catechism: Key Words to Know

ADAM: According to the creation story in Genesis, the first man. From this story the Church has learned that humanity was originally created in a state of holiness and justice, and that the first ancestors of the human race lost this state for themselves and all humanity by their sin ("original sin"). Christ is called the "second," or "new Adam," because He ushered in the new creation by forgiving sin and restoring humanity to the grace of God's friendship lost by original sin (359, 375, 388, 390, 402–404, 504; cf. 635, 655).

EVE: According to the creation story in Genesis, the first woman, wife of Adam. God did not create man a solitary being; from the beginning, "male and female He created them" (Gen. 1:27; CCC 369, 375). Mary is called the "New Eve" and the "Mother of the Living" in the order of grace because she is the mother of the eternal Son of God made man, Jesus Christ the "new Adam." (511).

ANGEL: A spiritual, personal, and immortal creature, with intelligence and free will, who glorifies God without ceasing and who serves God as a messenger of His saving plan (329–331).

SOUL: The spiritual principle of human beings. The soul is the subject of human consciousness and freedom; soul and body together form one unique human nature. Each human soul is individual and immortal, immediately created by God. The soul does not die with the body, from which it is separated by death and with which it will be reunited in the final resurrection (363, 366; cf. 1703).

DEVIL/DEMON: A fallen angel, who sinned against God by refusing to accept His reign. Satan, or the devil, the Evil One, and the other demons were at first good angels, created naturally good, but became evil by their own doing (391, 1707; cf. 2851).

EVIL: The opposite or absence of good. One form of evil, physical evil, is a result of the "state of journeying" toward its ultimate perfection in which God created the world, involving the existence of the less perfect alongside the more perfect, the constructive and the destructive forces of nature, the appearance and disappearance of certain beings (310). Moral evil, however, results from the free choice to sin that angels and men have; it is permitted by God who knows how to derive good from it and respects the freedom of His creatures (311). The entire revelation of God's goodness in Christ is a response to the existence of evil (309, 385, 1707). The devil is called the Evil One.

TEMPTATION: An attraction, either from outside oneself or from within, to act contrary to right reason and the commandments of God. During His life on earth, Jesus Himself was tempted (put to the test) to manifest both the opposition between Himself and the devil and the triumph of His saving work over Satan (538).

ORIGINAL SIN: The sin by which the first human beings disobeyed the commandment of God, choosing to follow their own will rather than God's will. As a consequence they lost the grace of original holiness, and became subject to the law of death; sin became universally present in the world. Besides the personal sin of Adam and Eve, original sin describes the fallen state of human nature that affects every person born into the world, and from which Christ, the "new Adam," came to redeem us (396–412).

Chapter 5

Who Is Jesus Christ?

Reading the Catechism: Paragraphs 422–483

> For, by his Incarnation, he, the son of God, in a certain way united himself with each man. He worked with human hands, he thought with a human mind. He acted with a human will, and with a human heart he loved. Born of the Virgin Mary, he has truly been made one of us, like to us in all things except sin.
>
> —Second Vatican Council, Pastoral Constitution on the Church in the Modern World *Gaudium et spes (December 7, 1965)*, no. 22

In the fullness of time, God's plan of salvation is fulfilled when the second Person of the Trinity becomes flesh in the Person of **Jesus Christ**, and God Himself walks in the presence of men.

In this chapter we will first discuss why Jesus had to come as truly God and truly man and explore how He redeems us through the Incarnation. We will then see how the doctrine concerning Jesus developed in the early Church as it had to respond to the numerous false teachings that circulated concerning Christ. Ultimately the Magisterium of the Church clarified and defended the fact that Christ is both fully God and fully man.

The Incarnation: Jesus Christ Is True God and True Man

Through the **Incarnation** (meaning "to become flesh") God becomes fully human in the Person of Jesus Christ, who is indeed Emmanuel, or "God with us." Jesus comes as God to fully reveal God the Father to man, but He also comes as a true human being (with respect to his operation, his "mode of human existence" through his sacred humanity) to reveal man to himself and to restore in us the likeness of God that was disfigured through sin.

Why Did Jesus Become both Fully God and Fully Human?

After the Fall of Adam and Eve a great chasm existed between God and man. Because of original sin each and every person is born into this world with a natural separation from God. Since sin entered the world through Adam's disobedience, and since he is the father of all the living, every member of the human family enters the world with a wounded and disfigured human nature.

The Fall of Adam and Eve presents a grave problem. First of all, this chasm, this rift between God and man, is so great that only God has the power to bridge it. No mere man, no matter how good, no matter how faithful to God, could ever fix it. But at the same time, since sin entered the world through a man, a man of unique and extraordinary faith and obedience is needed to atone and do justice for the sin of the first man, Adam. This is the impossible situation faced by humanity after the Fall.

God solved the problem. Immediately after the first sin God announced and inaugurated His plan of salvation in Jesus Christ. Through Christ, who is fully and truly God and fully and truly human, the redemption of the world would be accomplished. Jesus, being God, has the power to restore the communion between God and man. He can also, as a man, atone for the disobedience of Adam through His own extraordinary obedience to the Father. Thus, just as it was through the one man, Adam, that sin and death came into the world, it is through the one man, Jesus Christ, that all of humanity is restored to justification and life. This is why Jesus is the new Adam. Through His perfect obedience to the Father and His acceptance of the Cross, He accomplished the **redemption** and atoned for the disobedience of Adam.

Jesus Is Truly God

Jesus is the second Person of the **Trinity**—He is truly God and has assumed a human nature. Therefore, in Jesus Christ, God once again walks with man and restores to the human race that intimate communion with God that was lost through original sin. He comes to us as the Son of God to fully reveal to us the Fatherhood of God, to forgive us of our sins, and to make us partakers of divine life.

Jesus fully reveals the Fatherhood of God

Through the first sin, Adam and Eve separated themselves from God and no longer saw Him as their loving Father. Humanity lost intimate knowledge of God, but because we were made to be in communion with Him, man still craved union with and knowledge of Him. Throughout the Old Testament, God gradually revealed Himself and gathered His chosen people until, in the fullness of time, God Himself entered human history through His only Son, Jesus. Jesus fully reveals God to man. The Father, through Jesus Christ, restores man to the relationship of divine love for which He had created man. That merciful divine love, which set out to redeem all of humanity from slavery to sin, brings all men back into communion with God. Pope John Paul II speaks of this "divine dimension" of the Incarnation, and of what Jesus, as the Son of God, reveals about the Father and His love.

> This revelation [in Christ] of the Father and outpouring of the Holy Spirit, which stamp an indelible seal on the mystery of the Redemption, explain the meaning of the Cross and death of Christ. The God of creation is revealed as the God of redemption, as the God who is "faithful to himself," and faithful to his love for man and the world, which he revealed on the day of creation. His is a love that does not draw back before anything that justice requires in him. Therefore "for our sake (God) made him (the Son) to be sin who knew no sin." If he "made to be sin" him who was without any sin whatever, it was to reveal the love that is always greater than the whole of creation, the love that is he himself, since "God is love." Above all, love is greater than sin, than weakness, than the "futility of creation," it is stronger than death; it is a love always ready to raise up and forgive, always ready to go to meet the prodigal son, always looking for "the revealing of the sons of God," who are called to the glory that is to be revealed." *This revelation of love is also described as mercy; and in man's history this revelation of love and mercy has taken a form and a name: that of Jesus Christ.* (Pope John Paul II, Encyclical Letter on the Redeemer of Man *Redemptor hominis* [March 4, 1979], no. 9)

Jesus comes to forgive sins

Jesus forgives our sins and reestablishes our lost communion with God by restoring our wounded human nature to the fullness of life. Because He is God, Jesus has the power to both forgive sins and to bridge the great chasm between

God and man that was created through the first sin. He takes upon Himself the sins of the entire world so that through His Cross and Resurrection, all of humanity would be freed from both the slavery to sin and the power of death. Jesus is the "Lamb of God who takes away the sins of the world." He is the perfect and everlasting sacrifice to the Father that does not bring mere symbolic atonement, but is the full and definitive reconciliation of God and humanity.

Jesus Is Truly Human

Not only is Jesus the God who comes to fully reveal Himself to man and to forgive their sins, but Jesus is also fully human. His Incarnation marks the full and inseparable union between God and man. The entire reality and purpose of the Father's loving plan of salvation is contained in the one Person, Jesus Christ, truly God and *truly man*. Through the Incarnation, man, who lost his likeness to God through sin, once again receives a share in the very life of God.

Jesus fully reveals man to himself

Through this union of God and man in the Person of Jesus Christ, God fully reveals man to himself. Christ enters human history as the one and unique man who is not only the perfect reflection of the Father, but who also shows the dignity and destiny of each and every person as a son or daughter of God. God's love and mercy for us is so great and profound that He clothes Himself with our humanity, with all that entails, in order to redeem and restore our human nature. Jesus reveals to man his divine likeness that has been disfigured by sin. He is "the Way, the Truth, and the Life" who communicates to us through His words and deeds the fullness of life for which man was created and to which he is called.

> *The truth is that only in the mystery of the incarnate Word does the mystery of man take on light.* For Adam, the first man, was a figure of Him Who was to come, (Rom. 5:14) namely Christ the Lord. *Christ, the final Adam, by the revelation of the mystery of the Father and His love, fully reveals man to man himself and makes his supreme calling clear.* . . . He Who is "the image of the invisible God" (Col. 1:15), is Himself the perfect man. To the sons of Adam He restores the divine likeness which

> had been disfigured from the first sin onward. Since human nature as He assumed it was not annulled, by that very fact it has been raised up to a divine dignity in our respect too. For by His incarnation the Son of God has united Himself in some fashion with every man. He worked with human hands, He thought with a human mind, acted by human choice and loved with a human heart. Born of the Virgin Mary, He has truly been made one of us, like us in all things except sin. (*Gaudium et spes,* no. 22, emphasis added)

Jesus is fully human

Christ is fully human, and through His humanity *unites Himself with each and every person in all times, places, cultures, and circumstances*. By fully assuming our human nature and living a truly human life, Jesus redeems and restores each and every aspect of human nature and existence. Like us, He was conceived in His mother's womb and entered this world as a tiny baby cradled in the arms of Mary. He lived the life of a child, then an adolescent, and grew to manhood with all of the responsibilities and everyday struggles that each of us face in our own lives. He had a human soul, a human intellect, and a human will. He experienced human emotions like joy, fear, sadness, anger, and frustration in a fully human way but without the tarnish of sin. When Jesus suffered in His Passion and death upon the Cross, He fully experienced the pain. He truly died upon the Cross, just as did those crucified on either side of Him. By possessing a true human nature and living a fully human life, He was able to heal and restore our nature and every aspect of human life and existence. "For the Son of God became man so that man could become like God" (St. Athanasius, *On the Incarnation*, 54, 3).

Jesus had to be fully human in order to accomplish God's plan of salvation. For if He was not fully man, He would not have been able to atone for the disobedience of the one man, Adam. If Jesus were not truly human, He would not have been able to fully reveal man to Himself and totally heal our human nature. For example, if Jesus did not have a human will, then our wills would not have been redeemed. If Jesus did not truly have a human intellect, then our intellects would not have been healed. Jesus came to redeem our entire human nature; thus, He had to be fully and truly human.

Foundations of Doctrine concerning Christ

Since the time of the Apostles the Church has taught and proclaimed that Jesus Christ is truly God and truly man, and that these divine and human natures are completely and inseparably united in the one Person, Jesus Christ. However, throughout the Church's history, especially in the first five centuries, there were many false teachings concerning the Person of Christ who is fully God and fully human. This section will show how the true teaching concerning Jesus was taught, defended, and clarified by the Magisterium of the Church through the handing on of Sacred Tradition and the proper interpretation of Sacred Scripture.

Orthodoxy vs. Heresy

First, we must make an important distinction between *orthodoxy* and *heresy. Orthodoxy* comes from the Greek, meaning "right thinking" or "right opinion," and signifies that a person's faith is in conformity with the teachings of the Church. This implies belief in the fullness of the Church's teaching—acceptance of the whole of God's revelation. For example, we know that the Trinity is three Persons in one God. The nature of God is both three Persons and also one God. Thus, the true and complete teaching is "both/and," or *orthodox*. The same is true concerning the Person of Christ. Jesus is *both* fully human *and* fully divine. Thus, the teaching is complete, or *orthodox.*

Heresy, on the other hand, is from Greek, meaning "to make a one-sided choice." Heresy is not a denial of the whole and entire teaching, but is a choosing of only a part of the whole teaching. For example, a heresy would be to say that God is indeed One, but the three Persons in the Trinity are not really unique Persons; instead, they are different manifestations of the one God. Such a statement maintains the truth that God is One, but abandons the rest of the teaching that there are three unique and completely distinct Persons in the Trinity. It is making a one-sided choice, accepting one part of the teaching and abandoning the other part. This heresy described above is called *modalism* and has appeared several times throughout the history of the Church.

There have been more heresies concerning the union of Christ's two natures, human and divine, than there have been heresies concerning any other doctrine of the Church. The heresies concerning the natures of Christ are the result of a one-sided choice—not accepting that Jesus is both God and man.

Some proclaim that Jesus is truly God but not fully human, others that Jesus is human but not really God, and still others even deny both. The Magisterium of the Church, charged with preserving the orthodoxy of the revelation of Christ, has had to defend and clarify the fact that Christ is both fully God and fully human.

Heresies of the Early Church

As the preaching of the Apostles and their successors continued to spread throughout the ancient world, and the canon of Scripture continued to be written and then compiled by the Church, numerous heresies sprang up and circulated throughout the Church concerning the Person of Christ. Many of these heresies were the result of a misinterpretation of a passage or passages of Sacred Scripture—interpreted apart from Tradition and the whole of the Scriptures. Others evolved when theology or philosophies from other ancient religions and cultures were mixed with Christian doctrine inappropriately. The result was an erroneous view of the union of two natures, human and divine, in Christ. Here is a very small sample of the more popular and influential heresies of the early Church concerning Christ.

Gnostic Docetism

This was the earliest of the Christological heresies and developed out of the Gnostic religious and philosophical thought that was prevalent in the ancient world. It was a widespread heresy because Gnostic thought influenced many people. The Gnostics believed that there was a dualism between matter and spirit, and that all matter was evil and opposed to God, while all spirit was good. Thus, the Gnostics believed that Jesus was truly God, but that He could not have truly assumed a human body because it is matter and therefore, evil. They believed that Jesus only "appeared" to take on a human body, like a mirage, thus the name "Docetism" (from the Greek verb *dokeo,* meaning "to appear"). This heresy was an attempt to reconcile the nature of Jesus with the Gnostic philosophical and theological thought of the time.

Arianism

Arianism was an extremely popular and widespread heresy that was promoted by a priest from Alexandria named Arius. Arius and his followers were also influenced by Greek and Gnostic thought, especially that of *subordinationism.* Subordinationism is a product of Greek theology and mythology in which there was a hierarchy of immortal and mortal beings: gods and demigods. Arius was also influenced heavily by the philosophical thought of Plato, who shared these same ideas. It is very easy to see why someone like Arius, influenced by the thought and cultures of his time, could fall into error concerning both the divine and human natures of Christ. Arius believed that Jesus was not equal to the Father and not truly God. He believed that the Father was lonely and created the Son, Jesus, a demigod who was the first-born and greatest of all creatures. Arius denied that Jesus was truly God, and he also denied that Jesus was truly human, believing that He only assumed a human body, not a true human nature. This heresy was very influential and several bishops promoted this teaching. However, as we will see, the Magisterium of the Church condemned Arianism, and defined and clarified the teaching that Jesus' nature is true God and true man.

Nestorianism

Nestorianism was a heresy of a priest named Nestorius. This heresy overemphasized the humanity of Jesus to the degree that it separated His humanity and divinity. Nestorius refused to claim that the divine nature and human nature were intimately united in the one Person, Jesus Christ. Rather, he claimed that He is a manifestation of two persons: the divine Jesus and the human Jesus. He saw Him as a man who was bearing God, like the way someone dwells in a tent, or a baby dwells within his mother. Nestorius never intended to fall into error, but in his attempt to emphasize Jesus' humanity, he went too far and created this dualism between His divine and human nature. Nestorianism taught that Jesus is not forever the perfect and unbreakable union between God and man, but just simply the dwelling of God within a man.

Monophysitism

Monophysitism (Greek, meaning "one nature") was a heresy that developed as an overreaction to the heresy of Nestorianism. Monophysitism taught that Jesus' humanity was absorbed by His divinity. Thus, there no longer remained two natures intimately united, but one nature—the divine nature—in which His human nature was lost or absorbed.

Monothelitism

Monothelitism (Greek, meaning "one will") was an attempt by some to compromise and reconcile with the Monophysites in the face of the Muslim and Persian military threats to Eastern Europe. The sharp divisions within the Church had already resulted in the loss of Egypt. Monothelitism held that there was a union of Jesus' human and divine natures, but that He only had a divine will and not a human will. Monophysites insisted that there could only be one mode, or source, of operation: the divine will and nature. They believed that if Jesus had a human will and a divine will, there would be an innate opposition within Jesus Himself. Thus, the Monothelites tried to preserve Jesus' human nature while compromising with the Monophysites. What is the problem here? If Jesus has no human will, then He does not have a true human nature. Here we see the development of a new heresy from an effort to compromise with a different heresy.

The Magisterium Defended and Clarified the True Teachings Concerning Christ

The Magisterium of the Church, the successors of the Apostles in the pope and the bishops, defended and defined the true Person of Christ as human and divine. They were then and continue to be the authoritative teachers, with the mission of preserving, defending, and clarifying the sacred deposit of faith entrusted to the Church by Christ. When there has been the need to respond to heresy, and define or clarify true teaching, the bishops together with the pope have met in **ecumenical councils,** or gatherings. These ecumenical (meaning "household" or "whole") councils involved a majority of the bishops who assembled to clarify doctrine that affected the "whole household" of the Church. There have been twenty-one of these councils in the history of the Church. The first several ecumenical councils met within the first four centuries of the Church and clarified the true revelation of Christ concerning the nature of Jesus and of the Holy Trinity.

The Council of Nicaea (AD 325)

The first ecumenical council of the Church met to challenge the teachings of Arius. The goal of the council was to better define the divinity of Christ and His relationship to the Father. The issue at hand was whether or not Jesus was truly God, equal to God, and of the same nature as the Father, or whether Jesus was a creature of God and not equal to the Father. The Council of Nicaea taught that Jesus was "eternally begotten of the Father." In other words, Jesus, as the second Person of the Trinity, was not created by the "lonely" Father but was eternally in union and relationship with Him, having no beginning. The council also taught that He was *homoousion* (Greek, meaning "of the same substance" or "one in Being") with the Father. Jesus is of the same nature and is equal to God the Father. Indeed, He is truly God and in no way is subordinate to the Father. The council codified this teaching by adding clarifying language to the Eastern Baptismal Creed (known to us today as the Apostles' Creed).

The First Council of Constantinople (AD 381)

Only fifty-six short years after Nicaea, a second council was convened. Macedonius, the semi-Arian patriarch of Constantinople, had claimed that the Holy Spirit was not divine, but was a "super angel" and inferior to the Son. He had mustered a decent following called the Macedonians. The First Council of Constantinople confronted this false teaching and clarified the truth concerning the Holy Spirit. The Council taught that the Holy Spirit proceeds from the Father and the Son, He is of the same divine nature as the Father and the Son, and "with the Father and the Son He is adored and glorified." Thus, if He is adored in the same way as the Father and the Son, then the Holy Spirit is indeed God. The First Council of Constantinople added additional language to the Apostles' Creed that had already been expanded by the Council of Nicaea. This revised creed articulated the true and orthodox teaching concerning Christ, the Holy Spirit, and the Trinity. It is the **Nicene Creed** that has been handed on to us and which we recite today as the formal statement of what we believe as followers of Christ. (For a comparison of the Apostles' Creed and the Nicene Creed, see Catechism 184).

The Council of Ephesus (AD 431)

The Council of Ephesus was gathered in AD 431 to respond to Nestorianism, which denied the unity of Jesus' human and divine natures. The council emphatically taught that Jesus' human and divine natures are united in the one Person, Jesus Christ, and that you cannot in any way separate that union. Jesus is one Person with two natures, so you cannot speak of Him without speaking both of His humanity and His divinity. The Council of Ephesus proclaimed Mary as *Theotokos*, or "God-bearer." Mary did not create God, but she did give birth to the Person, Jesus Christ, who was conceived by the Holy Spirit in her womb. So if she gave birth to the Person Jesus Christ, and His divine and human natures are perfectly united within His Person, then Mary was indeed the God-bearer. The Council of Ephesus condemned the teaching of Nestorius, who claimed that Mary was only the "Christ-bearer," or the bearer of only Jesus' humanity. This teaching of Nestorius intrinsically placed a division between Jesus' human and divine natures, which the council clearly rejected.

The Council of Chalcedon (AD 451)

The Council of Chalcedon met only twenty years later. It further clarified and defined the unity of Jesus' human and divine natures in opposition to the Monophysites, who, as we have seen, claimed that the union of Jesus' natures was so profound that His divinity absorbed His humanity. The Council of Chalcedon taught that there indeed was a profound unity of the divine and human natures in the Person of Christ, and that both natures remain wholly and entirely without confusion. The council defined Jesus as "one and the same Christ, Son, Lord, only Son, in two natures (human and divine) without confusion, without transformation, without division, without separation."

The Third Council of Constantinople (AD 681)

The final "Christological" council was the Third Council of Constantinople in AD 681. It was convened to address Monothelitism, which claimed that Jesus was truly God and truly human, but that He only had one divine will and no human will. However, this teaching is contrary to what was taught at Chalcedon (i.e., that Jesus has a true divine nature and a true human nature without confusion, division, or separation). But if Jesus did not have a human will, then He would not have a human nature. Consequently, the Third Council of Constantinople further explicitly clarified Chalcedon and defined that Jesus has perfect divine and human natures; thus, He has two natural wills and operations: one that is human, and one that is divine. However, even though Jesus had a free human will, His will and His human operation were always in obedience and submission to the divine will.

Thus, the Magisterium of the Church clarified and defined the orthodox teaching concerning Christ and the Trinity in the first seven centuries of the Church. Notice that the Magisterium does not invent or change doctrine, but clarifies and defines it. The Church through the centuries has come to a better knowledge and grasp of the truth through the power of the Holy Spirit as it continues to ponder, live, and pray all that Christ has revealed to us. In addition, the early life of the Church shows us how Christ's revelation is transmitted to each generation through both Sacred Tradition and Sacred Scripture under the guidance and teaching authority of the Magisterium. Therefore, even today—over two thousand years after Christ's birth—we can still encounter the true and living Christ, who continues to come to us through the Church, who is the "pillar and foundation of truth" (1 Tim. 3:15).

From the Catechism: Key Words to Know

JESUS CHRIST: The eternal Son of God, who was born of the Virgin Mary, suffered crucifixion and death, rose from the dead, ascended into heaven, and will come again in glory to judge the living and the dead. *Jesus*, which means "God saves" in Hebrew, was the name given to Him at the Annunciation; "Christ" is a title which comes from the Greek translation of the Hebrew *Messiah* and means "anointed" (184 f.; 430, 436; cf. 727).

INCARNATION: The fact that the Son of God assumed human nature and became man in order to accomplish our salvation in that same human nature. Jesus Christ, the Son of God, the second Person of the Trinity, is both true God and true man, not part God and part man (461, 464).

REDEEMER/REDEMPTION: Jesus Christ, Redeemer of mankind. Christ paid the price of His own sacrificial death on the Cross to ransom us, to set us free from the slavery of sin, thus achieving our redemption (571, 601; cf. 517, 1372).

TRINITY: The mystery of one God in three Persons: Father, Son, and Holy Spirit. The revealed truth of the Holy Trinity is at the very root of the Church's living faith as expressed in the creed. The mystery of the Trinity in itself is inaccessible to the human mind and is the object of faith only because it was revealed by Jesus Christ, the divine Son of the eternal Father (232, 237, 249, 253–256).

HERESY: The obstinate denial after Baptism of a truth that must be believed with divine and Catholic faith (2089; cf. 465).

ECUMENICAL COUNCIL: A gathering of all the bishops of the world, in the exercise of their collegial authority over the universal Church. An ecumenical council is usually called by the successor of Saint Peter, the pope, or at least confirmed or accepted by him (884).

NICENE CREED: The profession of faith, common to the churches of East and West, which came from the first two ecumenical councils (Nicaea, AD 325 and Constantinoplc, AD 381; CCC 195–196)

Chapter 6

The Life and Ministry of Christ

Reading the Catechism: Paragraphs 512–594

> I am the good shepherd; I know mine and mine know me, just as the Father knows me and I know the Father; and I will lay down my life for the sheep.
>
> —John 10:14–15

Now that we know who Christ is, we need to turn our attention to His life and ministry on earth. In fact, most of what we know about Christ and His plan and mission was revealed through His life and ministry, through the many and various things He did and said. This chapter will explore in detail what Christ revealed through His humble birth in the stable in Bethlehem, His glorious teachings in the Sermon on the Mount, the establishment of His Church, and the fulfillment of His mission in His Passion, death, and Resurrection.

For thousands of years, the people of Israel waited in hopeful expectation of the promised Messiah. They knew from the many writings of the Jewish Scriptures, especially those of the great prophets, that God would send a Messiah to deliver Israel from its enemies and return it to the glory of God. Yet, the coming of this "Anointed One" was thought by many to be more political and military than spiritual. This was particularly prevalent in the days of Christ's coming when Israel was occupied by the Romans. The people of Israel believed that the Messiah would come as a great military king to overthrow the Roman occupation and bring peace and prosperity to Israel.

However, Jesus came into the world not to bring a military or political victory but to bring a spiritual and supernatural victory—a freedom not from earthly enemies but freedom from the slavery to sin, and the victory of the kingdom of God over the kingdom of Satan. Christ comes to once again restore the human family to communion with God and each other. He comes to conquer through love, faithfulness, humility, and peace.

The Birth of Christ

Christ's birth and the circumstances surrounding it reveal much about who Christ is and the mission that the Father has entrusted to Him. Most of us are very familiar with the Christmas stories of His birth. But what do these stories really reveal to us? You might be surprised how much meaning is contained within these simple and beautiful passages of Scripture.

Actually, the passages in Scripture concerning the childhood and adolescence of Christ are few. Of the four Gospels only Matthew and Luke have infancy narratives of the events surrounding His birth. Matthew's Gospel, written primarily to a Jewish audience, tells the story of Christ's birth from Joseph's perspective. In Luke's Gospel the story of Christ's birth surrounds Mary and her role and perspective. Since Luke traveled with Paul to Ephesus where Mary lived after Christ had ascended to heaven, he probably had a firsthand account from Mary about all the events that had occurred surrounding Christ's birth. Thus, Luke's account is longer, more detailed, and very personal, almost as if Mary herself is telling the story.

The Annunciation

In Luke's Gospel the narrative of Christ's birth begins with the beautiful story of the angel Gabriel's announcement to Mary of the coming birth of Christ. This event is crucially important concerning who Jesus is and how He fulfills the prophecies of the coming Messiah. Among these prophecies the writings of the prophet Isaiah provide a glimpse of who this Messiah would be, and how He would come into the world.

First, Isaiah prophesized that the Messiah, or "Anointed One," would come from the lineage of King David and would restore the house of David and shower new blessings upon it. He would indeed be anointed with God's spirit and come with the power and justice of God.

> But a shoot shall sprout from the stump of Jesse,
>   and from his roots a bud shall blossom.
> The spirit of the Lord shall rest upon him:
>   a spirit of wisdom and of understanding,
> A spirit of counsel and of strength,
>   a spirit of knowledge and of fear of the Lord,
>   and his delight shall be the fear of the Lord.

Not by appearance shall he judge,
    nor by hearsay shall he decide,
But he shall judge the poor with justice,
    and decide fairly for the land's afflicted.
He shall strike the ruthless with the rod of his mouth,
    and with the breath of his lips he shall slay the wicked.
Justice shall be the band around his waist,
    and faithfulness a belt upon his hips. (Is. 11:1–5)

Isaiah 7:14 also foretells that the Messiah will be born of a virgin and that His name shall be called Immanuel. "Therefore the Lord himself will give you this sign: the virgin shall be with child, and bear a son, and shall name him Immanuel."

In the Gospel of Luke, the **Annunciation** (1:26–38) is the fulfillment of both of these messianic prophesies foretold long before by Isaiah. Luke makes it very clear that Gabriel appears to "a virgin . . . and the virgin's name was Mary." Gabriel then continues to reveal that "the Holy Spirit will come upon you and the power of the Most High will overshadow you. Therefore the child to be born will be called holy, the **Son of God**." These words of Gabriel perfectly fulfill Isaiah 7:14. Jesus was truly conceived by a virgin, and not by a human father, but the Holy Spirit. Also, Immanuel in Isaiah 7:14 means "God with us." Jesus conceived of the Holy Spirit and being the "Son of God" is truly God with us. The Son of the Father becomes One like us in our humanity in every way except sin. The Messiah had come!

The Annunciation also fulfills the prophesy of Isaiah 11:1. The stump of Jesse, alluded to in Isaiah, represents the House of King David because Jesse is the father of David. The "stump of Jesse" refers to the House of David, or the kingdom of Israel, that has been rendered spiritually dead through sin. But from this House of David a "bud shall blossom," and this blossom of new life is the Messiah. Thus, the Messiah will come from the bloodline of David. Luke describes Mary as "a virgin betrothed to a man named Joseph of the House of David." Thus, Jesus is from the House of David because Joseph is His "father." We also know that Joseph was not the biological father of Jesus because Jesus was conceived of the Holy Spirit. However, Mary herself is of the bloodline of David, so Christ is also truly of the House of David through Mary.

We also see in the first chapter of Luke's Gospel that Gabriel reveals to Mary that her son "will be great and will be called the Son of the Most High and the Lord God will give him the throne of David his father and he will rule over the house of Jacob (Israel) forever, and of his kingdom there shall be no end." This too fulfills Isaiah 11 in that Jesus will rule and judge all Israel, coming forth from the House of David and judging and ruling over all until the end of time.

Scriptural Symbolism surrounding the Birth of Christ

Now let us turn our attention to the birth of Jesus. Although we are familiar with the Christmas stories as recorded by Scripture, we may not be aware that they are full of symbolism and deeper meaning providing insight into Jesus' identity and mission. Even on the day of His birth this symbolism was revealing Christ's fulfillment of Old Testament prophesies as well as foreshadowing His future mission.

Bethlehem

The fact that Jesus was born in the city of Bethlehem is of great meaning and importance. It was foretold by the prophet Micah that the Messiah would be born in Bethlehem, the birthplace of David.

> But you, Bethlehem-Ephrathah
> least among the clans of Judah,
> From you shall come forth for me
> one who is to be ruler in Israel;
> Whose origin is from of old,
> from ancient times. . . .
>
> He shall take his place as shepherd
> by the strength of the Lord,
> by the majestic name of the Lord, his God;
> And they shall dwell securely, for now his greatness
> shall reach to the ends of the earth:
> he shall be peace. (Mic. 5:1–4)

The name *Bethlehem* bears significant meaning concerning the mission of Christ. In Hebrew it means "house of bread," which is a foreshadowing of Christ who through His death and Resurrection will become the "bread of life" in the Eucharist. Jesus comes into the world to give Himself to the world so that "all may have life and have it more abundantly" (Jn. 10:10).

The swaddling clothes

After His birth, Mary wrapped Jesus in swaddling clothes. All parents know that it is still very much the norm to wrap a baby in a blanket or a cloth to keep the baby warm and safe. Why does Luke go out of his way to mention such a normal and seemingly insignificant practice? In the Jewish/Semitic culture, the baby was wrapped very tightly in a cloth not only to be kept warm and safe but to also give them good posture. It was a very tight wrapping with a thin cloth, a little different from how we do things today. For Luke, however, Jesus being wrapped in a cloth at His birth is already a foreshadowing of His death and burial, when Christ would once again be tightly wrapped in a cloth and placed in the tomb. Even at Christ's birth, His ultimate mission of reconciling the world to God through His blood on the Cross is already being revealed.

The manger

Christ was not laid in a crib or a bed but was placed in a manger in the stable. A manger is a feeding trough for animals. It held hay or other food. Again, we have the Eucharistic theme: Jesus who is the "true bread that comes down from heaven" is born in the city named the "house of bread" and is laid into a manger which feeds the flocks of the shepherd. Jesus is the Good Shepherd who gives His life so that He may feed His flock and give them eternal life.

The rejection at the inn

The rejection of Joseph and Mary (who carries the infant Jesus within her) at the inn because "there was no room," foreshadows the future rejection of Christ as the Messiah, leading to His crucifixion and death. The rejection at the inn also symbolizes humanity having no room for God in their hearts due to sin from which Christ comes to free us.

The finding of Jesus at the Temple

We know very little of Christ's life as a child or an adolescent. Luke does give us the account of the twelve-year-old Jesus who was left at the Temple for three days while Mary and Joseph frantically searched for Him. This story, as all the others, is rich in symbolism. First, it foreshadows how we will all lose Christ for three days after His death and before the Resurrection. It also marks the first time that Jesus, as a young man, is able to enter His Father's house in the Temple in Jerusalem. This is the first time we see Jesus teaching, and it foreshadows His public ministry when He will fully reveal the plan of His Father.

The Public Ministry of Christ

While we know little of His youth, all four of the Gospels resume the story of the life of Christ at the beginning of His public ministry, which is marked by His baptism by **John the Baptist** in the River Jordan. At Jesus' baptism the Spirit descends upon Him and He is anointed by the Father, who calls Him to begin the three years of His public ministry. It is during these years of ministry that Jesus communicates the revelation of the Father and teaches what it means to be and to live as the image and likeness of God.

The Baptism of Jesus

Baptism at the time of Christ was a rather new phenomenon in the Jewish faith. It was seen as a symbolic washing away of one's sins and as atonement for sin. It marked a moment of deeper repentance and the beginning of a more faithful and full living out of the covenant established by God for His people. Baptism was popularized and spread especially by John the Baptist who was the final herald making straight the way for the coming of Christ. John's baptism focused especially on repentance, a new and radical commitment to living out the covenant. He baptized with urgency, claiming that the Chosen One's coming was imminent. "I am baptizing you with water, for repentance, but the one who is coming after me is mightier than I. I am not worthy to carry his sandals. He will baptize you with the Holy Spirit and fire" (Mt. 3:11).

Many ask why Jesus needed to be baptized. After all, He had no sin. We discover that Jesus' baptism in the Jordan is one of the more crucial events in His life. While it marked the beginning of His public ministry, it also had much deeper meaning.

First, Jesus' baptism is a powerful revelation of His identity and mission as the Son of God. In a sense it is His commission by the Father revealing that He is truly the "Anointed One" who is filled with the Holy Spirit.

> After Jesus was baptized, he came up from the water and behold, the heavens were opened, and he saw the Spirit of God

> descending like a dove coming upon him. And a voice came from the heavens, saying, "This is my beloved Son, with whom I am well pleased." (Mt. 3:16–17)

Second, it was the will of the Father that baptism become the ordinary and necessary way in which we are literally and totally cleansed of sin and filled with God's grace. Although Jesus was free of sin and not in need of baptism, His acceptance of the Father's will elevated baptism to the level of a sacrament. Like Christ, when we come up out of the waters of baptism we are also anointed with the Holy Spirit, and the Father looks upon His new son or daughter in Christ with whom He is very pleased. So while Christ's baptism was not necessary, it did inaugurate His public ministry and establish the Sacrament of Baptism, through which we are cleansed of sin, filled with God's grace and love, and adopted as His sons and daughters.

Jesus Battles and Destroys the Kingdom of Satan

Immediately after His baptism in the Jordan Jesus is led by the Spirit into the desert where He prays and fasts for forty days. During this time Jesus prepares Himself spiritually for His work and mission that is yet to come. But after this time of prayer and fasting, Jesus is confronted and tempted by Satan. Satan tempts the New Adam as he tempted the first Adam. However, the circumstances are slightly different.

Adam was in a paradise where he enjoyed an abundance of pleasure and joy when Satan came to tempt him. He was lacking nothing. Jesus, however, is tempted by Satan in a desert after not eating for forty days. Jesus is hungry and tired. Satan tempted Adam once, and through Eve's influence he fell into sin. Jesus is not tempted once by the devil, but three times!

> Filled with the Holy Spirit, Jesus returned from the Jordan and was led by the Spirit into the desert for forty days, to be tempted by the devil. He ate nothing during those days, and when they were over he was hungry. The devil said to him, "If you are the Son of God, command this stone to become bread." Jesus answered him, "It is written, 'One does not live by bread alone.'" Then he took him up and showed him all the kingdoms of the world in a single instant. The devil said to

> him, "I shall give to you all this power and their glory; for it has been handed over to me, and I may give it to whomever I wish. All this will be yours, if you worship me." Jesus said to him in reply, "It is written: 'You shall worship the Lord, your God, and him alone shall you serve.'" Then he led him to Jerusalem, made him stand on the parapet of the temple, and said to him, "If you are the Son of God, throw yourself down from here, for it is written: 'He will command his angels concerning you, to guard you,' and: 'With their hands they will support you, lest you dash your foot against a stone.'" Jesus said to him in reply, "It also says, 'You shall not put the Lord, your God, to the test.'" When the devil had finished every temptation, he departed from him for a time. (Lk. 4:1–13)

Notice that each temptation brings an increased intensity. At first it is a very simple temptation to turn a stone into bread to eat since Jesus was so hungry. In the second temptation Satan offers to Jesus all the kingdoms of the world. Notice that the world belongs to Satan and sin. Jesus comes to establish the kingdom of God not in a vacuum but through the destruction of Satan's reign, which came to be through the sin of Adam. The temptation is to "sell His soul" to the devil to receive all the riches and power of the world. The third and final temptation is the strongest. Satan is asking Jesus to "prove Himself." All of these temptations are ultimately to separate Jesus from the Father and to bring about disobedience to the Father and abandonment of the plan of salvation. Jesus resists all three of the temptations perfectly, thus reversing the sin and disobedience of Adam. Notice also in Luke's Gospel it states that Satan departed from Him for a time. Satan returns again when he enters Judas who will betray Jesus. Satan's final temptation and Christ's ultimate victory will occur in Christ's Passion and death.

While the temptation in the desert is the time that we most powerfully see Jesus battling and overcoming the kingdom of Satan, Jesus continues to battle the powers of evil and evil spirits throughout His public ministry. We see Him performing numerous exorcisms, commanding the evil spirits to be quiet and leave. We see the story of the Gerasene demoniac who is possessed by legions of demons (Mk. 5:1–20). Jesus casts them out with power and authority, and they fall upon a herd of swine that cast themselves into the sea. Satan has no power or authority against God, and Jesus continues to establish the kingdom of God throughout His ministry by freeing His brothers and sisters from slavery to

Satan's power. These powerful exorcisms are only a small foretaste of the ultimate victory over Satan, sin, and death that will be accomplished through the Cross and Resurrection.

The Miracles of Jesus

The **miracles** of Jesus also play a very important role in His life and ministry. They signal the arrival of the Messiah and His kingdom. The miracles are mighty works and signs of God that complement the words and teachings of Jesus. They show that He was truly sent into the world by the Father. For those who witness Jesus' power, the miracles offer proof and reveal His identity as the Messiah and Son of God.

The miracles of Jesus are of two purposes, both of which invite belief in Him as the Son of God and strengthen the belief of those who have already begun to follow Him. The first purpose is to reveal Jesus' divinity, that He is truly "God with us." These miracles are largely miracles in which Jesus manipulates or changes nature, an ability only God would have. Examples include the calming of the storm (Mk. 4:35–41), the multiplication of the loaves and fish (Mt. 14:13–21), and the changing of water into wine (Jn. 2:1–11).

We also see miracles that not only clearly reveal Jesus as divine, but also have a second purpose: to restore and heal humanity, and to defeat Satan's kingdom. These include the numerous miracles of healing such as the healing of the paralytic (Lk. 5:18–25), the healing of the man born blind (Jn. 9:1–41), and the healing of blind Bartimaeus (Mk. 10:46–52). Included also are the many miracles of exorcism, and above all are the miracles of resuscitation from the dead in the case of Jarius' daughter (Mk. 5:35–42) and Jesus' friend Lazarus (Jn. 11:1–44).

All of these miracles involve physical healing, but in each case there is a deeper and more profound spiritual healing that takes place. In the case of the healing of the paralytic, the greater miracle is that Jesus forgives him of his sins. The restoration of physical sight is only a sign of restored spiritual sight. Blind Bartimaeus begins to follow Jesus, and the man born blind becomes a powerful witness of belief in Christ. Most importantly, the miracles of bringing people back from the dead are only a foreshadowing of the true resurrection of the dead, which will destroy death and bring about eternal life. Thus, the definitive purpose of the miracles is to bring about faith in Christ as the Messiah. Ultimately, miracles bring about spiritual healing and sight to all of us who have been wounded and blinded by sin.

The Teachings of Jesus

Jesus teaches throughout His public ministry. He reveals both the identity of God as our loving Father, and how we are to live and act as those made in the image and likeness of God. Jesus' teachings are numerous, and we will explore only some of the main themes and most important aspects.

Jesus as the new Moses

One of the more powerful images of Jesus in all the Gospels is the one portrayed by Matthew in chapters 5–7 of his Gospel. These chapters are traditionally called the Sermon on the Mount. Matthew begins chapter 5 with Jesus going up a mountain. He gives a long teaching based on the Mosaic Law, but greatly expands upon it and calls the children of Israel to a new and more radical way of loving and living the covenant with God. Matthew begins chapter 8 with Jesus coming down from the mountain. Matthew presents Jesus as the new Moses who has come as the Messiah, not to abolish the Mosaic Law but to fulfill it and to establish the law of the kingdom of the Messiah.

How is Jesus the new Moses? We have to go back to the Book of Exodus in the Old Testament. When the Israelites came to the foot of Mount Sinai, God called Moses to the top of Mount Sinai where He spent forty days before God. Then Moses came down the mountain with the Ten Commandments, which became the foundation of the Mosaic Law. In Matthew's Gospel, we see Jesus, the new Moses, going up upon the mountain teaching and presenting the New Law of the Everlasting Covenant to the people of Israel.

Parables

Throughout the Gospels Jesus teaches primarily through **parables.** They are a literary style of the ancient Semitic world in which a short story is told to bring out a crucial point. They are a type of analogy that helps one to understand difficult or crucial concepts. More times than not, Jesus would explain the meaning of the parable after it was told. This was a very effective and popular teaching style of the time. While there are numerous parables contained within the Gospels, we will explore some of the more important ones.

Parables of the kingdom

Many parables concern the nature of the **kingdom of God.** What do they teach us about the kingdom? The parable of the mustard seed (Mt. 13:31–32) teaches that the kingdom, like the mustard seed, begins as the smallest of seeds but grows to become the largest of plants. The kingdom began with the Twelve Apostles, but now extends to all the earth. The parable of the weeds (Mt. 13:24–30) teaches that within the kingdom there will be those who bear fruit and live selfless lives, and there will be others who, like weeds, will take for themselves and will try to choke the kingdom. The wheat is harvested for eternal life while the weeds will be burned. The parable of the treasure and the pearl (Mt. 13:44–46) reveals that the kingdom is the most treasured of possessions, and he who would possess it must give all. There is no greater importance in this life than being in the kingdom of God.

Parables of mercy

Luke chapter 15 contains some of the more famous parables in the Gospels. They teach us that God the Father is all merciful and He seeks out and finds those who are lost. The parables of the lost sheep (Lk. 15:1–7) and the lost coin (Lk. 15:8–10) illustrate powerfully how God will stop at nothing to find His lost children. However, the most powerful parable is the parable of the prodigal son (Lk. 15:18–24). A wayward son returns in sorrow to his father who offers him reconciliation. The father does not punish or shun his son, but embraces him with great joy over his conversion and repentance. This parable powerfully reflects the joy of heaven when a lost sinner repents and turns to Christ.

Parables of discipleship

The parables teach about discipleship more than anything else. This should not come as a surprise since Jesus instructs the Apostles and His other followers on what it means to be someone created in the image of God and how we ought to live in the kingdom of God. The parable of the sower (Mt. 13:1–9) teaches that we are to be open and ready to receive the Word of God in our hearts. The parable of the lamp (Mk. 4:21–25) teaches that we are to be a light to the world and to let God's glory shine through us for all to see. The parable of the salt (Lk. 14:34–35) shows us that we are to transform the world into the kingdom of God by letting God work through us in our daily lives. The parable of the persistent widow (Lk. 18:1–8) reveals to us that we must be persistent in prayer and trust in the loving care of our Father. While these are not all of the parables on discipleship, we can see through these examples that Jesus used them to teach His followers how to live and be faithful to God.

Jesus Establishes His Church

Finally, we clearly see in Jesus' public ministry that He set forth to establish a visible institutional Church that will be, until the end of time, the visible manifestation of the kingdom of God on earth. Christ did not leave us a book of instruction or merely a set of teachings, but He established a Church founded upon the Twelve Apostles that would faithfully hand on to each and every generation the fullness of all that Christ is and has revealed to us.

As we saw in chapter two, Jesus called the Twelve Apostles at the beginning of His public ministry to accompany Him throughout His ministry so that He may teach, train, and prepare them in a unique way to carry on His mission and work through the Church. Christ also appointed Peter to serve not only as the head of the body of the Apostles but also as the "rock" of His Church. He gave the Apostle Peter the authority to teach and govern the Church in a special way as the head of the Church. Since the very beginning, the successors of Peter and the successors of the Apostles have been the visible shepherds of the Church, tending and caring for Christ's sheep until the Shepherd returns at the end of time. Christ leaves for us His example for a way of life, as well as a visible, living, tangible Church that He will guide as we follow Him.

From the Catechism: Key Words to Know

ANNUNCIATION: The visit of the angel Gabriel to the Virgin Mary to inform her that she was to be the mother of the Savior. After giving her consent to God's Word, Mary became the mother of Jesus by the power of the Holy Spirit (484, 494).

SON OF GOD: A title frequently applied to Jesus in the Gospel, signifying His unique relationship to the Father. The second Person of the Blessed Trinity is called Son of God in reference to the Eternal Father. The revelation of His divine sonship is the principal dramatic development of the story of Jesus of Nazareth (441–445).

JOHN THE BAPTIST: The immediate precursor or herald of Jesus. John identified Jesus as the messianic Lamb of God and baptized Him in the Jordan River. With prophetic power John gave witness to Jesus by his preaching, by the baptism of conversion he announced, and finally by his martyrdom (523, 720).

MIRACLE: A sign or wonder such as a healing or the control of nature that can only be attributed to divine power. The miracles of Jesus were messianic signs of the presence of God's kingdom (547).

PARABLES: A characteristic feature of the teaching of Jesus. Parables are simple images or comparisons that confront the hearer or reader with a radical choice about his invitation to enter the kingdom of God (546).

KINGDOM OF GOD (OF HEAVEN): The reign or rule of God, "the kingdom of God is . . . righteousness and peace and joy in the Holy Spirit" (Rom. 14:17). The kingdom of God draws near in the coming of the Incarnate Word; it is announced in the Gospel; it is the messianic kingdom, present in the Person of Jesus, the Messiah; it remains in our midst in the Eucharist. Christ gave to His Apostles the work of proclaiming the kingdom, and through the Holy Spirit forms His people into a priestly kingdom, the Church, in which the kingdom of God is mysteriously present, for she is the seed and beginning of the kingdom on earth. In the Lord's Prayer ("Thy Kingdom come") we pray for its final glorious appearance, when Christ will hand over the kingdom to His Father (541–554, 709, 763, 2816, 2819).

Chapter 7

The Death and Resurrection of Christ

Reading the Catechism: Paragraphs 595–667

> Worthy is the Lamb that was slain to receive power and riches, wisdom and strength, honor and glory and blessing.
>
> —Revelation 5:12

"For God so loved the world that he gave his only Son, so that everyone who believes in him might not perish but might have eternal life" (Jn. 3:16). This powerful passage from Scripture summarizes the very heart and mission of Christ: to offer Himself as the definitive and perfect sacrifice for our sins, so that we may live in the freedom of the Father. The Passion, death, Resurrection, and Ascension of Christ are known as the Paschal Mystery. Jesus becomes for us the new Passover (Paschal) Lamb that frees us from the slavery of sin and destroys the power of sin and death forever. Through the Resurrection of Christ, who becomes for us the New Adam, we are destined to live forever with Him in the glory of the Father.

The Paschal Mystery is the source and center of the Christian life, the very saving action of Christ is packed with meaning. This chapter will explore in great detail the meaning and mysteries of Christ's Passion, death, Resurrection, and Ascension, and how these mysteries so perfectly fulfill the Father's plan of salvation which was promised many centuries before Christ.

The Agony in the Garden

The Passion of Christ begins with His agony in the Garden of Gethsemane immediately following the celebration of the Last Supper. This is the paradigm event in His life and mission. The agony in the garden defines everything that He is and came to do. Jesus faces the will of the Father—a will He is called to accept—knowing that it will result in His torture and cruel death on the Cross, a fate only hours away. The sin of all of humanity, past, present, and future, stares Jesus in the face. He falls to the ground in such agony that He begins to sweat blood. Here we see the real love of Jesus. He says yes to the Father and yes to us. For us He says yes to the cruel beatings He will receive after He is arrested. For us He says yes to the unimaginable scourging at the pillar. For us He says yes to being nailed to the Cross. For us He says yes to the piercing of His heart with a spear. To all of this He says yes out of merciful love for us. Jesus' yes in the Garden of Gethsemane is why the Cross becomes the instrument of salvation. Without Jesus willing it, without Him loving us through it all, it would have meant nothing. The agony in the garden reveals to us that God's love is greater than sin, greater than torture and death, greater than cruelty and hatred. By accepting the will of the Father, Jesus, the New Adam, reverses the disobedience of Adam and becomes the source of eternal life for us all. Saint Paul speaks of this love of Christ:

> For Christ, while we were still helpless, yet died at the appointed time for the ungodly. Indeed, only with difficulty does one die for a just person, though perhaps for a good person one might even find courage to die. But God proves his love for us in that while we were still sinners Christ died for us. How much more then, since we are now justified by his blood, will we be saved through him from the wrath. Indeed, if, while we were enemies, we were reconciled to God through the death of his Son, how much more, once reconciled, will we be saved by his life. (Rom. 5:6–10)

In the Garden of Gethsemane Jesus truly takes upon Himself the sin of the world, and through His love and obedience to the plan of the Father, Jesus destroys the power of sin and death forever.

The Sacrifice of Christ

In the Garden of Gethsemane, Jesus offers Himself as the definitive and eternal **sacrifice** for the forgiveness of sins. But why did Jesus have to sacrifice Himself and die? That is a question that needs closer examination.

The sin of Adam and Eve caused a great division, a vast chasm between humanity and God. Almost immediately in the Old Testament there develops the understanding of the need for sacrifice, or atonement, for sin. Something that is very good, a perfect calf or lamb, or the best fruits of harvest, ought to be sacrificed to God as a way of atoning or making satisfaction for our sins.

Sacrificial actions continued throughout the history of Israel. The Passover sacrifice, or sin offering, and the celebration Yom Kippur are the prime examples. As great and wonderful as these sacrifices were, they did not come close to atoning for the great sin of humanity. There was a twofold problem when it came to atoning for sin. First, there still existed the chasm between humanity and God caused by original sin, which was so great that it could be bridged only by God Himself. Nothing a mere person might be able to do, no matter how great, would even begin to suffice. Second, since sin entered the world through a man, Adam, another man would be required to pay the price for the sin of the first man. Sacrificing an animal, even the best of all the flocks, could never truly provide justice for the sin of humanity. It seemed that no matter what any person could do, the human race was hopelessly lost in sin.

This is where the merciful plan of the Father comes into play. The Father sends His only Son into the world to become fully human in His one divine Person. Suddenly there is a wonderful answer to the problem of sin. Jesus as God has the power to heal the massive wound of sin and bridge the gap that separates humanity from God. Jesus as a man, *without sin,* can Himself become the perfect sacrifice for the **expiation** of the sins of humanity. Thus, Jesus must offer Himself as the sacrifice, as the One who takes upon Himself the punishment for sin, so that all of us who have lived in sin may be freed from it. Jesus is the only answer to sin. In the end, the One who has no sin becomes sin so that, through His sacrifice, sin and death can be destroyed forever.

Jesus' sacrifice on the Cross is the one sacrifice that truly can and does atone for sin. It fulfills and surpasses all other sacrifices. All of the sacrifices in the Old Testament foreshadow and prepare for the sacrifice of Christ. Let's take a closer look at how the sacrifice of Christ is foreshadowed in, and also fulfills, the sacrifices of the Old Testament.

Yom Kippur Sacrifice

There are parallels between the sacrifice of Christ and the Jewish Yom Kippur sacrifice of the Old Testament. The Yom Kippur sacrifice was a sacrifice for the atonement of sin. It was and still is celebrated each fall and was and is one of the solemn Jewish feasts. In the Old Testament version of Yom Kippur, an unblemished male lamb was chosen from the flocks of the community and was presented to the priest for sacrifice. The priest would lay his hands upon the lamb, symbolically placing all the sins of the people on it. Then the lamb was dramatically taken out of the town and slaughtered. Once killed, all of its blood—blood was seen as the life-force—was drained. Then the lamb was burned as a holocaust to God.

When we look closely at Christ's sacrifice, we see that His crucifixion and death almost perfectly fulfills the Yom Kippur sacrifice. First, Christ is the perfect, "unblemished" sacrificial Lamb of the Father. He is the perfect man who knows no sin. Then, as seen in the agony in the garden, the Father places all the sin of humanity upon Christ, who accepts the will of the Father with love. Christ then takes up the Cross at the Praetorium inside Jerusalem, and is literally driven out of the city where He is crucified—sacrificed—outside the city walls. Once He is dead a soldier pierces His heart with a lance and immediately blood and water flow out. Jesus sheds every last drop of His blood out of love for us. He who becomes sin for us is completely obliterated. Christ's sacrifice on the Cross becomes the new and everlasting sacrifice for sin.

The Passover Sacrifice

Jesus' sacrifice on the Cross also fulfills another Jewish festival, the Jewish Passover sacrifice. As mentioned at the beginning of this chapter, we call the Passion, death, Resurrection, and Ascension of Christ the **Paschal Mystery** (meaning Passover) because Jesus becomes for us the new Passover Lamb. He is the Lamb of God who takes away the sin of the world. In fact, the Passion, death, and Resurrection of Christ take place during the celebration of Passover. Jesus fulfills the Passover sacrifice, the heart of the Old Covenant, and establishes the New and Everlasting Covenant sealed in His Blood shed upon the Cross.

Let us look closely at the Passover sacrifice as described in the Book of Exodus (see Ex. 12:1–26). The victim of the sacrifice is an unblemished lamb. It must be the best of all the flocks. It is to be slaughtered with all the assembly of Israel present. The blood of the lamb is to be sprinkled upon the wood of the lintel and doorpost of each house. Then they eat the roasted flesh of the lamb. If Israel completes the sacrifice, and the Lord sees the blood of the lamb on the houses of His chosen people, the death, which is to take the firstborn, will pass over them. The Lord commands the Israelites to hold Passover as a perpetual memorial feast for all generations. As a result of the Passover, the Israelites were freed from Egyptian slavery and passed through the waters of the Red Sea to freedom.

Now let's look at the sacrifice of Christ and how it fulfills the Passover sacrifice. In the Gospel of John, when John the Baptist first saw Jesus, he exclaimed,

"Behold, the Lamb of God, who takes away the sin of the world" (Jn. 1:29). Jesus is the Lamb of God, the sacrifice that the Father offers for the forgiveness of sins. He is sacrificed during the celebration of Passover, when the entire assembly of Israel is present in Jerusalem. In his Gospel John tells us that when Jesus was condemned to death by Pilate, "It was preparation day for Passover, and it was about noon" (Jn. 19:14). This is the exact time when the Passover lambs were being slaughtered in the Temple. Jesus indeed becomes for us the Lamb of God who is slain.

Christ's blood is shed on the Cross. When the Father sees the blood of His Son that is offered for all of humanity, the death we inherited from the first-born of humanity (Adam) passes over us and we are freed from slavery to sin. Jesus inaugurates the new and eternal Passover, the Paschal Mystery by which, through the blood of the Lamb of God who was slain for all, we are freed from sin and can now live in the freedom of the Father. The Passover of the Old Covenant is fulfilled by the Paschal Mystery of the New Covenant, the death and Resurrection of Christ.

The Eucharist as the New Passover

There is one final, crucial aspect of the Passover sacrifice that still needed to be fulfilled: the eating of the flesh of the lamb. During the Last Supper, the very celebration of the Passover meal itself, Jesus took unleavened bread and wine and changed them into His own Body and Blood so that we would be able to eat the flesh of the Lamb of God. Not only is Christ the new paschal sacrifice, He also institutes the new paschal banquet of the New Covenant where we come to partake of the very Body and Blood of Christ, who is our spiritual food.

Like the Passover of the Old Covenant, the Eucharist (the celebration of the sacrifice of the Mass) becomes the memorial feast and perpetual institution of the New Covenant. "This is my body that is for you. Do this in remembrance of me" (1 Cor. 11:24). The celebration of the Mass is the very heart and center of living and participating in the New Covenant. The Mass makes real and present once again the sacrifice of the Lamb of God for the forgiveness of sins. We come to really and truly participate in the redemptive act of Christ, and then we take into ourselves the flesh of the Lamb, Christ Himself, so that freed from sin and filled with the very life of God, we go forth into the world and build the kingdom of God. There is no greater way that we can live and participate in the New Covenant than in the celebration of the Eucharist. It is truly the "source and summit of the Christian life" (Second Vatican Council, Constitution on the Sacred Liturgy *Sacrosanctum concilium* [December 4,1963], no. 10).

Thus, the sacrifice of Christ is the definitive and eternal sacrifice for the forgiveness of sins that fulfills the Old Testament sacrifices and establishes the New and Eternal Covenant in His blood.

Jesus' Descent into Hell

In the Apostle's Creed we state that Jesus descended into hell before rising from the dead on the third day. What does this mean? Here, the word "hell" does not signify the place of eternal damnation, but rather it is from the Greek word *Hades* meaning the "place of the dead." Jesus' descent to this place of the dead has a twofold meaning.

First, Christ's descent to the dead means that Jesus suffered death in the same way we all suffer death. Jesus died a truly human death so that He might destroy death forever. Had He not truly died, He would not have been able to redeem us from death. He suffered physical death, that is, the destruction of His body and the separation of His body and soul. Profoundly, Christ also suffered spiritual death in a very human way; He suffered separation from the Father, which is the eternal and ultimate consequence of sin. This spiritual suffering can be seen on the Cross when Christ exclaims, "My God, my God, why have you forsaken me?" (Mt. 27:46). Out of love for us, Christ experienced death so completely that death may be redeemed and destroyed forever.

Second, Christ's **descent into hell** is also the first-fruits of the redemption in Christ. He descends to the place of the dead where the just souls of those who died before the redemption are awaiting the coming of Christ. He frees them from death and takes them into paradise. Jesus' descent to the dead is the culmination of His messianic ministry and shows the immediate power of the redemption for all humanity, past, present, and future. The mercy and love of Christ are available to all.

The Resurrection of Christ

Christ is truly resurrected from the dead and has destroyed sin and death forever. This is the very cornerstone of our faith. For as Saint Paul says, "And if Christ has not been raised, then empty (too) is our preaching; empty, too, your faith. . . . and if Christ has not been raised, your faith is vain; you are still in your sins" (1 Cor. 15:14, 17). The **Resurrection** fulfills and confirms Christ's entire mission, words, and actions, for He came to free us from sin and death and to establish an everlasting kingdom of God.

The Resurrection Brings about a New Creation

The Resurrection is not merely Christ's resuscitation from the dead. It goes far beyond that. Jesus brought people such as Jarius' daughter and Lazarus back to life during His public ministry. They were brought back to ordinary earthly life and would someday die again. The Resurrection of Christ is a resurrection to a new creation, a new way of being. The resurrected Christ truly had a human body, for He ate and drank, and Thomas placed his fingers in the nail marks in our Lord's hands. But it is a human body and a human nature filled with the grace and power of the Holy Spirit, and not bound by space and time. The resurrected Christ is the final fruit of a humanity freed from the power of sin and death, transformed by the grace of the Father. Through the Resurrection of Christ we truly become glorified sons and daughters of the Father living forever in His life and love.

> Behold, I tell you a mystery. We shall not all fall asleep, but we will all be changed, in an instant, in the blink of an eye, at the last trumpet. For the trumpet will sound, the dead will be raised incorruptible, and we shall be changed. For that which is corruptible must clothe itself with incorruptibility, and that which is mortal must clothe itself with immortality. And when this which is corruptible clothes itself with incorruptibility and this which is mortal clothes itself with immortality, then the word that is written shall come about:
>
> > "Death is swallowed up in victory.
> > Where, O death, is your victory?
> > Where, O death, is your sting?"
>
> The sting of death is sin, and the power of sin is the law. But thanks be to God who gives us the victory through our Lord Jesus Christ. (1 Cor. 15:51–57)

The Ministry of the Resurrected Christ

After His Resurrection Jesus spent forty days on earth with the Apostles and other disciples. This constituted the final phase of Jesus' earthly ministry. The resurrected Jesus confirmed the faith of the Apostles and continued to teach them about the kingdom. He commissioned them to the ministry of the forgiveness of sins (Jn. 20:19–23), and also commanded them to baptize all the nations and teach all that He had commanded them (Mt. 28:19). Jesus' post-Resurrection ministry to the disciples attests to the reality of the Resurrection as both a historical event and a spiritual reality. They experienced Jesus in a new and profound way and saw with their own eyes and touched with their own hands the reality of the saving power of God. Christ also promised to send the Spirit, the second Helper, who would confirm them in the faith and empower them to go out to the ends of the earth as His witnesses.

The Ascension of Christ

The **Ascension** completes the Paschal Mystery. It is a profound manifestation of Christ as the King of kings and the eternal High Priest of heaven. Jesus' entry into eternal glory opens for us access to the throne and grace of God.

> But when Christ came as high priest of the good things that have come to be, passing through the greater and more perfect tabernacle not made by hands, that is, not belonging to this creation, he entered once for all into the sanctuary, not with the blood of goats and calves but with his own blood, thus obtaining eternal redemption. For if the blood of goats and bulls and the sprinkling of a heifer's ashes can sanctify those who are defiled so that their flesh is cleansed, how much more will the blood of Christ, who through the eternal spirit offered himself unblemished to God, cleanse our consciences from dead works to worship the living God. For this reason he is mediator of a new covenant: since a death has taken place for deliverance from transgressions under the first covenant, those who are called may receive the promised eternal inheritance. (Heb. 9:11–15)

Jesus forever sits at the right hand of God as our glorious Mediator. Christ, sent by the Father, returns to Him with the fruits of His redemption and becomes the instrument of grace and life flowing from the Father.

Christ also becomes for us the way into the life of the Trinity. Through Christ we have access to the Father in and with the power of the Holy Spirit. The Ascension proclaims forever that the human race will never again be separated from the Father. We now joyfully await the second coming of Christ, when all things will be brought under His feet and the kingdom of Christ will be complete, and with all the angels and saints in heaven we can joyfully proclaim, "Worthy is the Lamb that was slain to receive power and riches, wisdom and strength, honor and glory and blessing" (Rev. 5:12).

From the Catechism: Key Words to Know

SACRIFICE: A ritual offering made to God by a priest on behalf of the people as a sign of adoration, gratitude, supplication, and communion (2099). The perfect sacrifice was Christ's death on the Cross; by this sacrifice, Christ accomplished our redemption as high priest of the new and eternal covenant (616). The sacrifice of Christ on the Cross is commemorated and mysteriously made present in the Eucharistic sacrifice of the Church (1357, 1544).

EXPIATION: The act of redemption and atonement for sin that Christ won for us by the pouring out of His Blood on the Cross, by His obedient love "even to the end" (Jn. 13:1; CCC 433, 616, 1475). The expiation of sins continues in the Mystical Body of Christ and the communion of saints by joining our human acts of atonement to the redemptive action of Christ, both in this life and in purgatory.

PASCHAL MYSTERY/SACRIFICE: Christ's work of redemption accomplished principally by His Passion, death, Resurrection, and glorious Ascension whereby "dying he destroyed our death, rising he restored our life" (1067; cf. 654). The Paschal Mystery is celebrated and made present in the liturgy of the Church, and its saving effects are communicated through the sacraments (1076), especially the Eucharist, which renews the paschal sacrifice of Christ as the sacrifice offered by the Church (571, 1362–1372).

DESCENT INTO HELL: An article in the Apostles' Creed referring to the victory over death and sin, which Christ won by being "raised from the dead." Jesus, like all people, experienced death and in His soul joined the others in the realm of the dead, where He descended as Savior, proclaiming the Gospel to the spirits imprisoned there in order to free the just ones who had gone before Him (632).

RESURRECTION OF CHRIST: The bodily rising of Jesus from the dead on the third day after His death on the Cross and burial in the tomb. The Resurrection of Christ is the crowning truth of our faith in Christ (638).

ASCENSION: The entry of Jesus' humanity into divine glory in God's heavenly domain forty days after His Resurrection (659, 665).

Chapter 8

The Holy Spirit

Reading the Catechism: Paragraphs 687–747

> Come, Holy Spirit, fill the hearts of your faithful and enkindle in them the fire of your love.
>
> —Pentecost Sequence from the *Roman Missal*

The **Holy Spirit** is the third Person of the Holy Trinity and the last of the Persons of the Trinity to be fully revealed. Through His presence and power we come to know Christ as the Son of God and have access to the Father. Through Baptism the Holy Spirit comes to dwell within our hearts and makes us holy temples of the living God. In this chapter we will discuss who the Holy Spirit is and His role in salvation history. We will also see how He empowers the followers of Christ and is present and working through the Church.

Who Is the Holy Spirit?

The Third Person of the Trinity

The Holy Spirit is not simply the presence or "spirit" of God, but is actually the third Person of the Trinity—a Person unique from the Father and the Son who with them is adored and glorified. For the first four hundred years after Christ sent His Holy Spirit at Pentecost, the Church struggled to define the mystery of His personhood and divinity, in the same way that it grappled with the questions concerning the doctrines of Jesus' humanity and divinity.

Many theologians during the infancy of the Church asserted that the Holy Spirit was merely the "spirit" of Christ or simply the presence of God, who forever remained with the Church. They did not believe that He was a true Person of the Trinity. It was the Council of Constantinople (AD 381) that clarified that the Holy Spirit "proceeds from the Father and the Son and with the Father and the Son is worshipped and glorified." The council defined the Holy Spirit as a distinct third Person of the Trinity equal to the Father and the Son, and worshipped and glorified because He is truly a divine Person, God Himself.

The Council of Constantinople also defined the relationship of the persons of the Trinity. The Trinity is a profound relationship of love that is so great that it unites three divine Persons in the one true God. The Holy Spirit proceeds from the Father and the Son because He is the love between the Father and the Son. How is this possible? The nature of love is to give a gift of self to another. The Father gives a complete gift of self to the Son and the Son gives a complete gift of self to the Father. This love of the Father and the Son does not remain contained between them, but is fruitful and efficacious in that it pours out from them as the third Person of the Holy Trinity. Therefore, although it is a mystery we can rightly assert that the Holy Spirit is the love between the Father and the Son. He is the very power and love of God that eternally pours forth from the heart of the Blessed Trinity.

The Names and Symbols of the Holy Spirit

The Holy Spirit is most often called the **Paraclete,** or Advocate, which mean "helper" (literally "called beside" or "called to one's aid"). He is the One sent by Christ to lead us in truth and fill us with His power so that we may know and be transformed into Christ. "But you will receive power when the Holy Spirit comes upon you, and you will be my witnesses in Jerusalem, throughout Judea and Samaria, and to the ends of the earth" (Acts 1:8). The Holy Spirit is our divine Helper who fills us with His power and love so that we can become the very vessels of God's love poured out for the sanctification of the world.

Many different symbols of the Holy Spirit are revealed in Scripture. At Jesus' baptism in the Jordan the Holy Spirit descended in the form of a dove, for He is the gentle Spirit of God who fills us with true peace and joy. At Pentecost, when descending on each of the Apostles, He was seen as the fire of God. He is the all-consuming fire of the love and power of God that purifies us of sin and fills our hearts with the burning desire to love God with all that we are, unafraid of the consequences. We see how the Apostles, consumed with the fire of this love, put aside all fear and boldly proclaimed Christ to the world.

The Gradual Revelation of the Holy Spirit

The Holy Spirit, together with the Father and the Son, always was and always will be; yet He was the last of the divine Persons to be fully revealed.

There is a progressive revelation of the Trinity, a divine "condescension" in which the Trinity was gradually revealed to mankind. The Father is first revealed as the God of the Old Testament, the Creator of heaven and earth and the Author of the plan of salvation history. The Son is revealed in the New Testament as the Redeemer sent by the Father to fully reveal the Father and redeem us from sin. Jesus often spoke of the One who was to come to lead us to all truth. Christ sent the Holy Spirit upon the Church to dwell within our hearts and fill us with the power and love of God. The Holy Spirit, fully revealed at Pentecost, leads us to Christ and empowers us to be His witnesses. Through the Holy Spirit the very love of God is poured forth from the Trinity, making us sharers in the divine life.

The Holy Spirit Sanctifies and Empowers the Church

Pentecost: The Coming and Revelation of the Spirit

The mission and presence of the Holy Spirit was fully revealed to humanity at Pentecost. (The word Pentecost means "fifty days." Pentecost was a Jewish feast that took place fifty days after Passover.) About fifty days after Easter, Christ sent the Holy Spirit upon the assembled Apostles and disciples, and they were filled with His presence, power, and gifts, and they began to proclaim the Gospel.

> When the time for Pentecost was fulfilled, they were all in one place together. And suddenly there came from the sky a noise like a strong driving wind, and it filled the entire house in which they were. Then there appeared to them tongues as of fire, which parted and came to rest on each one of them. And they were all filled with the Holy Spirit and began to speak in different tongues, as the Spirit enabled them to proclaim. Now there were devout Jews from every nation under heaven staying in Jerusalem. At this sound, they gathered in a large crowd, but they were confused because each one heard them speaking in his own language. They were astounded, and in amazement they asked, "Are not all these people who are speaking Galileans? Then how does each of us hear them in his own native language? We are Parthians, Medes, and Elamites, inhabitants of Mesopotamia, Judea and Cappadocia, Pontus and Asia,

> Phrygia and Pamphylia, Egypt and the districts of Libya near Cyrene, as well as travelers from Rome, both Jews and converts to Judaism, Cretans and Arabs, yet we hear them speaking in our own tongues of the mighty acts of God." (Acts 2:1–11)

The event of Pentecost is significant in two ways. First, the Holy Spirit is fully revealed, and as a result the Trinity is also fully revealed as a union of the Father, Son, and Holy Spirit. Additionally, the mission of the Holy Spirit of empowering and transforming the followers of Christ is inaugurated. The Holy Spirit transformed the disciples from weakness and fear to boldness and courage in proclaiming and witnessing the revelation of God. For it is only through the Holy Spirit that the early Church was able to exhibit empowered faith in God.

Second, the Pentecost event marks the birthday of the Church and launches the Church on a mission both visibly and spiritually. The Church is manifested visibly when the Apostles begin to preach to all the nations that were represented in Jerusalem. Each person heard the Apostles speaking in their own native tongue. The Catholic (universal) Church united the human race in Christ by the power of the Holy Spirit, and so we can say that Pentecost is the reversal of the scattering of humanity at the Tower of Babel as seen in the Old Testament. At Babel humanity was fractured into different languages and was no longer able to communicate and live together in peace because of sin. Only through the power of the Holy Spirit at Pentecost is the human family once again united in the Church where on a single day over three thousand people were baptized.

The Church also began her spiritual mission to teach and proclaim the Gospel of Christ. The Apostles burst out of the upper room filled with the fire of the Holy Spirit and began the missionary activity of the Church. The Holy Spirit not only leads us to the truth but also empowers us to go forth and proclaim the truth. Truly, the Holy Spirit is the source and soul of the Church, leading us always to Christ.

The Holy Spirit Sanctifies and Makes Us Like Christ

The Holy Spirit is sent by Christ to dwell within us so that we may be sanctified, or become holy (from the Latin *sanctus*). Christ redeems us from sin and opens the gates of heaven for us, but the Holy Spirit transforms us through our cooperation with His power and grace so that becoming holy, like Christ, we may have eternal life. The Holy Spirit accomplishes this work of sanctification in several ways.

The Holy Spirit frees us from both the law and the bondage of sin

Through the power of the Holy Spirit, we are set free from the old law written on stone and receive a new law written on our hearts. We now live in the freedom of Christ, and are no longer subject to the law and the desires of our flesh. Saint Paul states, "But now we are released from the law, dead to what held us captive, so that we may serve in the newness of the Spirit and not under the obsolete letter" (Rom. 7:6). The Holy Spirit frees us from the bondage of sin and death so that we enter into the freedom of life in God.

Through the Holy Spirit we are made righteous and become children of God

We are transformed from people bent over by the burden of sin to people able to stand upright before God. The power of the Holy Spirit is a transforming power that conforms us to the image of Christ and restores within us the likeness of God, which was disfigured through sin. The Holy Spirit sanctifies us, and we become the adopted sons and daughters of God.

> For those who are led by the Spirit of God are children of God. For you did not receive a spirit of slavery to fall back into fear, but you received a spirit of adoption, through which we cry, "Abba, Father!" The Spirit itself bears witness with our spirit that we are children of God, and if children, then heirs, heirs of God and joint heirs with Christ, if only we suffer with him so that we may also be glorified with him. (Rom. 8:14–17)

The Holy Spirit fills us with His seven gifts

The seven gifts of the Holy Spirit are the same seven gifts given to Christ.

> But a shoot shall sprout from the stump of Jesse, and from his roots a bud shall blossom. The spirit of the LORD shall rest upon him: a spirit of wisdom and of understanding, [a] spirit of counsel and of strength, a spirit of knowledge and of fear of the LORD, and his delight shall be the fear of the LORD. (Is. 11:1–3)

The seven gifts are given to us as the foundation or spiritual tools of the Christian life so that we too may continue the mission and work of Christ. For a more detailed look at the seven gifts, see chapter fifteen on Confirmation.

The followers of Christ bear the fruits of the Holy Spirit

As Christians, when we are set free from the law we are guided by the Holy Spirit to a fullness of life that bears the **fruits of the Holy Spirit**. He sets us apart, and our lives reflect His presence in the fruits that we bear when we walk under the guidance of the Holy Spirit. He works not only to free us from the desires of the flesh but also to produce the fruits of His holy presence within us.

> I say, then: live by the Spirit and you will certainly not gratify the desire of the flesh. For the flesh has desires against the Spirit, and the Spirit against the flesh; these are opposed to each other, so that you may not do what you want. But if you are guided by the Spirit, you are not under the law. Now the works of the flesh are obvious: immorality, impurity, licentiousness, idolatry, sorcery, hatreds, rivalry, jealousy, outbursts of fury, acts of selfishness, dissensions, factions, occasions of envy, drinking bouts, orgies, and the like. I warn you, as I warned you before, that those who do such things will not inherit the kingdom of God. In contrast, the fruit of the Spirit is love, joy, peace, patience, kindness, generosity, faithfulness, gentleness, self-control. Against such there is no law. (Gal. 5:16–23)

The Holy Spirit gives us individual charisms

In addition to the seven gifts of the Holy Spirit, each member of the Church is also given special gifts in order to build the kingdom of God and continue the mission of Christ. These gifts are many and varying, and certain gifts are given to certain people as the Spirit sees necessary. Saint Paul gives a clear teaching on these **charisms** in his letter to the Corinthians:

> Now in regard to spiritual gifts, brothers, I do not want you to be unaware. You know how, when you were pagans, you were constantly attracted and led away to mute idols. Therefore, I

> tell you that nobody speaking by the spirit of God says, "Jesus be accursed." And no one can say, "Jesus is Lord," except by the Holy Spirit. There are different kinds of spiritual gifts but the same Spirit; there are different forms of service but the same Lord; there are different workings but the same God who produces all of them in everyone. To each individual the manifestation of the Spirit is given for some benefit. To one is given through the Spirit the expression of wisdom; to another the expression of knowledge according to the same Spirit; to another faith by the same Spirit; to another gifts of healing by the one Spirit; to another mighty deeds; to another prophecy; to another discernment of spirits; to another varieties of tongues; to another interpretation of tongues. But one and the same Spirit produces all of these, distributing them individually to each person as he wishes. (1 Cor. 12:1–11)

This list of gifts is by no means exhaustive, but it shows how different gifts of the Spirit are given to different members of the Body of Christ for the good of the Church. Some gifts are greater than others, some more immediately evident, others more subtle. However, all are vital for the Church and each is crucial in God's plan. As we discern our own gifts we have the responsibility to offer them with love in service to Christ and His Church.

The Holy Spirit Inspires Our Prayer

The Holy Spirit is also the source and inspiration of our prayer. Our prayer is actually our soul responding to *the thirst of Christ for us* that comes to us through the Holy Spirit. When we pray, it is the Holy Spirit praying in and through us, leading us to the heart of Christ. We cannot even call Jesus "Lord" without the grace and inspiration of the Holy Spirit. As Saint Paul teaches, "the Spirit too comes to the aid of our weakness; for we do not know how to pray as we ought, but the Spirit itself intercedes with inexpressible groanings" (Rom. 8:26). We should always call upon the intercession of the Holy Spirit in our prayer, especially when prayer comes with difficulty or in times of spiritual dryness. (When we find it hard to pray, we are not alone.) The Holy Spirit is the inspiration of prayer, and it is only through His grace and power that we can lift our hearts like incense up to God.

The Holy Spirit Convinces Us Concerning Sin

The Holy Spirit works to sanctify us by convincing us of our sin. When we find ourselves in sin or straying away from God, the Holy Spirit calls us back to the Father. When we turn away from God, the Holy Spirit our Advocate does not abandon us but calls us to conversion and repentance. This loving call of the Holy Spirit comes to us through our conscience prompting the feeling of guilt or remorse.

In our present culture we are taught to avoid the feeling of guilt and that feeling guilty or remorseful is a bad thing. In fact, feeling remorse is a form of *suffering*, a feeling of loss and sadness. Even more profoundly, remorse is a form of redemptive suffering, for it is the voice of the Holy Spirit calling us back to the Father.

For example, if I touch a hot stove the feeling of pain is not a pleasant experience. But the pain I feel is *good* in that it triggers my brain to get my hand off the burning stove before more damage is done. In the same way, the pain of remorse is the Holy Spirit calling us away from sin and all its damaging effects back to the merciful heart of Christ.

We should never avoid this merciful call of the Spirit, because no sin is beyond the forgiveness of God. The only sin that is unforgivable is the sin against the Holy Spirit—when through hardness of heart we reject the call of conversion and the mercy of Christ, choosing not to open ourselves to the forgiveness of God. The sin against the Holy Spirit is unforgivable precisely because we refuse that very forgiveness.

The Holy Spirit in the Life and Mission of the Church

The Holy Spirit Is the Source of the Church's Communion

As we saw earlier, the Holy Spirit is the love between the Father and the Son, who proceeds or pours forth from them. The Spirit is the love that unites the Trinity in a communion of love that is so profound that the three divine Persons are one God. In the same way, the Holy Spirit is the source and unifying principle of the Church's communion. The Holy Spirit is sent from the Father and the Son upon the Church so that, like at Pentecost, the entire human family may be one as the Father and Christ are one. The entire mission of the Holy Spirit can be summed up in His role of bringing all of humanity into communion with God.

The Holy Spirit Guides the Church to the Truth

"When the Advocate comes whom I will send you from the Father, the Spirit of truth that proceeds from the Father, he will testify to me" (Jn. 15:26). The Holy Spirit manifests Christ to the disciples, leading and guiding them to the truth. The Holy Spirit recalls the mystery of the death and Resurrection of Christ, opening our minds and hearts to the truth that Christ reveals about God and about humanity.

He especially guides the Apostles and their successors, the magisterium, that they may faithfully preserve and proclaim the Gospel of Christ, unchanging, undefiled, and without error until the end of time. The pope and the bishops are guided by the Holy Spirit so that they may continue to manifest Christ in His fullness to each generation. This **infallibility** in regard to doctrines of faith and morals is essential to the protection and handing on of the truth, and it is viewed with reverence and great humility on the part of the Church. Christ Himself guaranteed that He would send His Holy Spirit upon the Church and that the gates of hell would not prevail against it. He also said He would be with the Apostles as they minister and teach the Gospel throughout the ages.

> Then Jesus approached and said to them, "All power in heaven and on earth has been given to me. Go, therefore, and make disciples of all nations, baptizing them in the name of the Father, and of the Son, and of the Holy Spirit, teaching them to observe all that I have commanded you. And behold, I am with you always, until the end of the age." (Mt. 28:18–20)

The Holy Spirit Makes Present the Mystery of Christ

The Holy Spirit makes present the mystery of Christ in the liturgy and sacraments, especially in the Eucharist. Through the liturgy, the Spirit makes real and present to us the entire plan of salvation accomplished in Christ, and through His presence we come into contact with God's saving power. The liturgy is not simply a memorial of Christ's Paschal Mystery, but through the Holy Spirit we actually experience God's saving grace. Through the sacraments the Holy Spirit communicates to us sanctifying and transforming grace. Each time we receive the sacraments we are overshadowed by the power of the Holy Spirit, who enables us to become more like Christ, to live according to the Gospel, and to continue the mission of Christ. The sacraments are rivers of grace through which the Holy Spirit accomplishes the work of salvation in us.

From the Catechism: Key Words to Know

HOLY SPIRIT: The third divine Person of the Blessed Trinity, the personal love of Father and Son for each other. Also called the Paraclete (Advocate) and Spirit of Truth, the Holy Spirit is at work with the Father and the Son from the beginning to the completion of the divine plan for our salvation (685; cf. 152, 243).

PARACLETE: A name for the Holy Spirit. The term was used by Jesus in the New Testament (cf. Jn. 14:16) to indicate the promised gift of the Spirit as another consoler and advocate, who would continue His own mission among the disciples (692).

FRUITS OF THE HOLY SPIRIT: The perfections that the Holy Spirit forms in us as the "first fruits" of eternal glory. The tradition of the Church identifies twelve fruits of the Holy Spirit (1832).

CHARISM: A specific gift or grace of the Holy Spirit that directly or indirectly benefits the Church, given in order to help a person live out the Christian life or to serve the common good in building up the Church (799, 951).

INFALLIBILITY: The gift of the Holy Spirit to the Church whereby the pastors of the Church, the pope and bishops in union with him, can definitively proclaim a doctrine of faith or morals for the belief of the faithful (891). This gift is related to the inability of the whole body of the faithful to err in matters of faith and morals (92).

Chapter 9

The Church

Reading the Catechism: Paragraphs 748–945

> And so I say to you, you are Peter, and upon this rock I will build my church, and the gates of the netherworld shall not prevail against it.
>
> —Matthew 16:18

We have seen that Pentecost was the birthday of the Church and the beginning of her missionary activity. But what exactly is the Church, and where do we find the true Church of Christ today? Modern Christianity has become a global marketplace for thousands of churches, and "church shopping" is a regular practice on Sunday mornings. Is this what Christ intended, or did Christ establish one Church as a visible instrument of truth, salvation, and unity?

In this chapter we will answer these tough modern-day questions. We will discover how the Catholic Church is the one true Church established by Christ. We'll look at the **four marks of the Church** and see that the Catholic Church truly is one, holy, catholic, and apostolic.

The Church as the Fulfillment of God's Plan of Salvation

The Church Prefigured and Gradually Revealed in the Old Testament

In the Old Testament God gradually revealed Himself to mankind. That revelation, as we have seen, culminated in the coming of Jesus—God's ultimate self-revelation. The Old Testament also shows God's desire to have a people in that covenantal relationship with Him. His covenants with Israel attest to that intent and plan. As Christ was the ultimate revelation of God, so the **Church** is the fulfillment of God's desire to establish a people in covenant with Him. In fact, "People of God" is a synonym for "Church." The Church is the vehicle of unity for the entire human race through Christ's grace and love in the power of the Holy Spirit.

The Old Testament reveals the gradual development of the People of God. First, we saw the beginnings of the human family in the *spousal union* of Adam and Eve, the first image of the Church. The Father then gathered the *family* of Noah as the faithful remnant in a world of chaos and sin. Later Abraham became our father in faith, and from his great faith emerged the *Twelve Tribes of Israel*, the foundation of God's chosen people. Moses led the *people* of Israel out of slavery to Egypt and into the Promised Land. David was anointed king of the *nation* of Israel that had become a great realm in the ancient world.

Through all of this history the Father was preparing His people for the coming of Christ. When He selected the Twelve Apostles at the very beginning of His ministry on earth, Christ began establishing the universal, or Catholic Church. It would be the People of God that encompasses all peoples of every time, place, and culture. The Church is the flowering of the Father's plan of salvation, the unity of the human race as one family of God in Christ.

Christ Established a Visible, Institutional Church

As we also saw in chapter two, Christ fulfilled the Father's plan by establishing a visible, institutional Church founded upon the teaching and authority of the Apostles. The Church was to be the instrument of salvation, the means through which all people would come into communion with Him and one another. From the very beginning of His ministry Jesus taught and prepared the Apostles to be the foundation of His Church. He gave them the authority to teach, minister, and govern in His name, promised to be with them until the end of time, and assured them that the gates of hell would not prevail against His Church.

After His Ascension Christ sent the Holy Spirit upon the Church at Pentecost, filling the Apostles with the power to go forth and teach the Gospel to all nations. Guided by the Spirit, the Apostles appointed other men to be successors to the apostolic ministry. They in their turn continued to faithfully teach and hand on the Gospel of Christ, guiding and governing the Church as she continued to grow and spread throughout the earth.

Thus, the Church emerged from Jerusalem as the new Israel founded upon the teaching and ministry of the Apostles, empowered by the Holy Spirit to be the visible sign and instrument through which Christ accomplishes His work of salvation.

The Catholic Church Is the One True Church

Today, where do we find this Church that Jesus established? With over thirty thousand Christian denominations in the United States, which one is the one true Church that Christ founded upon the Apostles and their successors? The Catholic Church is the only one that can claim its origins are in Jesus Christ Himself, founded by Him on the Apostles and their successors.

The papacy can be traced back in an unbroken line of authority to Peter himself, to whom Christ gave the keys to the kingdom and the authority as "rock" of the Church. Pope Francis was made the 265th successor to Peter to continue the ministry of "binding and loosing" in the Church (Mt. 16:18–19). The bishops in union with the pope continue the apostolic ministry of teaching, ministering, and governing in the name of Christ. They faithfully preserve, defend, and hand on the revelation of Christ contained in both Sacred Tradition and Sacred Scripture, so that the full revelation of Christ can be received by each generation. Christ established a visible, institutional Church with a clear and recognizable teaching authority, with one faith and one creed, and with a system of common worship that is the same today as it was in the earliest days of Christianity.

For the first thousand years of Christianity there was only one Church, the Catholic Church, with the pope and bishops leading and guiding it, with the sacraments and the Mass and a united faith and common doctrine based on the teachings of the Apostles. No other "church" existed until the split of the Eastern Orthodox in 1054 and the extensive fragmenting of the Church in the sixteenth century with the Protestant Reformation.

In truth, all other Christian churches trace their origins back to the Catholic Church, which existed in the first century, and in the eleventh century, and in the sixteenth century, and still exists today. No other Christian church has existed separately since apostolic times. Today the Catholic Church is in every country and has over on e billion members. Its unity in faith and worship is so profound that you can go to any Catholic Church in the world and find the same faith, the same system of worship, and the **communion** that makes the Church one.

The Four Marks of the Church

The Nicene Creed, which dates back to AD 325, states, "We believe in one, holy, catholic, and apostolic Church." These are the four essential features, or marks, of the one true Church. The Catholic Church is the only Church that possesses in fullness these four marks, as she is the one and original Church founded by Christ.

The Church Is One

At the Last Supper Jesus prayed for the unity and oneness of the Church:

> I pray not only for them, but also for those who will believe in me through their word, so that they may all be one, as you, Father, are in me and I in you, that they also may be in us, that the world may believe that you sent me. (Jn. 17:20–21)

Christ and the Father are completely one. They share the same mission, purpose, plan, and nature. They are not somewhat one, or basically one, but completely and truly one. Christ Himself willed and prayed that the Church be one in the same way that He and the Father are one.

The unity of the Church should be of the same nature as the union of Christ and the Father. When Christ prays for the Church to be one, it cannot mean a loose collection of different Christian denominations, each with different doctrines or systems of worship. It must mean a Church that is completely one in faith, teaching, doctrine, worship, and mission. For there is one Christ, and the Church is the bride of Christ. He cannot have many brides with different beliefs and teachings.

This is why Christ founded the Church upon the teaching authority of the Apostles and their successors. The pope and the bishops have preserved and continue to preserve the unity of the Church by ensuring that the one true faith, entrusted to them by Christ, is handed down preserved, unbroken, and undivided.

How can the Church be one if there are different interpretations of Scripture or different beliefs concerning faith and morals? Churches that have abandoned the teaching office of the Church have struggled to preserve the oneness of faith, and have been rocked with division and doctrinal turmoil.

Luther's cry of *sola scriptura* has massively divided the Church, harming its unity. In contrast, the Catholic Church has preserved the oneness of the Church through three very important visible means (see CCC, 815):

1. Through the profession of one faith received from the teaching of the Apostles.
2. Through the common celebration of divine worship established by Christ in the Mass and the sacraments.
3. Through apostolic succession and the teaching office (magisterium) of the Church, which preserves the fraternal accord of God's family.

Thus, we can rightly say that the Church of Christ in its fullness has been preserved intact and subsists in the Catholic Church, the one true Church that Christ Himself established and today has unbroken unity, authority, and a system of worship with origins in Christ Himself.

> For it is through Christ's Catholic Church alone, which is the universal help toward salvation, that the fullness of the means of salvation can be obtained. It was to the apostolic college alone, of which Peter is the head, that we believe that our Lord entrusted all the blessings of the New Covenant, in order to establish on earth the one **Body of Christ** into which all those should be fully incorporated who belong in any way to the People of God. (Second Vatican Council, Decree on Ecumenism *Unitatis redintegratio* [November 21, 1964], no. 3)

The Church Is Holy

The Church is holy because it is the very instrument Christ established through which He would accomplish His work of salvation. It is the means to holiness—the visible source and channel of grace through which He sanctifies the world. Holiness is also the goal or final end of the Church, for she is called to be the spotless bride of Christ, to be holy as Christ is holy. Each and every member of the Church is called to be like Christ, to no longer live for self but to live for Him and allow His glory to shine forth through their words and deeds. Every mission and activity of the Church should have the goal of holiness for its members.

While the Church is holy by its very nature and foundation as a divine reality, she is also filled with sinful people. Christ taught that the weeds would be mixed with the wheat, and it is indeed true that the Church is filled with people in various states of holiness. While here on earth, all of her members are called to strive for holiness and fight against sin and temptation. Thus the Church on earth is called the "Church Militant," fighting and struggling each day through ongoing conversion to be holy as Christ is holy.

The saints in heaven bear witness to the holiness of the Church and the power of the transforming grace of Christ. The Church in heaven is the Church perfected, the "Church Triumphant," which has won the crown of glory. Heavenly glory is the goal of the Church and all are called to sanctity and the perfection of charity.

For those who have died in the friendship of Christ but are still in need of further purification, there is the grace of purgatory. It is the final great act of God's mercy in which His sons and daughters are purified from any attachment to sin, so they may become holy and enter the glory of heaven. The "Church Suffering" in purgatory is also a witness to the call of holiness, the call to perfection in charity and transformation in Christ.

Finally, the martyrs of the Church, those who freely gave their lives out of love for Christ, most powerfully and profoundly witness the universal call to holiness and the holiness of the Church. "No one has greater love than this, to lay down one's life for one's friends" (Jn. 15:13). Martyrdom is the greatest expression of charity and the most powerful witness of holiness. The blood of the martyrs has been the seed of faith and the inspiration of holiness throughout the centuries. Although few are called to martyrdom through blood, we are all called to lay down our lives for Christ and one another in charity. This "white" martyrdom is the path of sanctification and perfection in charity. By offering ourselves to God as a spiritual sacrifice, even in the ordinary tasks of everyday life, we become clothed in His grace and love and become one with Christ. Saint Therese of Lisieux, who found a path to holiness in her "little way," expresses beautifully this desire for holiness and oneness with Christ:

> After earth's exile, I hope to go and enjoy you in the fatherland, but I do not want to lay up merits for heaven. I want to work for your love alone. . . . In the evening of this life, I shall appear before you with empty hands, for I do not ask you, Lord, to count my works. All our justice is blemished in your eyes. I wish,

> then, to be clothed in your own justice and to receive from your love the eternal possession of yourself. (Cf. CCC, 2011)

The Church Is Catholic

One of the most ancient names and designations of the Church is the term **catholic.** Saint Ignatius of Antioch first used this name in AD 110. The term *catholic* in Greek means "universal" or "all encompassing." The Church is fundamentally catholic in two ways.

First, the Church is catholic in that it is universal, encompassing all people in all times, places, and cultures. This was seen profoundly at Pentecost. Through the power of the Holy Spirit each person heard the Gospel preached in his own language, for the Church knows no cultural or geographical bounds. Through the Holy Spirit the Church becomes "incarnate" in every culture, bringing into herself those parts of the culture that are good and casting out those aspects that are contrary to the Gospel. The Church unites all cultures and sanctifies them, incorporating the richness of humanity. As stated earlier, the Catholic Church today is in every country of the world and continues to grow throughout the earth, consecrating all to Christ.

Second, the Church is catholic in that she encompasses within herself the fullness of truth revealed by Christ. He is fully present in the Church, which is the one instrument of salvation and grace through which all are saved and brought to Christ. There is no other means of salvation except through Christ and the one Catholic Church He established.

Members of other Christian churches, although lacking full communion with the Catholic Church, nevertheless receive grace and salvation through the Catholic Church. Even those who are non-Christian, who through no fault of their own do not know Christ, can receive salvation through the Catholic Church by their good will and active charity. There is simply no other means or instrument of salvation except the one true Church that Christ established. The Second Vatican Council reaffirmed the catholicity of the Church as the one instrument of salvation.

> Basing itself on Scripture and Tradition, the Council teaches that the Church, a pilgrim now on earth, is necessary for salvation: the one Christ is the mediator and the way of salvation; he is present to us in his body which is the Church.

> He himself explicitly asserted the necessity of faith and Baptism, and thereby affirmed at the same time the necessity of the Church which men enter through Baptism as through a door. Hence they could not be saved who, knowing that the Catholic Church was founded as necessary by God through Christ, would refuse either to enter it or to remain in it. (*Lumen gentium*, no. 14)

Even though there remain deep divisions within Christianity, it is the hope and mission of the Catholic Church that all may one day once again have full communion with the Church and fulfill the prayer of Christ that "they might be one." It is the work of **ecumenism**, the task of restoring the full communion of all Christians, that the Church continues to work toward tirelessly. However, true ecumenism and unity can only be accomplished through dialogue that is faithful to the truth concerning Christ and the Church, and only occurs with sincere charity.

The Church Is Apostolic

As we have seen, the Church is founded by Christ on the Apostles, and it is to the Apostles and their successors that Christ entrusted the fullness of His revelation, the sacred deposit of faith, so that it may be handed down faithfully and completely to each generation.

The pope and the bishops united with him are successors of the Apostles. They make up the magisterium of the Church. It is the function of the magisterium to preserve the apostolic faith by teaching, preserving, and defending the deposit of faith until the end of time and to interpret and apply it to the present day.

Throughout history, the magisterium has preserved and passed on the faith of the Apostles, often answering difficult questions and challenges. It was the magisterium that ultimately defined **doctrines** and **dogmas** that are held universally by all Christian faiths, doctrines such as those about Christ and the Trinity, the canon of Scripture, and the role of grace. None of these are defined or taught explicitly in Scripture, but have been handed on and interpreted by the magisterium. Any Christian who believes in the Trinity, or that Jesus is truly God and truly man, or that any book of the Bible is inspired by the Holy Spirit, is accepting and relying on the magisterium of the Catholic Church.

While many Christian churches continue to divide and face doctrinal controversies as the winds of society and culture blow, only the Catholic Church enjoys doctrinal purity and true unity through the teaching authority of the successors of the Apostles. Thus, the true Church of Christ, the Catholic Church, founded upon the Apostles and their successors, is the apostolic Church.

Therefore, when we look for the church that possesses in fullness the four pillars of the one true Church, she can be only found in the Catholic Church. Despite the trials and tribulations that often face her from both within and without, the Catholic Church continues today to be the "pillar and foundation of truth" (1 Tim. 3:15).

From the Catechism: Key Words to Know

MARKS (NOTES) OF THE CHURCH: The four attributes (marks) of the Church mentioned in the Niceno-Constantinopolitan Creed, "We believe in one, holy, catholic, and apostolic Church" (811).

CHURCH: The name given the "convocation" or "assembly" of the people God has called together from "the ends of the earth." In Christian usage, the word "Church" has three inseparable meanings: the People that God gathers in the whole world, the particular or local church (diocese), and the liturgical (above all Eucharistic) assembly. The Church draws her life from the Word and the Body of Christ, and so she becomes Christ's Body (752). In the creed, the sole Church of Christ is professed to be one, holy, catholic, and apostolic (811).

COMMUNION: Holy Communion is the reception of the Body and Blood of Christ in the Eucharist (1382). More generally, it is our fellowship and union with Jesus and other baptized Christians in the Church, which has its source and summit in the celebration of the Eucharist. In this sense, Church as communion is the deepest vocation of the Church (959).

BODY OF CHRIST: **(1)** The human body that the Son of God assumed through His conception in the womb of Mary and which is now glorified in heaven (467, 476, 645). **(2)** This same Body and Blood, together with the soul and divinity of our Lord Jesus Christ, are sacramentally present in the Eucharist under the appearances of bread and wine (1374). **(3)** The Church is called the (mystical) Body of Christ because of the intimate communion that Jesus shares with His disciples. The metaphor of a body, whose head is Christ and whose members are the faithful, provides an image which keeps in focus both the unity and the diversity of the Church (787, 790, 1396).

CATHOLIC: One of the four marks of the Church, taken from the Nicene Creed. The Church is catholic or universal because she possesses the fullness of Christ's presence and the means of salvation, and because she has been sent out by Christ on a mission to the whole of the human race (750, 830).

ECUMENISM: Promotion of the restoration of unity among all Christians, the unity that is a gift of Christ and to which the Church is called by the Holy

Spirit. For the Catholic Church, the Decree on Ecumenism of the Second Vatican Council provides a charter for ecumenical efforts (816, 820–822).

DOCTRINE/DOGMA: The revealed teachings of Christ that are proclaimed by the fullest extent of the exercise of the authority of the Church's magisterium. The faithful are obliged to believe the truths, or dogmas, contained in divine Revelation and defined by the magisterium (88).

Chapter 10

The Communion of Saints

Reading the Catechism: Paragraphs 946–962

> Therefore, since we are surrounded by so great a cloud of witnesses, let us rid ourselves of every burden and sin that clings to us and persevere in running the race that lies before us.
>
> —Hebrews 12:1

The Catholic practice of honoring and praying to the **saints** is one of the most misunderstood aspects of the Catholic faith. Many people wrongly believe that Catholics worship the saints, and that statues or images of them are graven images and products of idolatry. Nothing could be further from the truth. Catholics worship only God, not the saints, but they do honor these great people who throughout the history of the Church have shown heroic virtue in following Christ.

Honoring the saints is similar to honoring great heroes of the past for their heroic virtue, such as George Washington and Abraham Lincoln, for their heroic virtue. However, what is so amazing about the **communion of saints** is that not only do we honor these great spiritual giants of the past, but also we are still in relationship with them, benefiting from their prayers and examples every day.

In this chapter we will explore what the Church teaches and believes about the communion of saints and the many blessings we receive from this great "cloud of witnesses" (Heb. 12:1), always pointing to and leading us to Christ.

What Is the Communion of Saints?

The Church teaches that all believers in Christ share in an intimate union—those here on earth, those in heaven, and those preparing for entrance into heaven through purification in purgatory. This union is called the communion of saints because it is the intimate union of all who are living in the grace of Christ.

The communion of saints is a big family, although its members are in different stages on their journey to eternal life with Christ. From the last chapter you will remember that those saints in heaven are called the "Church Triumphant"; the saints in purgatory—they are indeed saints as they died in friendship with Christ—are called the "Church Suffering" because they are being purified of any remaining sins or attachment to sin so that they can enter heaven; and the saints on earth, those who live in the grace of Christ, are called the "Church Militant." They are still continuing the fight for holiness, justice, and peace through conversion of heart, turning away from darkness and sin, and turning toward and living in the grace and light of Christ.

Although these members of the communion of saints are in different stages of the pilgrimage toward heaven, all of the saints of God are intimately united in Christ and through Christ are in relationship with each other. The saints in heaven pray for and serve as great examples of faith for the Church Militant on earth and the Church Suffering in purgatory. The Church Militant pray for and offer sacrifices for the Church Suffering to expedite the purification of these souls and allow them to at last enjoy eternal glory in heaven. The saints on earth and those in purgatory ask the saints in heaven to pray for them. Thus, all the saints of God together reveal His glory through their lives, examples, and holiness, and also help one another in their pilgrimage of faith so that all may one day be perfectly united before the throne of grace in heaven.

This communion of saints is not new in Catholic Tradition, but has been believed from the earliest days of Christianity and is evident in Sacred Scripture.

- In the Book of Revelation, the saints in heaven are revealed as offering to God the prayers of the People of God: "Each of the elders held a harp and gold bowls filled with incense, which are the prayers of the holy ones" (Rev. 5:8).
- In the Letter to the Hebrews, the author describes the communion of saints as a "cloud of witnesses" that helps us to persevere in running the race of salvation in Christ: "Therefore, since we are surrounded by so great a cloud of witnesses, let us rid ourselves of every burden and sin that clings to us and persevere in running the race that lies before us" (Heb. 12:1).
- We also see throughout Scripture the relationship between the living and those who have died. The Transfiguration of Jesus is a great example in that Peter, James, and John are able to see and hear Moses and Elijah communicate with Jesus (Mt. 17:1–3, Mk. 9:2–4. Lk. 9:28–31).

- In the Second Book of the Maccabees (15:12–15) of the Old Testament, Maccabeus had a vision of the prophet Jeremiah and the martyred high priest Onias praying for the Jewish people.

We see that Scripture supports the belief that those who have died are still aware of and in relationship with those on earth, and that late Jewish belief reflected this idea.

The writings of the **Fathers of the Church** clearly support the belief and practice of the intercession of the saints.

- Clement of Alexandria writes in the year 208: "In this way is he [the true Christian] always pure for prayer. He also prays in the society of angels, as being already of angelic rank, and he is never out of their holy keeping; and though he pray alone, he has the choir of the saints standing with him [in prayer]" (*Miscellanies* 7:12 [AD 208]).
- The early theologian Origen also speaks of the saints in heaven joining with Christ in prayer for those who pray on earth: "But not the high priest [Christ] alone prays for those who pray sincerely, but also the angels . . . as also the souls of the saints who have already fallen asleep" (*Prayer* 11 [AD 233]).

Thus, the communion of saints has always been a part of the Catholic faith passed down to each generation through both Sacred Scripture and Sacred Tradition.

Do Catholics Worship Saints?

The idea that Catholics worship saints is one of the most common misunderstandings about the Catholic faith. A Catholic would never worship anyone or anything other than God, because only God alone is worthy of our **worship** and adoration.

However, the Church does honor or **venerate** the saints because of the heroic virtue they lived in following Christ. It is similar to the honor given to people throughout the history of our country for their heroic virtue in preserving liberty, justice, and peace, such as George Washington, Abraham Lincoln, and Martin Luther King, Jr. We also honor family members and friends for their lives and the love they gave us. We keep paintings, pictures, and even items they owned as a way of remembering and honoring them. Since the earliest beginnings of the Church, Catholics have honored the saints in the same way. The saints are powerful examples of what it means to be a true disciple of Christ in many different times, places, cultures, and circumstances. They also display many different personalities, spiritualities, states in life, and occupations, all of which were sanctified. They offered sanctification to the world through their great witness of Christ and the work of God's grace.

Like the heroes of our secular culture, we honor the saints through pictures, statues, and images as a way to remember them and to recall the great lives of faith and virtue they lived. Just because someone has a picture or statue of a saint does not mean that they are worshiping the saint. Nor is the statue a "graven image" of an idol, or a god, that Catholics "worships." Do we worship the statue of Abraham Lincoln at the Lincoln Memorial? Do we worship George Washington when we put his image on the dollar bill? Of course not. The same applies to the honoring of saints.

Far from worshiping saints, we honor them precisely for their example in bringing us closer to Christ. They are not a distraction from Christ, but through their lives and example, they point and lead us to a deeper love and relationship with Christ. They actually serve as a lens, focusing us more on the mystery and love of Jesus and on the effectiveness of His grace in our lives. Honoring the saints, far from being a diversion from Christ, is always a means to a deeper and more profound communion with Him.

Praying to the Saints

As we saw earlier, we not only honor the saints but we are also in relationship with them through the communion of saints. Because we are all joined in Christ through our communion in the Mystical Body of Christ, the Church does not end even after death. The saints in heaven are very aware of the people and events on earth. They pray for those on earth and those in purgatory to assist them on their journey toward heaven through grace. The saints' prayers in heaven are particularly powerful and efficacious for two reasons:

1. The saints in heaven have been perfected in their love for us. Their love is not darkened or distorted by any sin. They are fully immersed in God's grace. Therefore, their prayers are perfect and powerful because they are motivated by pure and great love for us.
2. The saints in heaven are in intimate communion with God. This profound closeness to Christ makes their prayers extraordinarily powerful and effective.

Thus, the prayers of the saints are a powerful means of grace and heavenly assistance for us as we continue to run the race and fight the good fight.

Often the question is asked, "Why bother to pray to the saints? Can't I just pray directly to God?" The answer is yes; we can and do pray directly to God. But we also have to understand that intercessory prayer on behalf of those of us on earth is a great gift given to us by Christ. When the saints in heaven pray for us or we pray for each other, Christ allows us to share in His own intercession before the Father. As the Catechism explains:

> Since Abraham, intercession—asking on behalf of another—has been characteristic of a heart attuned to God's mercy. In the age of the Church, Christian intercession participates in Christ's, as an expression of the communion of saints. In intercession, he who prays looks "not only to his own interests, but also to the interests of others," even to the point of praying for those who do him harm. (2635)

Intercessory prayer has always been practiced by the People of God. In the New Covenant established by Christ, He allows His followers to share in His own mediation so that through our prayers for each other we may be instruments of grace to one another. Our intercessory prayer and the intercessory prayers of the saints do not take away Christ's sole mediation between God and man, but augment it.

With all this in mind, the real question is why would one not take advantage of the incredible richness and power of the prayers of the saints who are standing before the throne of God? Christ Himself gives this gift to us and desires it for us. Yes, we can pray directly to God, *and* we can also benefit greatly from the perfected and powerful prayers of the saints. They love us tremendously and pray for us unceasingly that we may, through the grace of Christ, also share with them in the glory of eternal life.

The Canonization of Saints

The glossary of the Catechism defines a saint as anyone who "leads a life in union with God through the grace of Christ and receives the reward of eternal life." Thus, everyone who is in heaven is truly a saint and even those of us who are living in the state of grace on earth are rightly called saints of God. However, the Church honors certain saints in a special way by officially declaring them a saint through a process called "canonization."

Canonization is an official proclamation, or judgment, of the Church confirmed by the pope that declares a certain individual lived a life of heroic grace and virtue in following Christ, and is now enjoying the reward of eternal life in heaven. The Church began to "canonize" saints as early as the second century, and by the tenth century had developed a Vatican office to oversee the process of canonization.

The process is completed only after a lengthy and very thorough investigation of a person's life, verifying that the particular individual did indeed live a life of exceptional virtue and faith in conformity to the teachings of Christ and the Church. Canonization also requires two separate and verified miracles attributed to the intercession of that person after they have died. This serves as evidence that the person in question is truly in heaven interceding for us before God.

There are actually four steps toward canonization:

- First, the Church opens an official "cause" for sainthood. This begins the formal investigation and the process of canonization. At this stage the person is given the title "Servant of God."
- Second, after the investigation into the life of the person is completed, and if their life is affirmed as one of exceptional virtue and faith, the person is given the title "Venerable," meaning that they deserve special honor for their example as an exceptional disciple of Christ.
- Third, when a miracle is attributed to the intercession of the person and is confirmed, they are "beatified" and receive the title of "Blessed."
- Fourth, when there is a second verified miracle attributed to the intercession of the person, they are canonized by the pope and given the title of "Saint."

This process of canonization usually takes many years. Some only receive the titles "Venerable" or "Blessed" and are never canonized a saint. Some are finally canonized centuries after the Church opened their cause. The Church is always very careful and thorough in its investigation before officially declaring to the faithful that someone is a saint.

The Sanctoral Cycle

The Church also has what is called the sanctoral cycle of the liturgical calendar. It is a sequence of feast days by which the Church honors and asks the intercession of a saint who has been assigned a particular memorial or feast day. This liturgical calendar of saints gradually began to develop around the fourth century when the Church began to set aside certain days to celebrate the lives of the Apostles and martyrs.

The number of canonized saints in the sanctoral cycle continued to grow through the centuries up to the present day. The more popular and influential saints, such as the Apostles and martyrs, are given a feast day—a great celebration in the Church. Other saints are given a memorial day that recalls their life and example, and asks for their intercession. These commemorations may occur on the day of that saint's birth, but more often are celebrated on the day of their death since that is when they entered eternal life.

Over the years the sanctoral cycle has become so crowded with numerous saints that it has had to be revised several times. The sanctoral cycle is a great gift of the Church that allows us to ponder almost daily the great lives of the saints, and call upon their constant intercession for us as we continue on our pilgrim journey toward heaven.

Common Devotions to the Saints

There are countless prayers that have been written asking the intercession of a particular saint. These devotions can take various forms. One popular form of prayer is a novena, which is a prayer or series of prayers that is said over nine days asking the intercession of a saint. Another prayer form is the Litany of Saints. This long list invokes the intercession of many saints. It is often prayed before a person is baptized, or during some liturgies and on other important occasions. The Church contains an incredible treasury of devotions and prayers to many of the saints that has been handed down throughout the centuries.

The early Christians also honored the saints and recalled their memory by preserving a piece of their bone or clothing. These items were kept as relics of that particular saint and were often circulated throughout the Church. Many churches, especially in Europe, have within them several relics of saints. These relics provide occasions for honoring the saints, while making the spiritual presence and memory of the saints very close to us, even though they may have died centuries ago.

Other saints have been miraculously preserved from bodily corruption although they were dead for centuries. This is one of the signs of sainthood that the Church looks for. It is a sign of their profound holiness and a witness to the resurrection of the body that will occur at the end of the world. Many of these incorrupt bodies are displayed for all the faithful to see in their miraculous state. These saints provide great hope in the coming resurrection of the body, and the power of God's transforming and saving grace.

All of these different devotions are ways for the People of God to honor and ask the intercession of the saints who have gone before us, paving the way toward holiness and eternal life.

The "Cloud of Witnesses"

One of the most beautiful and inspiring aspects of the communion of saints is the amazing variety of saints. These men and women have lived lives of heroic virtue in following Christ in many different times, places, cultures, and circumstances. Saints are kings, queens, teachers, mothers, fathers, students, priests, nuns, boys, girls, rich and poor, all living extraordinary lives in the various circumstances of this world. Some lived their entire lives without committing a serious sin, while others lived much of their lives in the darkness of sin only to later come into the light of Christ and be counted among the greatest champions of faith and love.

This great and universal variety of saints shows us that no matter where we live, what we do, or whatever the circumstances of our lives are, we are called to holiness and are to live totally for Christ. Through their communion with us, the saints are truly a great "cloud of witnesses" that help us persevere in running the race that is salvation in Christ. May all of the saints, and our patron saints in particular, always pray for us and show us the way to everlasting life.

From the Catechism: Key Words to Know

SAINT: The "holy one" who leads a life in union with God through the grace of Christ and receives the reward of eternal life. The Church is called the communion of saints, of the holy ones (823, 946; cf. 828).

COMMUNION OF SAINTS: The unity in Christ of all the redeemed, those on earth and those who have died. The communion of saints is professed in the Apostles' Creed, where it has also been interpreted to refer to unity in the "holy things" (*communio sanctorum*), especially the unity of faith and charity achieved through participation in the Eucharist (948, 957, 960, 1474).

FATHERS OF THE CHURCH: Church teachers and writers of the early centuries whose teachings are a witness to the Tradition of the Church (78, 688).

WORSHIP: Adoration and honor given to God, which is the first act of the virtue of religion (2096). Public worship is given to God in the Church by the celebration of the Paschal Mystery of Christ in the liturgy (1067).

VENERATION (OF SAINTS): Showing devotion and respect to Mary, the Apostles, and the martyrs, who were viewed as faithful witnesses to faith in Jesus Christ. Later, veneration was given to those who led a life of prayer and self-denial in giving witness to Christ, whose virtues were recognized and publicly proclaimed in their canonization as saints (828). Such veneration is often extended to the relics or remains of those recognized as saints; indeed, honor is extended to many sacred objects and images. Veneration must be clearly distinguished from adoration and worship, which are due to God alone (1154, 1674, 2132).

CANONIZATION: The solemn declaration by the pope that a deceased member of the faithful may be proposed as a model and intercessor to the Christian faithful and venerated as a saint on the basis that the person lived a life of heroic virtue or remained faithful to God through martyrdom (828; cf. 957).

Chapter 11

Mary

Reading the Catechism: Paragraphs 484–511; 963–975

> But among creatures no one knows Christ better than Mary; no one can introduce us to a profound knowledge of his mystery better than his Mother.
>
> —Pope John Paul II, Apostolic Letter on the Rosary of the Blessed Virgin Mary *Rosarium Virginis Mariae* (October 16, 2002), no. 14

What Is True Devotion to Mary?

One of the significant and most common misconceptions about Catholicism is that Catholics worship **Mary**. As stated in the last chapter, Catholics worship only God; they do not worship Mary. Her whole mission and disposition as the mother of Jesus is to bring others into closer communion with her Son. She would be the most horrified if anyone were to worship her. However, the Church does hold a special honor for her because of who she is and her unique relationship with Christ. For a proper understanding, we need to make some important distinctions.

Latria or Adoration

Latria is the Latin word for "adoration or worship." **Adoration**, worship, and homage are reserved for God alone. Thus, it is only the Father, the Son, and the Holy Spirit who are due adoration or worship. No creature, no matter how good or holy, ever deserves worship or adoration. The same applies to Mary and the saints.

Dulia or Veneration

Dulia is the Latin word meaning "veneration." We venerate, or give honor, to a created person due to their excellence or virtue. We do this all the time with historical figures. For example, we give honor to George Washington for being the first president of the United States. We honor those who have fallen in battle or given their lives in the line of duty. We honor many people because of their heroic virtue and excellence in their lives.

In the same way we venerate *(dulia)* the saints because they achieved great excellence and holiness while on earth. During their lives they displayed heroic virtue in following the footsteps of Christ. The saints serve as exemplary models of what it means to be a follower of Christ and how to truly be transformed by His grace.

Our veneration of the saints does not end with them, but ultimately gives glory to God and fosters a greater union with Him, because it reveals to us His saving power and spurs us on to strive for greater holiness and communion with Christ. Far from worshipping saints, we honor them and look up to them so that we may better worship and love God.

Hyperdulia or Exalted Veneration

Hyperdulia is an exalted level of honor given to Mary because of her exceptional holiness and her unique role in God's plan of salvation as the Mother of God. Her excellence, heroic virtue, faith, and trust in God rise above that of every other creature. Mary is the perfect model of what it means to be a follower of Jesus. The Bible tells us that all generations will call Mary blessed (Lk. 1:47–48). As we will see later, it is proper and just to give Mary special honor or devotion for the unique and extraordinary role she played and the virtue and grace she possessed.

Therefore, we rightly give special veneration and honor *(hyperdulia)* to Mary, and in no way is this adoration or worship. She holds a special place in the heart of the Church and of all believers because she holds a special place in the heart of her Son. Far from being a distraction from God, Mary draws us closer to Him and always points us in the direction of her Son by her faith and example. She still is today as she was while on earth—the one through whom Christ comes to His people.

False Marian Devotions

We want to always have a true and right devotion to Mary so that we may know her and love her as the mother of Jesus and as our spiritual mother. There are two extremes to be avoided.

Marian excess

The most extreme form of Marian excess makes Mary equal to God or claims that she has divine qualities. Not so. She is a creature of God who was in need of salvation like all the rest of us. Another error is a devotion to Mary that "eclipses" or overshadows our relationship with Christ. Devotion to Mary should always bring us closer to Christ and not distract us from Him. This second form of Marian excess usually happens unintentionally and springs from an overemphasis on her in the spiritual life. Mary should always be a way to a deeper and more profound knowledge and communion with Christ, not a diversion or obstacle.

Marian defect

Marian defect is the opposite extreme of Marian excess. It minimizes the special role that Mary played in God's plan of salvation and undervalues the unique and unsurpassed heroic virtue she lived in her relationship with Him. Marian defect tends to claim that Mary was just another good disciple of Christ.

The goal of this chapter is to present a true knowledge of Mary and thus a true and balanced devotion to her. We will explore in detail the main Marian dogmas, identify where they are in Scripture, and see how they have been handed down through Sacred Tradition in the teachings of the Catholic Church. We will then discuss the different Marian devotions and prayers, especially the Rosary, and why our prayers to Mary are particularly efficacious.

The Immaculate Conception of Mary: Mary Was Created without the Stain of Original Sin and Remained Free from Sin throughout Her Life

If you ask people, including many Catholics, about the Immaculate Conception, there is a great chance they will tell you that it is the conception of Jesus in the womb of Mary. The **Immaculate Conception** is actually the conception of Mary. The Immaculate Conception reveals to us that Mary was freed from the stain of original sin at the moment of her conception, and remained free from sin for her entire life.

Why Was Mary Conceived without Original Sin?

It was intrinsic to God's plan of salvation that Mary was created without original sin. If you remember back in chapter four, we saw how sin entered the world through our first parents, Adam and Eve. Since Adam and Eve represented all of the human family when they fell away from God, all of humanity fell away with them. Original sin was passed on to their children and to their children's children, all throughout human history. When we are conceived we are born into a natural separation from God called original sin and with an inclination toward sin.

God's rescue plan was to have His only Son, the second Person of the Holy Trinity, assume a human nature so that as both God and man Jesus could accomplish the redemption of the human race. One problem arises: God is all-holy. Therefore, He is in complete and total opposition to sin. Sinners cannot even come into His presence without being purified. How then would God the Son be able to intimately join Himself with a fallen human nature? This is where God's plan for Mary comes in. God chose her to be conceived without original sin so that she would be able to give Jesus a pure and sinless human nature. Mary is the pure and stainless vessel through which Jesus receives a sinless and immaculate human nature so that He can enter the world to complete the Father's plan of salvation.

Scriptural References

Genesis 3:15: Let us go back once again to the Book of Genesis where God announced for the first time His plan of salvation that will be accomplished through Christ:

> I will put enmity between you and the woman, and between your offspring and hers; He will strike at your head, while you strike at his heel.

It is important that we identify exactly who God is addressing and talking about. God is speaking to the serpent, and He says that the offspring of the woman will strike at his head. Who is the one who will strike at the head of the serpent? Who is Satan? *Jesus* is the one who will come, strike at Satan's head, and destroy his power. So if the offspring of the woman is Jesus, then the woman must be Mary.

God speaks of *enmity* between the serpent and the woman, and between the serpent's offspring and the woman's offspring. The offspring of Satan is sin, with which Satan desires to multiply and fill the earth. Therefore, there is enmity between Mary/Jesus and Satan/sin. *Enmity means total and complete opposition.* If two things are in enmity with each other, they have nothing at all to do with one another; there is absolutely no cooperation or communion between the two. Consequently, both Jesus and Mary are completely opposed to Satan and sin. They would have absolutely no cooperation or communion with Satan and sin.

It was necessary that Mary not have a fallen nature since any participation in original sin or actual sin would destroy the enmity with Satan and sin. Thus, we see in the very first announcement of God's plan of salvation His intention to keep Mary totally free from sin so that Jesus would be able to assume a pure human nature.

Luke 1:28: We see an even more explicit reference to the Immaculate Conception of Mary in Luke's Gospel at the Annunciation. The angel Gabriel appears to Mary to announce God's plan for her to be the mother of Jesus. The angel Gabriel's greeting to Mary reveals her immaculate state. His greeting properly translated is "Hail, you who *have been filled* with grace." The Greek word *kekaritomene* is a perfect participle, "have been filled." Mary has already been filled with God's grace, for grace has already been infused into her at the moment of her conception.

The angel's greeting reveals another truth about Mary. Anytime someone sins, even the smallest sin, the person loses at least some of God's grace. That is the nature of sin: a choice a person makes that rejects the grace He offers to us, which is His very life and love. If Mary is *filled* with grace, then she would have been completely free from sin, because *any* sin, even the tiniest, would have caused her to be deprived of at least some grace.

The Immaculate Conception Has Been Constantly Taught Throughout Sacred Tradition

Not only do we see the Immaculate Conception in Sacred Scripture, but it has also been constantly and clearly taught through Sacred Tradition from the earliest times of the Church:

1. ***Saint Ambrose (d. 379):*** Mary is "free from all stain of sin."

2. ***Saint Severus, Bishop of Antioch (d. 538):*** "She (Mary) formed part of the human race, and was of the same essence as we, although she was pure from all taint and immaculate."

3. ***Saint Sophronius, Patriarch of Jerusalem (d. 638):*** "You (Mary) have found the grace which no one has received. . . . No one has been pre-purified besides you."

4. ***Saint Andrew of Crete (d. 740):*** "The Redeemer chose in all nature this pure and entirely Immaculate Virgin."

5. ***Theognastes of Constantinople (c. 885):*** "It was fitting indeed that she who from the beginning had been conceived by a sanctifying action should also have a holy death, holy in the beginning, holy in the end, holy her whole existence."

6. ***Infallible Ex cathedra definition of Pope Pius IX, Ineffabilis Deus, 1854:*** "We declare, pronounce, and define that the doctrine that holds that the Most Blessed Virgin Mary, at the instant of her conception, was preserved immune from all stain of sin, by a singular grace and privilege of the Omnipotent God, in view of the merits of Jesus Christ, the Savior of the human race, was revealed by God and must be firmly and constantly believed by all the faithful."

How Was Mary Preserved from Original Sin?

How exactly did God preserve Mary from original sin? In the above papal pronouncement, Pope Pius IX stated that she was preserved from sin "by a singular grace and privilege of the Omnipotent God, in view of the merits of Jesus Christ."

Mary needed Christ to redeem her just as much as we all do. She was redeemed by her Son's death on the Cross just like all of us. But how could Mary have been redeemed by Jesus' death on the Cross before Jesus was even born?

God is eternal and transcendent, and therefore He is not bound by either space or time. He sees all of time—past, present, and future—at once. It is like looking at a very long train from a helicopter. The engines are creation, the caboose the end of the world, and we are somewhere in between the two. God operates outside of time. Therefore, He took the graces and merits of Jesus' death on the Cross and applied them backwards in time to the moment of Mary's conception.

Mary was redeemed by Christ as we all are, but through a "singular (special) grace and privilege of the Omnipotent God" she was also completely preserved from original sin. The important distinction, however, is that Mary was redeemed but also *preserved* from sin. She never had sin, even for a second. From the very moment of her existence, Mary was completely preserved from sin and thus never knew or cooperated with sin her entire life.

Could Mary Have Chosen to Sin?

Even though Mary was preserved from original sin at the moment of her conception, she could have still chosen to sin since she had free will. She could have still rejected God's grace and His plan and fallen into sin. She could have said no to the Father at the Annunciation. She could have said no to the Father at the foot of the Cross where she surrendered her Son. She could have fallen into despair and cursed God. Rather, Mary perfectly cooperated and surrendered herself to the great gift of grace that God had given her and lived the most extraordinary Christian life. This is why Mary is the model of faith and the model of the Church. We are all called to cooperate with whatever graces God chooses to give us so that we humbly and lovingly walk whatever path He wills for us.

The Assumption of Mary: Mary Is Assumed Body and Soul into Heaven

The **Assumption** is the natural and logical consequence of the Immaculate Conception. If Mary was completely preserved from original sin and all sin, then she would not need to suffer the consequences of sin, which is death. Through the Assumption Christ took Mary into heaven body and soul where she enjoyed the full fruits of the redemption immediately upon the end of her earthly life.

How Could Mary Have Been Taken Directly to Heaven?

Note that Mary is taken to heaven not under her own power but by an act of Christ. This is the fundamental difference between Ascension and Assumption.

When Jesus ascended into heaven it was under His own power as the Son of God. However, Christ *assumes* Mary into heaven—she enters heaven by the power of her Son. This is entirely consistent with Scripture. In 2 Kings 2:11 Elijah was taken directly to heaven. Mary's Assumption is the same but infinitely more deserved.

Scriptural References

Genesis 3:15: The Assumption of Mary has its roots in the dogma of the Immaculate Conception. If Mary enjoys the same enmity to Satan and sin as Jesus, then she must also share in the same victory over sin. The consequences of sin are twofold: death and corruption of the body. "Until you return to the ground, from which you were taken; for you are dirt, and to dirt you shall return" (Gen. 3:19). Since Mary was preserved from sin, it follows that she would not suffer the consequences of sin. Thus, Mary does not experience separation from God or the corruption of the body, but shares fully in Christ's Resurrection immediately at the end of her earthly life.

Luke 1:28: Mary's bodily assumption again is a natural effect of being "filled with grace" and being completely free from sin.

The Assumption Is Seen throughout Sacred Tradition

1. ***Saint Gregory of Tours (d. 593):*** "The Lord commanded the holy body of Mary to be borne on a cloud to Paradise, where, united to its soul and exalting with the elect, it enjoys the everlasting bliss of eternity."

2. ***Lex orandi, lex credenda:*** "The law of prayer is the law of faith." By the sixth century, the first liturgical feasts dedicated to the Assumption appeared in the Alexandrian Church in Egypt. Western liturgical feasts dedicated to the Assumption took place in Gaul (France) in the seventh century. By the eighth century it was celebrated in Rome. From the thirteenth century on, the Assumption was taught with near unanimity by Church writers and theologians in both the East and West.

3. ***Infallible ex cathedra definition:*** In 1946, Pope Pius XII petitioned the bishops of the world asking whether the Assumption of Mary could be defined and whether they favored such a definition. Of the 1,232 bishops petitioned, 1,210 answered enthusiastically yes. In 1950, Pope Pius XII defined the Assumption of Mary: "The Immaculate Mother of God, the Ever Virgin Mary, having completed the course of her earthly life, was assumed body and soul into heavenly glory."

4. ***Vatican II, Lumen gentium, no. 59:*** "Finally the Immaculate Virgin preserved from all stain of original sin, was taken up body and soul into heavenly glory, when her earthly life was over, and exalted by the Lord as Queen over all things, that she might be the more fully conformed to her Son, the Lord of lords and conqueror of sin and death."

Mary Is the Mother of God: Mary Is the Mother of Jesus Christ Who Is the Son of God Made Man

As we saw in chapter five, the Council of Ephesus in AD 431 declared Mary the Mother of God, *Theotokos* or "God bearer" in Greek. Mary was proclaimed Mother of God to clarify and safeguard that Jesus was truly God and man. "If anyone does not confess that the Emmanuel (Christ) in truth is God and that on this account the Holy Virgin is the Mother of God made flesh . . . let him be anathema."

How Do We Define Motherhood?

Motherhood is the act of a woman giving to her offspring the same type of nature that she herself has. This gift of nature is given through the process of conception, growth or gestation, and birth. The fruit of this process, which we may call maternal gestation, is the whole child and not only the physical body.

Mary does not give Jesus His divine nature and personhood, for those had existed from all eternity. Mary did give to Jesus a human nature identical to her own. Since the human nature of Jesus is inseparable from the divine nature of Jesus, we can correctly say that Mary gave birth to a Son who is truly God, and through Mary, truly man. Mary gave flesh to the Word made flesh and is rightfully proclaimed the Mother of God.

Connection to Christology

Jesus is one divine Person with two natures, human and divine, which are absolutely inseparable. By the proclamation of Mary as the Mother of God, the truth of the unity of Christ's two natures in one Person was preserved, which refuted the Nestorian heresy that claimed that Christ's natures were two different persons. Hence, a proper understanding of Mary means a proper understanding of Christ.

Why Do Catholics Call Mary Their Mother?

Mary is not only the Mother of God, she is also the mother of the sons and daughters of God that have been redeemed through her Son. The last great gift that Jesus gave to the Church before His death was the gift of His mother:

> Standing by the cross of Jesus were his mother and his mother's sister, Mary the wife of Clopas, and Mary of Magdala. When Jesus saw his mother and the disciple there whom he loved, he said to his mother, "Woman, behold, your son." Then he said to the disciple, "Behold, your mother." And from that hour the disciple took her into his home. (Jn. 19:25–27)

Thus, Mary is also our mother, our spiritual mother. Like any mother she nourishes us, guides us, and protects us on our spiritual journey. She desires the best for us, which is union with her Son. Her intercession is powerful, and she is constantly praying for all of us that we may become holy. Devotion to Mary is a wonderful part of belonging to Christ's family the Church.

Perpetual Virginity of Mary: Mary Remained a Virgin before, during, and after the Birth of Jesus Christ

The Meaning and Importance of Mary's Virginity

In the Jewish tradition, virginity was seen as an outward sign of interior consecration to God. This tradition was carried on into the New Testament and is still present in the Church today. Mary's virginity was an outward sign of her total consecration to God. God preserved her virginity throughout her life so that she could perfectly fulfill her life of grace and faith as the mother of Christ and perfect model of the Church.

In addition, Mary's perpetual virginity preserved her as the unique vessel through which the Son of God was made flesh and entered the world. It would not be appropriate for any other person to pass through the Immaculate womb of Mary willed by God to bring forth the Savior of the world. Mary will forever be the unique and undefiled tabernacle through which God entered human history.

Scriptural References

Isaiah 7:14: "For behold, a Virgin shall conceive, and bear a son, and his name shall be called Immanuel." Here Scripture reveals that Mary was to be a virgin at the moment of Jesus' conception as well as during His birth.

Luke 1:26–38: The dialogue between the angel Gabriel and Mary during the Annunciation clearly shows that Mary was a virgin when she conceived Jesus. Mary says, "How can this be since I do not know man?" The word "know" in the Greek suggests carnal relations. Mary's question shows that she has had no sexual relations with a man and that she never plans to. This is very strong scriptural evidence that Mary had already taken a vow of lifelong virginity as a sign of her total consecration to God.

All of the Marian dogmas—the Immaculate Conception, the Assumption, Mary as Mother of God, and her Perpetual Virginity—point both to her special role in salvation and to the natures of Jesus, divine and human.

Magisterial Statements

1. ***Definition of Pope Martin I at the Lateran Synod of 649:*** "The blessed ever-Virgin and immaculate Mary, conceived without seed, by the Holy Spirit, and without loss of integrity brought Him forth, and after His birth preserved her virginity inviolate."

2. ***Pope Leo the Great in his Tome to Flavian:*** "Mary brought Him forth, with her virginity untouched, as with her virginity untouched she conceived Him."

3. ***Fifth Council at Constantinople in 553:*** Described Mary as the "Perpetual Virgin."

4. ***Pope Pius XII in his 1943 encyclical Mysterium Corpus, no. 110:*** "In a marvelous birth she brought Him [our Lord] forth."

5. ***Vatican II, Lumen gentium, no. 57:*** "This union of the mother with the Son in the work of salvation is made manifest from the time of Christ's virginal conception . . . then also at the birth of our Lord, who did not diminish his mother's virginal integrity but sanctified it."

Doesn't the Bible Say That Jesus Had Brothers, so Mary Must Have Had Other Children?

There are several scriptural references to the brothers of Jesus or the brethren of the Lord (Mt. 12:46, 13:55; Mk. 3:31). However, this is a translation problem rather than a doctrinal one. There is no specific word in Greek to mean "blood brother." The Greek word *adelphos* is used in the Scriptures to mean brother, cousin, uncle, or close relative.

The context of the conversation or writing determines the exact meaning of *adelphos*. It is used in instances where it cannot mean blood brother (for example, the relationships between Lot and Abraham in Genesis 13:8 and Jacob and Laban in Genesis 29:15). In the New Testament context, *adelphos* could even mean Jesus' close followers or disciples as "brothers in the Lord."

This is an interpretation issue. Remember, Scripture can never be translated or interpreted in a way that contradicts Sacred Tradition, through which the Church has already solemnly defined the perpetual virginity of Mary.

Doesn't the Bible Say That Joseph and Mary Had Relations after the Birth of Jesus?

A common objection to the perpetual virginity of Mary argues that the word "until" in Matthew 1:25 suggests that Joseph had relations with Mary after the birth of Jesus: *"He had no relations with her until she bore a son, and he named him Jesus."* This is a poor argument. The word "until" is used clearly by Matthew to show that Jesus' conception was virginal. That was his point. To suggest the word "until" means that it was absolutely necessary that Mary and Joseph had relations is not logically sound.

Mary Participated with Christ in the Redemption of the Human Family like No Other Creature

How Did Mary Participate with Christ in the Redemption in a Special Way?

God gave Mary a unique and unsurpassable role in His loving plan of salvation. No other creature participated with Christ in such a close and intimate way in helping him accomplish the redemption. Be careful: In no way does this say that Mary in any way redeemed the human race. Jesus and Jesus alone accomplished the redemption through His death and Resurrection. However, Mary played a crucial role in *helping* Him in His accomplishment in the redemption.

Instrument through which Jesus received His human body and human nature

Christ would not have been able to become a human being if it were not for the faith and total cooperation of Mary with God's plan of salvation. It is through Mary that Christ enters human history and the redemption of the human race is inaugurated. Thus, it is true and right to say that Mary participated in a unique and intimate manner in the Incarnation of the Son of God.

Participated in Christ's suffering on the Cross in a unique and intimate way as the mother of Christ

At the foot of the Cross Mary offered up her Son Jesus to the Father. She surrendered her will and maternal rights of protection and nurturing to the Father's will and plan of salvation. She perfectly offered her Son and herself to the Father. Mary's suffering and faith at the foot of the Cross is the perfect model of faith and surrendering to God that we are called to manifest in our own lives. Thus, Mary is called the Mother and Model of the Church.

Scriptural References

Luke 1:38: At the Annunciation, Mary says yes to the angel Gabriel and through the power of the Holy Spirit gives Jesus His body and human nature.

Genesis Chapter 3: Eve gave the fruit to Adam as the instrument of the Fall of humanity. Mary gave a human body and nature to Jesus as the instrument for the redemption of the human race. Mary is the "New Eve" who participates in the redemption with the "New Adam."

Luke 1:41–42: Elizabeth singles out Mary as blessed among all women. Mary is blessed because it was through her that Christ came into the world.

Luke 2:35: Simeon's prophesy at the Presentation of the Lord foreshadows the unique redemptive suffering that Mary will endure at the foot of the Cross.

Marian Devotion, Prayers, and Spirituality

We have already seen that Mary is our spiritual mother, and it is right and just that we as followers of Christ should have a special relationship with her. It must be a proper relationship that is not an end in itself, but one that fosters and brings about deeper union with Jesus her Son.

True Devotion and Prayers to Mary Should Always Lead Us to Christ

Devotion to Mary should always lead us to deeper union with Christ. We never pray to Mary as an end, but ask her to intercede for us to Christ. She would never want devotion to her to take away our focus on Him. Everything that she was and did was to bring about her own deeper communion with Christ and to bring others to a more intimate knowledge and union with Him. This is why we honor Mary as the perfect disciple of Christ.

Devotion to Mary does not take away from Christ, but rather augments our knowledge of His life and virtues. Mary shows us that salvation in Christ is real and possible, and what it looks like. If you want to know Christ, know His Mother. If you want to know Christ, know His Church. Hopefully, if you want to know Christ you will know others, because we are to be Christ to the world. Mary did it all perfectly and continues to show us how to come into a stronger and deeper relationship with Jesus.

Mary's Prayers and Intercession Are Particularly Powerful and Effective

Mary's prayers and intercession before Christ on our behalf are very powerful because of who she is and the role she played in God's plan of salvation. As the mother of Christ, she has a unique and special relationship with Him. He has a special place in His heart for His mother, and honors her prayers and requests in a very special way. Through Mary's prayers and intercession we have a unique and privileged way to the heart of Jesus. This is why prayers and devotion to her have been at the heart of the Church's life from the very beginning.

Additionally, Mary was created free from sin and was completely filled with grace and love throughout her life. She was created with a capacity to love God and others that far exceeds any capacity of ours. Thus, her love for us and her prayers for us are extraordinarily powerful.

Types of Marian Devotion

The Hail Mary

The Hail Mary is the most popular prayer to Mary. The first half is based upon Scripture. It begins with the angel Gabriel's greeting of Mary at the Annunciation (Lk. 1:28), and is followed by Elizabeth's greeting at the Visitation (Lk. 1:42). The second half is asks Mary to pray for us to her Son Jesus, especially at the hour of our death when we prepare to enter eternal life. Notice that the Hail Mary is actually a Christocentric (or Christ-centered) prayer. The name Jesus is the center of the prayer:

> Hail, Mary, full of grace, the Lord is with you. Blessed are you among women, and blessed is the fruit of your womb
> **JESUS**.
> Holy Mary, Mother of God, pray for us sinners, now and at the hour of our death, Amen.

Through the Hail Mary she draws us to her Son Jesus, and obtains for us His grace and mercy. Mary always leads us to her Son.

The Rosary

The **Rosary** is a very popular Catholic devotion to Mary, and is a meditation on the mysteries of Jesus' and Mary's lives. Each decade of the Rosary is a meditation on a particular aspect of Christ's life and ministry, or a profound event in Mary's life that reveals Christ's saving power. Through the Rosary we pray with Mary, who reveals and teaches us about her Son so that we can have greater union with Him. Like the Hail Mary, the Rosary is a Christ-centered prayer where, through Mary, we come to a more perfect knowledge of Jesus, and our prayer is perfected through her intercession. Pope John Paul II, the "pope of the Rosary," beautifully states:

> Christ is the supreme Teacher, the revealer and the one revealed. It is not just a question of learning what he taught but of "*learning him.*" In this regard could we have any better teacher than Mary? From the divine standpoint, the Spirit is the interior teacher who leads us to the full truth of Christ (cf. Jn. 14:26; 15:26; 16:13). But among creatures no one knows Christ better than Mary; no one can introduce us to a profound knowledge of his mystery better than his Mother.
>
> The first of the "signs" worked by Jesus—the changing of water into wine at the marriage in Cana—clearly presents Mary in the guise of a teacher, as she urges the servants to do what Jesus commands (cf. Jn. 2:5). We can imagine that she would have done likewise for the disciples after Jesus' Ascension, when she joined them in awaiting the Holy Spirit and supported them in their first mission. Contemplating the scenes of the Rosary in union with Mary is a means of learning from her to "read" Christ, to discover his secrets and to understand his message.
>
> This school of Mary is all the more effective if we consider that she teaches by obtaining for us in abundance the gifts of the Holy Spirit, even as she offers us the incomparable example of her own "pilgrimage of faith." As we contemplate each mystery of her Son's life, she invites us to do as she did at the Annunciation: to ask humbly the questions which open us to the light, in order to end with the obedience of faith: "Behold I am the handmaid of the Lord; be it done to me according to your word" (Lk. 1:38). (*Rosarium Virginis Mariae*, no. 14)

The Rosary is not vain, repetitious prayer. The repetition of the prayers, the movement of lips, and the handling of beads are all a means to deeper meditation on the mysteries contained in the lives of Jesus and Mary. While saying the prayers, our goal is to focus on and be drawn into the mysteries. This form of meditative prayer takes practice and concentration, and can be a very powerful and salvific prayer.

Through the Rosary and devotion to Mary we come to truly understand her love for us and her desire to make known the love of her Son. Mary is like the moon. She is not the source of light and life, but she perfectly reflects the light and grace of her Son so that through her we can come to a deeper love and knowledge of Him. Through her intercession and constant presence in the Church, Mary continues today to echo her last recorded words in Scripture: "Do whatever he tells you" (Jn. 2:5).

From the Catechism: Key Words to Know

MARY: The mother of Jesus. Because she is the mother of Jesus—Son of God and second Person of the Blessed Trinity—according to the flesh, she is rightly called *Theotokos,* the Mother of God (148, 495). Mary is also called "full of grace," "Mother of the Church," and in Christian prayer and devotion, "Our Lady," the "Blessed Virgin Mary," and the "New Eve" (722, 726, 963).

ADORATION: The acknowledgment of God as God, Creator and Savior, the Lord and Master of everything that exists. Through worship and prayer, the Church and individual persons give to God adoration, which is the first act of the virtue of religion. The first commandment of the law obliges us to adore God (2096, 2628; cf. 1083).

IMMACULATE CONCEPTION: The dogma proclaimed in Christian Tradition and defined in 1854 that from the first moment of her conception, Mary—by the singular grace of God and by virtue of the merits of Jesus Christ—was preserved immune from original sin (491).

ASSUMPTION: The dogma that recognizes the Blessed Virgin Mary's singular participation in her Son's Resurrection, by which she was taken up body and soul into heavenly glory when the course of her earthly life was finished (966).

ROSARY: A prayer in honor of the Blessed Virgin Mary that repeats the privileged Marian prayer Ave Maria or "Hail Mary" in "decades" of ten prayers. The Pater Noster ("Our Father") precedes each decade and the Gloria Patri ("Glory Be to the Father") concludes each decade. The entire prayer is accompanied by meditation on the mysteries of Christ's life. The Rosary was developed by medieval piety in the Latin Church as a popular substitute for the Liturgy of the Hours (2678, 2708; cf. 1674).

Chapter 12

Salvation, Purgatory, and the Rapture Theory

Reading the Catechism: Paragraphs 1987–2029; 1020–1060; 1471–1479

> Let us not hesitate to help those who have died and to offer our prayers for them.
>
> —Saint John Chrysostom,
> Homilies on First Corinthians 41:5 (c. AD 392)

Protestant Notions of Salvation

One of the most controversial and confusing debates between Catholics and Protestants is the question of salvation. Catholics are often asked, "Are you saved?" As simple and harmless as this question may seem on the surface, it has been at the very heart of the Catholic/Protestant debate since the Reformation. In order to make a proper defense of the Catholic position, we must first understand exactly what the Protestant notion of salvation is.

Most Protestants see salvation as a remarkably simple act. They believe that a person is justified by simply accepting and acknowledging Jesus as personal Lord and Savior, often by reciting the "acceptance prayer." Programs such as the 700 Club or other Protestant ministry shows invite people to say this prayer and accept Jesus as their Savior. In their view, when we sincerely say this prayer in our heart, we are **justified** or made righteous before God. God covers up our sins and allows us to stand rightly before Him. Once "saved," we cannot lose salvation because what we do—good or bad—has nothing to do with our salvation. God simply "forgets" our sin. Faith in Him alone is needed. Works do nothing to gain or take away salvation. To more fully understand the Protestant position we must examine a few points.

First, Protestant theology adheres to the doctrine of *sola fide* ("faith alone"), first proposed by Martin Luther in response to abuses (especially some abuses and tactics concerning the selling of indulgences) in the sixteenth century Church. Luther saw "works" as "magic tricks" and false promises of salvation.

He also was very scrupulous and tortured himself over whether or not what he did was good enough to bring about holiness and sanctification. Luther eventually denied that works have anything to do with salvation, and that salvation comes only through faith in Christ. (As we will see, Luther only has half of the big picture.)

Protestant theology separates what we do from who we are, which is a fundamental error concerning the human person. Protestant theology also has a very negative view of the human person. Luther believed that man is totally corrupt, so much so that man's ability to choose and do good is completely destroyed. He believed that God only "covers up" our sins and corruptness, but does not heal it.

Second, Protestant theology wants to grant assurance of salvation, which is very attractive and reassuring. If works are not necessary for salvation and only the saving power of Christ is, then once we have accepted salvation we can never lose it as long as we acknowledge Jesus as our personal Lord and Savior.

The Catholic View of Salvation

Now that we understand the Protestant view of salvation and its roots, let us look at the New Testament evidence and how it supports the Catholic position.

Faith without Works Is Dead

Mainstream Protestantism insists that we are saved by faith in Christ alone, and that there is nothing we can do to earn or effect salvation. This half-truth heavily emphasizes that salvation from Christ is a free gift that cannot be earned. Protestants often quote Romans 3:28 to make their point: "For we consider that a person is justified by faith apart from works of the law." While this seems to be a convincing argument, it only paints half of the whole. Yes, it is true that we are justified by faith in Christ and nothing we do can "earn" salvation. Salvation indeed is a free gift of Christ. When Paul speaks of "works of the law," he is saying that exterior works of the Old Covenant, such as circumcision or ritual cleansing, cannot bring salvation, but only faith in Christ.

Yet James says, "See how a person is justified by works and not by faith alone. . . . For just as a body without a spirit is dead, so also faith without works is dead" (Jas. 2:24, 26).

It seems as if the Word of God completely contradicts itself. Actually, it does not. These Scripture verses focus on two different aspects of justification, the process of being saved. In order to fully understand the Catholic and true New Testament notion of salvation, we need to make an important distinction between being *redeemed* by Christ and being *sanctified.*

For Catholics, justification is the process of being both redeemed *and* sanctified. For example, I know with complete certainty that Jesus died on the Cross and rose from the dead in order to expiate the sin of the world, opening the gates of heaven and the floodgates of grace for all mankind. I am *redeemed* by the Blood of the Lamb. He has paid the price and won for me the ticket to heaven. There is nothing that anyone can do to earn this gift. This is what Paul is referring to in Romans. Redemption is a free gift for all. This is God's part of the bargain.

However, I am *sanctified* (which means to become holy, i.e., a saint) in as much as I cooperate with the grace that flows from the redemption and the law of love revealed and perfected by Jesus Christ. I have to cash the ticket in! This is the response of faith. While salvation comes through faith alone and not works, faith requires a response of love that manifests itself in works, as James so clearly tells us. This is our part of the bargain.

Thus, justification or sanctification is a wondrous cooperation between the Redeemer and the sinner in which God desires to heal and transform the inner man so that he may literally become a son of God. It is a lifelong process of being a *handmaid* of the Lord. It is a daily yes to all God has for us and a rejection of sin. It is a process of ongoing conversion. God does not want to simply cover up our sins. He wants to make us a new creation. He wants us to literally and completely become pure and holy.

While works do not "earn" salvation, they are a prerequisite to *becoming* saved. Note the difference. We do nothing to *earn* God's act of redemption. That is a total and complete gift of utter love and mercy. However, works are necessary to *become* saved. Faith itself is not just an act of the intellect.

Consider this analogy. I do not simply know that I love my wife. I do not just love her with my mind. That would be preposterous. I love her with my whole being. Not only do I know I love her, but my love (or lack thereof) is manifested in my action. As the old saying goes, "Actions speak louder than words." What we do is intimately connected with who we are. If I am a faithful and loving husband it will show in what I do. If I commit an unfaithful act, I reveal a weakness in my love. Action follows from being. It is no different with God.

If I love God and have faith in Him, I am going to give all of myself to Him. Faith is not simply the submission of my intellect, but it is the complete submission of my intellect and will to God. He did not just say to love the Lord your God with your mind. He said, "Love the Lord your God with all your mind, your heart, your soul, and your strength and love your neighbor as yourself." The act of faith in itself implies that what we do *has everything to do with it*; it defines who we are. As James says, "faith without works is dead."

Jesus Himself and Many New Testament Authors Clearly Connect What We Do to Whether We Are Saved

It is very clear throughout the New Testament that what we do matters on whether or not we are accepting God's gift of salvation. The examples are numerous.

Matthew 19:16–17: The rich young man comes to Jesus and asks what he must do to possess everlasting life. Jesus answers, "If you wish to enter into life, keep the commandments." If all that was necessary was an acceptance of Jesus as his personal Lord and Savior, then why didn't Jesus just tell him that? The answer is because faith is more than an intellectual activity. It is loving God with our whole being and becoming what God wills for us.

Matthew 25:31–46: How will Jesus judge us at the Last Judgment? Is it by simply our faith in Him? No, it is how we loved and served our brothers and sisters in Christ, for in loving our neighbor we also love Him. Faith is love for God in action. We become holy as God is holy, by acting like God.

Luke 6:46–49: "Why do you call me 'Lord, Lord,' but do not do what I command?" We are not worthy to call Christ our Lord unless we follow His commands. If we truly love Christ and if He is Lord over our life, we will listen to His words and act on them.

John 14:21: "Whoever has my commandments and observes them is the one who loves me." Again, true faith and love in Christ will—indeed, must—manifest itself in what we do.

1 John 2:3–4: "The way we may be sure that we know him is to keep his commandments. Whoever says, 'I know him,' but does not keep his commandments is a liar, and the truth is not in him." That one speaks for itself.

Romans 2:5–8: "By your stubbornness and impenitent heart, you are storing up wrath for yourself for the day of wrath and revelation of the just judgment of God, *who will repay everyone according to his works: eternal life to those who seek glory, honor, and immortality through perseverance in good works, but wrath and fury to those who selfishly disobey the truth and obey wickedness"* (emphasis added).

Galatians 6:7–8: "Make no mistake: God is not mocked, for a person will reap only what he sows, because the one who sows for his flesh will reap corruption from the flesh, but the one who sows for the spirit will reap eternal life from the spirit." Our destiny is determined by how we live.

There Is No Assurance of Salvation or "Once Saved Always Saved" in the New Testament

There is also no evidence of a "once saved always saved" teaching in the New Testament, but plenty of evidence to support the opposite.

Matthew 24:13: "But the one who perseveres to the end will be saved." We must persevere and work to the end to obtain holiness and salvation.

Romans 11:22: "See, then, the kindness and severity of God: severity toward those who fell, but God's kindness to you, provided you remain in his kindness; otherwise you too will be cut off." Even those who were once saved can fall away. Salvation is conditional, depending upon our behavior—how we love God and others.

Hebrews 6:4–6: Another powerful text that shows that those "who have once been enlightened and tasted the heavenly gift and shared in the Holy

Spirit" can "then have fallen away" and be condemned. Clearly those who have been saved can reject and throw away God's gift of salvation. Notice we can either accept or reject God's gift. It is up to us.

Philippians 2:12–13: "Work out your own salvation with fear and trembling. For God is the one who, for his good purpose, works in you both to desire and to work."

I Corinthians 9:27: "I drive my body and train it, for fear that, after having preached to others, I myself should be disqualified." The holy Apostle Paul states that perseverance is necessary to attain salvation. He even fears that he may be disqualified from what he has already been given. If Paul is concerned about the race and the possibility of losing salvation, it behooves all Christians to follow his example.

God Does Not Want to Simply "Cover Up" or "Forget" Our Sins

God desires to completely heal and restore us to the goodness that was lost. Man is not totally corrupt, but has the capacity for sharing in God's life and doing good in His sight.

Protestants argue that man is totally corrupt after the Fall and that by accepting Jesus as Savior, a person's sins are "covered up" and God "forgets" that sin. Nonetheless, the person remains incapable of truly doing good.

If this Protestant teaching is true, then the All-Powerful, Omnipotent, Omniscient, Eternal God who created the entire universe out of nothing is only able to put a band-aid over my wound and forget my sin? God sent His only Son into the world to die a gruesome, brutal, and torturous death on the Cross only to cover-up what is corrupt in me? Our loving Father, who wills the best in all things for me, can only bandage but not heal my sin? No.

God desires to heal us, restore us, and make us perfectly clean from all stain of sin and corruption so that we can fully share in His life. Matthew 5:48 is a perfect example: "So be perfect, just as your heavenly Father is perfect." Jesus did not say, "You are saved, so don't worry about being perfect." He wants us to be perfect like He is. 1 Peter 1:15–16 echoes the same: "As he who called you is holy, be holy yourselves in every aspect of your conduct, for it is written, 'Be holy because I am holy.'" God wants us to be perfectly holy; He wants to purify and wash clean every part of us so we can be fully human and fully participate in His life.

Purgatory: God's Last Great Act of Mercy

Why Would We Need Purgatory?

As stated above, God does not desire to merely "cover up" or "forget" our sins, but rather He wills to completely heal, cleanse, and purify our souls from the very last speck of sin and corruption. Those who die in friendship with Christ but are still imperfectly purified (are still wounded or disfigured by already-forgiven sin) undergo a final purification in **purgatory** to prepare their souls for entrance into heaven. Purgatory is the great final act of God's love and mercy.

The Book of Revelation clearly shows that nothing unclean can enter heaven. "Nothing unclean will enter [heaven], nor anyone who does abominable things or tells lies. Only those will enter whose names are written in the Lamb's book of life" (Rev. 21:27). In other words, a soul with even the tiniest speck of sin or corruption would be unworthy of heaven and unable to enter into the presence of God. What are the options for a soul at the moment of death? There are three.

1. A soul that has fully cooperated with God's grace on earth is in the perfect state of grace and is completely detached from sin and the effects of sin, and thereby worthy of **heaven** and going straight into paradise.

2. A soul that has committed an unrepented mortal or deadly sin is completely deprived of all grace and is spiritually dead (see 1 Jn. 5:16–17; Jas. 1:14–15). It is as if a person arrived at the hospital clinically dead. Nothing can be done to save this soul, and it goes directly to **hell** where it will remain forever deprived of heaven and eternal life.

3. A soul that is in the state of grace and in friendship with God but still wounded by venial sin (a sin that diminished grace but does not destroy it) is not yet worthy of heaven. It is spiritually alive but needs final purification. This soul will go to purgatory until it is completely purified of all sin and corruption, and then it will go to heaven to be with the blessed for all eternity.

Purification in purgatory may also be needed for mortal sins that are forgiven through sacramental confession, but for which the **temporal punishment** of the sin still remains. For example, a drug addict can repent and confess his drug use, receive forgiveness for his sin and be restored to the state of grace. However, the temporal effects of that sin remain. The soul is in friendship with God, yet it remains in need of purification. In other words, through forgiveness of sin, God may free someone from eternal punishment of sin (damnation) and restore grace at the moment they repent (sacramental confession), but the residual effects of past or present sins remain and need to be expiated—temporal punishment.

While the Souls in Purgatory Are Purified Through Suffering, They Are Suffering Joyfully

While suffering is not enjoyable, all of us at some point in our life will subject ourselves to suffering to obtain a certain goal. For example, a person who desires to lose weight might willingly undergo a variety of sufferings such as eating less food or food that tastes bad, or engaging in painful and difficult exercise. Yet he wills it and perseveres in it because of the goal to lose weight.

Now let's consider how you would think as a soul in purgatory. In purgatory you are able to see sin for what it truly is and what it has done to you, others, and God. You know you could be and really deserve to be in hell if it were not for God's gift of mercy and salvation. With thanksgiving you see you are going to heaven and want to get there very badly. You know that through the purification of purgatory you will rid yourself of all horrible and disgusting sin. You would be praising God for His love and mercy while you suffer. Yes, it may hurt and will not be enjoyable, but you are being healed and prepared for heavenly glory.

Where Is Purgatory in the Bible?

While you will never find the word "purgatory" in the Bible, there are many implicit references to it that make clear it has always been a part of the Christian Tradition.

Matthew 12:32: "And whoever speaks a word against the Son of Man will be forgiven; but whoever speaks against the Holy Spirit will not be forgiven, either in this age or in the age to come." Here Jesus implies that some sins can be forgiven even in the next world. This would be impossible if there were only heaven and hell. Those in heaven do not need forgiveness, while those in hell cannot be forgiven.

1 Peter 4:6: "For this is why the gospel was preached *even to the dead* that, though condemned in the flesh in human estimation, they might live in the spirit in the estimation of God." Here Peter speaks of the Gospel being preached to the dead in order that they might live. Again this supports the possibility of salvation after death in purgatory.

1 Corinthians 3:13–15: Paul writes, ". . . the work of each will come to light, for the Day will disclose it. It will be revealed with fire, and the fire [itself] will test the quality of each one's work." He goes on to say that "he himself will be saved, but only as one passing through fire."

2 Maccabees 12:44–46: This is probably the clearest reference to purgatory in the Scriptures: "For if he were not expecting the fallen to rise again, it would have been superfluous and foolish to pray for the dead. *But if he did this with a view to the splendid reward that awaits those who had gone to rest in godliness, it was a holy and pious thought. Thus he made atonement for the dead that they might be absolved from their sin*" (emphasis added). If purification after death was not possible in purgatory, then why would there be offerings of atonement after death? The idea of purification of sin after death was a part of the Jewish tradition even before the coming of Christ.

The Souls in Purgatory Benefit From the Offering of Prayers and Sacrifices of Those on Earth, and the Intercession of the Saints in Heaven

As members of the Church we belong to the Mystical Body of Christ. The Church, however, does not simply exist on earth, but exists in heaven and purgatory. Since we belong to the same family, mysteriously and intimately united in the Holy Spirit, we all remain in relationship with one another even though we may be in different states. When we die we remain the same person, with the same relationships with others and with the Church.

As members of the Church, God in His loving plan allows each of us to merit or obtain graces for others by offering our prayers and daily sufferings for those who are in need of grace. Paul writes, "In my flesh I am filling up what is lacking in the afflictions of Christ on behalf of his body, which is the church" (Col. 1:24). Saint Paul is not saying that Christ's sufferings were somehow insufficient or incomplete, but rather that Christ wills that we assist in obtaining and applying the graces of the redemption for others through our prayers and sufferings.

The members of the Church in purgatory (the Church Suffering) are aided through grace obtained by the prayers and sufferings of the members of the Church on earth (the Church Militant) and the intercessory prayers of the saints in heaven (the Church Triumphant).

This idea of praying and performing practices for the purification of the dead is also seen clearly in Scripture.

2 Maccabees 12:44–46: We have already seen this marvelous text that gives proof of the existence of purgatory. It also proves that prayers and penitential practices are to be done by those on earth to benefit those in purgatory. "For if he were not expecting the fallen to rise again, it would have been superfluous and foolish to pray for the dead. But if he did this with a view to the splendid reward that awaits those who had gone to rest in godliness, it was a holy and pious thought. *Thus he made atonement for the dead that they might be freed from this sin*" (emphasis added).

2 Timothy 1:16–18: "May the Lord grant mercy to the family of Onesiphorus because he often gave me new heart and was not ashamed of my chains. . . . May the Lord grant him to find mercy from the Lord on that day."

1 Corinthians 15:29: "Otherwise, what will people accomplish by having themselves baptized for the dead? If the dead are not raised at all, then why are they having themselves baptized for them?" Here we see the offering of certain practices for the dead that would be completely meaningless unless there was a place of purgation after death.

Therefore, everyday sufferings and disappointments can become for those of us on earth moments of grace and merit, not only for ourselves, but also for others who are suffering on earth and in purgatory. This is the beauty of intercessory prayer and redemptive suffering. Uniting our suffering with Christ's suffering can be a means to personal holiness and a powerful aid to others in their struggle to overcome sin and grow closer to Christ. These powerful opportunities to grow in virtue and love for others—these "hidden" moments of grace that are given to us each and every day—should not be squandered.

By uniting our sufferings to Christ's sufferings with love, our suffering also becomes salvific, for we share in the redemption of Christ by becoming co-redeemers. Co-redeemer does not mean equal to Christ but rather with Christ.

He allows and expects us to participate in His redemptive suffering to obtain graces for ourselves and others. Remember, we share in every aspect of the mission of Christ, even in His redemptive suffering. Our participation in His redemptive suffering of the Cross does not diminish His perfect, full, and everlasting sacrifice. We simply share in it.

The Early Christians Also Believed in Purgatory

Numerous early Christian writings attest to a universal belief in the purification of the dead and the practice of praying for them. Here are just a few examples:

1. ***The Acts of Paul and Thecla:*** "And after the exhibition, Tryphaena again received her [Thecla]. For her daughter Falconilla had died, and said to her in a dream: 'Mother, you shall have this stranger Thecla in my place, in order that she may pray concerning me, and that I may be transferred to the place of the righteous'" (AD 160).

2. ***Tertullian:*** "We offer sacrifices for the dead on their birthday anniversaries [the date of death—birth into eternal life]" (*The Crown* 3:3 [AD 211]).

   "A woman, after the death of her husband . . . prays for his soul and asks that he may, while waiting, find rest; and that he may share in the first resurrection. And each year, on the anniversary of his death, she offers the sacrifice" (*Monogamy* 10:1–2 [AD 216]).

3. ***Cyril of Jerusalem:*** "Then we make mention also of those who have already fallen asleep: first, the patriarchs, prophets, Apostles, and martyrs, that through their prayers and supplications God would receive our petition; next, we make mention also of the holy fathers and bishops who have already fallen asleep, and, to put it simply, of all among us who have already fallen asleep, for we believe that it will be of very great benefit to the souls of those for whom the petition is carried up, while this holy and most solemn sacrifice is laid out" (*Catechetical Lectures* 23:5:9 [AD 350]).

What Is an Indulgence?

An **indulgence** is the removal of some or all of the temporal punishment due to sins that have already been forgiven. As we saw earlier, sin has an eternal consequence (loss of grace and separation from God) and a temporal consequence that may remain even after the eternal consequence is forgiven. The Church's authority given by Christ to grant indulgences comes from its power to bind and loose:

> An indulgence is obtained through the Church who, by virtue of the power of binding and loosing granted her by Christ Jesus, intervenes in favor of individual Christians and opens for them the treasury of the merits of Christ and the saints to obtain from the Father of mercies the remission of the temporal punishments due for their sins. Thus the Church does not want simply to come to the aid of these Christians, but also to spur them to works of devotion, penance, and charity. (CCC 1478)

The Church has the power to grant an indulgence to the faithful who do certain acts of charity or piety that the Church judges to be efficacious in the removal of temporal punishment. This is not a "magic trick." To obtain the indulgence the faithful must do the act of charity or piety with sincere and real love, and with the intention of doing it for the atonement for sin. The person's act merits grace, and through the intercession and authority of the Church also merits the partial or total remission of temporal punishment due to sin. An indulgence can only be obtained through a meritorious act of charity; we cannot just go through the motions with little care or concern and receive an indulgence.

Furthermore, an indulgence cannot be bought or be the source of a bribe. Because indulgences have been abused in this way in the past, the Church forbids the granting of an indulgence for the donation or paying of money, even though a monetary donation can be a charitable and meritorious act.

An indulgence can either be partial (removing some temporal punishment) or plenary (total removal of temporal punishment). The Church almost always sets conditions for the reception of indulgences, including true charity of heart and sacramental confession (usually required for plenary indulgences). In addition, the Church no longer designates a time period in purgatory—days, months, or years—for partial indulgences.

The Rapture Theory

What Is the Rapture Theory?

The rapture theory is another seriously misguided interpretation of salvation and the end times. It has grown immensely popular in Protestant circles and is even accepted as biblical truth by misinformed Catholics. The rapture theory was made popular particularly by the *Left Behind* fictional book series by Tim LaHaye and Jerry Jenkins. This interpretation of Scripture holds that before Jesus returns at the end of time to judge all the living and the dead (the Second Coming), there will be an additional "secret" coming of Christ. At this time the true believers on earth will be "caught up," or raptured (from the Latin *rapiemur,* "to be caught up"), to join the true Church in heaven before a "final tribulation" occurs on earth. Meanwhile, those "left behind" will fall victim to seven years of tribulation on earth. Those who were raptured will return with Christ (the "third coming") to destroy the Antichrist and to establish Christ's thousand-year reign on earth.

What Is the Origin of the Rapture Theory?

Although the rapture theory has become quite popular among many Protestants, most Protestant theologians reject the theory because it is not biblical. Not only is it not biblical, the idea of the rapture did not appear until the last half of the nineteenth century. The theory was first proposed by John Nelson Darby, an ordained priest in the Church of England.

Fed up with the laxity of many members of the Church of England, Darby started his own mini-Reformation and espoused a new and radical interpretation of Scripture called dispensationalism. He traveled around the United States and Canada preaching this new scriptural interpretation. With the publication of the popular Schofield Reference Bible in 1909, which was filled with Darby's extensive interpretive notes, the dispensationalist doctrine and the rapture theory rapidly grew. It fits in well with the "wealth and health" Christianity that was preached then and now, which minimizes suffering and assures salvation to those who accept Christ. It is "comfortable" Christianity at the expense of cheap grace.

Is There Any Evidence in the Bible That Supports the Rapture Theory?

Doesn't the Bible speak of a time when some people will suddenly be taken and others left as evidence of the true believers being raptured to heaven? In fact, there are several passages where there is a separation and some people are suddenly taken. However, it is the wicked that are taken first, not the blessed. These passages warn of the swift judgment of God that occurs at the second and final coming of Christ.

Luke 17:34–37: "I tell you, on that night there will be two people in one bed; one will be taken, the other left. And there will be two women grinding meal together; one will be taken, the other left. They said to him in reply, 'Where Lord?' *He said to them, 'Where the body is, there also the vultures will gather'*" (emphasis added).

Matthew 24:37–41: "For as it was in the days of Noah, so it will be at the coming of the Son of Man. . . . They did not know until the flood came and carried them all away. So will it be [also] at the coming of the Son of Man. Two men will be out in the field; one will be taken, and one will be left. Two women will be grinding at the mill; one will be taken and the other left."

Matthew 13:30: "Let them grow together until harvest; then at harvest time I will say to the harvesters, 'First collect the weeds and tie them in bundles for burning; but gather the wheat into my barn.'"

Rapturists also insist that Paul speaks of a separate and secret third coming in which the true believers are "caught up" into heaven. The following passages are at the core of their argument. If the rapture is to be a secret and separate coming from the Last Judgment, what's wrong with their claim?

1 Thessalonians 4:16–17: "For the Lord himself, with a word of command, with the voice of an archangel and with the trumpet of God, will come down from heaven, and the dead in Christ will rise first. Then we who are alive, who are left, will be caught up together with them in the clouds to meet the Lord in the air. Thus we shall always be with the Lord."

1 Corinthians 15:51–52: "Behold, I tell you a mystery. We shall not all fall asleep, but we will all be changed, in an instant, in the blink of an eye, at the last trumpet. For the trumpet will sound, the dead will be raised incorruptible, and we shall be changed."

There are loud trumpet blasts, a cry of command from Christ, and an archangel's call. This is not a secret coming but the final coming. In these two passages, Paul is clearly describing the last coming of Christ where the dead are raised (only at the Last Judgment). Paul even speaks of the "last trumpet" in 1 Corinthians.

Rapturists claim that through the rapture Christ desires to spare true believers from suffering through the Final Tribulation before His final return. What is wrong with this claim? It contradicts Jesus' own predictions of the Last Days. He tells His Apostles that it is the Church itself, the very followers of Christ, who will be persecuted and martyred and given over to synagogues and prisons. It is the ones who persevere to the end that will be saved (see Lk. 21:12–24; Mk. 13:9–13). The Church herself will go through a final purification, as will individuals at the end of their lives, to purify the Church to meet her Savior.

The Dangers of the Rapture Theory

The rapture theory is preposterous and contrary to the data of the New Testament. Although it may seem on the surface to be a rather harmless, ridiculous interpretation of Scripture, the rapture is a very dangerous theory that radically contradicts Catholic doctrine in two ways.

First, the rapture creates a radical dualism between believers on earth and the "true" Church in heaven. For the dispensationalist, believers on earth have accepted Christ in faith but can really do nothing to change or affect the corrupt culture or world around them. They wait to be "caught up" or "raptured" in the true Church in heaven. There is no sense of being a leaven within the world, bringing about the kingdom of Christ through their works or witness.

The Catholic teaching is quite the opposite. It is the Church Militant that strives and fights to build up the kingdom of God on earth. We participate with Christ in building His kingdom through faith lived out in charity. We "await in joyful hope" for Christ to come again to complete the work that we have already begun (see CCC 898 and 901). We are called to consecrate the world to Christ, not to sit around and bemoan our depraved surroundings as we wait for Him to reach down and snatch us out of this pit. There is a radical difference of consciousness and attitude.

Second, the rapture completely diminishes the value of redemptive suffering. Christ never promised that we would escape suffering. He said we must take up our own crosses and follow Him (Mt. 10:38; 16:24). He showed us that by embracing suffering with love and uniting ourselves to His Passion, we can bring about goodness, holiness, and love. Suffering actually strengthens the Church rather than weakens her, if we have the right attitude. Look at the witness of the martyrs whose blood is the "seed of faith."

So, yes, the Church on earth will pass through a final tribulation just as Christ predicted, but it will be her final purification and hour of glory. If we go through our lives avoiding and complaining about suffering, we miss out on this marvelous aspect of being followers of Christ. (For fabulous insight into the meaning of redemptive suffering, read Pope John Paul II's apostolic letter *Salvifici doloris,* "On the Christian Meaning of Human Suffering," written shortly after the attempt on his life. It will change the way you look at suffering in your own life.)

From the Catechism: Key Words to Know

JUSTIFICATION: The gracious action of God that frees us from sin and communicates "the righteousness of God through faith in Jesus Christ" (Rom. 3:22). Justification is not only the remission of sins, but also the sanctification and renewal of the interior man (1987–1989).

PURGATORY: A state of final purification after death and before entrance into heaven for those who died in God's friendship, but were only imperfectly purified; a final cleansing of human imperfection before one is able to enter the joy of heaven (1031; cf. 1472).

HEAVEN: Eternal life with God; communion of life and love with the Trinity and all the blessed. Heaven is the state of supreme and definitive happiness, the goal of the deepest longings of humanity (1023).

HELL: The state of definitive self-exclusion from communion with God and the blessed, reserved for those who refuse by their own free choice to believe and be converted from sin, even to the end of their lives (1033).

TEMPORAL PUNISHMENT: Purification of the unhealthy attachment to creatures, which is a consequence of sin that endures even after death. We must be purified either during our earthly life through prayer and conversion, which comes from fervent charity, or after death in purgatory (1472).

INDULGENCE: The remission before God of the temporal punishment due to sin that has already been forgiven. A properly disposed member of the Christian faithful can obtain an indulgence under prescribed conditions through the help of the Church, which, as the minister of redemption, dispenses and applies with authority the treasury of the satisfactions of Christ and the saints. An indulgence is partial if it removes part of the temporal punishment due to sin, or plenary if it removes all punishment (1471).

Part two

THE SACRAMENTS: THE CELEBRATION OF THE CHRISTIAN MYSTERY

Chapter 13

Introduction to the Sacraments

Reading the Catechism: Paragraphs 1113–1209

> You set a table before me
> in front of my enemies;
> You anoint my head with oil;
> my cup overflows.
>
> Indeed, goodness and mercy will pursue me,
> all the days of my life;
> I will dwell in the house of the LORD
> for endless days.
>
> —Psalm 23:5–6

Has anyone ever said or done something for you that really showed their love for you? It may have been heartfelt words of love or appreciation, or perhaps a special gift or something that the person went out of their way to do for you. If you think about it, love and friendship are almost always expressed to us through some sort of sign or words. We may understand the definition of love, but if I say, "Show me love," it must be expressed in some sort of concrete action. If I never told my wife or my children that I loved them or expressed it through my actions, would they really know I loved them?

It's not any different with our relationship with God. It is a relationship of love and gift of self like any human relationship, where love is expressed through words, signs, and actions. As we have seen, prayer is absolutely necessary in the Christian life. It is through prayer that we lift our hearts up to God and through our words and actions express our love.

But just as we desire to communicate our love to those we love and to God, even more so does God desire to communicate His love and share His life with us. He is not a distant and indifferent God, as some may assert. Rather, He is a passionate God who loves us with a love that far exceeds any stretch of our imagination.

In fact, God's love for us brings to mind the many romantic movies, or what we call "chick flicks," with which we are all so familiar. It usually goes something like this: A man meets a woman and they fall madly in love. After a short time of blissful love and companionship, something tragic happens that seriously endangers the relationship, and they find themselves drifting far apart. Finally, it is usually the man who comes to his senses, and realizing his great love will do anything to get his girl back—risking his life chasing her in a car to the airport before she leaves, or riding wildly through town on a motorcycle and bursting into the church to passionately express his love for her the moment before she gets married.

Well, our God is that same passionate lover, and the story of salvation history is much like a romantic movie. Even after man sinned and turned away from Him, God shows His passionate and undying love for us. He sets out on His plan to save us and does whatever it takes to get us back, even giving up His own life so that we can know His love and share in His life.

Even now, God desires that we know His great and undying love in a real and intimate way, as well as the great dignity and worth that He sees in each and every one of us. He desires to express His love for us in a way that we can know, feel, and understand. We can come to know this love especially through the special signs, words, and actions of God that we call **sacraments**. Furthermore, He not only desires to show us His love, He wants to share His very life with us. That life has healing and transforming power that heals us from sin and restores us as His sons and daughters. Thus, the sacraments are special moments in our lives through which God communicates His love and gives us **grace** to respond to it.

What Is a Sacrament?

A sacrament is a visible sign instituted by Christ that gives sanctifying grace. It is a unique moment in which, through visible and tangible signs, words, and actions, God imparts upon us the gift of His life and love. Through these signs we come to know in a real and intimate way His love, and we are transformed, healed, and strengthened. To better grasp an understanding of what a sacrament is, let us look in more detail at each part of the definition.

Sacraments Impart to Us Sanctifying Grace

In the sacraments God communicates grace to us—His very life and love. Grace is absolutely necessary to the spiritual life because without it we are spiritually dead. God created our human nature to live in intimate communion with Him. Our human nature needs and depends upon His grace in the same way that our bodies rely on oxygen; without it we would be physically dead.

Adam and Eve were created full of grace and lived in communion with God. After the first sin they lost the gift of grace, and as a result all of humanity fell away from God and was no longer filled with His grace. However, through Christ's death and Resurrection sin and death were conquered forever, and we were once again given access to God's grace. It is especially through the sacraments that He willed His grace to be communicated in a special way.

We call the grace given to us in the sacraments **sanctifying grace** because it transforms us and makes us holy and more like God. The word sanctifying comes from the Latin word *sanctus,* which literally means "to make holy." God's love is effective. When we come into contact with His love and life He enlivens us, heals us from the wounds of sin, and enables us to live a full human life freed from slavery to sin. With His grace we spiritually breathe again and once again become spiritually alive. The sacraments continue to communicate God's grace to us throughout our lives. They transform us to become more like Christ. They heal and strengthen us against sin, enabling us to live a life of faith, hope, and especially love. They keep us on the "narrow path" of salvation on our pilgrim journey toward heaven.

The Sacraments Are Instituted by Christ Himself

The sacraments are not an invention of the Church or of a pope; rather, they are of the will of Christ Himself. He instituted specific signs and actions, entrusting them to the Apostles and their successors to be the unique and powerful way in which He would communicate His life and love to us. The sacraments have their origin in Christ. The Church has neither the power nor the authority to create or eliminate the number of sacraments, or to change their essential signs, words, or actions. The Church, being faithful to its founder, continues to hand on to each generation the saving power of the sacraments.

We can clearly see the origins of some of the sacraments in the life and ministry of Christ as revealed to us in Scripture. Other sacraments are not necessarily seen in the life and actions of Christ, but are manifest in the apostolic Church and seen through the epistles of Paul and other scriptural writings. All seven of the sacraments are implicitly revealed in Scripture and have been handed on through Sacred Tradition from the very beginning of the Church's life. As we cover each sacrament in more detail, we will see how each one is at least implicitly revealed in Sacred Scripture.

The Sacraments Are Visible, Tangible Signs

Each sacrament is a visible, tangible, natural sign that communicates sanctifying grace to us. God's grace is effective in us whether or not we realize or understand it. However, He desires that we know exactly what He is doing in us so that we can respond to and accept His grace, making it more effective in our lives.

We can see, touch, or taste the sacramental signs, such as water, oil, bread and wine. These signs have universal meaning that peoples of all times, places, and cultures can know and understand. For example, water is used in the Sacrament of Baptism. If you ask someone from any time, place, or culture what they associate with water, they will almost always give the same answer. Water is universally associated with washing and cleansing. It is essential for life and is thirst quenching. Thus, water, as the sign of Baptism, communicates to us in a visible, real, and tangible way that God is washing and cleansing us from sin, bringing us into a new life with Christ, and satiating our thirst for union with God.

Sacramental signs are always accompanied by effective words and actions. As Christ revealed His transforming and healing power through both words and actions, He continues to work through the signs and words of the sacraments, filling us with His life and grace and transforming us with His power.

The Seven Sacraments

Both Sacred Scripture and Sacred Tradition affirm that Christ established seven sacraments that have been handed on by the Church through successive generations. The sacraments are broken up into three groups.

The sacraments of initiation

Baptism, the Eucharist, and Confirmation are called the sacraments of initiation because they bring us into communion with Christ and the Church. Once these three sacraments are received, we are said to be in full communion with and fully initiated into the Church.

The sacraments of healing

Penance (Confession) and Anointing of the Sick are called the sacraments of healing. They communicate to us God's healing and transforming grace in times of sin and repentance, and at times of physical, mental, or emotional suffering. These sacraments especially bring us into union with the Passion of Christ in order that we may be healed of sin, or that we may have the strength of Christ to endure our sufferings with patience, hope, and love.

The sacraments of vocation

Holy Orders and Marriage are called the sacraments of vocation. From the Latin word *vocare,* meaning "to call," these two sacraments are lifelong callings from God that are ordered to the service and building up of the Church. Through Holy Orders men are ordained bishops, priests, and deacons to serve and build the Church by proclaiming the Word of God and administering the sacraments. Marriage is a lifelong sacrament of life-giving love, through which a husband and wife love each other as Christ loves the Church. Sacramental marriages build and strengthen the Church through the procreation and education of children.

The Sacraments Are a Work of Christ Himself

We have already seen that Christ instituted the seven sacramental signs within the Church, through which He desires to communicate to us His life and bring us into communion with the Trinitarian life of God. However, not only did Christ institute the sacraments, He is also at work in the sacraments. As the Catechism states, "Celebrated worthily in faith, the sacraments confer the grace that they signify. They are *efficacious* because in them Christ himself is at work: it is he who baptizes, he who acts in his sacraments in order to communicate the grace that each sacrament signifies" (1127). Thus the sacraments are literally an encounter with the very Person of Christ, who comes to meet and embrace us, infusing within us His divine and transforming life.

"In Persona Christi"

How is it possible that each sacrament is a work of the Person of Christ Himself? He entrusted to the Apostles the authority and power to teach, govern, and minister in His name within the Church until the end of time. Through the imposition of hands in the Sacrament of Holy Orders, this apostolic ministry is handed on to each and every generation through apostolic succession within the Church. Through this unbroken line, bishops, priests, and deacons possess the same apostolic ministry that was given to the original Apostles.

Through the Sacrament of Holy Orders a man is received into the apostolic ministry, and through a special grace and charism of the Holy Spirit is conformed to Christ in a unique way that allows Christ to work through him in the administration of the sacraments. Thus we say that the priest stands *in persona Christi*, such that the Person of Christ is really present in the minister, and it is Christ who performs the sacrament through the priest (see CCC 1120).

Therefore, the role of a bishop, priest, or deacon in the administration of the sacraments is one of *instrumentality*—special instruments through which Christ performs each sacrament and communicates His grace to us. The sacraments are then a personal work of Christ, who comes to all of us to transform us, to heal us, to give us fullness of life, and to share with us the divine love that burns within His Sacred Heart.

The Sacraments Always and Necessarily Communicate God's Grace

Christ promised the Apostles and His Church that He would be with them until the end of time (Mt. 28:20). His presence within His Church is seen most profoundly in the sacraments, especially the Eucharist. He instituted the sacraments as the means through which He is made truly present to His Church—both in the signs themselves and in the apostolic ministry He established for their celebration. If the appropriate sign and words are present along with a properly ordained minister, Christ is really present and working in the sacrament. By virtue of His own will and authority, grace is communicated to the believer. Thus it is said that the sacraments act *"ex opere operato,"* which literally means "by the very fact of the action's being performed." This truth is crucial and important. Christ's presence and the grace that is communicated have nothing to do with the holiness or uprightness of the minister, or with the disposition or faith of the recipient. If this were not so, there would always be a question of whether the sacraments "worked" in any given situation. The Catechism clearly teaches that every time a sacrament is validly (truly and correctly) performed, it is Christ who performs the sacrament and grace is always and necessarily communicated:

> It follows that "the sacrament is not wrought by the righteousness of either the celebrant or the recipient, but by the power of God." From the moment that a sacrament is celebrated in accordance with the intention of the Church, the power of Christ and his Spirit acts in and through it, independently of the personal holiness of the minister. Nevertheless, the fruits of the sacraments also depend on the disposition of the one who receives them. (1128)

"When You Hear His Voice, Harden Not Your Hearts."

Although sacraments validly performed are always efficacious (as the Catechism teaches), the fruits of the sacraments depend on the disposition of the one receiving them. Although grace is communicated to us each time we receive a sacrament, we have to be open to those graces and allow them to penetrate our very being with their transforming and healing power. Through a nonchalant attitude, hardness of heart, or sin, we can choose to prevent God's grace from influencing our lives.

Our response to the sacraments should be the same reaction we should always give God: the response of faith. As we saw in chapter one, faith is the total surrendering to God of our entire being—opening ourselves completely and totally to all that God has for us. Faith is an unconditional surrendering to God. When we approach the sacraments we should throw open our hearts to the power of the Holy Spirit and to all the graces of Christ that God communicates to us in each and every sacrament.

In a very powerful way a priest illustrated this disposition of faith, so necessary in receiving the sacraments, to me when I was a child. He began with a big glass of milk, a rock, and a cookie.

He first took the rock and dropped it into the milk, letting it sink to the bottom. About thirty seconds later he pulled it out and it was no different. The milk simply ran off of it. He explained that the rock is like our hard hearts and the milk is like God's grace. The milk did nothing to the rock. It simply ran off without any change or effect.

Then he took the cookie and put it in the milk. Again, about thirty seconds later he took the cookie out. It was permeated with the milk to the point of falling apart. The priest explained that the cookie is like our hearts when we have faith and open ourselves completely to God. Like the cookie, our lives become permeated with Christ. He is incarnated in our hearts and lives, and we become Christ-bearers in the world.

The priest then put the cookie back into the milk and it began to dissolve. Eventually, the cookie and the milk became one substance. The milk had completely transformed the cookie and the two became one.

This is what God desires to do when we open our hearts to Him through the sacraments. He desires to transform us and to make us like Christ so that we, like the Apostle Paul, can say, "Yet I live, no longer I, but Christ lives in me" (Gal. 2:20). Therefore, when we hear the voice of Christ calling to us through the sacraments, we must not harden our hearts, but surrender ourselves completely to the transforming power of God's love.

From the Catechism: Key Words to Know

SACRAMENT: An efficacious sign of grace, instituted by Christ and entrusted to the Church, by which divine life is dispensed to us through the work of the Holy Spirit (774, 1131). The sacraments (called "mysteries" in the Eastern Churches) are seven in number: Baptism, Confirmation, Eucharist, Penance or Reconciliation, Anointing of the Sick, Holy Orders, and Matrimony (1210).

GRACE: The free and undeserved gift that God gives us to respond to our vocation to become His adopted children. As sanctifying grace, God shares His divine life and friendship with us in a habitual gift, a stable and supernatural disposition that enables the soul to live with God, to act by His love. As actual grace, God gives us the help to conform our lives to His will. Sacramental grace and special graces (charisms, the grace of one's state of life) are gifts of the Holy Spirit to help us live out our Christian vocation (1996, 2000; cf. 654).

SANCTIFYING GRACE: The grace that heals our human nature wounded by sin by giving us a share in the divine life of the Trinity. It is a habitual, supernatural gift that continues the work of sanctifying us—of making us "perfect," holy, and Christlike (1999).

Chapter 14

The Sacrament of Baptism

Reading the Catechism: Paragraphs 1213–1284

> Go, therefore, and make disciples of all nations, baptizing them in the name of the Father, and of the Son, and of the Holy Spirit, teaching them to observe all that I have commanded you. And behold, I am with you always, until the end of the age.
>
> —Matthew 28:19–20

The Sacrament of **Baptism** is the first that we receive. It is the sacrament that brings us out of slavery to sin and spiritual death, and introduces us into a new life in Christ. It is through Baptism that we are literally "born again," for we are made a new spiritual creation in and through Christ and come into a profound and intimate relationship with the Holy Trinity. We are filled with the Holy Spirit and become members of the Mystical Body of Christ, the Church (see CCC 1213).

From Death unto Life: The Effects of Baptism

The essential nature and purpose of the Sacrament of Baptism is a sharing in the death and Resurrection of Christ. We die to our old sinful self with Christ, and then rise with Him as a new creation, born again in the Spirit of God. The sacrament is called *baptism* from the Greek word *baptizein,* which means to "plunge" or "immerse." This plunge into the waters of Baptism symbolizes dying and being buried with Christ, before we rise up out of the water to a new and resurrected life. Baptism makes present the fruits and effects of Christ's Paschal Mystery (His death and Resurrection) in our lives in a real and powerful way. Christ's death and Resurrection are not distant events that we recall and remember in faith, but through this sacrament the reality of God's saving power in Christ is actually accomplished in us!

Baptism Frees Us from All Sin

Through plunging into the waters of Baptism we are washed clean of all sin as well as the punishment for sin. Baptism cleanses us from two types of sin, original and personal.

Baptism Frees Us from Original Sin

Original sin, recorded in the Book of Genesis, is the first sin committed in the Garden of Eden by Adam and Eve. They represent all of humanity and the choices we must face because we are creatures with a free will. Their first sin represents mankind's sins and the resulting separation from God. Thus, all of us who come into this world are born with a spiritual separation from God, and therefore all of us suffer from original sin.

Baptism cleanses and frees us from this. We no longer suffer the eternal consequences of original sin, which is separation from God. The sacrament restores our communion with Him and our sharing in His divine life. Baptism is a spiritual resuscitation, the divine defibrillator. We are literally brought back to spiritual life from being dead in sin. This is why Baptism is truly a new birth; we are "born again" in Christ.

However, while Baptism frees us from the eternal consequences of sin, we still suffer from the temporal effects of original sin. As we saw in chapter four, not only did the first sin cause Adam and Eve to be separated from God, it also wounded their human nature. Their relationship with each other and all of creation around them was dramatically affected by their sin. Original sin causes disorder within us; our passions, desires, emotions, even our intellect and will are wounded by it. These wounds still remain after Baptism, even though we are once again brought into union with God and have access to His kingdom. We still have attachment to sin and the tendency toward sin, even after receiving this sacrament. This we call **concupiscence**, and it is against this that we must struggle throughout our lives (see CCC 1264).

While we still suffer the temporal effects of original sin even after Baptism, the sacrament also fills us with God's grace and gifts that help us to battle against sin and transform us to be like Christ. Through faith and on-going conversion we cooperate with these graces and gifts to overcome our sinfulness and become holy and pleasing in the sight of the Lord.

Baptism Frees Us from All Personal Sin

Personal (or actual) sins are the sins that we ourselves commit. Those who are baptized as adults are also freed from and forgiven for all of the sins they have committed up to that point in their lifetime. Baptism is a clean slate, a completely new beginning in our life with Christ. Thus, it is not necessary for those who are baptized as adults to confess the sins they committed before Baptism (confession of sin will be discussed in more detail in the chapter on the Sacrament of Penance). However, like original sin, the temporal consequences of our personal sins may still remain with us even after Baptism, and we must cooperate with the grace of the sacrament to turn away from our sinful tendencies and embrace the life of Christ. This ongoing process of conversion and struggle against sin is also aided through the other sacraments, especially the Eucharist and Penance.

We Are Made a New Creation in Christ

We have seen that through Baptism we are cleansed of our sins by dying and being buried with Christ, but that is only the beginning of what He does in this wonderful sacrament. Baptism is about the forgiveness of sins, but it is even more profoundly a sacrament of re-birth and re-creation through the power of the Resurrection of Christ. As we literally die with Christ, we also literally rise with Christ. We are made a new creation in Him through Baptism (see CCC 1265).

That we are made a new creation in Christ is no mere metaphor. We are transformed, spiritually becoming an entirely new and different being. Raised to new life with Christ, we are "born again" through the power of the Holy Spirit in the waters of baptism. This reality of spiritual rebirth is clearly articulated by Christ Himself in the famous dialogue with Nicodemus in John's Gospel:

> Amen, amen, I say to you, no one can see the kingdom of God without being born from above." Nicodemus said to him, "How can a person once grown old be born again? Surely he cannot reenter his mother's womb and be born again, can he?" Jesus answered, "Amen, amen, I say to you, no one can enter the kingdom of God without being born of water and Spirit. What is born of flesh is flesh and what is born of spirit is spirit. (Jn. 3:3–6)

This spiritual rebirth is made possible through the sanctifying grace infused into the soul through this sacrament. This grace of Baptism makes us new creatures in Christ in several ways.

We Become Adopted Sons and Daughters of God

Baptism frees us from sin and brings us into right relationship with God, but it goes much further. We become adopted children of the Father through Christ. *In the same way that Christ enjoys His sonship with the Father, we too enter into that same relationship.* In fact, adoption is not entirely an adequate word to use. It is true that we are adopted sons and daughters of God insofar as adoption implies that God, out of His own free initiative and gracious love, brings us into a filial relationship with Himself. However, an adopted child can never become the blood son or daughter of the adoptive parent. But through Baptism, we truly become a real son or daughter of God, sharing in the relationship that Christ enjoys with His Father. Thus, Baptism is a spiritual transformation of who we are. This is why Paul is able to boldly proclaim to the new Christians in the Church of Rome:

> For you did not receive a spirit of slavery to fall back into fear, but you received a spirit of adoption, through which we cry "Abba, Father!" The Spirit itself bears witness with our spirit that we are children of God, and if children, then heirs, heirs of God and joint heirs with Christ, if only we suffer with him so that we may also be glorified with him. (Rom. 8:15–17)

We Become Co-Heirs with Christ

As Saint Paul tells us, Baptism makes us co-heirs with Christ. If we are truly sons and daughters of God, then all that belongs to and is given to the Son of God, Jesus Christ, also belongs to and is given to us.

Through this sacrament, Christ unites Himself with all who receive it, and we are given a share of His life and mission. Even the sufferings we endure in life, when united to the sufferings of Christ, become meaningful and can even bring about redemption and conversion. Although the glory of the Resurrection will only be fully revealed and realized when we reign with Christ in the presence of the Father for all eternity, through Baptism it is already manifested in our lives in the here and now. Baptism also gives us a share in the threefold mission of Christ as priest, prophet, and king:

- We are grafted into the priesthood of all believers. With Christ, we present to the Father a sacrifice of worship and praise, offering ourselves "as a living sacrifice holy and pleasing to God."
- We share in Christ's mission as prophet by proclaiming the Gospel, and witnessing to the presence of God in our daily lives through our words and deeds. We literally are called to bear Christ in the world through our faith and good works.
- We participate in the mission of Christ the King as we reign with Him over sin and death. Through mastery over sin in our lives, we are truly free to serve others in the building up of the kingdom of God.

Through this great sacrament, we become Christ present and working in the world—His living instruments through which He continues to accomplish His work of salvation.

We Receive the Grace of Justification

Through Baptism we receive sanctifying grace, which is called the grace of justification. Justification, or becoming justified, is synonymous with being righteous, or living in righteousness. Baptism allows us to stand before God in justice. Thus, we are transformed from once being "bent over" in sin to being filled with the life of Christ and His Spirit, and standing before God in a true and right relationship as His child. The sanctifying grace of Baptism brings us into the life of the Trinity and empowers us to live the Christian life.

We receive the virtues of faith, hope, and charity

Baptism infuses within us the theological virtues of faith, **hope**, and **charity**. These are basic virtues that allow us to have a relationship with God. Faith and hope are only needed in this present life. Faith allows us to know, accept, and live according to God's revelation and will for our lives. We have faith in this life because we do not yet see God face to face or the fullness of His plan for us. But through faith we trust in His word and promise of salvation, entrusting ourselves entirely to Him. Baptism also helps us to hope in God and His promise of salvation and to know that it is only in God that we will realize true fulfillment, freedom, and fullness of life.

The virtue of love (charity), however, is not only present in this life, but will endure forever. God is love, and it is through love that we share in His life. Love is the foundation of Christian life. Through the perfection of love for God and others, we will know the fulfillment of our vocation and the true meaning and purpose of life. Once in heaven, as we finally gaze upon the face of God, faith and hope will pass away and we will forever live fully immersed in the love of God.

We receive the presence and gifts of the Holy Spirit

"He will baptize you with the Holy Spirit and fire" (Mt. 3:11). This testimony of John the Baptist reveals that through this sacrament the Spirit of God comes to dwell within each of us, filling us with His power and His love. The Holy Spirit is the animating force of our life in Christ. Baptism allows us to live and act in accordance with His inspiration and promptings. The Holy Spirit also frees us from sin and the desires of the flesh. Through His presence and grace we are justified and made righteous before God. Through His indwelling we become temples of God, and no longer live for ourselves but for God and in the very power of God.

We grow in the moral virtues

Baptism allows us to grow in goodness and live the moral virtues. It strengthens within us the natural virtues of prudence, justice, fortitude, temperance, and all of the other moral virtues that surround and are rooted in these. The Holy Trinity, through the grace of Baptism, gives us all the natural and supernatural gifts and tools that we need to live out the Christian life so that we "might have life and have it more abundantly" (Jn. 10:10).

Baptism Imprints Upon Us a Permanent Spiritual Mark

In addition to making us a new creation in Christ, Baptism also imprints upon our soul a permanent, or indelible, spiritual mark, or **sacramental character**, of belonging to Christ forever. This "fingerprint" of Christ, given through this sacrament, can never be erased or taken away. Baptism conforms us to Christ and makes us His "chosen race, a royal priesthood, a holy nation, a people of his own" (1 Pet. 2:9). This spiritual mark consecrates us, or sets us apart, as belonging to the household of God. It enables us to love and serve Him through worship, service, and charity (see CCC 1273).

This permanent mark of Baptism is given once and cannot be repeated. The Church recognizes that any Baptism celebrated in the Trinitarian formula, "In the Name of the Father, and of the Son, and of the Holy Spirit," is a real and valid Baptism and cannot be repeated. This is why those that enter the Catholic Church who were baptized in another Christian denomination are never "re-baptized."

Even sin cannot take away or diminish this permanent spiritual mark. While we can certainly reject God's grace and salvation through our sinful choices, sin can never take away the reality that Christ redeemed us and we belong to Him. This is why Baptism intrinsically and necessarily calls us to conversion. Even though we may sin, the Father still sees the "fingerprint" of His Son on our soul, and He will always go to great lengths to call us back to Him. Through our repentance, He welcomes us back and restores us to life.

Only through hardness of heart and persistence in sin do we choose to reject God's salvation offered in Jesus Christ. God never revokes His promise or the inheritance we receive through Baptism. Only through free will can we reject it. The greatest suffering of those in hell is their separation from God, and the realization that they rejected the great and marvelous love that God has for them in preference for love of self.

Baptism Incorporates Us into the Body of Christ, the Church

By joining us to Christ and marking us with His seal, Baptism also incorporates us into the Mystical Body of Christ, which is the Church. We are not only united to Christ, but through Him we are united to each other as brothers and sisters of Christ who make up the People of God. In this family of the Church, we are both nourished and strengthened by Christ. As members of the Church, the "household of God," we no longer live for our own sake but we live in, through, and for Christ. We are called to make Him present to others through our words and deeds. This provides for us a new and entirely different existence, which entails certain duties, rights, and responsibilities.

> Having become a member of the Church, the person baptized belongs no longer to himself, but to him who died and rose

> for us. From now on, he is called to be subject to others, to serve them in the communion of the Church, and to "obey and submit" to the Church's leaders, holding them in respect and affection. Just as Baptism is the source of responsibilities and duties, the baptized person also enjoys rights within the Church: to receive the sacraments, to be nourished with the Word of God and to be sustained by the other spiritual helps of the Church. (CCC 1269)

Baptism opens to us the spiritual wealth and graces of the Church. It also calls us to be faithful to the teachings and commands of Christ and to be a responsible and loving member of God's chosen people, rejecting sin and striving for holiness through an ardent love for God and neighbor. We are reminded of this each time we enter a Catholic Church and make the sign of the cross with holy water. That water reminds us of our own Baptism through which we were made a new creation in Christ, and to which we must always be faithful in our daily lives. Each time we sign ourselves with holy water, we are thanking God for the gift of salvation given to us through the sacrament, and we renew the promises we made: to renounce Satan and sin, and to believe in the saving power of the Holy Trinity, which we should make present through our witness and holiness.

The Waters of Life: The Sign of Baptism

Water is one of the more common substances known to humanity. Yet in the Sacrament of Baptism, God uses this common and ordinary sign to be the means through which He communicates to us His saving grace and power. Why did God choose water? As explained earlier, water universally communicates to humanity the ideas of cleansing, washing, new life, and creation. Water communicates to us in a visible, tangible way what God is doing for us invisibly and supernaturally. God also used water throughout His unfolding plan of salvation in both the Old and New Testament to prepare His chosen people for the institution and effects of Baptism. We will now explore the full meaning of water in Baptism and how God gradually unfolded its meaning and reality throughout salvation history.

The Symbolism of Water

Water has universal meaning and significance that crosses all historical and cultural lines. It is unanimously associated with cleansing and washing, quenching of thirst, creation, and life. Water as the sign of Baptism communicates to us these very same meanings as God accomplishes His work in us and communicates to us His sanctifying grace.

Water Signifies Our Cleansing from Sin

Water is always associated with cleansing and washing. We use it to remove impurities and stains from many things. In Baptism it signifies to us that we are indeed being washed clean of all sin and impurities. The baptismal water washes away both original and personal sin and leaves the soul clean and free from the stain of sin.

Water Signifies Our New Life and Creation in Christ

Water is always associated with life. All living things depend on it, and it has often been seen as the very source of life. Where there is no water, life is impossible. Through the waters of Baptism we are brought into new life in Christ and made a new creation through Him. In the same way that winter rains transform a desert into a haven of life, so too do the waters of Baptism deliver us from spiritual death to new life and power with Christ.

Water Signifies God's Thirst for Us and Our Thirst for God

Water quenches thirst. When we are deprived of it, we pine for it, and our life quickly fades without it. This aspect of the waters of Baptism has a twofold significance. First, Baptism signifies our own thirst for God and the divine life for which He created us. Without Him our life fades and diminishes, but when we have communion with Him and share in His life and grace, we enjoy fullness of life. Through the baptismal water our thirst for God is quenched and fulfilled.

Second, Baptism signifies God's thirst for us and His desire to have communion with us. When Christ uttered the words "I thirst" from the Cross, He spoke not only about a human thirst for water, but also about a divine thirst for human souls and God's desire to share His life with us. The waters of Baptism are the floodgates of divine love, showering upon humanity the Father's tears of desire for communion with all of us.

The Waters of Baptism Are Prefigured in the Old Testament

The symbol of water in this sacrament is powerfully prefigured throughout the Old Testament. As God gradually revealed Himself and gathered His chosen people, He began to prepare them for the wonderful gift of new life. Certain events, in the light of the New Testament and teachings of Christ, foreshadow the Sacrament of Baptism.

The Waters of Creation

In both creation stories, water is present and active at the beginning of creation.

In the first story, "the earth was without form and void, and darkness was upon the face of the deep, and the spirit of God was moving over the face of the waters" (Gen. 1:1–2, RSVCE). This water, seemingly filled with the presence and power of the Holy Spirit, is identified as the source of creation and life.

In the second story of creation we see water flowing up from the ground as the source of all life:

> There was no field shrub on earth and no grass of the field had sprouted, for the Lord God had sent no rain upon the earth and there was no man to till the ground, but a stream was welling up out of the earth and watering all the surface of the ground. (Gen. 2:5–6)

Thus, water from the very beginning is seen as an important element in the first creation, and as the creative power and love of the Holy Spirit. This foreshadows the waters of Baptism, through which the power of the Holy Spirit becomes the source of the new creation in Christ, and in which we are transformed into the children of God and restored to the likeness of God in which we were created.

The Flood

We see a more explicit prefiguring of Baptism in the story of Noah and the flood. After the Fall of Adam and Eve, a great proliferation of sin overshadowed all of humanity. The world's first murder occurred when their son, Cain, killed his brother Abel. Finally, sin became so rampant that God even regretted having created man (Gen. 6:5–6). So He decided to send a great flood to destroy wicked man. However, we see that the flood was not the final punishment of humanity, but rather an act of God's mercy. For God did not destroy humanity but brought about a new beginning, born of a faithful remnant in Noah and his family.

The waters of the flood prefigure Baptism in two ways. First, they destroy evil and sin, just as the waters of Baptism destroy evil and sin within us. Second, the flood brings about a new creation, one that is born from the faith of Noah. We see a new humanity and a new earth. Noah is a type of Christ whose faithfulness to the Father brings about the ultimate redemption of humanity and all of creation. The ark prefigures the Church, in which we pass through the waters of Baptism to new life in Christ.

The Crossing of the Red Sea

The most powerful prefiguring of Baptism in the Old Testament is the Israelites crossing the Red Sea, as told in the Book of Exodus.

God's chosen people passed through the waters of the Red Sea freed from slavery to the Egyptians, and began their journey to the Promised Land. In the same way we pass through the waters of Baptism freed from slavery to sin and death, and enter freedom and new life in Christ as we begin our journey toward heaven. The waters of the Red Sea destroyed Pharaoh and his army in the same way that Baptism destroys the power of Satan and sin.

Just as the redemption of the Israelites was sealed and accomplished by passing through the waters of the Red Sea, our redemption in Christ is sealed and accomplished through Baptism.

The Crossing of the Jordan

A final prefiguring of Baptism is in the Book of Joshua when the Israelites crossed the Jordan River to enter the Promised Land. This is a powerful foreshadowing of how the Church, the New Jerusalem, will pass into the heavenly glory of the eternal Promised Land through the power of the waters of Baptism.

The Waters of Life and Grace

Baptism is the sacrament of eternal life established by Christ to free us from sin and bring us to new life. Through it we are truly born again, transformed by the power of the Holy Spirit to become sons and daughters of God. Baptism fulfills the Father's loving plan of salvation, freeing His chosen people from the bondage of sin and death and restoring them to the very life of God. The splendor of the Sacrament of Baptism, in the plan of the Father and the life of the Church, is beautifully presented to us in the blessing of the baptismal water:

> Father, you give us grace through sacramental signs, which tell us of the wonders of your unseen power. In baptism we use your gift of water, which you have made a rich symbol of the grace you give us in this sacrament. At the very dawn of creation your Spirit breathed on the waters, making them the wellspring of all holiness. The waters of the great flood you made a sign of the waters of baptism, that make an end of sin and a new beginning of goodness.
>
> Through the waters of the Red Sea you led Israel out of slavery, to be an image of God's holy people, set free from sin by baptism. In the waters of the Jordan your Son was baptized by John and anointed with the Spirit. Your Son willed that water and blood should flow from his side as he hung upon the cross.
>
> After his resurrection he told his disciples: "Go out and teach all nations, baptizing them in the name of the Father, and of the Son, and of the Holy Spirit." Father, look now with love upon your Church, and unseal for her the fountain of baptism. By the power of the Spirit give to the water of this font the grace of your Son. You created man in your own likeness: cleanse him from sin in a new birth to innocence by water and the Spirit.
>
> We ask you, Father, with your Son to send the Holy Spirit upon the water of this font. May all who are buried with Christ in the death of baptism rise also with him to newness of life. We ask this through Christ our Lord. Amen.

May the grace and power of Baptism bring us to eternal life and empower us to be a people of faith, hope, and love.

From the Catechism: Key Words to Know

BAPTISM: The first of the seven sacraments and the "door" which gives access to the other sacraments. Baptism is the first and chief sacrament of forgiveness of sins because it unites us with Christ, who died for our sins and rose for our justification. Baptism, Confirmation, and the Eucharist constitute the "sacraments of initiation," by which a believer receives the remission of original and personal sin, begins a new life in Christ and the Holy Spirit, and is incorporated into the Church, the Body of Christ. The rite of Baptism consists in immersing the candidate in water or pouring water on the head, while pronouncing the invocation of the Most Holy Trinity: the Father, the Son, and the Holy Spirit (977, 1213 ff.; 1275, 1278).

CONCUPISCENCE: Human appetites, or desires, that remain disordered due to the temporal consequences of original sin, which remain even after Baptism and produce an inclination to sin (1264, 1426, 2515).

HOPE: The theological virtue by which we desire and expect from God both eternal life and the grace we need to attain it (1817).

CHARITY: The theological virtue by which we love God above all things for His own sake, and we love our neighbor as ourselves for the love of God (1822).

SACRAMENTAL CHARACTER: An indelible spiritual mark which is the permanent effect of the Sacraments of Baptism, Confirmation, and Holy Orders, by which a person is given a new, permanent configuration to Christ and a specific standing in the Church. The reception of these sacraments is never repeated (1272, 1304, 1582).

Chapter 15

The Sacrament of Confirmation

Reading the Catechism: Paragraphs 1285–1321

> But you will receive power when the Holy Spirit comes upon you, and you will be my witnesses in Jerusalem, throughout Judea and Samaria, and to the ends of the earth.
>
> —Acts 1:8

The Sacrament of **Confirmation** seals or "confirms" us in the grace and power of the Holy Spirit and commissions us to go out into the world to be the witnesses of Christ to all the nations.

It is very closely united to Baptism because it completes and confirms all that we received in that sacrament. The grace and power of the Holy Spirit received in Baptism is given to us in superabundance through Confirmation.

Thus, Confirmation is our own "personal" Pentecost, in which the Holy Spirit descends upon us, fills us with an overflowing presence of His gifts, and calls us forth to **evangelization** and service in the building of the kingdom of God.

Scriptural Foundation

Confirmation, as a separate sacrament of the outpouring of the Holy Spirit, is seen clearly in the ministry of the Apostles in the Acts of the Apostles:

> Now when the Apostles in Jerusalem heard that Samaria had accepted the word of God, they sent them Peter and John, who went down and prayed for them, that they might receive the Holy Spirit, for it had not yet fallen upon any of them; they had only been baptized in the name of the Lord Jesus. Then they laid hands on them and they received the Holy Spirit.
>
> (Acts 8:14–17)

Notice in this passage that Confirmation is a separate sacrament from Baptism, in that those disciples in Samaria had already been baptized. However, the Holy Spirit had not yet fallen upon them, so Peter and John laid hands upon them so they would receive the Holy Spirit.

Calling down the Holy Spirit upon those who have been baptized is a separate sacramental action. This is why Confirmation is called the "sacrament of the Holy Spirit," because it is through this powerful sacrament that one is sealed with His gifts and power.

In Baptism we are conformed to Christ, and in Confirmation we are marked with the seal of the Holy Spirit. When the Father looks upon us after Confirmation, He sees the image of His Son and the seal of the Spirit. *Confirmation completes our union with the life and mystery of the Holy Trinity.* We belong totally and unconditionally to the Triune God!

The Effects of Confirmation

Confirmation completes baptismal grace. That is, everything that is given to us in Baptism is now given to us in superabundance through the outpouring of the Holy Spirit. In Baptism we initially receive the Holy Spirit and become children of God and are intimately united to Him. In Confirmation, the presence and power of the Holy Spirit is now overflowing within our souls. Our union with Christ is also strengthened, and through the power and grace of the Holy Spirit, we are called forth to witness Christ to the world.

The Gifts of the Holy Spirit Are Given in Superabundance

The first and greatest effect of Confirmation is that the seven **gifts of the Holy Spirit** are given in superabundance. Through this sacrament, we are overshadowed by the Holy Spirit who comes upon us in the same way that He came upon the Apostles at Pentecost. The gifts of the Holy Spirit well up in our souls as an eternal fountain of grace and powerfully help us live the Christian life, striving to build the kingdom of God through word and action. These gifts are the tools and foundation blocks of the Christian life.

Wisdom

The gift of Wisdom is a sharing in God's vision for our life and His will for us and the Church. It is literally seeing things as God sees them and knowing His plan. It allows us to become instruments of God's will for others and the Church.

Understanding

The gift of Understanding is a God-given insight to see the truth about God's presence in the world and the meaning of our faith.

Counsel

The gift of Counsel enables us to make the best moral decisions in our life of faith and on our journey to heaven. We especially need the gift of Counsel in our present day to make our way through the fogginess of moral relativism and indifference that surrounds us in our culture.

Fortitude

Fortitude is a gift of the Spirit that, even in times of fear and difficulty, enables us to bravely speak out in faith when called upon and to stand up for what is right and just. As the disciples experienced at Pentecost, Fortitude enables us to witness to the Gospel of Christ especially when it may be frightening or difficult.

Knowledge

Enhancing what we know naturally through reason, the gift of Knowledge reveals to us the truths about God and about the human person so that we are able to love God with all our hearts and love our neighbor as ourselves.

Piety (Reverence)

Through the gift of Piety the Holy Spirit helps us to be people of faith and prayer and be aware of God's holy presence.

Fear of the Lord (Awe)

The gift of Fear of the Lord instills in us a healthy fear or awe of God's power, majesty, and justice. It enhances our understanding of the greatness of God and all He is and all that He deserves from us.

These seven gifts are given to all of us, first through Baptism and in superabundance through Confirmation, allowing us to share in Christ's mission and be His faithful witnesses in all times and circumstances. We must always rely on the powerful presence of these gifts as we journey with Christ in this world.

We Are Called to Be Witnesses of Christ to the Ends of the Earth

Confirmation is our own personal Pentecost. The Holy Spirit overshadows us with His presence, power, and gifts. Like the Apostles we should step forward and proclaim the Gospel from the rooftops. This is the very heart of this sacrament. Sealed with the gifts of the Holy Spirit, we should become Christ's witnesses, spreading the Gospel to the very ends of the earth and building up the kingdom of God. Christ Himself called the Apostles and us to this very mission through the Sacrament of Confirmation.

> "But you will receive power when the Holy Spirit comes upon you, and you will be my witnesses in Jerusalem, throughout Judea and Samaria, and to the ends of the earth." (Acts 1:8)

Pentecost fulfilled Christ's prophecy. The Church began her life and mission the day when more than three thousand were baptized, and the Apostles did truly preach to all the nations.

Each of us is called by the power of that same Spirit to bring the Gospel to the very ends of the earth. That may not be another country or a far away land. It may be our own families, the workplace, school, the political process, friends, acquaintances, or the person sitting next to us on a flight. We are called to witness the Gospel of Christ in every place we go. Sometimes it is through what we say, sometimes through what we do. Sometimes we witness simply by being faithful to our calling. Confirmation calls us out of ourselves, out of our own upper room, to be the Apostles in our day and age.

Many of the great saints who witnessed Christ and even gave their lives for Him were ordinary men and women who, filled with the grace and power of the Holy Spirit, left a lasting impression upon us all. Each of us is called by this sacrament to be that witness. For some of us it may be in really big ways, but for many of us it will be in little ways or little acts of charity like praying before a meal at McDonalds, or simply not being afraid to let our life of faith be known.

Never underestimate the great things God can do through us in the little ways we are faithful to Him. When we are confirmed we accept Christ's challenge to be His witness to the whole world. We are not to be afraid because we are given the grace and power of the Holy Spirit to guide and strengthen us as we journey in faith, working to consecrate the world to God through Christ.

We Are Forever Sealed in the Presence and Power of the Holy Spirit

Like Baptism, Confirmation imprints a permanent mark or seal upon the soul. In Baptism our soul was shaped or conformed to Christ forever, and in Confirmation our soul forever bears the mark of the power of the Holy Spirit. This mark clothes us with power and enables us to walk forever in the grace and consolation of the divine Helper, the Holy Spirit. Thus, Confirmation completes the image of the Trinity within us. Not only is our initiation into the Church completed, but our initiation into the intimate life of the Holy Trinity is also completed. Forever we are children of the Father, conformed to the Son, and sealed with the Spirit.

The Signs of the Sacrament of Confirmation

There are two powerful signs of the Sacrament of Confirmation, both signifying and communicating the power and presence of the Holy Spirit.

Laying On of Hands

During the celebration of Confirmation, the bishop extends his hands over the people to be confirmed as he says the prayer (**epiclesis**) calling down the power of the Holy Spirit. Specifically, he calls for the outpouring of the seven gifts of the Holy Spirit, who is at the heart of the sacrament:

> All-powerful God, Father of our Lord Jesus Christ,
> by water and the Holy Spirit
> you freed Your sons and daughters from sin
> and gave them new life.

Send Your Holy Spirit upon them
to be their helper and guide.
Give them the Spirit of Wisdom and Understanding,
the Spirit of Right Judgment and Courage,
the Spirit of Knowledge and Reverence.
Fill them with the Spirit of Wonder and Awe in Your presence.
We ask this through Christ our Lord.
Amen.

Anointing with Chrism

The **anointing** or sealing with sacred **chrism** on the forehead follows immediately after the laying on of hands. Sacred chrism is one of the three oils used in sacramental life, possessing the characteristic of consecrating power. The anointing with chrism consecrates, or sets aside, a person or place as belonging to God forever. When they are baptized, infants are anointed with chrism as a sign of their union with Christ forever. A man who is ordained a priest or bishop is anointed with chrism as being consecrated and conformed to Christ the High Priest forever. When a new church is built, the bishop anoints the altar and walls to consecrate it to God as a place of worship. In Confirmation, we are anointed with the sacred chrism as being consecrated forever in the power and presence of the Holy Spirit. This anointing is the Father clothing us with the power of the Holy Spirit, and at the same time commissioning us to be Christ's witness to the ends of the earth. The anointing with chrism is both an act of consecration and an act of commissioning. Saint Ambrose speaks powerfully of this anointing received in Confirmation:

> Recall then that you have received the spiritual seal, the spirit of wisdom and understanding, the spirit of right judgment and courage, the spirit of knowledge and reverence, the spirit of holy fear in God's presence. Guard what you have received. God the Father has marked you with his sign; Christ the Lord has confirmed you and has placed his pledge, the Spirit, in your hearts. (De Mysteriis, 7, 42 PL 16, 402–403)

Who Can Receive Confirmation?

Strictly speaking, any person who is baptized may receive Confirmation, and the age at which we receive it has varied in different times and places throughout the Church's history. In the Latin rite, the age of discretion or reason has been given as the minimum age for the reception of Confirmation, which would mean the age of seven. Since it completes Christian initiation and calls us to "Christian maturity" and "full and active participation in the Church," many dioceses delay receiving the sacrament until junior high or high school age following adequate preparation and catechesis for the sacrament. However, recently some bishops have changed the age of Confirmation to seven. Either practice is theologically acceptable. It is ultimately up to the local bishop to determine the appropriate age of Confirmation in his diocese.

However, adults and children seven and older who are becoming Catholic through RCIA and RCIC, are confirmed immediately after they are baptized. If they have been baptized in another Christian tradition, they are confirmed after making an Act of Reception into the Catholic Church.

The Minister of Confirmation

The ordinary minister of Confirmation is the bishop, but he may delegate the authority to priests to administer the sacrament if necessary. In the danger of death, any priest may administer Confirmation even without delegation from the bishop.

In conclusion, graces begun in us at Baptism reach their fullness through the Sacrament of Confirmation. Following the example of the Apostles at Pentecost, we are called to go out and be witnesses to the world. The fire of the Holy Spirit burning within us should shine forth to all so we may use the gifts God has given us in our own way, to build the kingdom of God.

From the Catechism: Key Words to Know

CONFIRMATION: One of the ensemble of the Sacraments of Initiation into the Church, together with Baptism and Eucharist. Confirmation completes the grace of Baptism by a special outpouring of the gifts of the Holy Spirit, which seal or "confirm" the baptized in union with Christ and equip them for active participation in the worship and apostolic life of the Church (1285).

EVANGELIZATION: The proclamation of Christ and His Gospel (from the Greek *evangelion,* meaning "good news") by word and the testimony of life, in fulfillment of Christ's command (905; cf. 861).

GIFTS OF THE HOLY SPIRIT: Permanent dispositions that make us docile to follow the promptings of the Holy Spirit. The traditional list of seven gifts of the Spirit is derived from Isaiah 11:1–3: wisdom, understanding, knowledge, counsel, piety, fortitude, and fear of the Lord (1830, 1831).

EPICLESIS: The prayer petitioning God to send the Holy Spirit so that the offerings at the Eucharist may become the Body and Blood of Christ and thus the faithful, by receiving them, may themselves become a living offering to God. In every sacrament, the prayer asking for the sanctifying power of God's Holy Spirit is an "epiclesis" (1105, 1127).

ANOINTING: A symbol of the Holy Spirit, whose "anointing" of Jesus as Messiah fulfilled the prophecies of the Old Testament. Christ (in Hebrew, *Messiah*) means the one "anointed" by the Holy Spirit. Anointing is the sacramental sign of Confirmation, called Chrismation in the Churches of the East. Anointings form part of the liturgical rites of the catechumenate and of the Sacraments of Baptism and Holy Orders (695).

CHRISM: Perfumed oil, consecrated by the bishop, which signifies the gift of the Holy Spirit. Chrism is used for consecration in the Sacraments of Baptism, Confirmation, and Holy Orders (1241, 1289, 1291, 1294).

Chapter 16

The Sacrament of the Eucharist

Reading the Catechism: Paragraphs 1322–1419

> For I received from the Lord what I also handed on to you, that the Lord Jesus, on the night he was handed over, took bread, and, after he had given thanks, broke it and said, "This is my body that is for you. Do this in remembrance of me." In the same way also the cup, after supper, saying, "This cup is the new covenant in my blood. Do this, as often as you drink it, in remembrance of me." For as often as you eat this bread and drink the cup, you proclaim the death of the Lord until he comes.
>
> —1 Corinthians 11:23–26

The **Eucharist** is truly at the very heart of Catholicism. It sets Catholics apart from all the other Christian denominations. In fact, it is so important in the life of the Catholic Church that it is called the "source and summit of the Christian life."

Why is it so important, so adored, and so central to what it means to be a Catholic? The Catholic Church teaches and believes that the bread and wine are literally changed into Jesus Himself. At every Mass Jesus makes Himself really and totally present to us in this Most Blessed Sacrament. The Eucharist is not a symbol of Christ but *is* Christ!

How can what looks and tastes like bread and wine be Christ? It is really a rather simple miracle for almighty God to perform (which we will address later). When Jesus said, "I am with you always, until the end of the age" (Mt. 28:20), the reality is that He wasn't kidding. As we will see, it is Jesus Himself who commands us to eat His flesh and drink His blood so that we may have eternal life. It is Jesus who gives us His flesh and blood to eat and drink at the Last Supper on the night before He died on the Cross. In fact, the Old Testament prepares God's chosen people for the gift of God present in the Eucharist, which is at the heart of the New Covenant established by Christ and is at the very heart of what it means to be His follower.

This chapter will lead us through how the Church has always believed that the Eucharist is really and truly Christ. It was not until Martin Luther and the Protestant Reformation that anyone ever believed it was merely a "symbol" or memorial of Christ. The belief that it was a symbol went squarely against more than fifteen hundred years of Christian belief and practice. Today, many Christian denominations have altogether abandoned the Eucharist as a part of the Christian walk.

We will also show that the Eucharist is scriptural, explicitly taught and practiced by Jesus, and was at the very heart of the New Testament Church. We will explain how it was foreshadowed in and fulfills the Old Testament.

We will see how this sacrament is the most explicit and important way in which we participate in and live out the New and Eternal Covenant established by Christ. We will come to understand how through the Eucharist we receive the very life and presence of God.

A Hard but True Teaching

Let's begin with the words and teachings of Christ Himself by turning to the Scriptures. In the sixth chapter of John, Jesus teaches about the Eucharist in a long and elaborate passage. Jesus teaches His disciples more clearly and more comprehensively on the Eucharist than any other doctrine. We do not find such an elaborate and clear teaching from Christ on the Trinity. Nor do we find one from Christ on the nature of who He is. Yet, all Christian churches agree on those two doctrinal points. But Jesus gives a very passionate and painstakingly clear teaching on the Eucharist in the Gospel of John. We will look carefully at everything Jesus has to say regarding this important doctrine (see Jn. 6:22–71).

First, Jesus takes us back to the Book of Exodus in the Old Testament, where the Israelites are journeying through the desert. Remember, they had been freed from Egyptian slavery and were journeying toward the Promised Land. They grumbled against Moses when they became hungry, so God promised to send them bread from heaven. The next morning they awoke, and there was bread called manna scattered over the ground for them to eat, nourishing them for their journey toward the Promised Land. God did this for His people throughout their pilgrimage. Now Jesus said, "Your ancestors ate the manna in the desert, but they died." His Father had sent the bread that came from heaven, yet in the end the people still perished. But Jesus promises to send bread from heaven so that they can eat and *not* die.

Take a moment and count how many times Jesus says that *He* is the bread that comes down from heaven or that *He* is the bread of life. He says it twelve times in the passage! He is being emphatic about this reality. It is He who will become this bread that will give eternal life.

But Jesus takes it a radical step further. He says that this bread is "my flesh for the life of the world," and that "Whoever eats my flesh and drinks my blood will have eternal life, and I will raise him on the last day. For my flesh is true food and my blood is true drink." In fact, four different times in this passage Jesus commands us to eat His flesh and drink His blood in order to have eternal life. He even invites us to literally "feed on" Him.

Jesus uses precise and graphic language in John's Gospel, teaching us that He is the new manna, the new bread that comes down from heaven. He commands us to eat His flesh and drink His blood, and explains that having eternal life is conditional upon eating His flesh and drinking His blood. Unlike the Israelites who ate the manna and died, those who partake of the Body and Blood of Jesus will not die, but will have eternal life.

Of course, this was very scandalous to those who heard it. Imagine yourself present and listening to those words. Many became angry and confused and said, "This is a hard teaching, who can accept it?" Now Jesus' response is so important here. Many Protestants will say that Jesus was just teaching symbolically and not literally. It is true that many times Jesus teaches symbolically through parables and other stories. But in each of those instances when there is confusion or doubt, Jesus always taught the true meaning of the story. Jesus does no such thing here. He says, "The words I have spoken to you are spirit and life."

Jesus knew that many did not believe and as a result of this teaching He would ultimately be betrayed. Many Bible scholars believe that Jesus' teaching on the Eucharist was the final cause for Judas to betray Him.

Finally, Scripture tells us that many of Jesus' disciples left and no longer followed Him. Do we see Jesus chasing after them saying, "No, stop, I really didn't mean that"? No, because what He taught is the truth. No excuses, no further explanation. Instead, He turns to the Twelve and says, "Do you also want to leave?" Peter leads the Apostles in the truth and responds, "Master, to whom shall we go? You have the words of eternal life."

Jesus wasn't joking. He wasn't teaching symbolically. What He was teaching was so important and so true that He risked everything: His whole mission,

His reputation, all of His disciples and Apostles, and ultimately His life. That is how important and true the Eucharist was to Jesus, and that is why it is always at the heart of His Body, the Church.

The Last Supper

Another passage in which we see Jesus speaking explicitly about the Eucharist was during the **Last Supper** on the night before He embraced the Cross. The Last Supper was the celebration of the Jewish Passover meal in which all of Israel was commemorating their deliverance from Egypt. In the Gospels of Matthew, Mark, and Luke, Jesus teaches us about the Eucharist during the Last Supper when He gives us the Eucharistic sacrifice of His Body and Blood:

> Then he took the bread, said the blessing, broke it, and gave it to them, saying, "This is my body, which will be given for you; do this in memory of me." And likewise the cup after they had eaten, saying, "This cup is the new covenant in my blood, which will be shed for you." (Lk. 22:19–20)

Jesus does not say, "This is a symbol of my body" or "This is like a cup of my blood," but rather, "This *is* my body" and "This *is* my blood." It is very clear that the bread and wine literally become the actual Body and Blood of Christ.

If it is the Body and Blood of Jesus, why do Catholics believe that it is Christ *totally* present? We believe this because Jesus said in John 6 that *He* is the bread of life. It is His whole Person and divinity that is given to us.

In addition, in the Semitic world in which He lived and taught, the blood is the life-force, the essence of a person or animal. This is why blood is so important in sacrifice and other Jewish practices. The same applies in our own culture, but to a lesser degree. Those who become "blood brothers" are pledging their whole selves to each other. If Jesus is giving to us His Body and Blood, He is giving to us His entire self: His Body, Blood, Soul, and Divinity.

Another important aspect of the Last Supper is Jesus' injunction, "Do this in memory of me." He is commanding His Apostles to continue and repeat the actions of the Last Supper. Just as the Jewish Passover is the commemoration of the Israelites' deliverance, the Eucharistic sacrifice is the constant memorial of Jesus' new and eternal sacrifice on the Cross for the forgiveness of sins. With this command, Jesus gave the Apostles authority and power to change bread and wine into Himself, so that He could be continuously present to His people, and that His sacrifice on the Cross could be constantly re-presented and made efficacious until the end of time.

Thus, every Catholic Mass is a memorial of Christ's life, death, and Resurrection, and it is also a participation in the very same sacrifice that Christ made on the Cross. It is not a re-crucifixion of Christ, but the same sacrifice miraculously made present again for the atonement of our sins. At Mass, we are in all actuality at the foot of the Cross, adoring, asking forgiveness, and offering ourselves to Christ who loved us even unto death. This was Christ's command to His Church, and the Church has faithfully followed it for over two thousand years.

Finally, at the Last Supper, Jesus associates the chalice of His Blood with the New Covenant. His death on the Cross seals and begins a new relationship between God and man. The Eucharist is an essential part of our participation in this New Covenant. Eating the Body and drinking the Blood of Christ is the most important and efficacious way in which we fulfill and participate in the New Covenant that God has made with man.

It should not surprise us that God asks us to consume His sacrifice. Whenever God established a new covenant in the Old Testament, it involved "eating" laws. For example, the first covenant with Adam and Eve allowed them to eat any and all of the fruit in the garden, especially from the tree of life, but it did not allow them to eat of the fruit from the tree of knowledge of good and evil. The covenant with Moses was full of very detailed eating laws, which are still a part of the Jewish faith today. Central to participating in the New and Everlasting Covenant established by Christ is His command to eat His Body and drink His Blood in this Holy Sacrifice.

Christ's Church humbly remains faithful to this day, and honors Christ by centering all of its liturgical and sacramental life around this great mystery. The Eucharist is truly the "source and the summit of Christian life" (*Lumen gentium*, 11; CCC 1324).

The Eucharist in the Old Testament

To better understand the Eucharist and its central role in the New Covenant and God's entire plan of salvation, we need to see how it was foreshadowed in the Old Testament and how it fulfills and completes many parts of these sacred writings.

From the beginning God gradually prepared His people for the gift of the Eucharist. When we see this gift in light of the Old Testament, the importance and significance of this great sacrament becomes clear.

The Eucharist Is the Fruit of Christ, the New Tree of Life

As we saw in chapter four, after the first sin in the Garden of Eden, Adam and Eve were banned from eating from the tree of life whose fruit gave eternal life. Christ, through His perfect obedience to the Father's will in the Garden of Gethsemane, not only became the New Adam, but by embracing the Cross became the new tree of life whose fruit we eat in the Eucharist so that we once again may have eternal life.

The Offering of the Priest-King Melchizedek, Genesis 14:17–20

Melchizedek prefigures the Eucharistic sacrifice of Christ, who will be the Priest of the Most High God and will offer a sacrifice of Himself under the appearances of bread and wine.

The Passover Lamb and the Lamb of God

As we saw in chapter seven, Christ is the new Passover Lamb. Eating the flesh of this "Lamb" brings about the Passover from the "death of the firstborn," Adam, and frees us from sin. Just as the Israelites were commanded to eat the flesh of the Passover Lamb, we are commanded to eat the flesh of Christ, the new Passover Lamb. As the Passover was commemorated and placed at the head of the Jewish calendar, the Mass as the Feast of the Lamb of God is the "source and summit of the Christian life."

The Manna in the Desert and Jesus as the Bread of Life: Exodus 16:4–36/Jn. 6:22–71

Finally, as seen in John's Bread of Life discourse, Jesus Himself is the new bread that comes down from heaven and gives us life eternal. As the manna nourished and strengthened the Israelites in their journey to the Promised Land, the Eucharist nourishes and strengthens the Pilgrim Church as she journeys toward heaven.

The Eucharist in the New Testament

The Eucharist has a central place in the Church of the New Testament as well. During the first sixty years after the death and Resurrection of Christ, the New Testament gives us ample evidence that the celebration of the paschal sacrifice was a central and essential part of early Christianity.

One of the most amazing Eucharistic events comes at the end of Luke's Gospel. It happens on the very day of Christ's Resurrection, as two disciples were walking on the Road to Emmaus from Jerusalem. The two were joined by Christ, whom they did not recognize. He walked with them for the entire journey, explained the Scriptures to them, and showed how Christ fulfilled all that Moses and the prophets spoke of concerning the Messiah. Yet they did not know they were talking with Jesus. At the end of the journey they invited this "stranger" to stay with them. It was not until they witnessed His breaking of the bread, the celebration of the Eucharist, that Jesus was finally revealed to them.

> And it happened that, while he was with them at table, he took bread, said the blessing, broke it, and gave it to them. With that their eyes were opened and they recognized him. (Lk. 24:30–31)

Two points are crucial here. First, the disciples only recognize Jesus after He gives them the Eucharist. This shows that the fullness of the mystery and identity of Jesus is revealed to us in the Eucharist. Through receiving Jesus in the Most Blessed Sacrament we come to know Him and experience His presence on our journey through life.

Second, in choosing the Eucharistic meal to reveal Himself, Jesus underscored its importance in the life of the Church. He celebrated the Eucharistic sacrifice on the very day of His Resurrection, which demonstrates its necessity as the center and source of our relationship with Christ. He desires above all things to come into communion with us in the Holy Sacrifice of the Mass.

More evidence for the development and importance of the Eucharistic meal in the early Church is seen in the Acts of the Apostles where Luke explains, "They devoted themselves to the teaching of the Apostles and to the communal life, to the breaking of the bread and to the prayers" (Acts 2:42).

We clearly see that the "breaking of the bread," which was the earliest form of the celebration of the Eucharistic sacrifice and meal, was one of the central aspects of the early Church.

We have seen how Jesus celebrated the Eucharist with His disciples and how it began to develop as the summit of the early Christian Church, where the disciples of Jesus came to recognize Him and be in His presence. However, the most explicit example of the celebration of the Eucharist in the New Testament Church comes from the teaching and instruction of Paul in his first letter to the Corinthians. He wrote this letter to the Church in Corinth for two important reasons.

First, Paul had been told that there were many divisions among the members of the Church in Corinth, so he wrote to dispel those divisions and teach that there is only one faith that comes to them from Christ through the Apostles.

Second, Paul desired to specifically correct abuses and confusion that had arisen in the celebration of the Eucharist. Paul gives his guidance and teaching because the Eucharist was obviously a central part of the Church. He wanted the Eucharist to be celebrated rightly and with purity of heart.

In this letter there are three key passages concerning the Eucharist. The first is in chapter ten where Paul warns against false idols and false worship, and he proclaims the true worship given to us by Christ Himself is the Eucharist:

> Therefore, my beloved, avoid idolatry. I am speaking as to sensible people; judge for yourselves what I am saying. The cup of blessing that we bless, is it not a participation in the blood of Christ? The bread that we break, is it not a participation in the body of Christ? Because the loaf of bread is one, we, though many, are one body, for we all partake of the one loaf. Look at Israel according to the flesh; are not those who eat the sacrifices participants in the altar? So what am I saying? That meat sacrificed to idols is anything? Or that an idol is anything? No, I mean that what they sacrifice, (they sacrifice) to demons, not to God, and I do not want you to become participants with demons. You cannot drink the cup of the Lord and also the cup of demons. You cannot partake of the table of the Lord and of the table of demons. (1 Cor. 10:14–21)

This passage clearly illustrates that the Eucharist was certainly celebrated by the Church in Corinth, and that Paul believed that the bread and wine were truly the Body and Blood of Christ.

The second passage is from chapter eleven, and here we find Paul teaching and reaffirming the Tradition of the celebration of the Lord's Supper, which he has handed on to them from Christ. Paul is giving a clear description of the celebration of the Eucharist:

> For I received from the Lord what I also handed on to you, that the Lord Jesus, on the night he was handed over, took bread, and, after he had given thanks, broke it and said, "This is my body that is for you. Do this in remembrance of me." In the same way also the cup, after supper, saying, "This cup is the new covenant in my blood. Do this, as often as you drink it, in remembrance of me." For as often as you eat this bread and drink the cup, you proclaim the death of the Lord until he comes. (1 Cor. 11:23–26)

Paul's teaching distinctly shows that the New Testament Church was faithfully carrying out Christ's command to "do this in memory of me," and that it was the central aspect of the Church's worship and life.

Also in chapter eleven, Paul instructs the Corinthians not to come and receive the Eucharist unworthily:

> Therefore whoever eats the bread or drinks the cup of the Lord unworthily will have to answer for the body and blood of the Lord. A person should examine himself, and so eat the bread and drink the cup. For anyone who eats and drinks without discerning the body, eats and drinks judgment on himself.(1 Cor. 11:27–29)

These are very strong words that Paul uses. First, they again show his belief that the Eucharist is the Body and Blood of Christ, since anyone who approaches the altar unworthily "sins against the Body and Blood of the Lord." Second, this teaching of Paul stands as the foundation for the Church's teaching that those who are in the state of serious sin, or who have separated themselves from the Church, cannot receive Holy Communion.

This unambiguous evidence shows that in the early years of the Church there was a clear belief in the Eucharist as truly the Body and Blood of Christ, and that the celebration of this Paschal Mystery stood at the center of the New Testament Church's worship and life.

Early Church Fathers

We also see in the writings of the early Church fathers that the Christians of the early Church, only a mere twenty to one hundred years after the death of the last Apostle, believed in the real presence of Christ in the Eucharist, and that the celebration of the Mass was at the very heart and center of the Church's life and worship. Here are a few powerful examples.

> I have no taste for corruptible food nor for the pleasures of this life. I desire the Bread of God, which is the Flesh of Jesus Christ, who was the seed of David; and for drink I desire His Blood, which is love incorruptible.
>
> **Saint Ignatius of Antioch,**
> ***Letter to the Philadelphians*, AD 110**

> They abstain from the Eucharist and from prayer, because they do not confess that the Eucharist is the Flesh of our Savior Jesus Christ, Flesh which suffered for our sins and which the Father, in His goodness, raised up again.
>
> **Saint Ignatius of Antioch,**
> ***Letter to the Smyrnaens*, AD 110**

> We call this food Eucharist, and no one else is permitted to partake of it, except one who believes our teaching to be true and who has been washed in the washing which is for the remission of sins and for regeneration [i.e., has received baptism] and is thereby living as Christ enjoined. For not as common bread nor common drink do we receive these; but since Jesus Christ our Savior was made incarnate by the word of God and had both flesh and blood for our salvation, so too, as we have been taught, the food which has been made into the Eucharist by the Eucharistic prayer set down by him, and by

the change of which our blood and flesh is nurtured, is both the flesh and the blood of that incarnated Jesus.

Saint Justin Martyr,
***First Apology* 66, AD 150**

If the Lord were from other than the Father, how could he rightly take bread, which is of the same creation as our own, and confess it to be his body and affirm that the mixture in the cup is his blood?

Saint Irenaeus,
***Against Heresies* 4:33–32, AD 169**

He has declared the cup, a part of creation, to be his own blood, from which he causes our blood to flow; and the bread, a part of creation, he has established as his own body, from which he gives increase unto our bodies. When, therefore, the mixed cup [wine and water] and the baked bread receives the Word of God and becomes the Eucharist, the body of Christ, and from these the substance of our flesh is increased and supported, how can they say that the flesh is not capable of receiving the gift of God, which is eternal life—flesh which is nourished by the body and blood of the Lord, and is in fact a member of him?

Saint Irenaeus,
***Against Heresies* 5:2, AD 186**

"Eat my flesh," [Jesus] says, "and drink my blood." The Lord supplies us with these intimate nutrients, he delivers over his flesh and pours out his blood, and nothing is lacking for the growth of his children.

Clement of Alexandria,
***The Instructor of Children* 1:6:43:3, AD 191**

[T]here is not a soul that can at all procure salvation, except it believe whilst it is in the flesh, so true is it that the flesh is the very condition on which salvation hinges. And since the soul is, in consequence of its salvation, chosen to the service of God, it is the flesh which actually renders it capable of such

> service. The flesh, indeed, is washed [in baptism], in order that the soul may be cleansed . . . the flesh is shadowed with the imposition of hands [in confirmation], that the soul also may be illuminated by the Spirit; the flesh feeds [in the Eucharist] on the body and blood of Christ, that the soul likewise may be filled with God.
>
> **Tertullian,**
> ***The Resurrection of the Dead*, AD 210**

Transubstantiation

For Catholics and non-Catholics alike, one of the major stumbling blocks concerning the **real presence** of Christ in the Eucharist is that it seems impossible that He could really and substantially be present when it looks, tastes, smells, and feels like bread and wine. It is a mystery that goes against what our senses tell us. Our senses perceive what appears to be bread and wine, when in fact, the substance itself has been changed from bread and wine into Christ Himself. **Transubstantiation** means "change of substance."

In fact, this mystery is more comprehensible than the mysteries of the Trinity, the Incarnation, or the Resurrection of Christ, and is a relatively simple miracle for us to understand. Let's look at how this happens.

To better understand this doctrine, we need to do a little philosophy. We need to delve into some *metaphysics*, or the study of being. Everything that exists has what we call its substance and its accidents, or properties.

For example, the substance of an apple is what it is objectively—an apple, or its "appleness"—apart from its individual characteristics. The accidents of the apple are things like size, color, shape, taste, and texture. If I am holding an apple, the substance is an apple, and the accidents would be red, round, sweet, crunchy, and smooth. Now, it is possible to change the accidents of a substance while the substance remains the same. If I put the apple in a blender, the accidents change, but the substance remains the same. It is still an apple, but now it is liquid or yellow.

Let's take another example. How about water? Here is a substance that remains the same while the accidents change quite drastically. It can be a liquid, solid, or gas, but regardless, it remains water.

Now that we have a better understanding of the accidents and substance of an object, we can comprehend what God does in the Eucharist, through the power of the Holy Spirit. Instead of the accidents changing in the bread, *it is the substance that changes*. When the priest says the words of Jesus over the bread, "This is my body," the Holy Spirit suspends (or keeps the same) the accidents and appearance of bread, but changes the substance from bread to Christ Himself. The very substance of the Eucharist is Jesus, although the accidents remain the same. We see the appearances of bread and wine—its color, taste, and texture—while the reality of the substance is truly the Son of God, who chooses such a humble means to present Himself to us and come in our hearts to dwell. Not a hard miracle for God to perform, but it really throws our minds for a loop!

Now we need to do some *epistemology*, or the study of knowledge. How do we come to know things? Well, our intellect, or mind, is part of our soul. It interacts with the physical world, gathering information through our senses. This is how we come to know things. Our mind relies on our senses of sight, touch, taste, smell, and hearing to know and understand the physical world. Our senses, however, only perceive the accidents of a substance. When my mind perceives furry, small, four legs, and bark, it knows the object as "dog." Our minds completely rely on the accidents of a substance to know what it is.

However, in the Eucharist, God has changed the substance of bread and wine into Jesus, but has kept all the accidents the same. Thus, our senses are still telling our mind that the Eucharist is bread and wine, which is all that our senses can perceive. This is where we must make that intellectual and spiritual "leap of faith." Christ, who guides us into union with Himself, has revealed through His own words and the teaching of the Church that He is truly present in the Eucharist. So while our senses are screaming to our intellect that what we hold in our hands is ordinary bread, our faith tells us that God has changed the substance to Christ Himself.

Saint Thomas Aquinas wrote a beautiful depiction of this mystery in a much-loved traditional hymn of the Church, the *Tantum Ergo*:

> Down in adoration falling,
> This great sacrament we hail.
> Over ancient forms of worship,
> Newer rites of Grace prevail:
> Faith will tell us Christ is present,
> When our human senses fail.

Consider also two finer points regarding transubstantiation. First, Christ's substantial presence is totally dependent on the accidents of bread or wine being present. Once the accidents have ceased to exist, through digestion or dilution, Christ's substantial presence also ceases to exist. When the Eucharist is preserved, and the accidents remain, Christ's sacramental and substantial presence remains. This is why we can come and be with Jesus when we pray before the tabernacle, where the Most Blessed Sacrament is kept in the church, or in adoration, when the Body of Christ is exposed to be adored.

Second, Jesus is totally present—Body, Blood, Soul and Divinity—in even the smallest crumb of "bread" or tiniest drop of "wine." One does not get more or less of Jesus depending on the amount of Eucharist received. Very ill patients who cannot eat can receive a very tiny drop of the Blood of Christ and receive all of Christ. While receiving both "species" or forms gives a more complete sign of the Body and Blood of Christ, one may receive only the consecrated bread or Body and still be receiving the entire Person of Jesus Christ.

Fruits of the Eucharist

The word Eucharist means "thanksgiving." In and through this sacrament we give thanks to God for the gift of salvation. The thanks that we ultimately give Him is the gift of ourselves. Herein lies the true beauty of this Sacrament of sacraments. Jesus gives Himself totally, completely, and unconditionally to us in the Eucharist. His gift to us is so profound that He desires to physically enter into our being. Our response is to be the gift of ourselves to Him.

We surrender ourselves to God so that He may heal and transform us so we may become His instruments of grace and love. This is why we also call the Eucharist "Communion," because it is literally the communion of God and man. It reaches even beyond our individual communion with Christ. It also brings about the communion of the whole Church, which is the Mystical Body of Christ on earth. Through the Eucharist, we are not only united to Christ, but we are also intimately united to each other as brothers and sisters of Christ.

The Eucharist Augments Our Union with Christ

The Eucharist is often called the Blessed Sacrament, or the Sacrament of Sacraments, because each time we receive His Body and Blood, we literally welcome Jesus into the very depth of our being—into our hearts. This union is so profound that it can be efficacious in transforming us to be more like Christ. The more we devoutly receive Jesus in the Eucharist, the more we become like Him and mirror His virtues, His wisdom, and His strength.

The Eucharist Separates Us from Sin

Since the Eucharist transforms us to be more like Christ, it can't help but separate us from sin. The more we receive Jesus in this sacrament, the easier it is to avoid sin. The Eucharist cleanses us from all venial sins and heals the wounds caused by them. We are also given grace by Christ to transform our desire for sin into dislike and hatred of it. The Eucharist heals our intellect and strengthens our will so that, literally, it becomes harder for us to sin. It enables us to see how sin both offends God and wounds us.

The Eucharist is medicine for our souls and food for our journey to heaven. In the same way that the manna came down from heaven to nourish and sustain the Israelites as they journeyed toward the Promised Land, so this heavenly food of Christ's Body and Blood nourishes our souls and protects us from sin as we journey toward our heavenly home.

The Eucharist Unites the Church

As already mentioned, through the Eucharist all the members of the Church are both united to Christ and intimately to each other as brothers and sisters in Christ. With Christ as the Head, our union makes up the Mystical Body of Christ, which is the Church present and working in the world.

The Eucharist is truly the source of this unity, giving life and power to the Church. This is why it is the source and summit of the Christian life. It is the source because it gives life and unity to the Church. It is the summit because the celebration of the Eucharist is the greatest and most powerful prayer or action of the Church. The whole life, unity, and mission of the Church have their source and climax in this Most Blessed Sacrament.

As stated earlier, the Eucharist is also called "Communion." This signifies our union with God and with each other in the Body of Christ. This is why those in mortal sin who have separated themselves from God and the Church cannot receive Communion until they go to Confession to restore this relationship. They cannot participate in such an intimate union with Christ and His Church having chosen to willfully separate themselves through their actions.

The same applies to those who willfully and publicly reject Church teachings. One cannot say yes to Christ and reject the teachings of His Church, especially regarding serious issues of faith and morals such as abortion or euthanasia.

This is why the Catholic Church does not have "open communion" or "interfaith communion." The Eucharist brings about the unity of the Mystical Body of Christ and it deepens our union with the Church. The reception of His Body and Blood is the most visible and powerful statement we can make about our faith. When we receive the Eucharist, we say "**Amen**" ("Yes, it is true") to Jesus. As we accept Him we surrender ourselves completely to Him. This means accepting and saying yes to all He has revealed. We say yes to His teachings (both the easy and the difficult), and we say yes to the Mystical Body of Christ, the Church. Through the Church Christ established He is present working in and sanctifying the world. Therefore, each time we say "Amen" as we receive the Eucharist, we are saying yes to all that Christ's Church believes, teaches, and proclaims. This Most Holy Sacrament is at the heart of the Catholic faith. One cannot receive Christ while at the same time rejecting His Body, the Church.

> If you are the body and members of Christ, then it is your sacrament that is placed on the table of the Lord; it is your sacrament that you receive. To that which you are—you respond "Amen" ("yes, it is true!") and by responding to it you assent to it. For you hear the words, "the Body of Christ" and respond "Amen." Be then a member of the Body of Christ that your *Amen* may be true. (Saint Augustine, quoted in CCC 1396)

Through Baptism we become members of the Body of Christ, through Confirmation we assent to her teachings, and through the Eucharist we give witness to our membership and our belief. Therefore, these three sacraments taken together complete our initiation into the Mystical Body of Christ. Those who desire the Eucharist must first seek union with the Church.

The Eucharist Commits Us to Evangelization and Service

Finally, by its very nature the Eucharist heals, prepares, and strengthens us for evangelization and service. As we will see in the next chapter, the entire goal and purpose of the Mass is to feed and transform us so that we can go into the world to be Christ's instruments. We are especially sent to those who are most in need, the vulnerable, the alone, and those desiring God's love and mercy. The word "Mass" comes from the Latin "missa," which means to be sent. The Eucharist intimately unites us to Christ our Savior, who then calls us to continue His mission of building the kingdom of God. We are His hands, His voice, and His instruments in a world that is crying out for the message of the Gospel. The Eucharist is truly the source of our mission of evangelization and service.

Preparing to Receive the Eucharist

The celebration of the Eucharist is the most sacred and important event in the Catholic Church. The faithful must be consciously and spiritually prepared to receive Jesus in this Holy Sacrament. We have already mentioned Paul's warning to the Corinthians to approach the altar with discernment and seriousness. The Church requires every Catholic to prepare carefully to accept the gift of the Eucharist. In order to receive the sacrament worthily, one must do three things.

Be in the State of Grace

Those who willingly separated themselves from God and His Church cannot participate in the intimacy of the Sacrament of Holy Communion. Anyone conscious of committing a mortal sin must first receive the Sacrament of Penance before receiving Communion. "State of grace" means being in union and friendship with God. This is lost when we choose to separate ourselves through grave sin. Those who are conscious of venial sins may receive the Eucharist without sacramental absolution, and our venial sins are forgiven through the grace of the sacrament. That said, the Catechism strongly recommends confessing venial sins because regular confession helps us form our conscience, resist evil tendencies, and progress in the spiritual life (1458).

Believe That Jesus Is Truly Present in the Eucharist

Belief comes before reception of the Eucharist in Communion. There must be faith that the Eucharist is Jesus. Faith, however, does not mean total understanding. That is why it is faith—we must go beyond what our senses tell us. We must accept that the God who created the universe chose to unite Himself to us in such a humble form as a tiny wafer of bread through the work of human hands. We must believe we truly receive Christ's Body and Blood in the Eucharist.

Fast for One Hour before Receiving Communion

The Church asks Catholics to fast for one hour from all food and drink (except water and medicine) before receiving Communion. This discipline helps to prepare us both physically and spiritually for the reception of the Eucharist. This act of humble obedience reminds us of the extraordinary event in which we are about to participate. The Eucharistic fast is not meant to be a burden. In fact, a generation ago the fast was observed from midnight the night before we received the Eucharist. Today the Church has eased this obligation to one hour. The hour fast is a practical and important way to prepare ourselves to have communion with our Savior.

Eucharistic Devotions

While the Mass is the greatest and most efficacious form of worship in the Church, there are also other devotions and practices in which we adore Christ present in the Eucharist.

Adoration

Eucharistic adoration is a powerful devotion to the Eucharist outside the context of the Mass. Exposition is when the host, the consecrated Body of Christ, is visibly exposed in a special vessel called a monstrance, so that the faithful may physically see and worship Jesus present in the Eucharist. This time of adoration is spiritually efficacious because we sit in His very presence and gaze upon His precious Body.

Certainly Christ is always present in the soul of a Christian in the state of grace, yet He desires to come into our hearts more deeply and more profoundly in the Eucharist. Adoration is an extension of Communion at Mass because Jesus He is still physically present (substantially and sacramentally). This time of closeness to Him makes our prayers especially powerful and brings about great spiritual healing and strength.

Some parishes offer Eucharist adoration on a regular basis and others offer what is called Perpetual Adoration, which is Eucharistic exposition twenty-four hours a day. Jesus is always waiting for us to come and share our lives with Him so that He can shower us with His burning love, His presence, and His grace.

Visiting the Tabernacle

Every Catholic Church has the **Blessed Sacrament** reserved in the tabernacle, a special place for the safekeeping of the Eucharist. Although the host is not visibly exposed, a visit before the tabernacle provides an opportunity to spend time in prayer and meditation in the physical presence of Jesus. It is a worthy practice to make the Sign of the Cross when passing by a Catholic Church in reverence to Jesus present in the tabernacle.

Benediction

Benediction is a special Eucharistic liturgy apart from the Mass that usually includes exposition of the Eucharist for adoration or a "holy hour." Benediction means "blessing," and within this special liturgy a priest or deacon blesses the congregation with the consecrated Body of Christ exposed in the monstrance. It is the greatest and most efficacious blessing in the Church because we are blessed by Christ Himself present in the Eucharist. Like the Mass, Benediction is a time of surrendering ourselves to Christ so that He may bless and strengthen us to go into the world to continue His work of loving and serving others and spreading the Gospel.

In conclusion, although there are many ways for Christians to worship and come into union with Christ, there is no union on this earth that brings us as close to Christ than when we receive Him in Holy Communion. He comes to us as the "bread from heaven," the manna in the desert that strengthens for our journey. His Eucharist fulfills the saving plan of God begun in the Garden of Eden and culminated at the Cross on Calvary. It unites us to Christ in the deepest sense, strengthening and unifying His Mystical Body, the Church, through which He sanctifies the world. An "inexhaustible richness" given to us by Christ Himself, the Eucharist is truly the source and summit of all that we are as Catholics.

From the Catechism: Key Words to Know

EUCHARIST: The ritual, sacramental action of thanksgiving to God that constitutes the principal Christian liturgical celebration of and communion in the Paschal Mystery of Christ. The liturgical action called the Eucharist is also traditionally known as the Holy Sacrifice of the Mass. It is one of the seven sacraments of the Church; the Holy Eucharist completes Christian initiation (1322 ff.). The Sunday celebration of the Eucharist is at the heart of the Church's life (2177).

LAST SUPPER: The last meal, a Passover supper, which Jesus ate with His disciples the night before He died. Jesus' passing over to His Father by His death and Resurrection, the new Passover, is anticipated in the Last Supper and celebrated in the Eucharist, which fulfills the Jewish Passover and anticipates the final Passover of the Church in the glory of the kingdom. Hence, the Eucharist is called "the Lord's Supper" (610–611, 1329, 1340).

REAL PRESENCE: The unique, true presence of Christ in the Eucharist under the species, or appearances, of bread and wine. The Church invites the faithful to deepen their faith in the real presence of Christ through adoration and communion at the Eucharistic liturgy, and through adoration outside its celebration (1378–1379).

TRANSUBSTANTIATION: The scholastic term used to designate the unique change of the Eucharistic bread and wine into the Body and Blood of Christ. "Transubstantiation" indicates that through the consecration of the bread and the wine there occurs the change of the entire substance of the bread into the substance of the Body of Christ, and of the entire substance of the wine into the Blood of Christ—even though the appearances or "species" of bread and wine remain (1376).

AMEN: A Hebrew word meaning "truly; it is so; let it be done," signifying agreement with what has been said. The prayers of the New Testament, the Church's liturgy, and the creeds conclude with "Amen." Jesus used the word to introduce solemn assertions, to emphasize their trustworthiness and authority (1061, 1345, 1396, 2856, 2865).

BLESSED SACRAMENT: A name given to the Holy Eucharist, especially the consecrated elements reserved in the tabernacle for adoration or for the sick (1330).

Chapter 17

The Mass

Reading the Catechism: Paragraphs 1076–1112; 1135–1209

> Nevertheless the liturgy is the summit toward which the activity of the Church is directed; at the same time it is the font from which all her power flows. For the aim and object of apostolic works is that all who are made sons of God by faith and baptism should come together to praise God in the midst of His Church, to take part in the sacrifice, and to eat the Lord's supper.
>
> —Second Vatican Council, Constitution on the Sacred Liturgy, *Sacrosanctum concilium* (December 4, 1963), no. 8

Christ, the new and eternal Passover Lamb, instituted the Eucharist during the Jewish Passover. Through His sacrifice on the Cross we are freed from slavery to sin. In the same way that the Passover was at the very heart of the faith of Israel, the Eucharist is at the very heart of the New Covenant established by Christ. It is the "source and summit" of the Christian life. In every celebration of the Mass, we participate in Christ's death and Resurrection and are transformed by His grace.

The Mass is a sacrifice. It is a re-presentation (making present) of the sacrifice of the Cross and an application of its fruit. The sacrifice of the Cross and the sacrifice of the Eucharist are one and the same. It is the same victim and the same offering, only the manner is different. It is truly Christ we offer to the Father in the sacrifice of the Mass.

Here is an important caveat: The Mass does not re-sacrifice Christ but re-presents the one sacrifice of Calvary. We are not crucifying Christ again, but rather we are mystically participating in the very same sacrifice. Jesus Christ, Body, Blood, Soul, and Divinity, is being offered to the Father for the forgiveness of sins as a continuation of the one and same sacrifice of the Cross.

The members of the Church also offer themselves with Christ as a sacrifice to the Father. God does not desire the sacrifice of bulls and rams, but a sacrifice of our hearts and lives. We are to be active participants at Mass as we offer all that we have and all that we are, so we may be transformed into Christ and participate in the priesthood of all the faithful.

The word "Mass" comes from "*Ite missa est*," a command spoken at the conclusion of the Roman liturgy that means "Go, it is the dismissal." We go to Mass to be healed and transformed, so we can go into the world and consecrate it to God through our words and actions. We are sent forth to "love and serve the Lord and one another."

The Mass is the source and summit of the Christian life. It is the source because we are transformed, nourished, and empowered by Christ to go into the world and faithfully live as His followers. It is the summit because it is the greatest act of worship in which we can participate, bringing us into union with Christ.

The Mass is the wedding feast of the Lamb of God in which Christ's union with His Bride, the Church, is made complete. During this celebration Christ offers Himself completely to His Bride, first through His Word, and then through the gift of the Eucharist where He gives Himself completely, Body, Blood, Soul and Divinity. In turn, the Church gives herself completely to her Bridegroom with each person offering themselves to the Father with Christ. Through the reception of the Eucharist Christ literally becomes "one flesh" with His Church. By becoming "one flesh" with Him, we are transformed to be like Him and are sent out to be Christ to the world and accomplish His work.

We will now take a closer look at the Order of the Mass, which is the heart of our worship as Catholics. Within the Mass we come into union with the divine, where the angels and all of heaven unite with us as we offer ourselves to the Father through Christ in the power of the Holy Spirit.

THE ORDER OF THE MASS

The Liturgy of the Word

Within the first part of the Mass we celebrate Christ's unique presence in the Scriptures and are nourished by the Word (Jesus). The inspired Word of God reveals to us the good news of salvation in Christ, guides us to put it into action in our daily lives, and prepares us to receive Jesus in the Eucharist.

I. PREPARATORY RITES/We Pray With Our Words and Our Hearts

The Mass begins with the members of the community preparing themselves to encounter Christ in the Scriptures and in the Eucharist.

A. The Processional: The priest and ministers process into the church while a song is sung. The priest then kisses the **altar** as an act of reverence for the altar of sacrifice. (Stand)

B. The Greeting: The priest begins with the Sign of the Cross and then greets the community in the name of the Holy Trinity. The Mass is an action of the Holy Trinity, and during the Mass we enter into the intimate life of the Trinity. (Stand)

C. The Penitential Rite: This is a time in which we examine our lives and seek forgiveness from Christ for our sins. We do this in order to prepare to immerse ourselves into the mysteries of faith. Sin blocks our spiritual sight. By being cleansed of our sins we will be able to open ourselves completely to Christ in both the Scriptures and, especially, in the Eucharist. NOTE: The Penitential Rite only obtains forgiveness for venial (lesser) sins. If we are conscious of committing a mortal (grave) sin, we must first receive the Sacrament of Penance before we can receive the Eucharist. (Stand, Kneel during Lent)

D. The Gloria: A prayer of praise and adoration in which we lift up our hearts in love to God in thanksgiving for His works of salvation. The Gloria draws us into the mysteries of God and prepares us to listen to His Word in the Scriptures. (Stand)

E. The Opening Prayer: The priest reads a short prayer with the intentions of the Church for that day. This prayer is addressed to the Father through Jesus in the Holy Spirit. We are truly participating in the life of the Trinity. (Stand)

II. THE LITURGY OF THE WORD/We Listen to God's Word Proclaimed

The reading of the Scriptures, a service of instruction.

A. The First Reading: The first reading is usually from the Old Testament, except during Easter season when it is from the Acts of the Apostles. The Old Testament reading is always thematically tied to the Gospel reading. (Sit)

B. The Responsorial Psalm: The Church then prays one of the Psalms from the Old Testament. These are the ancient prayers of Israel. The responsorial psalm is usually sung and always requires the participation of the community. (Sit)

C. The Second Reading: The second reading is from one of the New Testament letters. (Sit)

D. The Gospel: The priest or deacon reads from one of the four Gospels, which tell about the life and ministry of Christ. The Gospels are the most sacred of all the Scriptures because they contain the actual recorded words of Christ. Before the Gospel, we make the Sign of the Cross with our thumb over our foreheads, mouth, and hearts, asking God that the Gospel will forever be in our minds, upon our lips, and in our hearts. *We are bearers of the Gospel.* (Stand as a sign of the special importance of the Gospel. Standing is also a sign of attention.)

E. The Homily: The priest speaks to the community about the Scriptures and how we can live its message in our daily lives. (Sit)

III. THE CREED/We Respond to God's Word

The Church stands together as one in faith and responds to hearing the Word of God by proclaiming our belief in the Triune God and all He has revealed.

A. The Creed: We join as one in reciting this prayer as a visible sign of our unity in one faith that will be actualized in the Eucharist. Our assent to the articles of the creed allows us to participate in what will happen next. It is like passing through a door into the mysteries of God. (Stand)

B. The Prayers of the Faithful: We end the Liturgy of the Word by bringing before the Lord our intentions that will be offered to the Father with the Eucharist. We especially pray for the Church, the world, the sick, and the dying. Other appropriate intentions can also be added. (Stand)

The Liturgy of the Eucharist

After being nourished by Christ through the Scriptures, the Liturgy of the Eucharist makes Christ present in the Eucharist and offered to the Father for the forgiveness of sins. We participate in the Eucharistic sacrifice by offering ourselves with Jesus to the Father so that we may more perfectly know and accomplish His will on earth. We are intimately united with Christ by receiving Him in Communion, and sent forth on a mission into the world to love and serve the Lord and each other.

IV. THE OFFERTORY/With the Bread and Wine, We Offer Ourselves to God

The gifts of bread and wine to be used in the Eucharistic sacrifice are offered by the community. The priest prepares and offers the gifts to the Father on behalf of the community. We also offer ourselves with the gifts of bread and wine as a spiritual sacrifice to the Father.

A. The Prayer over the Gifts: The priest prays a special prayer over the gifts asking the Lord to bless them and the community. (Stand)

V. THE EUCHARISTIC PRAYER OF SACRIFICE/God Transforms the Bread and Wine

This is the most solemn part of the Mass when the bread and wine are changed into the Body and Blood of Christ and offered to the Father in sacrifice.

A. The Preface: This is the final preparation before the Eucharist is made present and offered in sacrifice. The community is asked to lift up their hearts in thanksgiving to the Father through the Son in the Spirit for the gift of His salvation. This is when we offer ourselves as a spiritual sacrifice to the Father with Jesus. (Stand)

B. The Holy, Holy, Holy: A prayer that is usually sung that announces the coming of Jesus our God and king. Taken from two scriptural texts:

  1. Isaiah 6:3–4: Isaiah has a vision of the throne of God in heaven surrounded by angels who sing, "Holy, holy, holy is the Lord of Hosts. All the earth is filled with his glory." At the Mass, heaven is mystically brought down to earth. In the Eucharist, heaven and earth touch in the Person of Jesus. We are being brought into the throne room of God!

  2. Matthew 21:9: When Jesus entered Jerusalem before His death, the people welcomed Him as their king. They threw palm branches before Him and said, "[B]lessed is he who comes in the name of the Lord; hosanna in the highest." We are about to welcome Christ our King into our midst. We acknowledge Him as our king and look forward to thc day when His kingdom will be completed. As His subjects we seek to accomplish His will.

C. The **Consecration**: While holding his hands over the gifts (Epiclesis), the priest calls down the power of the Holy Spirit upon the bread and wine to change them into the Body and Blood of Christ. Then he says the words of Jesus, "This is my Body," and "This is the chalice of my Blood," which make the Eucharist present. The priest holds up both the sacred host and the chalice for all to adore. (Kneel)

D. The Canon of the Mass: The priest then prays the prayers of sacrifice offering Jesus to the Father for the reparation of sins, to strengthen the mission and unity of the Church, for the holiness and salvation of the community present, and for those who have died. The Canon ends when the priest holds up the Body and Blood of Jesus as sacrifice for the glory and honor of God, offering all things to the Father through Jesus in the Holy Spirit. (Kneel)

E. The Final **Doxology**: This is the climax of the whole Mass. Jesus has been made present in the Eucharist and is being offered in sacrifice to the Father. Here we offer all of ourselves, our joys, sufferings, struggles, all that we are and have to the Father through, with, and in Christ. It is a prayer of total surrender at the foot of the Cross!

F. The Our Father: Those present join as one in praying the perfect prayer that Jesus taught us. The Our Father is followed by a prayer asking God to free us from all anxiety and evil. (Stand)

G. The Sign of Peace: We then give those around us a sign of peace and unity in Christ before receiving Jesus in the Eucharist. We are not to approach the altar of sacrifice if we have an unforgiving heart. We pray for that in the Our Father and we act upon it in the sign of peace. (Stand)

VI. THE COMMUNION RITE/We Receive Jesus, by Whom We Are Transformed

This is the part of the Mass in which we have union with Christ by receiving Him in the Eucharist. We have already given ourselves to Him, and now this union becomes a complete reality, physically and spiritually. We literally become one flesh with Christ, embracing the Cross of Christ in the same way He did and offering ourselves to the Father ready to do His will.

A. The Lamb of God: This is the final prayer of preparation before receiving Jesus. Three times we ask Him to take away the sins of the world, and once to grant us peace. We then behold Jesus, the Lamb of God, who died on the Cross for our sins, and we adore Him. We are not worthy to receive Him; no one is. But we throw ourselves upon His mercy and ask Him to heal us. (Kneel)

B. The Reception of Communion: The community goes forward to receive Jesus. We finally have union with Him. We should spend the next few minutes with Him in prayer. We speak, but we must also remember to listen. (Kneel, Receive, Kneel)

C. The Prayer after Communion: The priest prays that the Eucharist will produce abundant fruit in us and help us to continue Christ's work. (Stand)

D. The Final Blessing: The priest bestows upon the community a special blessing and then dismisses them, using one of four formulas, such as "Go in peace, glorifying the Lord by your life." The Mass is only the beginning. We must then go and live it. (Stand)

E. The Recessional: A song is sung and the priest and ministers exit the church. (Stand)

From the Catechism: Key Words to Know

MASS: The Eucharist or principal sacramental celebration of the Church established by Jesus at the Last Supper, in which the mystery of our salvation through participation in the sacrificial death and glorious Resurrection of Christ is renewed and accomplished. The Mass renews the paschal sacrifice of Christ as the sacrifice offered by the Church. It is called "Mass" (from the Latin *missa*) because of the "mission" or "sending" with which the liturgical celebration concludes (Latin: *Ite, Missa est*; 1332; cf. 1088, 1382, 2192).

ALTAR: The center and focal point of a church where the sacrifice of Christ on the Cross is made present under sacramental signs in the Mass. Among the Israelites the altar was the place where sacrifices were offered to God. The Christian altar represents two aspects of the mystery of the Eucharist: the altar of sacrifice where Christ as the sacrificial victim offers Himself for our sins; and the table of the Lord where Christ gives Himself to us as food from heaven (1182, 1383).

CONSECRATION: The dedication of a thing or person to divine service by a prayer or blessing. The consecration at Mass is that part of the Eucharistic Prayer during which the Lord's words of institution of the Eucharist at the Last Supper are recited by the priestly minister, making Christ's Body and Blood—His sacrifice offered on the Cross once for all—sacramentally present under the species of bread and wine (1352, 1353).

DOXOLOGY: Christian prayer which gives praise and glory to God, often in a special way to the three divine Persons of the Trinity. Liturgical prayers traditionally conclude with the doxology "to the Father, through the Son, in the Holy Spirit." The final doxology of the Lord's Prayer renews the prayer's first three petitions in the form of adoration and praise (2639, 2855).

Chapter 18

Introduction to Morality: Preparing for Penance

Reading the Catechism: Paragraphs 1699–1986

> I came so that they might have life and have it more abundantly.
> —John 10:10

"I came so that they might have life and have it more abundantly" (Jn. 10:10). These words of Jesus the Good Shepherd in John's Gospel are the basis of the moral life. Jesus comes not only as the One who reveals the love of the Father, but also as the God who created and redeemed us, the God who knows what is best for us, and the God who desires to give us human life to the full measure. This is what morality is all about, and we need to start out with the right attitude and perspective.

It can be easy to view **morality** and the moral teachings of the Church as a no to this and a no to that, limiting our freedom and becoming a source of burden and guilt. However, both are part of God's wise and loving plan for us. They are the path to fullness of life and eternal life. Morality is not so much a no but rather a yes to life, to a full human life, to the best God can give us. This is the attitude and perspective we must have toward morality.

This chapter introduces the basic foundations and principles of Catholic moral teaching handed down to us through Sacred Tradition and Sacred Scripture. These principles are not necessarily answers to specific moral questions, but they can and should be used in making good moral decisions and in forming our conscience according to the teachings of Christ and the Church. We will discuss specific moral questions and issues in later chapters.

Human Freedom

The first issue to address with morality is human freedom. Man is created in the image and likeness of God. He created each of us as a rational being with the dignity of a person who can initiate and control his own actions. We are created with free will so that we can have the ability to love, which requires a freely chosen gift of self. Love cannot be forced or coerced. It must be freely given. This freedom, however, is not a radical or unfettered freedom; it comes with immense responsibility.

This profound reality of human freedom is clearly visible in Genesis chapter three. Adam and Eve have the freedom to eat the fruit of almost all of the trees in the Garden of Eden. Of all the trees, two are specifically mentioned. The first is the tree of life that is in the center of the garden. The second is the tree of knowledge of good and evil, the fruit of which God specifically forbids Adam and Eve to eat.

Why are these two trees so important? The author of Genesis is teaching about the reality of human freedom. The tree of life is at the center of the Garden because it represents eternal life and the goodness that come from being in communion with God. The tree of knowledge of good and evil represents the reality that we can abuse the freedom God gave us and choose evil. We can turn away from Him and His goodness and choose to experience evil, which is separation from Him and from what is good.

God has given us free will so that we can choose to love Him and live in His life. Only in choosing Him and His good will for us we know and experience true human freedom. True and authentic human freedom is found only in embracing God's wisdom and plan for the human family.

On the other hand, human freedom must halt before the tree of knowledge of good and evil, because God alone determines what is good and what is evil. By eating of the fruit of that tree, Adam and Eve abused their freedom, chose to disobey God, and committed the first sin. This sin was a sin of pride, a false sense of freedom. Thus, their freedom became enslaving, diminishing life.

In answering this fundamental question about human freedom, Pope John Paul II beautifully writes:

> In the Book of Genesis we read: "The Lord God commanded the man, saying, 'You may eat freely of every tree of the garden; but of the tree of the knowledge of good and evil you shall not eat, for in the day that you eat of it you shall die'" (Gen. 2:16–17). With this imagery, Revelation teaches that *the power to decide what is good and what is evil does not belong to man, but to God alone*. The man is certainly free, inasmuch as he can understand and accept God's commands. And he possesses an extremely

> far-reaching freedom, since he can eat "of every tree of the garden." But his freedom is not unlimited: it must halt before the "tree of the knowledge of good and evil," for it is called to accept the moral law given by God. In fact, human freedom finds its authentic and complete fulfillment precisely in the acceptance of that law. God, who alone is good, knows perfectly what is good for man, and by virtue of his very love proposes this good to man in the commandments. (*Veritatis splendor*, no. 35)

Unfortunately, our culture glorifies a misguided human freedom that sees man as autonomous in determining his own destiny. Moral laws and the teachings of the Church are regarded as limits to freedom and a hindrance to human potential. The knowledge of what is good and evil no longer belongs to God alone, but becomes a product of human freedom in which man himself becomes a god who knows what is good and what is bad. Sound familiar? It is the same sin of pride with which Satan tempted Adam and Eve. Do we alone know what is good and what is evil? Does my five-year-old know what is truly good for him? Or does he need his loving parents to show him what is truly good for him? Only in choosing God and His goodness do we come to know true freedom and fullness of life! Only in the truth God reveals to us do we become truly free. Again Pope John Paul II states:

> God's law does not reduce, much less do away with human freedom; rather, it protects and promotes that freedom. In contrast, however, some present-day cultural tendencies have given rise to several currents of thought in ethics which centre upon *an alleged conflict between freedom and law*. These doctrines would grant to individuals or social groups the right *to determine what is good or evil*. Human freedom would thus be able to "create values" and would enjoy a primacy over truth, to the point that truth itself would be considered a creation of freedom. Freedom would thus lay claim to a *moral autonomy* which would actually amount to an *absolute sovereignty*. (*Veritatis splendor*, no. 35)

Moral relativism within our culture is rooted in our misunderstanding of human freedom. God did not make us free to do whatever we want. God made us free so that we can choose to love God and one another. In doing so we live in His goodness and love. Then and only then do we experience true freedom and life.

The Moral Law

As a wise and loving Father, God reveals to us our goodness and His plan for us through the moral law. The **moral law** is a participation in the eternal law, which is God's governance and providence over all of creation. The eternal law encompasses physical laws (such as physics and chemistry) and the moral law (the truths of God's plan for the human family).

Because the moral law is part of the eternal law, it is objective and unchanging. This is what we call objective moral norms. Some actions are inherently good (always and everywhere), and some are inherently evil (always and everywhere), no matter the time, place, or culture. Furthermore, the moral law is not a product of history or cultures as many often claim. In fact, history and culture are the means by which objective moral norms are transmitted from generation to generation.

The moral law has been revealed to us in two ways. The first is through the natural law, which is God's law written in creation itself and the creatures He created. It can be known through reason alone. The second is through divine Revelation. God directly reveals to us the moral truths about good and evil, first through His gradual revelation to Israel in the Old Testament, and then through His full revelation in Jesus Christ, whose teachings are handed down to us this day through the Church.

Let's take a closer look at these two means through which we come to know the moral law.

Natural Law

The natural law is a reflection of the moral order as intended by the Creator. Certain moral norms can be known and understood through reason alone by experiencing and understanding our own human nature. The first principle of the natural law is to do good and avoid evil. Every human being from the age of reason understands that fundamental moral principle. It is written in our nature. Thus, we can reason that certain moral actions (such as the killing of innocent human life and rape) are always and everywhere morally evil. They are an offense against the created order as written upon the human heart and are actions against reason and human nature as created by God. Since it is written within our very nature, the natural law can be known without the help of divine Revelation.

Saint Paul speaks of this in Romans when he points out that even the pagans and the Gentiles come to know the wise and eternal plan of God through the natural law:

> The wrath of God is indeed being revealed from heaven against every impiety and wickedness of those who suppress the truth by their wickedness. For what can be known about God is evident to them [Gentiles], because God made it evident to them. Ever since the creation of the world, his invisible attributes of eternal power and divinity have been able to be understood and perceived in what he has made. As a result, they have no excuse; for although they knew God they did not accord him glory as God or give him thanks. (Rom. 1:18–21)

> For when the Gentiles who do not have the law by nature observe the prescriptions of the law, they are a law for themselves even though they do not have the law. They show that the demands of the law are written in their hearts, while their conscience also bears witness and their conflicting thoughts accuse or even defend them on the day when, according to my gospel, God will judge people's hidden works through Christ Jesus. (Rom. 2:14–16)

The natural law can be seen in the basic moral laws of almost every culture and civilization in human history. For example, the Code of Hammurabi in the Babylonian Empire, written fifteen hundred years before Christ, is very similar to the Ten Commandments. Murder, rape, stealing, and adultery are universally seen as morally wrong. Thus, the plan of the Father is written in our very nature, and good and evil can be known through our reason alone.

However, because humanity has fallen away from God and is wounded by sin, the natural law gives us only a limited understanding of the moral law. It is like what I see without my glasses. I can make out certain images, shapes, and forms, but not any of the detail. It is through God's revelation that our understanding of good and evil becomes clear and complete.

Divine Revelation

God has revealed to us through salvation history, culminating in Christ, how to live according to the divine plan. *Divine Revelation enlightens and perfects our knowledge of the natural law.* Saint Thomas Aquinas describes the divine law as "the additional law given by God, whereby man shares more perfectly in the eternal law" (*Summa* I–II, q. 91 a. 4). It takes what we have come to know through our reason alone and reveals to us the fullness of the moral law and the Father's plan for humanity.

Christ not only reveals to us who God is, but also what it means to be fully human and to have fullness of life. Through Him, we see what is good and what is evil. The moral teachings of Christ have been handed down as a part of the sacred deposit of faith through Scripture and Tradition. Therefore, *the Church has not only the authority to teach on doctrine, but she safeguards, preserves, and teaches the moral Gospel as well.* The Church constantly has to interpret and apply the divine law to new circumstances and situations that arise each day, especially in the areas of medical ethics and bioethics. As science and technology move forward, we must always safeguard the dignity of the human person and the moral Gospel. As Pope Paul VI states:

> No member of the faithful could possibly deny that the Church is competent in her magisterium to interpret the natural moral law. It is in fact indisputable, as Our predecessors have many times declared, that Jesus Christ, when He communicated His divine power to Peter and the other Apostles and sent them to teach all nations His commandments, constituted them as the authentic guardians and interpreters of the whole moral law, not only, that is, of the law of the Gospel but also of the natural law. For the natural law, too, declares the will of God, and its faithful observance is necessary for men's eternal salvation. (Encyclical Letter Concerning the Regulation of Birth *Humanae vitae* [July 25, 1968], no. 4)

The moral law—through both the natural law and the divine law—continues to guide us in our search for the fundamental truths of what it means to be human and to direct us to our ultimate destiny in Christ.

The Morality of Human Actions

It is very important that we know and understand what makes a specific moral action good or evil so that we can make good moral decisions. As followers of Christ we do not ever want to will, commit, or cooperate with evil. Thus, we need to be sure that our actions are totally good. There are three criteria that have always been used in Catholic Tradition to determine whether a specific moral action is good or evil (see CCC 1750).

- The object chosen (what is done).
- The end in view, or the intention (why it is done).
- The circumstances of the action (important elements surrounding the action).

To determine if an act is morally good, all three of the criteria must be examined. This is called the "principle of totality." For an action to be morally good, two of the criteria, both the object chosen (what is done) and the intention (why it is done), have to be good. If either the object chosen or the intention is evil, then the entire act is morally evil. Let's examine each of these more closely.

The Object

The object of the choice can by itself render an act morally good or evil, regardless of the good intentions or surrounding circumstances. *There are some specific acts that are always and everywhere wrong because they are objectively evil* (rape, murder, and adultery). We may have the best intentions, but if what we do is objectively evil we have committed a morally evil act. For example, our intention may be to provide for our family, but if we rob a bank to obtain money, we have committed evil despite the noble intentions. *Good intentions cannot make a morally evil action good.* The end can never justify the means.

The Intention

The intentions of a moral act may also render the act morally evil if the intentions are evil, even though the action may be good. For example, a person who fasts and gives alms is doing something objectively good. However, if his intentions are to obtain the praise of others, then the evil intentions render the entire action evil.

The Circumstance

The circumstances of a moral act are secondary. *They in themselves cannot change whether or not an action is morally good or evil.* They do, however, increase or diminish the goodness or evilness of human acts. They can also diminish or increase the agent's responsibility (such as acting out of the fear of death). For example, let's go back to the person trying to provide for his family. If the circumstances are that his family is very poor and in great need, then those circumstances reduce the evilness of the act, but don't change the fact that it was still evil. However, if the man was stealing to provide a trip to Disneyland for his well-off family, then that would increase the evilness of the act. Notice that the circumstances do not change the fact that the act was evil, but increase or decrease the evilness of the act. *You can never use the consequences or the proportional outcome of a specific action to make an objectively evil action good.* An objectively evil action can never be rendered good in any circumstance, or in view of the consequences or proportional outcome. This would be consequentialism or proportionalism, which is condemned by the moral Tradition of the Church.

Principle of Double Effect

Sometimes we encounter a specific moral situation that is very difficult to judge and seems to leave no choice but to commit evil. Remember, we may never deliberately choose or will evil, but at times a morally good action has unintended side effects that are evil. This is called the "principle of double effect." This principle is often used to justify proportionalism, that is, claiming that an objectively evil action can be rendered good because of the circumstances. However, the principle of double effect, when correctly understood, is very different because it upholds the moral criteria that *the object chosen and intended can never be objectively evil.* The principle of double effect holds that it is morally allowable to perform an action that has a bad effect only under the following conditions:

- The object chosen cannot be objectively, morally evil.
- The resulting and foreseen moral evil cannot be intended, but must be an unintended result of the chosen object.
- The unintended resulting moral evil cannot outweigh the moral good that is chosen.
- There must not be any other reasonable course of action to take.

The frequently used case to explain the principle of double effect is uterine isolation, in which a woman has uterine cancer that must be excised if she is to live. She has a right to self-preservation, and removal of the cancerous uterus will likely result in saving her life. If there also happens to be a fetus in her womb, it is known that the fetus will die if the cancerous uterus is removed. But the foreseen death of the unborn child, though not intended, is not a greater evil than the good brought about by preserving the life of the mother through this medically necessary surgery.

Sin

Now let us turn our attention to the topic of sin. **Sin** is not a topic that many like to discuss, but it is a reality of life. We are all sinners and we are all in need of God's salvation in Christ. As His followers we must always battle against sin and temptation so that we continue to live in the freedom of God. In order to do that we must understand the nature of sin and its terrible consequences. The Catechism defines sin as "an offense against reason, truth, and right conscience; it is failure in genuine love for God and neighbor caused by a perverse attachment to certain goods. It wounds the nature of man and injures human solidarity. It has been defined as 'an utterance, a deed, or a desire contrary to the eternal law'" (1849). We sin through deeds, thoughts, words, and omission.

Sin is utterly unreasonable because it destroys our humanity. Do we ever think of it in that way? Sinning is like saying 2+2=5; it just doesn't make sense. Sin is contrary to the reality that we were made in the image and likeness of God, and were created to share in God's life and to live in His goodness. To sin is to live in opposition to what it means to be human.

It is unreasonable because instead of loving God we love things and make them like God, things like money, drugs, alcohol, sex, power, work, and even other people. It is not fun (contrary to what the media says) and it destroys who we are.

It is amazing that in such a health-conscious society where we worry so much about what we eat, we often do not concern ourselves with sin, which can destroy the divine life of God within our soul. Sinning does to our soul what eating candy 24/7 would do to our body. Serious sin does to our soul spiritually what a .45 caliber pistol shot to the head would do to our body. The battle against sin should be the number one concern in our lives.

Original Sin

As we described previously, we all come into the world with original sin. Since all of humanity has fallen away from God, we enter this world in a natural separation from Him. In essence, we are born spiritually dead. However, through Baptism we are freed from original sin and filled with the life of God. While the eternal effects of original sin are washed away, we still live with its temporal effects. We still remain attracted to sin and continue to struggle to be perfected. Even after Baptism, we can choose to sin.

Actual Sin

Actual sins are sins we commit during our lifetime. They are the times when we choose evil through our actions, thoughts, words, or by not doing something we should have done (omission). Actual sins wound our relationship with God and others, and wound or even destroy grace and charity in our souls. There are two kinds of actual sin: mortal and venial.

Mortal sin

Mortal sin is a grave sin that destroys charity in our heart and deprives us of sanctifying grace. It is called mortal from the Latin *mors,* which means death. Mortal sin is an engagement of the will that is so serious that it separates us from God and the Church. Those who persist in mortal sin without repentance are excluded from heaven. Under normal circumstances mortal sins are forgiven through the Sacrament of Reconciliation (Penance).

Three criteria must be examined to determine if a sin is (1) objectively mortal, and (2) if the one committing the sin is fully culpable for their actions:

- Grave matter
- Sufficient knowledge
- Sufficient freedom

Grave matter

The first criterion concerns the objective nature of the sin. Some acts are "of themselves" light matter, such as complaining, faultfinding, and impatience. Other acts are of themselves serious matter, such as murder and adultery. Apart from what is going on in the person's mind, acts have an objective degree of moral seriousness. For a sin to be mortal the object of the act must be of grave matter; in other words, it must be a very grave evil. Mortal sin is something so wrong that it violates the virtue of charity, results in the loss of the grace of charity in our souls, and causes complete separation from God. By it the person has been seriously unfaithful to the Covenant established by Christ (see CCC 1858).

There are some acts that are always and clearly grave by their nature, such as murder, abortion, rape, blasphemy, or adultery. Other acts may not always rise to the level of serious matter, such as stealing, lying, or jealousy. For example, if someone steals a dollar from another's purse, that most likely is not serious. If, however, someone steals 100,000 dollars that becomes grave matter.

Whether a sin is mortal or not is often judged by the circumstances surrounding the action and the person committing the sin. As we saw earlier, this is not to say that circumstances make an evil action good. The circumstances surrounding an action can increase the gravity of sin, causing an already evil action to become gravely evil, resulting in a mortal sin.

Sufficient knowledge

For a person to be culpable or responsible for committing any sin, they must have sufficient knowledge that what they are doing is wrong. For someone to be guilty of committing a mortal sin, they must have sufficient knowledge that what they are doing is gravely wrong.

For example, if we know that it is grave matter to miss Mass on Sunday and choose to miss it anyway, we make the choice with the awareness that the act is gravely wrong. But if someone did not know that missing Mass on Sunday was a mortal sin and they missed Sunday Mass, they would not be guilty of mortal sin. A person must know that the sin committed is of grave matter to be held responsible. However, intentional ignorance does not remove culpability but increases it (see CCC 1859).

Sufficient freedom

A mortal sin is committed only when the grave wrong is freely chosen. Fear of death, heat of passion, pathological disorders, or external pressures may diminish or even remove the person's culpability.

For example, a teenage girl chooses to have an abortion because her boyfriend threatened to kill her if she didn't go through with it. In that case she lacks sufficient freedom to avoid that horrible crime, and her culpability for the action may be reduced or removed. However, it is important to remember that lack of sufficient knowledge and/or freedom does not change the objective nature of the action. The girl still committed a morally evil act. Whether an action is a mortal sin for a particular person rests on whether they are fully or at all culpable for their action. That is a question left between a penitent and their confessor, and ultimately only God can judge the human heart (see CCC 1860).

Venial sin

Venial sins are less serious sins and are characterized as our everyday faults. Venial sin wounds charity and diminishes our ability to do good. It impedes the soul's progress of practicing the moral virtues and merits temporal punishment (purgatory). However, venial sins do not exclude one from heaven. They do not require sacramental confession for forgiveness and can be forgiven when the person expresses contrition for the sin and ask God's forgiveness. We should try to avoid all sin, even venial sin. Habitual venial sin weakens our will to resist sin and may eventually lead us to commit mortal sin (see CCC 1855).

The Human Conscience

> Deep within his conscience man discovers a law which he has not laid upon himself but which he must obey. Its voice, ever calling him to love and to do what is good and to avoid evil, sounds in his heart at the right moment. . . . For man has in his heart a law inscribed by God. . . . His conscience is man's most secret core and his sanctuary. There he is alone with God whose voice echoes in his depths. (*Gaudium et spes,* no. 16)

These beautiful and powerful words of the Second Vatican Council describe the gift of our **conscience**. It is the presence of God in our souls always calling us to the truth and to fullness of human life. It is a judgment of reason, enlightened by the Holy Spirit, that enjoins us to do what is good and to avoid what is evil. It judges an action before it takes place, while it is being performed, or after it has taken place.

Our conscience is at the heart of our human dignity as beings created in the image and likeness of God. Through it we are able to judge good from evil and recognize the divine plan written in our heart. Each of us has the duty and responsibility to act in accordance with our conscience. The dignity of the human person demands that each person is always free to act in accordance with their conscience and is never forced or coerced to do otherwise.

Formation of Conscience

While we must follow our conscience, we also have the grave responsibility of forming it according to the truth that God has revealed. It is only a true conscience when it is formed according to the teachings of Christ.

We act in good faith when we follow our conscience, but we must always strive to have it well informed. If we act in good conscience and our conscience is true, then we have made a good moral decision. Sometimes our conscience is true, but we act against it or in bad conscience. This is what happens when we sin.

But there are other times in which we follow our conscience, acting in good conscience, but our conscience is in error and is not formed correctly according to God's law. This would be a false conscience. When we act in good conscience, but it is false, that is called erroneous judgment.

Someone may make an erroneous judgment for several reasons. They simply may not have known something was wrong, or they may have misunderstood or not been properly informed of the teachings of the Church. When a person has not deliberately ignored the duty to form their conscience, this ignorance is called "invincible." However, ignorance is vincible when a person does not take the responsibility of forming their conscience seriously or when they deliberately ignore the moral law. Vincible ignorance is a grave sin and seriously undermines the moral life.

Conscience must be formed and moral judgment enlightened. A well-formed conscience formulates its judgments according to reason and in conformity with the true good willed by God. The education of conscience is the responsibility of all and is a lifelong task. It requires interiority, to enter our hearts to recognize the voice of the Creator. The Word of God (Scripture and Tradition) is the light to our path, and our conscience should always be formed in accordance to God's law and revelation. We have a grave moral obligation to form it according to the teachings of the Church. We can't just say, "I just follow my conscience." We have to be sure that the conscience that we are following is conformed to the teachings of Christ and the Church. Many people use the excuse of "I just follow my conscience" to dissent from various Church teachings. Deliberately acting against Church teaching is either disingenuous or the result of a poorly formed conscience.

Conscience is not the source of truth but rather the witness of a truth that is beyond us, unchanging, and eternal. To act against that truth degrades both the human conscience and the human person, bringing about grave confusion and error.

Pope John Paul II addresses this intimate relationship between conscience and truth, which cannot be separated:

> Like the natural law itself and all practical knowledge, the judgment of conscience also has an imperative character: man must act in accordance with it. If man acts against this judgment or, in a case where he lacks certainty about the rightness and goodness of a determined act, still performs that act, he stands condemned by his own conscience, *the proximate norm of personal morality*. The dignity of this rational forum and the authority of its voice and judgments derive from the *truth* about moral good and evil, which it is called to listen to and to express. This truth is indicated by the "divine law," *the universal and objective norm of morality*. The judgment of conscience does not establish the law; rather it bears witness to the authority of the natural law and of the practical reason with reference to the supreme good, whose attractiveness the human person perceives and whose commandments he accepts. "Conscience is not an independent and exclusive capacity to decide what is good and what is evil. Rather there is profoundly imprinted upon it a principle of obedience vis-a-vis the objective norm which establishes and conditions the correspondence of its decisions with the commands and prohibitions which are at the basis of human behavior." (*Veritatis splendor*, no. 60)

God's Mercy

Finally, we turn our gaze to the merciful love of God. You can never talk about sin without talking about the **mercy** of God, which is greater than all sin. We all sin; yet God so loved the world He sent His only Son, not to condemn the world but to save it. God calls us to conversion. He desires that we be freed from sin and live eternally with Him. When we sin we separate ourselves from Him, but He always gently calls us back. The first step in conversion is realizing our own sinfulness and our need for God and His mercy.

The story of the prodigal son in the Gospel of Luke (Lk. 15:11–32) is the most powerful story of God's mercy. Even though the son squandered his inheritance through a life of sin, his father still loved him. When the son returned, his father ran to him, embraced him, and restored him fully as his beloved son. God the Father has the same response to us if we turn away from our sins, come to our senses, and return to Him. In the Sacrament of Penance, the Father comes running to us to embrace us and restore us to life. No sin can separate us from the love of Christ if we trust in His great mercy and love.

The moral life is challenging, especially in our day and age when the culture is so opposed to the Gospel of Christ. As Christians we are not only called to be holy, but also to change the culture through our lives and examples. We are called every day through ongoing conversion to offer ourselves as a spiritual sacrifice to God, holy and pleasing to Him. In that way we can truly consecrate our world to God.

Let us conclude with the powerful words of Saint Paul:

> I urge you therefore, brothers, by the mercies of God, to offer your bodies as a living sacrifice, holy and pleasing to God, your spiritual worship. Do not conform yourselves to this age but be transformed by the renewal of your mind, that you may discern what is the will of God, what is good and pleasing and perfect. (Rom. 12:1–2)

From the Catechism: Key Words to Know

MORALITY: Referring to the goodness or evil of human acts. Human freedom makes a person a "moral subject" or agent able to judge the morality (goodness or evil) of the acts that are chosen. The morality of human acts depends on the object (or nature) of the action, the intention (or end foreseen), and the circumstances of the action (1749; cf. 407).

MORAL LAW: A rule of conduct established by competent authority for the common good. In biblical terms, the moral law is the fatherly instruction of God, setting forth the ways that lead to happiness and proscribing those that lead to evil. The divine, or eternal, law can be either natural or revealed (positive). Natural moral law is inscribed in the heart, and known by human reason. Revealed law is found in the ancient law (Old Testament), notably the Ten Commandments, and in the New Law (Law of the Gospel), the teaching of Christ, notably the Sermon on the Mount, which perfects the ancient law (1950–1974).

SIN: An offense against God as well as a fault against reason, truth, and right conscience. Sin is a deliberate thought, word, deed, or omission contrary to the eternal law of God. In judging the gravity of sin, it is customary to distinguish between mortal and venial sins (1849, 1853, 1854).

MORTAL SIN: A grave infraction of the law of God that destroys the divine life (sanctifying grace) in the soul of the sinner, constituting a turn away from God. For a sin to be mortal, three conditions must be present: grave matter, full knowledge of the evil of the act, and full consent of the will (1855, 1857).

VENIAL SIN: Sin that does not destroy the divine life in the soul, as does mortal sin, though it diminishes and wounds it (1855). Venial sin is the failure to observe necessary moderation, in lesser matters of the moral law, or in grave matters acting without full knowledge or complete consent (1862).

CONSCIENCE: The interior voice of a human being, within whose heart the inner law of God is inscribed. Moral conscience is a judgment of practical reason about the moral quality of a human action. It moves a person at the appropriate moment to do good and to avoid evil (1777–1778). An examination of conscience is recommended as a preparation for the reception of the Sacrament of Penance (1454).

MERCY: The loving kindness, compassion, or forbearance shown to one who offends (e.g., the mercy of God to us sinners; 1422, 1829).

Chapter 19

The Sacrament of Penance

Reading the Catechism: Paragraphs 1422–1498

> Jesus said to them again, "Peace be with you. As the Father has sent me, so I send you." And when he had said this, he breathed on them and said to them, "Receive the Holy Spirit. Whose sins you forgive are forgiven them, and whose sins you retain are retained."
>
> —John 20:21–23

The **Sacrament of Penance** is one of the two sacraments of healing. Penance cleanses us of sin committed after Baptism and restores us to new life in Christ whenever our soul has been wounded by sin. This sacrament is the great sacrament of healing, one that ought to be approached often with great confidence and trust. It is a fountain of mercy flowing from the heart of Christ through the Church.

This chapter will explore what the Sacrament of Penance is, the common questions asked about it, and address how to go to confession.

Penance Was Instituted by Christ Himself

Like the other six sacraments, Penance was instituted by Christ. It is the perpetual instrument and ministry of the forgiveness of sins through the Church. How do we know that Christ instituted the Sacrament of Penance? The institution of the sacrament is recorded explicitly in the Gospel of John immediately following the Resurrection:

> On the evening of that first day of the week, when the doors were locked, where the disciples were, for fear of the Jews, Jesus came and stood in their midst and said to them, "Peace be with you." When he had said this, he showed them his hands and his side. The disciples rejoiced when they saw the Lord. (Jesus)

> said to them again, "Peace be with you. As the Father has sent me, so I send you." And when he had said this, he breathed on them and said to them, "Receive the Holy Spirit. Whose sins you forgive are forgiven them, and whose sins you retain are retained." (Jn. 20:19–23)

Let's look closely at what exactly happens here, because it is very important for our understanding of the sacrament. First, Jesus says to the Apostles, "As the Father has sent me, so I send you." He is commissioning the Apostles to share in and be instruments of the same mission that the Father gave Him. This mission of Jesus was to come into the world and bring about the forgiveness of sin. He accomplished this by His death on the Cross and Resurrection from the dead. When His earthy mission was complete, Jesus gave the Apostles the authority to carry it on.

Jesus then breathed upon them the power of the Holy Spirit and said, "Whose sins you forgive are forgiven them, and whose sins you retain are retained." Jesus gave the Apostles the power of the Holy Spirit because only through this power given from the Father through the Son can sins be forgiven. In sharing the same mission of Christ and empowered by the Holy Spirit, the Apostles and their successors have the power and authority to forgive and retain sin.

This powerful Scripture passage makes clear that Jesus gave authority to His Apostles to forgive sins. Only God can forgive sins, but empowered by Jesus the Apostles are His unique instruments of mercy and forgiveness through the Sacrament of Penance. This authority has been handed down through apostolic succession through the bishops and priests who share in the same apostolic ministry of the forgiveness of sins. Through the Sacrament of Holy Orders, our bishops and priests today have the same authority to forgive and retain sins as did the first Apostles.

Why Must I Confess My Sins to a Priest? Can't I Just Ask God for Forgiveness?

This is a great question asked by Catholics and non-Catholics. There are several reasons why we confess our sins to a priest, ranging from the will of Christ to the way our human nature works. Let's explore these reasons more closely.

Christ Is Present and Working through the Priest

As we have already seen, Christ established the Sacrament of Penance and entrusted the power to forgive or retain sins to the Apostles and their successors. Accordingly, we confess our sins to a priest because it is the will of Christ. But it goes much deeper than that. As with any sacrament, the priest is ministering *in persona Christi,* which means in the Person of Christ. It is a simple but powerful truth: Christ is really present and ministering through the priest. It is Christ who baptizes, Christ who confirms, and Christ who hears and forgives our sins. We tell our sins not to a mere man, but to Christ Himself who is really present and working through the priest.

The Priest Represents both Christ and the Church

The second reason to confess to a priest has to do with the nature of sin and the healing needed to bring about true penance or reconciliation. When we deliberately choose to disobey God and reject His goodness, it wounds (or in the case of mortal sin, severs) our relationship with Him. We sever the relationship, not God. God always searches for us and calls us back to Him through Christ, just as He did with Adam after the first sin.

This is called the *divine dimension* of sin. Sin always affects our relationship with God. When we confess our sins to the priest we confess them to Christ. He restores our relationship with the Father through the power of the Holy Spirit. We come to the foot of the Cross and lay our sins before the Lamb of God, who washes them away through the blood and water that flowed from His side. That is what *really* happens when one goes to confession.

Also, there is no such thing as a "private sin." Yes, it can be done privately in that no other person knows about it (but God does). However, even a sin that is done in private hurts and affects others. *Every* time we sin it affects our ability to love—to relate and live in communion with others. This is certainly true when we commit a sin that directly affects or hurts another, but even those committed in private, even our sinful thoughts hurt others indirectly. Sin by its nature isolates us and wraps us in ourselves. Every sin has social consequences, harming and even destroying our relationship with others. Since we are members of the Church, the Mystical Body of Christ, sin also harms our communion with the Church, and in the case of mortal sin severs our relationship with her. This is why we cannot receive the sacraments (except

Penance) in the state of mortal sin—because we have separated ourselves from the life of the Church.

This is called the *human dimension* of sin. Every time we sin it wounds our relationship with others and the Church. By confessing our sins to the priest, we are also confessing to a leader and representative of the community and the Church, and therefore our relationship with others and the Church is also reconciled.

Confessing our sins to a priest addresses both the divine and human dimensions of sin and fully restores us to communion with God and the Church.

The Confession of Sin to Another Heals Our Human Nature

The third reason we confess our sins to a priest has a lot to do with our human nature. God in His wisdom knows that confessing our sins brings about a deeper and more complete healing of ourselves. As we said before, by its nature sin isolates us and causes us to become wrapped up in ourselves. The more isolated we become the more sin festers and worsens. Sin loves to operate in the dark. Keeping sin inside ourselves becomes like cancer eating at our souls and our humanity. The best way to defeat sin, like defeating cancer, is to remove it and bring it into the light. That may not be the most pleasant experience, similar to surgically removing cancer, but we will not be truly healed unless sin is brought into the light and removed.

This is the beauty of the Sacrament of Penance: it brings about true healing. When we confess our sins to another we are required to look the sin squarely in the eye, take ownership and responsibility for it, and admit it to another. We literally empty ourselves of sin so we may be filled with the grace of Christ. The Catechism powerfully brings out this aspect of the confession of sins.

> The confession (or disclosure) of sins, even from a simply human point of view, frees us and facilitates our reconciliation with others. Through such an admission man looks squarely at the sins he is guilty of, takes responsibility for them, and thereby opens himself again to God and to the communion of the Church in order to make a new future possible. (1455)

We Know and Experience in a Human Way Christ's Forgiveness

This is the most powerful aspect of the Sacrament of Penance. Remember that all the sacraments are visible, tangible signs that make present to us in a natural way what God is doing supernaturally. God is communicating His grace and love for us in a way we know and understand. Penance is an extraordinarily human and tangible experience of God's mercy and forgiveness.

If we were to simply ask God for forgiveness, we could only trust that He has forgiven us. But through confessing our sins in the Sacrament of Penance, we have a tangible means to give our sins over to Christ. Through the ministry of the priest, we experience Christ's forgiveness in a human and tangible way, through our senses of hearing, feeling, experiencing, and knowing. At the end of confession the priest extends his hand over us calling down the power of the Holy Spirit, allowing us to us hear and know the reality and power of Christ's merciful forgiveness through the priest's prayer of absolution.

By confessing our sins to a priest we participate in the Sacrament of Penance that Christ established. Through the sacrament Christ forgives us and brings about a real healing of our human nature. We also experience in a powerful way God's love and mercy that pours forth from the heart of Christ.

The Effects of the Sacrament of Penance

As we have seen, the Sacrament of Penance forgives our sins and restores our relationship with God and the Church. It is our "second baptism" in the sense that we are once again brought out of the darkness of sin and into the life and light of Christ. We also must remember that Penance not only gives us the grace of forgiveness, but also the grace and the power of the Holy Spirit to overcome sin, fight against temptation, and avoid the near occasion of sin. In other words, the more we receive Penance the more grace and power we will have to overcome sin in the future. Penance restores us to life and is extraordinary medicine against temptation and sin.

There is also an intrinsic link between Penance and the Eucharist; both defeat sin and give grace to help us grow in holiness and become like Christ. Penance destroys not only sin, but also the roots of sin within our souls. Frequent recourse to the Sacrament of Penance uproots sin and tills the soil of our soul, making it fertile and ready to receive the gift of Christ in the Eucharist. The Eucharist by its nature separates us from sin and transforms us to become like Christ. Penance and the Eucharist together are not only the antidote against Satan and sin, but are the most efficacious means to holiness.

The most important thing Catholics can do in their spiritual lives is to have frequent recourse to Penance and the Eucharist. Pope John Paul II powerfully states:

> It is certain that the Church of the new Advent, the Church that is continually preparing for the new coming of the Lord, must be the Church of the Eucharist and of Penance. (*Redemptor hominis*, no. 84)

How Often Should One Go to Confession?

One of the precepts of the Church is that the faithful are to confess serious sin at least once a year. That is the bare minimum. But that is like saying that one should take a shower at least once a year. As we explained, Penance is a great gift of Christ we should have frequent recourse to.

A person who commits a mortal sin must receive Penance in order to receive forgiveness. A mortal sin is so serious that it requires the confession of the sin and the action of sacramental grace to restore one to spiritual life. Someone who is very seriously hurt in an accident should immediately be taken to the hospital. It is even worse for someone guilty of mortal sin. They are spiritually dead and need the Divine Physician in the Sacrament of Penance to bring them back to life. A soul in the state of mortal sin should receive the Sacrament of Penance as soon as possible. A person cannot receive the Eucharist in the state of mortal sin; they must go to confession before receiving Communion.

Even if there are only venial sins on our consciences, it is highly recommended to receive Penance every month to three months or more frequently. Remember that the grace of the sacrament helps us overcome and battle the sins we confess.

> Without being strictly necessary, confession of everyday faults (venial sins) is nevertheless strongly recommended by the Church. Indeed the regular confession of our venial sins helps us form our conscience, fight against evil tendencies, let

> ourselves be healed by Christ and progress in the life of the Spirit. By receiving more frequently through this sacrament the gift of the Father's mercy, we are spurred to be merciful as he is merciful. (CCC 1458)

Avoiding Penance for long periods of time deprives us of great graces to overcome sin. The grace of the sacrament helps us avoid sin, particularly in our battle against sins with which we frequently struggle, before they become more serious in nature. Penance should be a normal and frequent part of our life.

Don't let guilt or shame keep you from the Sacrament of Penance. There is no sin that you could commit that God cannot or will not forgive if you go to Him with a contrite heart. Especially, do not let embarrassment be a reason to stay away from confession. There is nothing you could say that would shock a priest or be something he has not already heard. These tools and tactics of the devil to keep people away from confession must be resisted. Furthermore, priests are forbidden by severe penalty from disclosing to anyone what someone has confessed in confession. This is called the "**seal of confession**" or "sacramental seal" obligating a priest to keep absolutely secret what a penitent has told to him in the Sacrament of Penance.

If you have been away from this sacrament for many years, know that there is nothing that gives a priest and God greater joy than one who returns to this great sacrament. Confession is not a time for lecturing and belittling, but is a place of mercy and forgiveness. As long as you approach the sacrament with a sincere and contrite heart, there is nothing but the love and mercy of Christ awaiting you.

How to Go to Confession

The celebration of the Sacrament of Penance has four essential parts: contrition, confession, satisfaction, and absolution. All four parts take place when we receive Penance, and are very important steps in making a good confession and reconciling with God and the Church.

Contrition

The first and absolutely necessary step in the celebration of Penance is **contrition**. Contrition entails sorrow for the sins we have committed and the intention of avoiding and overcoming those sins. Confession is not a magic trick. We can't sin and expect forgiveness without being sincerely sorry.

Contrition precedes reception of the sacrament. Time should be taken before going to confession to recall our sins and express sorrow for them. This process is called an examination of conscience, which we should do often in our spiritual lives. We are called to do so at the beginning of Mass during the Penitential Rite, and we should do one at the end of each day, asking God to forgive us of any sins we committed during the day. It is simply accounting for the sins we have committed in preparation for what we will confess, and more importantly to express sorrow for these sins and ask God for mercy and forgiveness.

Before making an examination of conscience, we should say a prayer to the Holy Spirit, asking Him to help us to have a true accounting of our sins and to be sincerely sorry for them. One of the roles of the Holy Spirit is to help us see our sins and how ugly and evil they are. This is part of tilling the soul's soil, uprooting the evil so that Christ's grace may be fruitful within us.

In making our examination of conscience, we also prepare the list of sins we need to confess during the sacrament. This process may take place immediately before confession, or perhaps over a longer period of time before we actually go to confession. What do you actually need to confess?

First you need to confess any serious sins of which you are guilty. These are usually specific events and need to be confessed clearly. In other words, don't use code language or try to sugarcoat it. Just be out with it. Take responsibility for what you have done and get it out. Christ wants you to claim it so He can take it. Do not intentionally withhold a serious sin, for that is a serious sin in itself. It is permissible to accidentally forget a sin, but never to intentionally withhold a serious sin in confession.

For venial sins a list of every instance and example is not as important as realizing and confessing the nature of the sin and the root of it. For example, if you struggle with the sin of judging others, you likely won't remember every instance when you judged someone. It is important that you confess your struggle with that sin and perhaps why. Is it insecurity? Pride? Jealousy? Getting to the root will bring about healing. A good way to confess would be to say, "I really struggle with judging others based on their appearance and actions. It really makes it hard to love others because I am judging people a lot. I think it is because I feel insecure and it makes me feel better about myself when I judge others. I am very sorry for doing this." We all have areas in which we struggle, such as anger, judging, lying, foul language, impure thoughts, and other things. In a good confession we confess specific serious sins, but also confess the venial sins with which we struggle and why.

Confession of Sins

The second step is the actual **confession** of sins. This takes place in the presence of the priest. After his greeting you begin together with the Sign of the Cross. He might offer some words of encouragement to trust in God's mercy. Before you confess your sins you offer any information helpful to the priest such as the time since last confession, state in life (married, single, children), or the need for his help getting through the celebration of the sacrament. Many Catholics begin with the formula, "Bless me Father for I have sinned. It has been [time period] since my last confession." Then you will confess your sins as you have prepared. When you have completed confessing your sins, it is good to end with something like, "For these sins and for all my sins I am truly sorry." This not only lets the priest know you are finished confessing your sins, but it also is an expression of sorrow for any sins you did not recall or any sins you unintentionally forgot to confess. After you are finished, the priest may or may not counsel you with practical advice on how to overcome sin.

Satisfaction

The third step is what is called **satisfaction for sin**. This is the penance that the priest will give you after you confess your sins. A penance is usually prayers or small actions that the priest asks you to do in repentance for your sins. It may be three Hail Mary's or a Rosary, reading a passage from Scripture, or even doing a kind act for someone. A penance may be specific to a sin you confessed. You must complete your penance as soon as possible.

In addition to your penance the priest will also ask you to say an Act of Contrition in his presence before he gives you absolution. There is an Act of Contrition at the end of this chapter for you to learn. This is a formal act of sorrow you express before Christ. It should be done with sincerity. Taking a copy of the Act of Contrition into confession to pray is acceptable.

Absolution

The fourth and final step is **absolution**. This is the formal sign of the sacrament when, through the power of the Holy Spirit, the priest, in *persona*

Christi, forgives you of your sins. The priest will extend his hand over you, calling down the power of the Holy Spirit and saying the formal prayer of absolution:

> God, the Father of mercies,
> through the death and the resurrection of his Son
> has reconciled the world to himself
> and sent the Holy Spirit among us
> for the forgiveness of sins;
> through the ministry of the Church
> may God give you pardon and peace,
> and I absolve you from your sins
> in the name of the Father, and of the Son, and of the Holy Spirit.

As the Sign of the Cross is made over you, you are to make the Sign of the Cross yourself. The priest may conclude with, "Give thanks to the Lord for he is good." Your response is, "His mercy endures forever." At that point it is appropriate to thank the priest and conclude the celebration of the sacrament.

The Sacrament of Penance is the river of mercy through which Christ heals and reconciles us to God. Penance, along with the frequent reception of the Eucharist, must be at the very center of the Christian life as the greatest means to holiness.

EXAMINATION OF CONSCIENCE

Before receiving the Sacrament of Penance, we should spend time in prayerful reflection examining the ways in which we have failed to love God and neighbor. Below is a helpful guide for an **examination of conscience**.

Prayer before Confession

> **Come Holy Spirit into my soul. Enlighten my mind that I may know the sins I ought to confess, and grant me your grace to confess them fully, humbly, and with a contrite heart. Help me to firmly resolve not to commit them again. Grant for me the grace to make a good confession, that I may repent from my sins, and that my heart may be forever united with Yours in eternal love. Amen.**

THE TEN COMMANDMENTS

1. **I AM THE LORD THY GOD: THOU SHALT NOT HAVE STRANGE GODS BEFORE ME.**

   COMMANDS: faith, hope, love, and worship of God; reverence for holy things; prayer.

   FORBIDS: idolatry, superstition, spiritism, tempting God, sacrilege, and attendance at false worship.

2. **THOU SHALL NOT TAKE THE NAME OF THE LORD THY GOD IN VAIN.**

   COMMANDS: reverence in speaking about God and holy things; the keeping of oaths and vows.

   FORBIDS: blasphemy, the irreverent use of God's name, speaking disrespectfully of holy things, false oaths, and the breaking of vows.

3. **KEEP THE SABBATH HOLY.**

   COMMANDS: going to Mass on Sundays and holy days of obligation.

   FORBIDS: missing Mass through our own fault, unnecessary servile work on Sunday and holy days of obligation.

4. **HONOR THY FATHER AND THY MOTHER.**

   COMMANDS: love, respect, obedience on the part of children, care on the part of parents for the spiritual and temporal welfare of their children, obedience to civil and religious superiors.

   FORBIDS: hatred of parents and superiors, disrespect, disobedience.

5. THOU SHALT NOT KILL.

COMMANDS: safeguarding of our own life and bodily welfare and that of others.

FORBIDS: unjust killing, suicide, abortion, sterilization, contests to the death, endangering life and limb of self or others.

6. THOU SHALT NOT COMMIT ADULTERY.

COMMANDS: chastity in word and deed.

FORBIDS: obscene speech, impure actions alone or with others, pornography, sexual relations outside of marriage, contraception.

7. THOU SHALT NOT STEAL.

COMMANDS: respect for the property and rights of others, paying just debts, paying just wages to employees, integrity in public office.

FORBIDS: theft, damage to the property of others, not paying just debts, not returning found or borrowed articles, giving unjust measure or weight in selling, not paying just wages, bribery, cheating, fraud, accepting stolen property, not giving an honest day's work for wages received, breach of contract.

8. THOU SHALT NOT BEAR FALSE WITNESS AGAINST THY NEIGHBOR.

COMMANDS: truthfulness, respect for the good name of others, the observance of secrecy when required.

FORBIDS: lying, injury to the good name of others, slander, tale bearing, rash judgment, contemptuous speech, violation of secrecy.

9. THOU SHALT NOT COVET THY NEIGHBOR'S WIFE.

COMMANDS: purity in thought.

FORBIDS: willful impure thought and desires.

10. THOU SHALT NOT COVET THY NEIGHBOR'S GOODS.

COMMANDS: respect for the rights of others.

FORBIDS: the desire to take, keep, or damage the property of others.

Act of Contrition

My God, I am sorry for my sins with all my heart. In choosing to do wrong and failing to do good, I have sinned against you whom I should love above all things. I firmly intend, with your help, to do penance, to sin no more, and to avoid whatever leads me to sin. Our Savior Jesus Christ suffered and died for us. In his name, my God, have mercy. Amen.

From the Catechism: Key Words to Know

PENANCE, SACRAMENT OF: The liturgical celebration of God's forgiveness of the sins of the penitent, who is thus reconciled with God and with the Church. The acts of the penitent—contrition, confession of sins, and satisfaction or reparation—together with the prayer of absolution by the priest, constitute the essential elements of the Sacrament of Penance (980, 1422, 1440, 1448).

SEAL OF CONFESSION: The confessor's obligation to keep absolutely secret what a penitent has told to him in the Sacrament of Penance; also known as the "sacramental seal" (1467).

CONTRITION: Sorrow of the soul and hatred for the sin committed, together with a resolution not to sin again. Contrition is the most important act of the penitent and is necessary for the reception of the Sacrament of Penance (1451).

CONFESSION: An essential element of the Sacrament of Penance and Reconciliation, which consists in telling our sins to the priestly minister. By extension, the word "confession" is used to refer to the Sacrament of Penance itself (1455).

SATISFACTION (FOR SIN): An act whereby the sinner makes amends for sin, especially in reparation to God for offenses against Him. The penance given by the confessor in the Sacrament of Penance constitutes such satisfaction. All true satisfaction for sin must be a participation in the satisfaction for sin made by Christ through His death on the Cross (1459). See Penance; Penitent/Penitential; Reparation.

ABSOLUTION: An essential element of the Sacrament of Penance in which the priest, by the power entrusted to the Church by Christ, pardons the sin(s) of the penitent (1424, 1442, 1449, 1453, 1480).

EXAMINATION OF CONSCIENCE: Prayerful self-reflection on our words and deeds in the light of the Gospel to determine how we may have sinned against God. The reception of the Sacrament of Penance ought to be prepared for by such an examination of conscience (1454).

Chapter 20

The Sacrament of Anointing of the Sick

Reading the Catechism: Paragraphs 1499–1532

> Even though I walk through the valley of the shadow
> of death,
> I fear no evil for you are with me;
> your rod and your staff comfort me.
>
> —Psalm 23:4

The second of the two sacraments of healing is the Sacrament of the **Anointing of the Sick**. For many centuries it was considered to be a final preparation for death and was only administered to those who were at the end of their lives. While it is certainly appropriate and crucial to those who are dying, the fathers of the Second Vatican Council made the sacrament available to the faithful who are seriously sick or chronically ill.

This great sacrament imparts upon us a grace of healing, and the grace to accept and embrace our suffering with faith, hope, and love. Suffering is an inescapable part of human life, and the Anointing of the Sick joins our suffering with the suffering of Christ so that we may more fully share in His strength and love.

Origin of the Anointing of the Sick

The Sacrament of the Anointing of the Sick has always been a part of the sacramental life of the Church, and its origins can clearly be seen in Scripture in the Letter of James.

> Is anyone among you sick? He should summon the presbyters of the church, and they should pray over him and anoint (him) with oil in the name of the Lord, and the prayer of faith will save the sick person, and the Lord will raise him up. If he has committed any sins, he will be forgiven. (Jas. 5:14–15)

This reference explicitly shows the sacrament was already developed and being practiced in the New Testament Church. It also gives a remarkably simple but clear theology of the sacrament.

Vatican II Expands the Use of the Sacrament

Prior to Vatican II the common title for this sacrament was Extreme Unction (from Latin *unctio*, "anointing"). It was generally only administered to someone who was in immediate danger of dying. Vatican II clarified and broadened the understanding of the Anointing of the Sick, explaining that it is not just for the dying. The official commentary on the rite states: It is for anyone "whose health is seriously impaired by sickness or old age." Also, it is for the healing of the whole person. Illness and suffering are not limited to the physical realm; physical illness affects us mentally and emotionally.

Any baptized person who is seriously ill or suffering is eligible to receive the Anointing of the Sick. Many parishes will periodically offer it after Mass, especially on the first Friday of the month when we celebrate the Sacred Heart of Jesus. It can also be received by simply meeting with a priest. Ordinarily, priests make the sacrament available regularly at hospitals and health care centers. The sacrament is certainly appropriate right before surgery or in the case of serious illness.

The Sacrament of the Anointing of the Sick should *always* be given when someone is in danger of death. In these situations the Church encourages not only the Anointing of the Sick, but also Penance and the Eucharist. When one of the faithful is in danger of death, the "last rites" are celebrated in the following order. First, the Sacrament of Penance is celebrated for forgiveness of all sin. This is followed by the Sacrament of the Anointing of the Sick, which gives the person Christ's healing grace to prepare him for death. Then the dying person receives the Sacrament of the Holy Eucharist (called **viaticum**, Latin for "traveling provisions"), which unites the sufferer to Christ and is the spiritual food for one's "passing over" into eternal life.

If a dying person is unconscious and cannot make a confession of sins, the Anointing of the Sick grants a grace of absolution of sin. Ordinary reception of this sacrament does not grant absolution; one would still need to receive the Sacrament of Penance.

Grace for Strength and Peace in Suffering

In discussing the Anointing of the Sick, it is important to understand what is meant by healing. Often, when we hear the word "healing" we think only of physical healing. But there are many other types of healing. Certainly complete physical healing is possible, but many times physical suffering may simply lessen or the illness might depart more quickly than expected. The grace we receive in the Anointing of the Sick may also bring healing and peace to help us embrace our suffering. There may be deeper spiritual healing that frees us from sin and helps us to see God's plan and purpose to our suffering. Sometimes God's ultimate healing is death and the passing into eternal life. God knows what healing we need most.

So, the healing through the Anointing of the Sick goes deeper than the physical, and that is the real grace of the sacrament. Peace and healing do not always bring about the alleviation of suffering. Suffering often calls us to greater love, greater faith, and greater sacrifice. The Anointing of the Sick gives the healing grace of the Holy Spirit that heals us in ways we may not even expect.

The Signs of the Sacrament's Healing Grace

Saint James describes two visible signs of the Anointing of the Sick: the laying on of hands and the anointing with oil. "Pray over him and anoint him with oil in the name of the Lord." Both of these sacramental signs are signs of healing and power. The laying on of hands calls down the healing power of the Holy Spirit, and the anointing with oil is a sign of healing and strength.

Laying On of Hands

As we have seen in many of the sacraments, the laying on of hands (or epiclesis) is the calling down of the power of the Holy Spirit. In the Sacrament of the Anointing of the Sick, the healing power of the Holy Spirit is called upon the person to immerse them in the grace and strength of Christ. Jesus Himself often healed by laying hands on those brought to Him. The priest lays his hands on the head of the ill person and prays silently for God's grace and power to overshadow them.

Anointing with Oil

After the laying on of hands, the priest will anoint the forehead and hands of the person with the *oil of the infirm.* This is one of the three sacramental oils that are blessed by the bishop every Holy Week. This oil is blessed and consecrated specifically to be an oil of healing and comfort. Oil has always been used as a healing medication that cleanses and soothes pain. The oil of the infirm is a sign of Christ's grace and strength seeping into the ill person to give a special grace of healing and strength to suffer with faith, hope, and love.

The Effects of the Anointing of the Sick

Like all the other sacraments the Anointing of the Sick is efficacious; it gives us grace and transforms us to be like Christ. It unites us to the suffering Christ, so like Him, we may entrust ourselves into the hands of the Father and more perfectly do His will, even in our suffering.

Imparts a Special Gift of the Holy Spirit

This gift of the Holy Spirit is a gift of strengthening, peace, and courage to overcome the difficulties that come with our suffering and illness. It strengthens us against the temptation of despair and deepens our faith in Christ. This gift of healing the soul may lead to healing the body if that is God's will.

Unites Us More Fully to the Passion of Christ

The grace of the Anointing of the Sick enables us in a unique and mysterious way to unite our suffering with the Passion of Christ. By being sacramentally united to Christ's Passion we receive His strength, and by offering our suffering to be united with His we also participate in His saving mission. *Suffering presents us with a unique and powerful opportunity to love.* We are given a special grace to offer our suffering with Christ to the Father for our own salvation and the salvation of others.

Unites Us More Closely to the Church

Through the Sacrament of the Anointing of the Sick we are more closely united to the suffering Christ and to His mystical body, the Church. The sacrament calls for the intercession of the communion of saints to pray for the sick person to receive the consoling grace of the Spirit. In turn, the suffering of the sick person is offered for the sanctification and holiness of all the Church.

Gives Us the Grace of Final Preparation

For those who are dying, the Anointing of the Sick gives the grace of final preparation for the passing into eternal life. It marvelously brings to completion within us all the fruits and graces of the sacramental life received in our lifetime. Along with Penance and the Eucharist, the Anointing of the Sick completes our transformation into Christ and participation in His death and Resurrection. The Catechism beautifully states:

> The Anointing of the Sick completes our conformity to the death and Resurrection of Christ, just as Baptism began it. It completes the holy anointings that mark the whole Christian life: that of Baptism which sealed the new life in us, and that of Confirmation which strengthened us for the combat of this life. This last anointing fortifies the end of our earthly life like a solid rampart for the final struggles before entering the Father's house. (1523)

Who May Administer the Sacrament?

We see in the Letter of Saint James that it is the presbyters or priests of the Church minister the Sacrament of the Anointing of the Sick. "Let him call for the presbyters of the Church." Only a priest or bishop may administer the sacrament. We should never hesitate to call a priest to receive the Anointing of the Sick if we or others we love become ill, especially when there is danger of death. Through this sacrament we receive strength, courage, peace, and grace to face life's most difficult moments in union with Christ.

From the Catechism: Key Words to Know

ANOINTING OF THE SICK: One of the seven sacraments, also known as the "sacrament of the dying," administered by a priest to a baptized person who begins to be in danger of death because of illness or old age. The priest prays and anoints the body of the sick with oil. The proper effects of the sacrament include a special grace of healing and comfort to the Christian who is suffering the infirmities of serious illness or old age, and the forgiving of the person's sins (1499, 1520, 1523, 1526–1532).

VIATICUM: The Eucharist received by a dying person. It is the spiritual food for one's "passing over" to the Father from this world. With Penance and the Anointing of the Sick, the reception of Holy Communion as Viaticum constitutes the "last sacraments" of the Christian (1524).

Chapter 21

The Sacrament of Holy Orders

Reading the Catechism: Paragraphs 1533–1600

You are a priest forever according to the order of Melchizedek.
—Hebrews 7:17

The Sacrament of **Holy Orders** is called the sacrament of "apostolic ministry." Christ entrusted the Apostles with the ministry of teaching, ministering, and governing His people. Through this sacrament the "apostolic ministry" has been handed on throughout the history of the Church. Men **ordained** in the Sacrament of Holy Orders come to share in apostolic ministry. Through the power and presence of the Holy Spirit, they teach, minister, and govern with the authority of Christ.

The word "order" comes from the Roman tradition meaning a recognized governing body. To receive orders or to be ordained means to become a member of that body. Thus, through the Sacrament of Holy Orders bishops, priests, and deacons are consecrated or set apart by Christ to be His instruments in teaching, guiding, and ministering to His Church.

Holy Orders is also one of the sacraments in service of the communion of the Church. While it confers great authority and responsibility, it is an authority that serves the People of God, faithfully dispenses the graces of the sacraments, and preserves the communion and oneness of the Church by faithfulness to the truth revealed by Christ. Holy Orders is not about power and prestige; it is about being a sign and presence of Christ, who washed the feet of the Apostles.

The Three Degrees of Holy Orders

The Sacrament of Holy Orders has three degrees or levels of participation: the *episcopate* (bishops), the *presbyterate* (priests), and the *diaconate* (deacons). Let us take a more detailed look at each.

Episcopal Orders

The **episcopate** (bishop) is the highest degree of Holy Orders. The bishops possess the fullness of Holy Orders and share fully in the apostolic ministry. They are the high priests of the Church and the New Covenant. By receiving the fullness of the apostolic ministry, they are the direct successors of the Apostles. Within the Catholic Church there is a historically unbroken line of apostolic succession from the Apostles to the bishops today. As successors of the Apostles, the bishops in communion with the pope are the authoritative teachers and interpreters of the Word of God passed on through Sacred Scripture and Sacred Tradition. They are the ministers of the sacramental life of the Church and have the authority to perform all of the sacraments, including ordaining other bishops, priests, and deacons. They also have the authority to govern the Church both spiritually and materially.

Most bishops are the leaders of what is called a *diocese,* or a local church, comprised of several parishes. He is the overall shepherd of his diocese with particular authority to teach, minister, and govern his local church. All bishops and their dioceses are in communion with the pope who is the bishop of Rome. Thus, while each bishop shepherds his own diocese, the Church is one through communion with the successor of Peter, the pope.

While all bishops possess the fullness of Holy Orders and the apostolic ministry, there are different levels of bishops that denote different levels of governance in the Church. In other words, some bishops have greater responsibilities than others.

The Pope

The pope is the successor of Peter and has universal and supreme authority in the Church. Like Peter, Christ gives him the keys to the kingdom and he has the power to bind and loose in the name of Christ. He is the visible center of unity and communion within the Church and is the head of the college of bishops. All new bishops are appointed by him and are ordained with his blessing. *The pope preserves and maintains the visible and spiritual communion of the Church.*

Cardinals

The word "cardinal" comes from the Latin word meaning "hinge." Cardinals are considered the hinges, or ambassadors of the pope. They wear the red zucchettos (skullcaps) and in almost all cases assume significant responsibility in the Church. Many of them work in the Roman Curia, the pope's governing office at the Vatican. The Curia is very similar to the President's Cabinet consisting of the heads of specific governing offices and advisors. Those promoted to cardinal are usually bishops. Many cardinals are heads of large archdioceses such as New York or Chicago. The cardinals are also responsible for electing a new pope. For most of the history of the Church, while not strictly necessary, the pope chosen has been a cardinal.

Archbishops

Archbishops shepherd a large diocese called an archdiocese. An archdiocese is also the metropolitan or principal diocese in a certain geographical region. An archbishop has certain oversight and authority over the bishops in the dioceses of his region. For example, the Denver Archdiocese oversees the dioceses of Cheyenne, Colorado Springs, and Pueblo. Unless an archbishop is a cardinal, he wears a violet zucchetto.

Bishops

Bishops shepherd a diocese and also wear the violet zucchetto. Some bishops as well as archbishops may not head a diocese but are in charge of a department or organization within the Church.

Bishops also have and wear special symbols that point to their role and mission.

- The miter, or arch-shaped headdress: The miter is a sign of the bishop's authority and points toward heaven from which his authority comes. This "crown" of authority is not to lord over the People of God, but to serve the faithful in bringing them to the truth of Christ.

- The *crosier* or shepherd's staff: The crosier is a symbol that the bishop represents Christ the Good Shepherd, and like Christ he shepherds his flock toward heaven.
- The ring: The ring is a sign of authority, and in generations past was the authoritative stamp the bishop used to seal letters. The ring also symbolizes the bishop being wed to the Church and accepting the Church as his bride. The bishop's role is to protect and serve his unblemished bride.
- The *cathedra* (or chair): From this chair the bishop officially teaches and governs. The church with the bishop's cathedra is called the *cathedral* and is the main church within a diocese.

Presbyterate Orders

The presbyterate (priesthood) is the second degree of Holy Orders. While priests do not possess the fullness of Holy Orders and the apostolic ministry, through the bishop they do *share* in the apostolic ministry and ministerial **priesthood.** They act as the associates of the bishop, assisting him in preaching and administering the sacraments in his diocese. The authority and ministry of priests is intrinsically connected to the bishop and come from him; however, priests cannot ordain other priests or bishops, nor can they perform the Sacrament of Confirmation without delegation or explicit permission from the bishop.

Diaconate Orders

The **diaconate** is the third degree of Holy Orders. Deacons fundamentally differ from bishops and priests in that they do not share in the ministerial priesthood. However, they are ordained through the Sacrament of Holy Orders and are given a special gift and grace of the Holy Spirit to preach the Word of God and act in service to the People of God. The main function of the deacon is to assist the bishops and priests in preaching, serving at the altar, and pastoring the faithful through various ministries. In addition, deacons can baptize and witness marriages.

There are two types of deacons in the Church, transitional and permanent. A transitional deacon is a man in his final year of preparation for the priesthood. In this case, the diaconate is the transition between the lay state and the priesthood. A permanent deacon is a man who is ordained a deacon without an intention of becoming a priest. A permanent deacon may be married, and serves a unique role by living in the secular world and fulfilling his ordained role in the Church.

Signs and Effects of the Sacrament of Holy Orders

The Imposition of Hands

The essential sign for all three degrees of Holy Orders is the imposition or laying on of hands by the bishop. This powerful sign of Holy Orders confers the sacrament in two important ways.

First, it calls down the Holy Spirit to fill the candidate for ordination (ordinand) with the power and gifts of the Holy Spirit, thereby enabling him to serve and minister in the name of Christ. For a bishop or priest, this calling down of the Holy Spirit joins him to the ministerial priesthood of Christ, enabling him to act in the Person of Christ through the celebration of the sacraments.

Second, the imposition of the bishop's hands, especially in the ordination of a bishop, is the handing on of the apostolic ministry and authority of teaching, ministering, and governing in the name of Christ. This handing on of apostolic succession continues the unbroken line of authority in the Church that Christ established and will continue to the end of time. Only a bishop can hand on apostolic succession and Holy Orders.

The Anointing with Sacred Chrism

Bishops, priests, and deacons are also anointed with sacred chrism by the bishop. As seen in Confirmation, sacred chrism is consecratory in nature; it sets apart the priest as belonging to God forever.

In Holy Orders, the man receives a permanent spiritual mark of belonging to Christ. For priests and bishops, it signals their union with Christ the High Priest. For deacons, Holy Orders unites them to Christ who serves all. The ordinand's soul is conformed for all eternity to Christ in a unique and unchangeable way.

This permanent spiritual mark can never be removed, and once a man is validly ordained he remains ordained forever. While ordination can never be removed, a bishop, priest, or deacon may have the functions, obligations, and responsibilities of his ordination discharged or removed for grave reasons. But he still remains forever a bishop, priest, or deacon. In addition, Holy Orders can never be repeated.

Celibacy and the Ordination of Women

Celibacy and the Priesthood

In the discipline of the Latin rite, priests and bishops make a promise of chastity and **celibacy** as a way of dedicating their whole hearts and lives to the service of the Church. Virginity and celibacy have always been outward signs of one's total consecration to God. There is also a practicality to the Church's discipline of unmarried priests and bishops, for they are able to give total devotion and service to the People of God without the concerns of family and secular life. In speaking on celibacy and the priesthood, there are two important points that must be clarified.

First, the Church's discipline of celibacy for the priesthood is exactly that, a discipline. It has changed in the past and could be changed by the pope if in his wisdom he decided to do so. There are priests in the Latin rite who have converted from the Episcopal or Presbyterian tradition and are married. In many of the Eastern rites, priests are allowed to be married (although bishops are celibate) and even the Apostles were married. The Church's discipline on celibacy and the priesthood is not part of Sacred Tradition and divine Revelation and therefore could change.

Second, those who are called to the priesthood embrace celibacy out of love for the Church, because through celibacy they are able to give themselves totally to the Church. In our highly sexualized society, many believe that committing oneself to a life of celibacy is either impossible or unhealthy. Contrary to popular belief, this is not true. Through the Sacrament of Holy Orders God gives the grace of the Holy Spirit to the priest so he can faithfully live a celibate life. The Church is careful in interviewing, admitting, and forming those seeking to enter the priesthood, ensuring they are able to freely and willingly enter the celibate state. When God calls a man to the priesthood, He places in the man's heart the desire to serve him in this way.

The Reservation of Ordination to Men Alone

Unlike celibacy, which is a discipline of the Church, the ordination of only men is part of Sacred Tradition and divine Revelation and is not open for change. The Church has no authority to ordain women to the priesthood because Christ Himself chose only men, and the example of the Apostles and their immediate successors also witnesses to this divinely instituted Tradition. Christ certainly could have chosen women to be among the Apostles, for many of the women who followed Him showed greater faith and fidelity to Christ than the Apostles. Mary, His mother, was the perfect disciple and would have been the perfect Apostle, but Christ did not choose women, nor did the Apostles or their immediate successors. Christ showed that He was willing to break with the social customs of the time, so the mores of the time cannot be the reason why he chose only men. The reasons are more profound than that.

Christ chose men because He was a man, and God revealed Himself to us in the Person of a man, Jesus Christ. The Apostles and their successors act in the Person of Christ in the sacraments. Humanly speaking, only a man can act as a man. Does this degrade or lessen women in any way? No. Look at what God did with Mary. Mary is the perfect disciple, the Model of the Church. If we want to know how to love, follow, and be like Christ, Mary is the standard. Christ reveals God to us, while Mary reveals to us how to love God and live in His life. Christ and Mary complement each other just like man and woman complement each other.

Although women cannot be ordained, their role within the Church is indispensable. Motherhood is one of the holiest and most necessary roles in the Church. There would be no Church, no popes, no bishops, and no priests without mothers. Although men and women are different and have different roles in the Church, both are indispensable. In the ministries and activities of the Church, both men and women contribute to its sanctification and the building of the kingdom.

Those who are upset or offended by the reservation of the priesthood to men alone are often missing the point. The priesthood is not about power and prestige; it is about serving the People of God. We are all called to serve, and authority is given in order to serve others, not "lord over" others. The priesthood is a calling, not a right. God calls those He chooses to the priesthood; it is not anyone's "right" to become a priest.

In order to respond to any confusion and define the Church's position on the ordination of women, Pope John Paul II forcefully stated:

> Although the teaching that priestly ordination is to be reserved to men alone has been preserved by the constant and universal Tradition of the Church and firmly taught by the Magisterium in its more recent documents, at the present time in some places it is nonetheless considered still open to debate, or the Church's judgment that women are not to be admitted to ordination is considered to have a merely disciplinary force.
>
> Wherefore, in order that all doubt may be removed regarding a matter of great importance, a matter which pertains to the Church's divine constitution itself, in virtue of my ministry of confirming the brethren (cf. Lk. 22:32) I declare that the Church has no authority whatsoever to confer priestly ordination on women and that this judgment is to be definitively held by all the Church's faithful. (Apostolic Letter on Reserving Priestly Ordination to Men Alone *Ordinatio sacerdotalis* [May 22, 1994], no. 4)

Christ hands on the apostolic ministry and ministers to His people through the Sacrament of Holy Orders. As Catholics, we should keep in our prayers the men to whom Christ has entrusted the Church, that they may be faithful to their calling and powerful witnesses of Christ's grace and love to the Church and the world. We must constantly pray for men to respond to the call to the priesthood, so that the sacraments of the Church will continue to be the source of rivers of grace and mercy to a broken world.

From the Catechism: Key Words to Know

HOLY ORDERS: The Sacrament of Apostolic Ministry by which the mission entrusted by Christ to His Apostles continues to be exercised in the Church through the laying on of hands. This sacrament has three distinct degrees or "orders": deacon, priest, and bishop. All three confer a permanent, sacramental character (1536).

ORDINATION: The rite of the Sacrament of Holy Orders by which the bishop, through the imposition of hands and the prayer of consecration, confers the order of bishop, priest, or deacon to exercise a sacred power that comes from Christ on behalf of the Church (1538).

EPISCOPAL/EPISCOPATE: Pertaining to the office of bishop (in Greek *episkopos*), hence episcopal consecration, the episcopal college, and episcopal conferences (883, 887, 1557). "Episcopate" is a collective noun referring to all those who have received sacramental ordination as bishops.

PRIESTHOOD: The ministerial priesthood received in the Sacrament of Holy Orders differs in essence from this common priesthood of all the faithful. It has as its purpose to serve the priesthood of all the faithful by building up and guiding the Church in the name of Christ, who is Head of the Body (1547).

DEACON, DIACONATE: A third degree of the hierarchy of the Sacrament of Holy Orders after bishop and priest. The deacon is ordained not to priesthood but for ministry and service. Deacons are ordained to assist the bishop and priests in the celebration of the divine mysteries, above all the Eucharist, in the distribution of Holy Communion, in assisting at and blessing marriages, in the proclamation of the Gospel and preaching, in presiding over funerals, and in dedicating themselves to the various ministries of charity. While the Churches of the East have always had a functioning order of deacons, in the West the permanent diaconate was reestablished by the Second Vatican Council (1569, 1571).

CELIBACY: The state or condition of those who have chosen to remain unmarried for the sake of the kingdom of heaven in order to give themselves entirely to God and to the service of His people. In the Latin Church, celibacy is obligatory for bishops and priests. In some Eastern Churches, celibacy is a prerequisite for the ordination only of bishops; priests may not marry after they have been ordained (1579, 1580).

Chapter 22

The Sacrament of Marriage

Reading the Catechism: Paragraphs 1601–1666

> For this reason a man shall leave his father and his mother and be joined to his wife, and the two shall become one flesh.
>
> —Ephesians 5:31

The Sacrament of **Marriage** is the sacrament of lifelong and life-giving love in which spouses, filled with the grace of Christ, become a living and visible sign of Christ's love for the Church and of the mystery of the Trinity. Like Holy Orders, Marriage is a sacrament of **vocation** at the service of the communion of the Church. As the domestic church, the family is irreplaceable in the building of the Body of Christ.

In this chapter we will see how God's plan for marriage was revealed in creation, and how Christ instituted the Sacrament of Marriage to be the visible, living sign of His love for the Church. We will explore the vital role of the family in the Church and society, and answer the common questions and misunderstandings concerning annulments in the Church.

The Sacrament of Lifelong and Life-Giving Love

In the Book of Genesis, the two creation stories reveal God's plan for the Sacrament of Marriage. He created man and woman in His image and likeness and called them to live in an intimate union of lifelong and life-giving love.

Lifelong Love

Marriage unites a man and a woman in lifelong love: "That is why a man leaves his father and mother and clings to his wife, and the two of them become one body" (Gen. 2:24). In the Sacrament of Marriage the couple is called to a profound union of love. In living out their marriage vows, they give a complete gift of self to each other, physically, emotionally, and spiritually. Through this complete self-giving, spouses (while remaining two separate distinct persons) become "one flesh," a new reality.

This intimate union is revealed in Genesis 2:25: "The man and his wife were both naked, yet they felt no shame." Nothing separated the oneness that united Adam and Eve. In the New Covenant the complete union of spouses in Marriage is strengthened and sealed by Christ's grace, which sustains the one-flesh union of husband and wife. The declaration of love between the man and the woman before God and His Church seals a bond that cannot be broken except by death. With the help and presence of God's grace, husband and wife are called to grow in love and communion every day through all the hardships and sufferings of life.

Life-giving Love

Marriage is fruitful through life-giving love: "God blessed them and God said to them: Be fertile and multiply; fill the earth and subdue it" (Gen. 1:28). The union of husband and wife is ordained by God to be fruitful in the creation of new human life. Through their sexual union, they participate in the creative power of God and give life to a new person in the image and likeness of God. They become co-creators with God!

Because a sacramental marriage is a profound union of love involving husband, wife, and God, the married couple can witness to the world a fruitfulness of charity, hospitality, and *sacrifice* even if they are not blessed with children (see CCC 1654).

The Sign of the Sacrament of Marriage

The sign of the Sacrament of Marriage is unique. It is not oil or the laying on of hands or some other external sign. It is love pledged and lived out between husband and wife. That love is the visible and tangible sign of a supernatural reality. The minister of the Sacrament of Marriage differs from the other sacraments. In the Latin rite the spouses administer the Sacrament of Marriage to one another through the exchanging of their vows.

Visible Sign of Christ's Love for the Church

The love between husband and wife in the Sacrament of Marriage is a visible sign of Christ's love for the Church. In a mystical way Marriage makes this love of Christ present. Paul speaks of this reality in the Letter to the Ephesians:

> Husbands, love your wives, even as Christ loved the church and handed himself over for her to sanctify her, cleansing her by the bath of water with the word, that he might present to himself the church in splendor, without spot or wrinkle or any such thing, that she might be holy and without blemish. So (also) husbands should love their wives as their own bodies. He who loves his wife loves himself. For no one hates his own flesh but rather nourishes and cherishes it, even as Christ does the church, because we are members of his body. "For this reason a man shall leave (his) father and (his) mother and be joined to his wife, and the two shall become one flesh." This is a great mystery, but I speak in reference to Christ and the church. In any case, each one of you should love his wife as himself, and the wife should respect her husband. (Eph. 5:25–33)

The love between husband and wife should mirror the love of Christ for the Church, a love that is complete, unconditional, self-sacrificing, unending, nourishing, and cherishing. To be faithful to the reality to which they are to bear witness, spouses are called through their daily commitment to faithfully live the love they have pledged to one another. Marriage is a daily yes, a daily commitment of spouses to love one another as Christ loved the Church, even through the sufferings, hardships, sicknesses, and hurts of life.

Christ did not abandon the Church but embraced the Cross for her salvation. At times marriage requires spouses to bear the cross for one another. Even in difficult times, Christ's grace can strengthen their love and union. Lived faithfully, marriage is a living witness and sign of the sacrificial love of Christ that knows no boundaries. Marriage literally makes Christ's love incarnate in the world and society.

Visible, Living Sign of the Nature and Life of the Trinity

Marriage and the family are also visible signs of the nature of the Trinity, the manifestation of the Trinitarian love of God. In the same way that the Father and the Son give a complete and total gift of self to one another, spouses in marriage are called to give a complete gift of self to one another. The love between the Father and the Son is fruitful, pouring forth from them in the third Person of the Trinity, the Holy Spirit. The love between spouses is also by its nature fruitful, and through the marital embrace, the love between husband and wife bears fruit in the creation of a new human life. In the same way that the Holy Spirit is the love between the Father and the Son, it can be said that a child is the incarnation of the love between husband and wife. Thus in the most profound way marriage and the family bear witness to the love and unity of God in which we are created, manifesting to the entire world the mystery of the love of the Holy Trinity.

The Role and Mission of the Family

The Family Is the Domestic Church

From the beginning of time the family has been the source of human life and the place where the divine life of faith is nurtured. Within the family the love of Christ is first witnessed to children. Through the parents the seeds of faith are planted and carefully nurtured in children so they produce great fruit. The family is called the "domestic church" because it is called to be a model of the Church, and also because the Church gains strength, grows, and flourishes through the family. Parents have a particular responsibility to bring children up in the faith. They are the first heralds of the Gospel, bringing to their children the light and life of Christ. Through the family the Church becomes "incarnate" in society. As Pope John Paul II states, "The Church thus finds in the family, born of the sacrament, the cradle and the setting in which she can enter the human generations and where these in their turn can enter the Church" (Apostolic Exhortation on the Christian Family *Familiaris consortio* [November 22, 1981], no. 15).

The Family Is a Witness of Faith to the World

The family has an indispensable role in society as the living witness of faith, hope, and charity in an often dark and hostile world. Within holy families children first learn the basic virtues of justice, charity, forgiveness, and generosity. Within this framework these virtues and lessons of life are lived and nurtured, forming citizens of good will for society. The family is the vital cell of society on which civilization itself depends.

Family members are called through Baptism to be living witnesses of Christ and the Church to the secular world. They have a unique and indispensable role of witnessing and proclaiming the Gospel in their schools, workplaces, and even places of leisure. Through their words and examples Christian families become leaven in the world, making the presence of Christ incarnate in the ordinary places of society and culture. By its very nature the family is the first place of evangelization within both the Church and society.

Annulments

In concluding our survey of marriage and family, we must consider the question of annulments in the Church. An annulment or "declaration of nullity" is not just a form of "Catholic divorce" as many think. It is a declaration by the Church that a sacramental marriage never took place. Therefore, a marriage never existed in the eyes of the Church—the Sacrament of Marriage did not happen. The Church does not recognize **divorce.** A valid sacramental marriage exists until the death of one of the spouses and cannot be dissolved or broken. The question addressed in the case of an annulment is whether a valid sacramental marriage existed.

Valid vs. Invalid

The administration of a sacrament can be either valid or invalid. To be valid certain essentials of the sacrament must be present. If any of those essentials are missing, the sacrament is invalid; it never happened.

For example, Baptism must precede Confirmation because Confirmation perfects baptismal grace. If a non-baptized person attempted to receive Confirmation, the sacrament would be invalid even if the rite were properly "performed."

The annulment process investigates whether a marriage is valid even though it was performed. A sacramental marriage can be rendered invalid if any of the essentials required for a valid marriage are missing. If so, the sacrament never happened. Thus, an annulment is not a divorce but a declaration by the Church that a sacramental marriage never took place.

What Is Necessary for Marriage to be Valid?

There are several essentials for a sacramental marriage to be valid in the eyes of the Church. Let's look at them more closely.

Form

The first essential is form, or how the sacrament was performed. Regardless of the spouse's religion, a person who is baptized Catholic must be married in a Catholic Church in the presence of a bishop, priest, or deacon with at least two witnesses. Any deviation from that form, such as being married by a justice of the peace, would automatically render the marriage sacramentally invalid. In the eyes of the Church, the marriage never happened (even though civilly it may be recognized). This is called lack of form.

Catholics who were married outside the proper form may have their marriage regularized in the Church through convalidation or sanation, a process that sacramentally validates their marriage. The Church recognizes marriages that take place in other Christian traditions as valid marriages. If two Baptists are married in the Baptist Church, the Church recognizes that as proper form and a sacramentally valid marriage. This is why converts to the Catholic faith who are married in their faith tradition do not have to go through convalidation in the Catholic Church in most cases.

Consent

For a sacramental marriage to be valid it must be entered into freely with the consent of both spouses. Sometimes people withhold their consent to one of the minimum requirements for marriage (openness to having children, for example). If for some reason the marriage was not entered into with the consent of one or both spouses, it is sacramentally invalid. Lack of consent may be very obvious or it may not be. This is one of the essentials investigated by the Church in the annulment process.

Impediments

There are also various **impediments** that can keep a person from entering into a valid sacramental marriage. For example, only two baptized people can enter into a sacramental marriage, and if one of the participants is not baptized he is impeded from entering into a valid marriage. Another impediment would be marrying below a certain age. Impotence can also be an impediment to marriage (infertility, however, is not an impediment).

For grave or serious reasons a bishop may grant a dispensation from form, or in some cases impediment issues. Consent on behalf of both spouses, however, must always be real and free. For a marriage to be sacramental it must be consummated; a non-consummated marriage can also be considered invalid. Within the annulment process all those issues are considered.

The Annulment Process

The annulment process involves a very in-depth investigation by the Church to verify whether a marriage was entered into validly. The person seeking the annulment, as well as the other spouse, complete paperwork and are interviewed. Witnesses are also summoned and interviewed. Based upon the evidence gathered, the Church makes a judgment on the validity of the marriage. If it is judged invalid, the annulment is granted and the couple are free to enter into a sacramental marriage. If the marriage is judged to be valid, the two remain sacramentally married and cannot remarry. Remember, the judgment of the Church on the sacramentality of marriage is separate from any civil judgments concerning the marriage.

Each diocese has a tribunal or judicial court in which matters of Church law (**canon law**) are investigated and settled. The annulment procedure takes place through the tribunal of the diocese in which the person seeking the annulment was married. For any questions concerning annulments, you can contact your local parish or diocese for assistance.

In conclusion, the Sacrament of Marriage is the sacrament of lifelong and life-giving love that is the real and visible sign and witness of Christ's love for the Church. Marriage and the family are at the very heart of the Church's life and mission. Those who are called to this sacrament must, with prayer and sacrifice, build up the Church through holy families contributing to the future of the Church. Holy families are rich gardens in which the seeds of vocations grow. In the face of the modern day "culture of death" that seeks to attack and degrade the family, families must be courageous heralds for the "culture of life," instruments of God's life and love in a world so often lost in darkness.

From the Catechism: Key Words to Know

MARRIAGE: A covenant or partnership of life between a man and woman ordered to the well-being of the spouses and to the procreation and upbringing of children. When validly contracted between two baptized people, marriage is a sacrament called Matrimony (1601).

VOCATION: The calling or destiny we have in this life and hereafter. God has created the human person to love and serve Him; the fulfillment of this vocation is eternal happiness (1, 358, 1700). Christ calls the faithful to the perfection of holiness (825). The vocation of the laity consists in seeking the kingdom of God by engaging in temporal affairs and directing them according to God's will (898). Priestly and religious vocations are dedicated to the service of the Church as the universal sacrament of salvation (cf. 873; 931).

DIVORCE: The claim that the indissoluble marriage bond validly entered into between a man and a woman is broken. A civil dissolution of the marriage contract (divorce) does not free persons from a valid marriage before God; remarriage would not be morally licit (2382; cf. 1650).

IMPEDIMENT: An obstacle that makes a person ineligible for performing an act or receiving a sacrament, such as Holy Orders or Matrimony (cf. 1635).

CANON LAW: The rules (canons or laws) that provide the norms for good order in the visible society of the Church. Those canon laws that apply universally are contained in the Codes of Canon Law. The most recent Code of Canon Law was promulgated in 1983 for the Latin (Western) Church and in 1991 for the Eastern Church (*The Code of Canons of the Eastern Churches*).

Chapter 23

Sexual Morality

Reading the Catechism: Paragraphs 2331–2400

> Married love particularly reveals its true nature and nobility when we realize that it takes its origin from God, who "is love," the Father "from whom every family in heaven and on earth is named."
>
> —Pope Paul VI, Encyclical Letter Concerning the Regulation of Birth *Humanae Vitae* (July 25, 1968), no. 8

The Morality of Human Sexuality

Human sexuality is intimately connected with the Sacrament of Marriage. Sexual union of spouses is ordained and willed by God to be the highest and most perfect expression of marital love. Therefore it must remain faithful to that love and the invisible realities it expresses: Christ's love for the Church and the life and love of the Holy Trinity. Spouses must be faithful to each other and express faithful sexual love "for richer, for poorer, in sickness and in health." Thus, the expression of sexual love cannot be separated from the marriage vows.

The Church's teachings concerning sexuality are not based upon theological opinions, but on the very nature of love and the human person as created in the image and likeness of God. Conjugal love is good and holy, and a moment of grace.

However, sexuality is a powerful force that can be quite harmful and addictive if abused or distorted. The Church strives to preserve and protect the nature of human love and sexuality. Her teachings are based on the natural law, that is, God's plan for human nature already written in the very being of humanity. They are also based on the divine law revealed by Christ, which makes known to us God's plan for marriage and sexuality.

The Conjugal Act Is both Unitive and Procreative

The marital act is established by God to be both unitive (the complete expression of self giving) and procreative (open to the creation of human life). These two aspects expressed in the conjugal act cannot be separated. Doing so distorts the true meaning and nature of sexuality as well as the nature of the human person, who is created in the image and likeness of God.

The *unitive* aspect of the conjugal act is total gift of self to another. It is a mutual gift and acceptance of the whole person. This complete gift of self can only happen through lifelong and life-giving love of spouses. *Sexual union is the total and unconditional expression of love, withholding nothing from one another, physically, emotionally, or spiritually.* In conjugal love the spouses literally become one flesh.

The *procreative* aspect of the conjugal act acknowledges that sexual intercourse is for the creation of human life. God willed that through conjugal love we participate with Him in creating human life. Although each act of sexual union does not result in the creation of a new human being, the conjugal act must always remain open to life and God's participation in it. Love by its very nature is fruitful, as especially seen in the nature of the Trinity and Christ's love for the Church. Marital love must always be faithful to the reality that it expresses.

Therefore, we come to a basic moral principle within sexual morality. *You cannot separate marriage, the sexual act (and expressions of), and procreation.* We are called to adhere to the following basic moral principles. To intentionally separate procreation from the sexual act is a grave moral wrong. Using contraception to close the procreative aspect of the sexual act is a grave moral wrong. Marriage, the sexual act, and openness to procreation are inseparable.

Why are sexual sins considered grave or mortal sins? They are objectively grave because they involve the deepest and most personal areas of the person. Sexuality and our expression of it affect us tremendously. Sexual sin can affect our ability to love others, can cause us to see others as mere objects, and can become habitual and addictive, causing serious harm to the person. Sexual sin also harms others. They undermine the family and society. They are considered grave sins because the consequences are serious whether we realize them immediately or not. Many times the consequences are not immediately evident, but they gradually erode a person's freedom and ability to give of self to another.

Offenses against Sexuality

Our culture is very sexualized and constantly bombarding us with sexual images. Many television shows and movies contain sexual situations, innuendos, and even outright pornography. The internet is filled with pornography that can be freely and easily accessed. These are serious "structural sins" within our society that are having disastrous consequences. The Catechism defines structural sins as both "the expression and effect of personal sins" in society, which make its members "accomplices of one another and causes concupiscence, violence, and injustice to reign" (CCC 1869).

Those of us who are followers of Christ need to examine our consciences concerning these sins and make our lives witnesses of **chastity** and purity. As Saint Paul says, "Do not conform yourselves to this age but be transformed by the renewal of your mind, that you may discern what is the will of God, what is good and pleasing and perfect" (Rom. 12:2).

The first step to overcome sexual sin is to know what these sins are and why they are so wrong.

Premarital or extramarital sex

Sex outside of marriage, **fornication,** violates the unitive nature of the marital act because it is not a complete, total, and unconditional gift of self to the other. Two unmarried people who have sex are speaking with their bodies a language of total lifelong and unconditional love and commitment, while that is not at all their intent. Even if a man and a woman are "in love," sex outside of marriage lacks lifelong and life-giving commitment in God's grace. Their relationship lacks a total giving of self. For many, premarital or extramarital sex is primarily for self-gratification and becomes recreational activity. This seriously degrades the gift of sexuality as God intended and devalues the human person.

Masturbation

Masturbation violates both the unitive and procreative aspects of sexual love. It distorts sexuality to complete selfish love, stripping it of any meaning beyond self-gratification. Combined with pornography it is terribly addictive and sometimes leads one to a lifetime of sexual addiction very difficult to overcome. Sadly, many psychologists and even some educators tout masturbation as a healthy and normal expression of sexuality. In reality it is one of the more destructive sins against sexuality and has devastating effects on a person emotionally and spiritually.

Pornography

Pornography is seriously wrong, violates human sexual love, and is also highly addictive. It objectifies the human person, reducing women and men to mere objects to be used for self-gratification. Pornography degrades human beings and the sexual act. It undermines the ability to give ourselves fully through sexual love, and in marriage the spouse is seen not as a person but simply as an object of pleasure. Internet pornography is a serious problem in our society due to its private and easy access. It so degrades and objectifies the person that it has even led several known serial killers to begin their murderous ways.

Homosexuality

Homosexuality distorts both the unitive and procreative aspects of sexual love. Sexuality was created by God so the unitive love between man and woman would allow mankind to share in the creative power of God. Homosexuality obviously violates the procreative aspect of God's plan. People with homosexual tendencies are called to live a chaste life in the same way that a single person is called to live. Even married people are called to chastity and must avoid lust in expressions of affection with their spouse. The Church does not condemn the person with homosexual tendencies but expects them to live a life that respects the dignity of sexuality. People with same-sex attraction enter into sin when they act upon it, or indulge in impure thoughts in the same way that heterosexual people can fall into sin.

Technological fertilization

Human procreation cannot be separated from married sexual love. Procedures such *in vitro* fertilization are a violation of the nature of human sexuality. This will be covered in much more detail in chapter twenty-six.

Church Teaching Concerning Contraception

One of the serious and most widespread violations of marriage and sexual love is **contraception**. This is one of the most controversial teachings of the Catholic Church because it is so countercultural, and because on the surface contraception seems to be so good and responsible. Unfortunately, most people, including most Catholics, know the Church teaches that contraception is wrong, but they do not know *why* it is wrong or how seriously it harms and undermines marriage and sexual love. This section will explain the Church's teaching concerning contraception.

History of Contraception

The Church has always taught that contraception is a violation of human love and sexuality. Even after the Protestant Reformation in the sixteenth century, all Christian churches taught the immorality of contraception up until 1930.

At the Lambeth Conference in 1930, the Anglican Communion, which includes the Episcopal Church, was the first Christian church to split from Scripture and Tradition and allow contraception in very grave situations. However, many other Christian churches began to relax the prohibition on contraception soon after.

Responding to the Episcopalian approval of contraception, Pope Pius XI promulgated his 1930 encyclical letter "On Christian Marriage," *Casti Connubii*. It strongly condemned the use of contraception as "an offense against the law of God and of nature" and a "foul stain" on the Sacrament of Marriage. He accused some of "departing from the uninterrupted Christian Tradition" by allowing the use of contraception.

During the 1960s the contraception debate was again pushed to the forefront with the emergence of the birth control pill. In 1968, Pope Paul VI issued the encyclical letter "On Human Life" *Humanae vitae,* again reaffirming the Church's teaching concerning the use of contraceptives. Both Pope Pius XI and Pope Paul VI were:

- reaffirming Sacred Tradition and the natural law.
- safeguarding the true nature, purpose, gift, and responsibility of human love that was questioned and under attack.
- *not* changing or making up new teaching.

Why Is Contraception Wrong?

Contraception violates both the unitive and procreative aspects of the conjugal act. It completely distorts the purpose and nature of sexual love as established by God.

First, contraceptives violate the unitive aspect of sexual intercourse because there no longer exists a total and complete gift of self between husband and wife. Why not? Contraceptives reject the fertility of the woman or the man, and the ability of one's spouse to be a co-creator with God in bringing about new human life. It rejects one of the most remarkable and fundamental realities that make us beings created in the image and likeness of God. With contraception, the language spoken between spouses is no longer a language of complete gift and surrender. It is now a language of rejection, of refusal to give self totally to the other, and of mistrust and selfishness. It is the same language Adam and Eve spoke when they covered their bodies with fig leaves. Contraception prevents and destroys the spouses' ability to become one flesh. Pope John Paul II clearly describes this distortion of the sexual act through contraception:

> When couples, by means of recourse to contraception, separate these two meanings that God the creator has inscribed in the being of man and woman and in the dynamism of their sexual communion, they act as "arbiters" of the divine plan and they "manipulate" and degrade human sexuality—and with it themselves and their married partner by altering its value of "total" self-giving. Thus the innate language that expresses the total reciprocal self-giving of husband and wife is overlaid, through contraception, by an objectively contradictory language, namely, that of not giving oneself totally to the other. This leads not only to a positive refusal to be open to life, but also to a falsification of the inner truth of conjugal love, which is called upon to give itself in personal totality. (*Familiaris consortio,* no. 32)

Second, contraceptives violate the procreative aspect by intentionally and artificially closing the marriage act to the creation of human life. Sexual intercourse is no longer about self-giving and life-giving love but becomes merely about self-pleasure and self-gratification. Spouses remove themselves from procreative responsibility. Even more sadly, God is removed from the process. Contraception renders the sexual act both physically and spiritually infertile. Sexuality is no longer a mysterious participation of man and woman as co-creators in God's grace.

Contraception introduces a grave distortion of the conjugal act. The sexual embrace is no longer a mutual and unconditional gift of self, but rather a withholding of self. What was meant to be an expression of total self-giving now becomes explicitly selfish. The sexual act is no longer a participation with God as co-creators of human life, but a separation from fertility and openness to God. Fertility is no longer understood as a gift, but as a burden that must be squashed, a disease that must be avoided through "preventative medicine."

Contraception Is the "Pandora's Box" of Sexual Immorality

In *Humanae vitae,* Pope Paul VI made four predictions of what would happen if society accepted the use of contraception as a moral means for regulating birth. Unfortunately, 90 percent of married couples (including Catholics) use contraception. The results have been disastrous, and all of his predictions have come true. Contraception has become a "Pandora's Box" that once opened has brought about many evil consequences that seriously affect society.

First, Pope Paul VI warned that conjugal infidelity would increase, and there would be the general lowering of morality throughout society. This has certainly come true. The divorce rate in 1960 was about 15 percent. Today the divorce rate is about 50 percent. Over 60 percent of married people admit having had an adulterous affair. There is also a serious, general lowering of morality in society, especially in the areas of sexual morality and life issues. Our culture is immersed in sexual immorality in the media, in the schools, in the workplace. Contraception certainly changed the way our society views sex, and it is not for the better.

Second, Pope Paul VI predicted that man would lose respect for woman and see her only as a means for his sexual pleasure and power, no longer viewing her as his beloved companion. (It is also happening vice-versa). Who are the real beneficiaries of contraception? Men. Men are freed from the responsibility of procreation and are free to have sexual domination over women. Consider the explosion of the pornography industry. It is by far the number-one grossing industry on the Internet, making over six billion dollars in 2005. Many feminist groups defend contraception and the right of a woman to control her own body, touting it as "liberation." Unfortunately, contraception has enslaved women to the sexual desire and objectification by men. The dignity of women as the heart of the family and as mothers has been nearly destroyed because of contraception. The role of the father and husband has been degraded as men have become enslaved to their own sexual needs and desires at the expense of the family. Ultimately, the family suffers the consequences of contraception.

Third, Pope Paul VI warned that contraceptives would become a dangerous weapon in the hands of public authorities to solve certain social, economic, or family problems without any regard for the moral and divine law. This has also come true. The United Nations for years now has made contraception and population control a major agenda item, and it is part of almost every aid package to third world countries. In 1994 the Cairo Conference attempted to make population control, contraception, and forced abortion major components of the mission of the UN. China uses contraception and forced abortion as a way of silent genocide against minorities within its borders. Even the United States under several administrations advocated population control and forced contraception as part of foreign aid.

Finally, Pope Paul VI warned that widespread use of contraceptives would mislead human beings into thinking they have unlimited dominion over their own bodies and human nature—apart from the truth and meaning of human nature and life itself. Contraception has opened the door to widespread legal abortion to the count of over 4,600 *per day* in the United States alone. If fertility is a disease that needs to be attacked and destroyed at all cost, what stops a person from destroying the unwanted fruit of fertility? This is the connection between contraception and abortion. This physical dominance of man over the body has also led to in vitro fertilization, cloning, embryonic stem cell research, and genetic manipulation, all of which destroy and subvert new human life.

Spiritual and Physical Side Effects

As previously shown, the spiritual side effects of contraception are enormous. Contraception violates the fundamental relationship between human beings and God. We no longer see ourselves as created in the image and likeness of God, dependent on Him, and co-creators with Him in the creation of new human life. Rather, like the first sin, contraception is spiritual suicide that excludes God from the most fundamental aspect of what it means to be human. It denies our humanity and God's role in our humanity.

Contraception destroys the spiritual relationship between husband and wife. No longer do they become one flesh; instead, selfishness, distortion, and infidelity to the nature and purpose of marriage infiltrate their relationship. The result? Since contraception has become widely used, the divorce rate has risen to 50 percent or higher. However, among couples that embrace and live the Catholic teaching on contraception, the divorce rates are *much* smaller. Some studies show that the incidence of divorce is as low as 0.5 percent! Sexuality is a much deeper spiritual reality than many realize. There are serious consequences any time we abuse or distort sexual love, and this is why sexual sins are serious sins.

Contraception, especially the birth control pill, is known to have many serious physical side effects. Groups such as Human Life International have chronicled many health risks associated with oral contraceptives. Even the U.S. Department of Health and Human Services warns that there is "the risk of blood clots, heart attack, and stroke" with the use of the pill.

Natural Family Planning

Natural Family Planning (NFP) involves monitoring the woman's natural cycle of fertility and infertility to either achieve or avoid pregnancy. If spouses choose to avoid pregnancy, they abstain from sexual relations during the woman's fertile period. With this approach, each time spouses engage in sexual union, both the unitive and procreative aspects remain intact, and the spouses remain faithful to the nature of love and human sexuality. Thus, NFP is never "Catholic contraception" because it differs fundamentally from contraception. It remains faithful to God's plan for marriage, sexuality, and the creation of new human life. Pope John Paul II describes this fundamental difference:

> When, instead, by means of recourse to periods of infertility, the couple respect the inseparable connection between the unitive and procreative meanings of human sexuality, they are acting as "ministers" of God's plan and they "benefit from" their sexuality according to the original dynamism of "total" self-giving, without manipulation or alteration. . . . [The difference between contraception and NFP] is a difference which is much wider and deeper than is usually thought, one which involves in the final analysis two irreconcilable concepts of the human person and of human sexuality. The choice of the natural rhythms involves accepting the cycle of the person, that is, the woman, and thereby accepting dialogue, reciprocal respect,

> shared responsibility and self-control. To accept the cycle and to enter into dialogue means to recognize both the spiritual and corporal character of conjugal communion and to live personal love with its requirement of fidelity. In this context the couple comes to experience how conjugal communion is enriched with those values of tenderness and affection which constitute the inner soul of human sexuality in its physical dimension also. In this way sexuality is respected and promoted in its truly and fully human dimension and is never "used" as an "object" that, by breaking the personal unity of soul and body, strikes at God's creation itself at the level of the deepest interaction of nature and person. (*Familiaris consortio,* no. 32)

Due to significant scientific research over the past twenty-five years, NFP has become highly effective, reliable, and accurate. It is not the rhythm method, nor is it mere guesswork, or throwing darts at a calendar. Rather, NFP uses the cycles of the woman's fertility and the signs within that cycle to determine times of fertility and infertility. When used correctly it has the same efficacy as the pill in avoiding pregnancy (98 percent), but it remains essentially different as each sexual act remains open to both the unitive and procreative aspects as God intended. That essential difference of mindset is the reason why couples using NFP are often parents and even parents of large families. They view children as a blessing from God, generously opening their hearts and homes to the responsibility and gift of children. NFP is also a great aid to many couples in conceiving children. In addition, NFP helps in the early diagnoses of infertility and reproductive problems more easily and accurately than other forms of modern gynecology.

Benefits of Natural Family Planning

There are several benefits of Natural Family Planning that address the questions of fertility and family planning, and also serve to strengthen the marriage both spiritually and emotionally as NFP is faithful to our human nature and the plan of God for human sexuality and marriage. Information on NFP is available on the USCCB website (www.usccb.org) under Marriage and Family.

98 percent effective

As stated above, when done correctly, NFP is 98 percent effective, which is as effective as the Pill (but with no side effects). NFP is more effective than any barrier contraceptives (condoms, jellies, foams, IUDs, etc.), which are on average 85–88 percent effective.

Fosters a respect for women and their fertility

NFP fosters respect for women and their fertility, and helps the woman be in tune with her fertility cycle. Husbands are made aware of the beauty of womanhood, of her fertility, of her cycle, and of her potential to be a bearer of new life. It is not an illness for which she must be treated. A woman should never feel ashamed or apologetic for her fertility. It is truly a gift from God in which she and her spouse are able to become "co-creators" with God.

Fosters communication between spouses

Spouses using NFP must communicate with each other concerning the woman's cycle and fertility. As they will together bear the responsibility of caring for and raising each new life, so they should together prayerfully bear the responsibility of planning for their children.

Spouses learn to find different ways of loving each other and renewing their courtship

During periods of abstinence spouses find different ways of expressing their love for each other. This often leads to a renewal of their courtship and allows their relationship to grow in other aspects, enhancing their love and respect. This helps foster true love in a marriage. Sacrifice always deepens love.

Responsible Parenthood

The Church teaches that all conjugal acts must be open to the possibility of life, but it also teaches that parents must be responsible in bringing new life into the world. While we should always be open to life and the blessings of children, there may be times when for serious reasons the spouses may not wish to conceive new life. In *Humanae vitae,* article 10, Pope Paul VI gives four reasons why couples may want to avoid pregnancy for a time: physical, economic, psychological, and social conditions. This list of reasons is certainly not exhaustive. There may be other serious reasons why a couple may choose to avoid pregnancy, but such a decision must be taken seriously.

God does not desire our faith to be totally blind. He gives us our reason so we can make sound judgments, and He gives us our conscience so we can behave in a way that is in accord morally with God's plan for humanity. The decision to have a child at any point in time is truly one between the parents and God. This decision is not to be taken lightly by the spouses. Conceiving a child is one of the greatest gifts that we can give to God as well as one of the greatest that we can receive from Him. In making decisions concerning responsible parenthood, we should do and consider the following:

- ***Pray:*** What is God's will for our family right now?
- ***Conscience:*** Are we using our sexuality according to God's plan? Are we using the gifts and resources that God gives us as He would have us use them?
- ***Consider the circumstance of the family:*** At this point in time, can we handle this responsibility?
- ***Consider the blessings of new life:*** Are we open to the blessings and responsibilities that God wishes to give us?

However, even if a couple uses moral means to avoid pregnancy such as NFP, they can still have a *contraceptive mentality*. This mentality or outlook is anti-procreation, and harbors an attitude that human life is an inconvenient and unnecessary burden rather than a sacred gift from God. The couple must seek God's will and follow the teachings of the Church, taking into account the situation of their family, while always being open to life both in *mentality and action*

Contrary to the messages of our society (and even other Christian churches), the Holy Spirit teaches responsible parenthood through the Church, which is perfectly balanced and wise. While the Church, on the one hand, praises the generosity and benefits of large families, it also recognizes that not all couples have that capacity. While being open to life some couples (for serious reasons) may not have many children or any children at all. No one should judge a family on how faithful they are to the Church's teaching by the number of children they have. That decision is only between the couple and God. It is possible for a couple to be completely open to life and heroically generous but be childless, just as it is possible for them to be selfish and resentful of each child in their large family. This illustrates the very personal, intimate nature of our fidelity in our sexual union and our relationship with God.

Any discussion of the gifts of fertility and children must acknowledge with great compassion those who cannot conceive and bear children. For many, this is painful suffering that has no easy answers. As with any suffering, the reasons are often unclear and the couple is called to seek in faith God's plan for them. The Church praises couples that adopt children, fulfilling both their own longing for the fruits of love and the child's longing to be loved. Adoption is a gift that requires great courage, and the graces of this love will undoubtedly bear great fruit in the lives of those families who choose it. The Church also praises couples that give expression to their generosity by performing demanding services for others.

In conclusion, the discussion of human sexuality must not be based on the passing whims of society, but on the truth of human nature and God's guidance in revealing to us the truths that give "fullness of life." God desires that each child be created as an act of love between spouses, reflecting the love of the Holy Trinity. It is a great gift to be able to become co-creators of life through the will of God! The Church continues to guide us to the true nature of human sexuality so that we can live in the freedom of God's plan for the human family.

Frequently Asked Questions about Contraception and NFP

What is the difference between Contraception and NFP? Isn't NFP just Church-approved birth control?

There is a fundamental difference between contraception and NFP. Contraception is a willful act to make sexual union infertile. It is doing something or taking something with the sole purpose of making the sexual act sterile. Thus, the nature of the sexual act as both unitive and procreative is destroyed.

Natural Family Planning uses the woman's cycle of periods of fertility and infertility to either achieve or avoid pregnancy. If spouses choose to avoid pregnancy, they rightly use a faculty provided them by nature—abstinence from sexual relations during the woman's fertile period. With NFP, each time spouses engage in sexual union both the unitive and procreative aspects remain intact, and the spouses remain faithful to the nature of love and human sexuality.

NFP is fundamentally different from contraception because it remains faithful to the nature of human sexuality and God's plan for marriage, sexuality, and the creation of new human life.

A lot of families I know that use NFP have a lot of kids. I don't think NFP works.

Not true. NFP has been proven to be 98 percent effective. The question here is not whether NFP works, but what are the motives and mentality of those who use NFP. Couples who use NFP with right intention view children as a blessing and the greatest gift that God can give—a gift that is worthy of sacrifice. Although they are using NFP, they are very open to life and the blessing of children, and they often decide to have more children. This is in contrast to the "contraceptive mentality" of our society that views children largely as a burden and a hindrance, and believes that having more than one or two kids is crazy. So the issue is not the effectiveness of NFP but whether or not one views children as a blessing from God.

But doesn't the Catholic Church teach that you have to have as many children as possible?

No, the Church asks spouses to always be open to life and to discern God's timing for the blessings of children, cognizant of the awesome responsibility of bringing new life into the world. However, because this responsibility is so great, the Church does teach that for serious reasons spouses may space children or avoid pregnancy altogether. If there are serious economic, psychological, physical issues or concerns in a marriage, spouses must prayerfully consider whether it is an appropriate time to bring a child into the family.

God does not ask a couple to have "blind faith," nor does He want them to act recklessly or irresponsibly. For example, one would never jump off a cliff and hope that if it is God's will He will save him. The same applies to responsible parenthood.

However, one can never use immoral means (contraception) to avoid pregnancy. In addition, raising children will always require sacrifice, and spouses should avoid a "contraceptive mentality" that views children as a burden or hindrance to their freedom and happiness in life.

Doesn't the Church teach that sex is all about having kids? Can we only have sex when my wife is fertile?

Absolutely not. Procreation of children is one of the twofold ends of marriage; it is not the only end. What is important here is that *each and every conjugal act is open to life; nothing is done to the act to purposefully render it infertile.* Sexual intercourse while the woman is infertile in her cycle is still open to life and remains faithful to the nature of conjugal love. God designed our sexual nature so spouses could be united in a total gift of mutual love and become one flesh. Even during the infertile time of a woman's cycle, or if a couple is infertile, sexual union is still the highest and most perfect way spouses express their love for each other.

Does the Church frown upon smaller families or those couples that cannot have children?

Again, absolutely not. While the Church does praise the generosity of those parents who do raise large families and the benefits of large families, she would never look less favorably upon a small family or spouses who are infertile. Having a big family is not a litmus test of being a good family. Not every couple has the means or the capacity to have a large family. What is important is openness to life and the exercise of responsible parenthood. The rest is between the couple and God.

From the Catechism: Key Words to Know

CHASTITY: The moral virtue (under the cardinal virtue of temperance) that provides for the successful integration of sexuality within the person leading to the inner unity of the bodily and spiritual being (2337). Chastity is called one of the fruits of the Holy Spirit (1832).

FORNICATION: Sexual intercourse between an unmarried man and an unmarried woman. Fornication is a serious violation of the sixth of God (2353).

HOMOSEXUALITY: Sexual attraction or orientation toward persons of the same-sex and/or sexual acts between persons of the same sex. Homosexual acts are morally wrong because they violate God's purpose for human sexual activity (2357).

CONTRACEPTION: The intentional prevention or interference of conception as a result of sexual intercourse; contraception offends against the openness to procreation required of marriage and also the inner truth of conjugal love (2370).

Part three
LIVING AND WITNESSING THE CHRISTIAN LIFE

Chapter 24

Human Life Issues

Reading the Catechism: Paragraphs 2258–2330

> The Gospel of life is at the heart of Jesus' message. Lovingly received day after day by the Church, it is to be preached with dauntless fidelity as "good news" to the people of every age and culture.
>
> —Pope John Paul II, Encyclical Letter on the Gospel of Life *Evangelium Vitae* (March 25, 1995), no. 1

The dignity of the human person and the right to life is at the very heart of any society or civilization. Today we see the so-called "culture of death" ever more invading our society through grave issues such as **abortion** and **euthanasia**. This culture of death cheapens the sacredness of human life and views it as something to be manipulated or simply thrown away.

In this chapter we will address these serious life issues that face our modern world. We will study the Church's unwavering teachings in defense of the sacredness of human life and the dignity of the human person in all stages of life, from the miraculous moment of conception to natural death, when we are called by God to live forever in His presence. We will see that the "gospel of life" is at the very heart of the life of Christ and of His Church: "I came so that they might have life and have it more abundantly" (Jn. 10:10).

The Sacredness of Human Life

Unique Dignity: Created in the Image and Likeness of God

The dignity of the human person and the sacredness of human life are revealed from the very beginning in the Book of Genesis, as God completes the wondrous work of His creation:

> God created mankind in his image; in the divine image of God he created them; male and female he created them. God blessed them and said to them: Be fertile and multiply; fill the earth and subdue it. Have dominion over the fish of the sea, the birds of the air, and all the living things that crawl on the earth. (Gen. 1:27–28)

This profound passage reveals that human beings, man and woman, are the pinnacle of God's creation. As creatures created in His image and likeness, we *possess a dignity that far exceeds the rest of creation.* Human beings were created like God, to share in and possess His life. The dignity of the human person is at the heart of the commandment, "Thou shall not kill." The commandment is strongly negative and prohibitive, expressing the moral norm that absolutely prohibits the willful killing of innocent life. However, the commandment in the light of Genesis is *far more positive,* revealing the absolute dignity of each and every human life, and the responsibility of every person to respect, defend, and promote human life in all stages and circumstances. Life is a great gift, and the gift of life is entrusted to humanity by the Creator:

> In giving life to man, God *demands* that he love, respect, and promote life. The *gift* thus *becomes a commandment* and the *commandment is itself a gift*. (*Evangelium vitae*, no. 52)

God Alone Is the Master of Life

Human life is indeed sacred and it belongs to God, not man. *God alone is Lord and Master of life.* He is the Source and Creator of Life, who creates us out of His love. In His mysterious plan of love, He alone has authority to call men and women to Himself through the sleep of death. This sacredness of human life is entrusted to the human family as both gift and responsibility. Life is entrusted to man, but it does not belong to him. Man is to welcome, treasure, and cultivate life. He is not the arbiter of life, but rather its recipient and treasurer. *It does not belong to man to determine when life begins or ends, but man has the grave responsibility of protecting, promoting, and defending the gift God entrusted to him.* As Pope John Paul II states:

> With regard to things, but even more with regard to life, man is not the absolute master and final judge, but rather—and this is where his incomparable greatness lies—he is the "minister of God's plan." Life is entrusted to man as a treasure which must not be squandered, as a talent which must be used well. Man must render an account of it to his Master. (*Evangelium vitae,* no. 52)

Human Life Is Real and Sacred from the Moment of Conception . . .

The dignity and sacredness of human life must be respected and defended from its very beginning, from the mysterious and remarkable moment of conception. That moment, when the gametes of man and woman meet, speaks profoundly of the sacredness of life. For at conception the divine and the human meet in a marvelous miracle of creation. The man and the woman cooperate with God as co-creators of a new human life that bears both the image of God and the unique image of the parents.

Far from being a mere biological act or phenomenon, conception is the beginning of the journey of life for a unique human being. Although in a very simple cellular form, this new human life is a person who contains everything that is human, a physical body and a spiritual soul.

Through the capabilities of modern science, conception of human life has been studied from its earliest moments. Science profoundly reveals the mystery and sacredness of life, the miracle of conception, and the complexity of the human body from the miraculous growth of two cells.

Unfortunately, today the same science that bears witness to this miracle of life often attacks and seeks to destroy life at its very beginnings, claiming that a new human embryo is only a "potential person" or "biological material."

Pope John Paul II forcefully defends the fact that life begins at conception and from that moment must be protected and defended:

> Some people try to justify abortion by claiming that the result of conception, at least up to a certain number of days, cannot yet be considered a personal human life. But in fact, "from the time that the ovum is fertilized, a life is begun which is neither that of the father nor the mother; it is rather the life of a new human being with his own growth. It would never be made human if it were not human already. This has always been clear,

and . . . modern genetic science offers clear confirmation. It has demonstrated that from the first instant there is established the programme of what this living being will be: a person, this individual person with his characteristic aspects already well determined. Right from fertilization the adventure of a human life begins, and each of its capacities requires time—a rather lengthy time—to find its place and to be in a position to act." Even if the presence of a spiritual soul cannot be ascertained by empirical data, the results themselves of scientific research on the human embryo provide "a valuable indication for discerning by the use of reason a personal presence at the moment of the first appearance of a human life: how could a human individual not be a human person?"

Furthermore, what is at stake is so important that, from the standpoint of moral obligation, the mere probability that a human person is involved would suffice to justify an absolutely clear prohibition of any intervention aimed at killing a human embryo. Precisely for this reason, over and above all scientific debates and those philosophical affirmations to which the Magisterium has not expressly committed itself, the Church has always taught and continues to teach that the result of human procreation, from the first moment of its existence, must be guaranteed that unconditional respect which is morally due to the human being in his or her totality and unity as body and spirit: *"The human being is to be respected and treated as a person from the moment of conception;* and therefore from that same moment his rights as a person must be recognized, among which in the first place is the inviolable right of every innocent human being to life." (*Evangelium vitae,* no. 60)

. . . Until Natural Death

Human life must be respected until natural death, the moment when through His providence God calls someone from this life into the next. Man can never determine for himself when life ends, nor can he deliberately kill any innocent human life at any stage of their existence. This prohibition of killing *innocent life* is absolute and unwavering. However, in situations of legitimate defense, the killing of an aggressor may be the only means of protecting the life of oneself or others. This is a gravely different situation than the direct and willful killing of an innocent human life. As Pope John Paul II states:

> Moreover, "legitimate defense can be not only a right but a grave duty for someone responsible for another's life, the common good of the family or of the State." Unfortunately, it happens that the need to render the aggressor incapable of causing harm sometimes involves taking his life. In this case, the fatal outcome is attributable to the aggressor whose action brought it about, even though he may not be morally responsible because of a lack of the use of reason. (*Evangelium vitae,* no. 55)

The commandment "Thou shall not kill" prohibits the willful taking of another's or our own life, whether through direct action or acts of omission, even when the argument is that death will relieve suffering or the pain of a disease or injury. Authority over life and death belong to God alone. A dangerous Pandora's Box is opened when man begins to determine when someone should live or die, or who should live or die. Humanity was not given the right or providential knowledge to make such decisions; those belong to the Creator and Lord of Life alone.

Thus the willful decision or action to end or deprive an innocent human being of life is never permitted and is always and everywhere an intrinsic and objective moral evil. Pope John Paul II definitively states:

> Therefore, by the authority which Christ conferred upon Peter and his Successors, and in communion with the Bishops of the Catholic Church, *I confirm that the direct and voluntary killing of an innocent human being is always gravely immoral.* This doctrine, based upon that unwritten law which man, in the light of reason, finds in his own heart (cf. Rom. 2:14–15), is reaffirmed by Sacred Scripture, transmitted by the Tradition of the Church and taught by the ordinary and universal Magisterium.
>
> The deliberate decision to deprive an innocent human being of his life is always morally evil and can never be licit either as an end in itself or as a means to a good end. It is in fact a grave act of disobedience to the moral law, and indeed to God

himself, the author and guarantor of that law; it contradicts the fundamental virtues of justice and charity. "Nothing and no one can in any way permit the killing of an innocent human being, whether a fetus or an embryo, an infant or an adult, an old person, or one suffering from an incurable disease, or a person who is dying. Furthermore, no one is permitted to ask for this act of killing, either for himself or herself or for another person entrusted to his or her care, nor can he or she consent to it, either explicitly or implicitly. Nor can any authority legitimately recommend or permit such an action." (*Evangelium vitae,* no. 57)

Abortion

Never Justified

Abortion is the willful and direct killing of an innocent human life within the mother's womb from the moment of conception until birth. It is intentionally murdering a human being and can never be justified as a means or an end.

Even in cases of incest and rape, as horrible as those circumstances are, the rights of the mother never negate the rights of the human life that is living and growing in the mother's womb. Similarly, in the case of the health and life of the mother, the direct killing of the unborn child can never be justified even if it will save the life of the mother. Despite tragic circumstances, one cannot willfully murder even to save the life of the other. There are no situations or circumstances that can ever morally justify abortion.

Certainly abortion cannot be used as a form of birth control or family planning. Contrary to popular belief and the reporting of the mass media, 95 percent of abortions performed in the United States are not performed due to rape, incest, or the health of the mother, but are simply due to unwanted pregnancies. Mass abortion has become the last line of defense and last resort of birth control; hence, again, there is a fundamental connection between contraception and abortion.

Pope John Paul II defines the Church's constant and unchanging teaching that abortion can never in any circumstance be morally justified:

> Given such unanimity in the doctrinal and disciplinary tradition of the Church, Paul VI was able to declare that this tradition is unchanged and unchangeable. Therefore, by the authority which Christ conferred upon Peter and his Successors, in communion with the Bishops—who on various occasions have condemned abortion and who in the aforementioned consultation, albeit dispersed throughout the world, have shown unanimous agreement concerning this doctrine—*I declare that direct abortion, that is, abortion willed as an end or as a means, always constitutes a grave moral disorder,* since it is the deliberate killing of an innocent human being. This doctrine is based upon the natural law and upon the written Word of God, is transmitted by the Church's Tradition and taught by the ordinary and universal Magisterium.
>
> No circumstance, no purpose, no law whatsoever can ever make licit an act which is intrinsically illicit, since it is contrary to the Law of God which is written in every human heart, knowable by reason itself, and proclaimed by the Church. (*Evangelium vitae,* no. 62)

The Modern and Invisible Holocaust

Many abortion advocates of *Roe v. Wade,* such as Planned Parenthood and the National Abortion Rights Action League, want the average American to believe that abortion is "rare and safe." Let's look closely at the falsehood of both of these claims.

First, abortion is not rare. The numbers are staggering and unimaginable. In the 1980s the reported annual abortion rate averaged about 1.25 million, peaked in 1990 at 1.6 million before declining again to about 1.2 million. The average annual live births in that same time period were about 4 million. *That means that almost one out of four conceived babies was murdered through abortion!* Based on data from both the Centers for Disease Control and the pro-abortion Guttmacher Institute (a former Planned Parenthood research arm), the National Right to Life Committee estimates there have been over 55 million babies killed since the Supreme Court handed down its 1973 *Roe v. Wade* decision. The number boils down to this: every thirty seconds in the United States a baby is killed in an abortion. Does that sound rare?

Furthermore, these are only the reported numbers in the United States. At least 10 percent of abortion providers do not report their abortions, which would make the real number even higher. It bears repeating: 95 percent of these abortions have nothing to do with rape, incest, or saving the life or health of the mother. They are simply unwanted pregnancies. Abortion is not rare! It has truly become the silent modern-day holocaust, claiming millions and millions of innocent lives.

There is another very disturbing side to all of this. Why are so many groups like Planned Parenthood so vigilantly fighting for abortion? Again, according to a May 2013 report from the Guttmacher Institute, "the average cost of a first-trimester abortion was $470 in 2009." Take the 1.2 million annual number of abortions and multiply it by $470 each. That earned income exceeds $500 million per year for the abortion industry. Carry that number over the past forty years and more than *$20 billion* in cold, hard cash was earned with the blood of innocent human life. It's not about women's rights or the health and well-being of women. The abortion industry is a lucrative business that is making some people very rich.

Second, abortion is not safe. Hundreds of women each year are injured through this procedure, and some even die. There are also many long-term physical side effects that cause serious complications, for example Pelvic Inflammatory Disease. In addition, the spiritual and emotional consequences are devastating. Post-Abortion Syndrome (PAS) is a form of Post Traumatic Stress Disorder (PTSD). This well-known and often-diagnosed disorder affects women psychologically and emotionally for years after having an abortion. It is not safe physically, emotionally, or spiritually. The bottom line is that no one ever wins with abortion, not the baby, not the mother, not the family, not society.

Partial Birth Abortion

Partial birth abortion is a particularly hideous procedure that is performed on babies that are twenty weeks or older (the time most doctors think a baby can survive a premature birth). The baby is delivered feet first with only the head remaining in the birth canal. The abortionist then pierces the base of the skull and removes the brain, murdering the child. Those who support partial birth abortion claim that this procedure is rare and is only done when there is danger to the life of the mother. However, this is not true. According to the Guttmacher Institute, in the year 2000 about 2,200 partial birth abortions were performed. Abortionists have admitted to doing thousands of these gruesome procedures each year. Over 80 percent of them are elective, that is, not medically necessary for the life of the mother.

In 2003 Congress finally passed into law a Federal ban on partial birth abortion. We must pray and let our voices be heard that this hideous procedure will never again become legal in our country and that all abortion will be outlawed.

Difficult Situations

At times there are difficult situations in which the life or health of the mother comes into question. One such situation is an ectopic pregnancy, usually tubal, in which the fertilized egg does not implant in the uterus. It might instead implant in the fallopian tube, endangering the mother because of the possibility of rupture or excessive bleeding. In this case, morally acceptable procedures focus on treatment of the damaged tissue of the fallopian tube. Obviously, with the embryo inside, the unintended and unfortunate result will be the death of the developing child. Note that there is no willful and direct killing of the baby. The principle of double effect applies here. The intention is to remove the infected tissue and the unintended result, although foreseeable, is the death of the child.

Occasionally there is a very difficult and tragic situation when a late term baby affects the life of the mother. Even in this case, it can never be morally justified to directly and willfully abort the baby, even to save the life of the mother. This is especially the case today when modern medical technology can now help babies, even as early as five months, survive premature birth. Even in the case of the life or health of the mother, late-term or partial-birth abortion is absolutely unjustified and completely unnecessary because those babies could be delivered by caesarean section and be viable (be able to survive outside the womb).

Fertility and Biomedical Research

Another area where human life is under attack at its very beginnings is the arena of fertility and biomedical research. Here new human life is often destroyed and cruelly manipulated. New life can never be willfully destroyed, even to bring about the healing of disease or the creation of other new life. These serious issues are discussed in detail in chapter twenty-six.

Euthanasia

At the other end of life's spectrum, there is the issue of euthanasia or "mercy killing." In these instances the killing is ostensibly to relieve the pain and suffering of someone very ill or dying. However, like abortion, euthanasia is never justified. No one, under any circumstance, can directly and willfully take the life of another and no one can take their own life to end pain or suffering. This applies to situations such as permanent disability or coma, either through direct means or acts of omission.

End of Life Decisions: Ordinary vs. Extraordinary Means

Spouses and families often face very difficult medical decisions concerning their loved ones. The morally right course of action considers the means used and examines the intention of the will. In making these decisions there must be a clear distinction between ordinary and extraordinary means of sustaining life.

Ordinary means

Ordinary means includes nursing care, hygiene, and palliative care. It also includes nutrition and hydration, orally or with artificial assistance. *Food and hydration are always ordinary means of sustaining life and can never be intentionally removed or deprived in order to end one's life.* Especially in the case of the severely disabled and the permanently comatose, food and water, including feeding tubes, cannot be removed. In addition to basic care, ordinary medical procedures are reasonable when they do not place an undue burden on the patient and are proportionate to the prospects for improvement.

Extraordinary means

Extraordinary means are medical procedures that are experimental or rare, have a high degree of complexity or risk, or are exceptionally expensive. They are judged to be disproportionate when they impose an excessive burden on the patient or their family, cause excessive pain or prolonged suffering, or provide a low expectation of success. Extraordinary means often cause a significant financial burden on the patient and the family.

Extraordinary care would include breathing machines and use of other life-sustaining devices when the patient is either clinically dead or not able to survive without those extraordinary means. Examples of extraordinary means are a massive chemotherapy treatment for an aggressive cancer, an experimental or extremely risky surgery, or a breathing machine that extends the life of a person so seriously ill or injured that they would not be able to survive without it and there is no reasonable expectation of recovery.

These are only a few examples. Each medical decision must be weighed carefully and the best judgment made through prayer, the consideration of all medical options, and the teachings of the Church. However, ordinary means of sustenance and treatment can never be deprived to hasten the death of an individual.

Mercy Killing

Certainly, direct and willful euthanasia or "mercy killing" can never be justified. Suffering is a part of human life and an element of Christian revelation. Christ revealed that suffering can be redemptive—a means through which we can grow in love and faith by offering our suffering for the salvation of others. Jesus revealed that suffering is not without purpose. It is an opportunity to unite our suffering to Christ's and, in doing so, participate in a way of loving. This in no way diminishes the recognition of serious and long-term suffering that many experience, but in the light of Christian revelation suffering can have great meaning and should never be the reason for ending our life.

Pope John Paul II witnessed to the whole world the Christian meaning of human suffering. Even in his intense suffering for many years, his love for Christ and the Church only increased as he continued his ministry of leading and guiding the Church. Through his suffering he revealed to the entire world the intense love to which suffering calls us. Our model is the suffering of Christ on the Cross, which is not meaningless, but bears great fruit in the redemption of the human family. As the Holy Father stated:

> [W]e could say that suffering, which is present under so many different forms in our human world, is also present in order *to unleash love in the human person,* that unselfish gift of one's "I" on behalf of other people, especially those who suffer. The

> world of human suffering unceasingly calls for, so to speak, another world: the world of human love; and in a certain sense man owes to suffering that unselfish love which stirs in his heart and actions. (Apostolic Letter on The Christian Meaning of Human Suffering *Salvifici doloris* [February 11, 1984], no. 29)

Thus, human suffering is not something to be squashed or conquered in every circumstance. Instead, it calls man out of himself and gives him an opportunity to love as Christ loved. God is the Lord and Master of life, and only His providence and wisdom can call one from this life into the next. It is also through the providence and wisdom of God that, even in our suffering, He brings about goodness and redemption. We need to see and accept suffering with the eyes of faith.

Euthanasia Is Never Justified

Pope John Paul II defines the Church's universal and unchanging opposition to euthanasia:

> Taking into account these distinctions, in harmony with the Magisterium of my Predecessors and in communion with the Bishops of the Catholic Church, *I confirm that euthanasia is a grave violation of the law of God*, since it is the deliberate and morally unacceptable killing of a human person. This doctrine is based upon the natural law and upon the written word of God, is transmitted by the Church's Tradition and taught by the ordinary and universal Magisterium. Depending on the circumstances, this practice involves the malice proper to suicide or murder. (*Evangelium vitae,* no. 65)

The Death Penalty

Here, let us take up the issue of the death penalty. The morality of the death penalty is different from that of abortion or euthanasia. Abortion and euthanasia are objectively evil; they are always and everywhere wrong and can never be justified. On the other hand, *the death penalty is not objectively evil.* The Church recognizes the right of society and the state to protect its citizens, and that the death penalty in certain situations can be morally justified if it is the only means of protecting society. Yet from the Church's perspective the death penalty should be used only as a means of last resort.

The Story of Cain

In *Evangelium vitae*, Pope John Paul II uses the story of Cain from the Book of Genesis to show that even those who have committed a serious crime still have the opportunity for redemption and reconciliation (cf. Gen. 4:8–16). Cain committed the first murder by killing his brother, and God severely punished him by exiling him and sending him out to live like a wild beast. However, *in the end God spared his life.* This revelation in Scripture provides the foundation for the Church's teaching on the death penalty in the modern world. The pope explains:

> And yet God, who is always merciful even when he punishes, *"put a mark on Cain,* lest any who came upon him should kill him" (Gen. 4:15). He thus gave him a distinctive sign, not to condemn him to the hatred of others, but to protect and defend him from those wishing to kill him, even out of a desire to avenge Abel's death. *Not even a murderer loses his personal dignity,* and God himself pledges to guarantee this. And it is precisely here that the *paradoxical mystery of the merciful justice of God* is shown forth. As Saint Ambrose writes: "Once the crime is admitted at the very inception of this sinful act of parricide, then the divine law of God's mercy should be immediately extended. If punishment is forthwith inflicted on the accused, then men in the exercise of justice would in no way observe patience and moderation, but would straightaway condemn the defendant to punishment. . . . God drove Cain out of his presence and sent him into exile far away from his native land, so that he passed from a life of human kindness to one which was more akin to the rude existence of a wild beast. God, who preferred the correction rather than the death of a sinner, did not desire that a homicide be punished by the exaction of another act of homicide." (no. 8)

The Death Penalty in the Modern World

Although the worst criminals lose many of the rights of citizenship and freedom, they still have the right to life and the promise of reconciliation and conversion.

Today's society has the means and capabilities of protecting society from violent criminals through incarceration. Therefore, the need for the death penalty as a means to protect society from further harm is not a necessity, and should not be used as an ordinary means of capital punishment.

Of course this moral principle is dependent upon a fair and reasonable criminal justice system. Such a system should be capable of removing dangerous criminals from society for life or bringing about their adequate and permanent correction. This should be a vital and essential part of any modern society. The death penalty is a grave and serious matter that should not be taken lightly.

The Just War Doctrine

War Is Sometimes Necessary

War should be avoided as much as humanly possible. However, because evil and the powers of darkness are present and working in the world, war is sometimes the only means through which a nation or a community of nations can protect freedom, goodness, and the basic human rights of civilizations and societies (see CCC 2308). Thus, while war is unbelievably tragic, it is not always objectively evil. It can be the means in which goodness and peace are achieved and established, and by which regimes and programs of hatred are abolished.

Conditions of the Just War Doctrine

The Church has established a just war doctrine that lays out the strict conditions through which legitimate military defense can take place. These conditions must be interpreted and applied to any specific situation that arises, and great care must be taken by leaders of nations to insure that any military action is done reasonably within these guidelines. The Catechism (2309) gives the following guidelines:

- ***The damage inflicted by the aggressor on the nation or community of nations must be lasting, grave, and certain.*** In other words, the decision to go to war must be in response to a threat that is very serious and poses a lasting, immediate, and certain danger.
- ***All other means of putting an end to it must have been shown to be impractical or ineffective.*** In today's world this is the equivalent to exhausting all reasonable diplomatic or economic solutions.
- ***There must be serious prospects of success.*** Before initiating military action, there must be a reasonable expectation that the action proposed will be successful and will not bring about a worse situation.
- ***The use of arms must not produce evils and disorders graver than the evil to be eliminated. The power of modern means of destruction weighs very heavily in evaluating this condition.*** The military action cannot bring about a situation or an evil that is worse than the evil being confronted. This would apply particularly to the use or possible use of weapons of mass destruction. Another factor implicit in the above is the need to limit civilian casualties as much as humanly possible.

The decision to go to war and the responsibilities of ensuring the conditions of a just war belong to the authorities responsible for the common good, particularly the leaders of nations and governments. They have the grave responsibility to see that war is only used as a last resort and only as a legitimate response to counter aggression.

In conclusion, the threats to human life and dignity in our modern world are grave and serious concerns to the Church and her members. As followers of Christ, we must make our voices known to protect and defend human life in all stages and in all circumstances. In order for the gospel of life and the culture of life to take permanent hold in our society, we must be the ones who courageously plant the seeds of justice and ensure the right to life of every person. There is no issue in today's world that has greater importance or consequence.

From the Catechism: Key Words to Know

ABORTION: Deliberate termination of pregnancy by killing the unborn child. Such direct abortion, willed either as an end or a means, is gravely contrary to the moral law. The Church attaches the canonical penalty of excommunication to this crime against human life (2271–2272).

EUTHANASIA: An action or an omission that of itself or by intention causes the death of handicapped, sick, or dying persons—sometimes with an attempt to justify the act as a means of eliminating suffering. Euthanasia violates the fifth commandment of the law of God (2277).

Chapter 25

Principles and Themes of Catholic Social Teaching

Reading the Catechism: Paragraphs 1877–1948

> Above all, the common outcry, which is justly made on behalf of human rights—for example, the right to health, to home, to work, to family, to culture—is false and illusory if the right to life, the most basic and fundamental right and the condition for all other personal rights, is not defended with maximum determination.
>
> —Pope John Paul II, Apostolic Exhortation on the Laity *Christifideles laici* (December 30, 1988), no. 38

What Is Catholic Social Teaching?

Catholic **social teaching** has developed over her two-thousand-year history, but has been more explicitly developed by the papal magisterium relatively recently, after the rise of industrial capitalism. The first social encyclical, *Rerum novarum* by Pope Leo XIII in 1891, primarily addressed the rights of workers during the peak of the industrial revolution. The popes of the twentieth century continued to draw from the richness of Sacred Scripture and Sacred Tradition to expound upon the Church's social teachings and apply them to present day economic and societal issues.

The foundation of Catholic social teaching is the dignity of the human person as created in the image and likeness of God. Catholic social teaching does not provide many black-and-white doctrinal statements. Instead, these teachings provide guidelines and criteria to be used in those varying times, circumstances, and situations in which the dignity of the human person may be threatened or diminished. These guidelines should be used so true **social justice** and peace may be established by a proper ordering of the state, the family, and the rights of persons.

In this chapter we will look at what these criteria and principles are and how they are applied. Then we will explore seven key themes of Catholic social teaching.

The Three Categories of Catholic Social Teaching

Many good Catholics will disagree on how certain social issues should be addressed or solved. This reasonable debate is possible within Catholic social teaching because there are few issues and social situations that have clear-cut solutions. There are many ways to approach and deal with issues like the role of the state, care for the poor, the welfare system, immigration, and just economic systems. In her social teaching the Church is not so much articulating doctrine, but providing principles for reflection and criteria for judgment to help bring about true justice and peace in these often difficult social issues.

Catholic social teaching can be grouped into three categories: principles for reflection, criteria for judgment, and guidelines for action.

Principles for reflection

Catholic social teaching provides principles for reflection that can be used across many different times, places, cultures, and circumstances. These principles are based firmly on the dignity of the human person and the dignity of the family as the basic and vital cell of society. While they are founded on this objective good, their application may change and develop as new situations and issues are encountered. Also because societies vary from one another and the social, economic, and cultural landscape is continuously developing and changing, the Church provides these principles to guide the development of specific applications. A Catholic can use the principles of Catholic social teaching and apply them to any given situation to help promote the dignity of the human person and find ways to help best bring about true justice and peace.

Criteria for judgment

The Church provides criteria for judgment that act as a bridge between the highly authoritative but necessarily general principles for reflection and the action needed for particular social issues. These criteria help a Catholic best apply the principles given by the Church to specific social concerns. They can be applied to a specific issue at a certain time or to an ongoing social concern. Again, these are not concrete black-and-white teachings, but criteria that focus the principles for reflection more closely on a particular issue or circumstance.

Guidelines for action

Guidelines for action spring from the above principles and criteria. They are based upon the guidance of the Church and the knowledge, circumstances, and intricacies of a social issue in a specific time and place. A properly informed conscience is indispensible in making guidelines for action. Frequently there are legitimate differences among Catholics on how to approach a specific issue, and reasoned debate can be a healthy way of coming to the best possible solution. As has been said, within Catholic social teaching there may be a variety of solutions to a specific issue based upon the principles and criteria present within Church teaching.

A simple way of understanding these elements is the method of "see, judge, and act." When a social issue arises and needs to be addressed, we look to the basic principles of Catholic social teachings to *see* the right perspective. Then we *judge* how best to apply these principles concerning the specific issue at hand. Finally we *act* to develop a specific plan to address and resolve the issue. By using these basic elements, a Catholic can apply sound principles of teaching and develop effective plans of action to bring about justice and peace, even in difficult social issues.

Seven Key Themes in Catholic Social Teaching

Catholic social teaching addresses numerous social issues. It is impossible to list all of the specific issues that have been or may be addressed by the Church in her teaching, but the United States Conference of Catholic Bishops has developed seven key themes that are at the heart of Catholic social teaching. These themes serve as a basic introduction to the Church's social teaching, and we will explore each theme and the basic issues and elements each address.

1. Life and Dignity of the Human Person

At the very heart of Catholic social teaching is the dignity of the human person as created in the image and likeness of God. This teaching exists wholly and primarily to protect the dignity of the human person and the basic human rights of every human being. Of all the basic human rights, the first and most foundational is the right to life. As Pope John Paul II powerfully explains, all other rights flow from and are dependent upon this first and basic right:

> Above all, the common outcry, which is justly made on behalf of human rights—for example, the right to health, to home, to work, to family, to culture—is false and illusory if the right to life, the most basic and fundamental right and the condition for all other personal rights, is not defended with maximum determination. (*Christifideles laici,* no. 38)

As we saw in the last chapter, the crime of abortion undercuts human life at its most innocent and vulnerable state, resulting in the killing of well over one million lives each year in the United States alone. *There is no issue that is of graver concern in our society today.* Abortion is intrinsically evil, and there are no circumstances whatsoever that can ever justify the direct killing of an unborn child. *Abortion and other attacks on innocent human life such as euthanasia, embryonic stem cell research, and cloning must always and everywhere be opposed.* If we, as a society, cannot uphold the basic human right to life, then all of the other rights are endangered and subverted. The right to life and the protection of all human life from the moment of conception to natural death is at the very heart and essence of Catholic social teaching.

2. Call to Family, Community, and Participation

Human beings by their nature are social beings. This is most profoundly seen in the Book of Genesis. God creates woman as a fitting companion for Adam. Adam's loneliness is overcome when he finds communion with another like himself. Thus, man and woman are called to live in community, and the basic and vital cell of all communities and society is the family. Catholic social teaching has always recognized the family as the foundation of society and vigorously defends its dignity and rights. The Church also recognizes that how communities and governments are formed and operate are of great importance and consequence. She continuously upholds that the goal and purpose of all communities is to support and enhance the dignity of the human person and the family. Let's take a closer look at some of the important teachings that fall under this theme.

Dignity of the family

Catholic social teaching recognizes the importance of the family as the foundation for all communities and societies. It emphasizes that the family is the first social consideration in order and importance. In fact, the family surpasses all other societies in the community or state and serves as the model and the basic foundation for all of society. Because of this, it is important that the state and society foster stable marriages where children are welcomed and educated. The family wage is one important way of supporting and fostering strong and stable families.

Society must oppose any social conditions that degrade or minimize the role and basic structure of the family and must protect the natural institution of marriage as between one man and one woman. Catholic social teaching recognizes that if the family is degraded, if its rights and structure are not defended and allowed to flourish, society as a whole will suffer and decline.

Pope Benedict XVI forcefully defends the rights and dignity of the family and its importance and role within society:

> Consequently, whoever, even unknowingly, circumvents the institution of the family undermines peace in the entire community, national and international, since he weakens what is in effect the primary agency of peace. This point merits special reflection: everything that serves to weaken the family based on the marriage of a man and a woman, everything that directly or indirectly stands in the way of its openness to the responsible acceptance of a new life, everything that obstructs its right to be primarily responsible for the education of its children, constitutes an objective obstacle on the road to peace. The family needs to have a home, employment and a just recognition of the domestic activity of parents, the possibility of schooling for children, and basic health care for all. When society and public policy are not committed to assisting the family in these areas, they deprive themselves of an essential resource in the service of peace. The social communications media, in particular, because of their educational potential, have a special responsibility for promoting respect for the family, making clear its expectations and rights, and presenting all its beauty. (*Message for World Day of Peace*, January 1, 2008, 5)

Role of the state

Catholic social teaching also provides principles and guidelines for the proper role of the state in social and economic affairs. The Church's teaching affirms that the basic role of the state is to help secure the common good and promote the dignity of the human person and basic human rights. It recognizes that the state is necessary to accomplish tasks that are proper to the government such as national defense, interstate cooperation, treaties with other nations, and the criminal justice system. However, it also warns against a state becoming too large, involving itself in all problems, or taking upon itself the functions and duties that are proper to smaller institutions such as faith-based groups, charities, local communities, and the family. Within Catholic social teaching this is called the **principle of subsidiarity,** a very important and fundamental principle in Catholic social teaching (see CCC 1883).

The Church also opposes any type of collectivism (communism) and any form of unchecked capitalism. Both of these economic systems degrade the dignity and rights of the human person and the social nature of man. Communism exalts the role of the state to the point of removing basic human rights and freedoms, including the right to own private property. Unchecked capitalism can exalt radical individualism that can destroy basic social institutions, such as the family. It can lead to treating human persons as objects that are only the means to an economic end. While the Church does not support any one specific economic system, it does caution against these extremes and strongly encourages the principle of subsidiarity in both the role of the state and within basic economic systems.

Political participation

Whenever possible, all are called to participate in the public square. This is a fundamental part of our responsibility as Christian citizens in society (see CCC 1913). Some are called to direct and active participation in political life through public service. All of us, however, should be involved in the public square through the right and duty to vote. It is our duty to call on those entrusted with political and governmental responsibility to protect the dignity of the human person and the family, to promote the **common good**, and ensure justice for all.

All participation in the public square and political life should be based upon a proper formation of conscience. It should bring to light the basic message of the Gospel as well as our moral convictions based on the natural law and the teachings of Christ and the Church. In the document *Forming Consciences for Faithful Citizenship* (November 2007), the United States Bishops urgently call all Catholics to this kind of participation in the public square:

> Unfortunately, politics in our country often can be a contest of powerful interests, partisan attacks, sound bites, and media hype. The Church calls for a different kind of political engagement: one shaped by the moral convictions of well-formed consciences and focused on the dignity of every human being, the pursuit of the common good, and the protection of the weak and the vulnerable. The Catholic call to faithful citizenship affirms the importance of political participation and insists that public service is a worthy vocation. As Catholics, we should be guided more by our moral convictions than by our attachment to a political party or interest group. When necessary, our participation should help transform the party to which we belong; we should not let the party transform us in such a way that we neglect or deny fundamental moral truths. We are called to bring together our principles and our political choices, our values and our votes, to help build a better world. (14)

Contrary to popular belief, participation in the political arena, whether through holding public office or exercising the right and privilege to vote, calls us to not abandon our moral convictions. Rather, we must be a moral voice in the public square, vigorously defending and promoting the dignity of the human person. Issues such as the right to life, liberty, adequate living conditions, just wages, health care, and care and concern for the poor are not just Catholic issues, but are the basic moral foundations and rights upon which our society and any just society is built.

While all of these issues are important and should be of concern and importance to all Catholics, *not all of the issues have equal moral weight.* Some issues, such as abortion, euthanasia, embryonic stem cell research, and cloning that involve the direct killing of innocent human life, often on a massive scale, are intrinsically evil and should always be opposed.

While Catholics should be concerned with all issues of social justice and peace, a candidate's support of any of thc intrinsically evil acts listed above can and often should disqualify a candidate for consideration, even if their position on other issues may be favorable. Other important issues like immigration, the death penalty, national security, health care, and the economy are issues where principled debate on how to best address them can be possible, because they are not intrinsically evil in themselves.

At times there may not be a candidate or a political party that totally adheres to the principles of Catholic social teaching. In such a case the Catholic voter must first address and consider the candidate's position on the non-negotiable issues such as abortion, as a major factor in determining which candidate or party best adheres to the principles of Catholic social teaching.

It is important that all Catholics take seriously their role and participation in the public square, and see that their consciences are properly formed and rooted in the teachings of Christ articulated, taught, and handed on by the Church to whom Christ has entrusted the fullness of truth.

3. Rights and Responsibilities

According to Catholic social teaching every person has the inalienable right to life and the basic necessities of life. This right covers what is required to live a full and decent life including the right to work, education, health care, and the basic necessities of food, water, and adequate living conditions. In addition, all people have the responsibility to see that these rights are safeguarded and preserved so the common good of all is established and protected.

The common good is a fundamental principle of Catholic social teaching. "As a result the common good, that is, the sum of those conditions of social life which allow social groups and their individual members relatively thorough and ready access to their own fulfillment" (*Gaudium et spes,* no. 26). The Catechism gives three basic elements of the common good and the rights and responsibilities concerning it: respect for the person, social well-being and development, and the requirement of peace (see 1907, 1908, 1909).

4. The Poor and Vulnerable

Another important theme in Catholic social teaching is the preferential option for the poor and the most vulnerable. This principle is derived directly from the teaching and action of Jesus. We see throughout His earthly ministry that Jesus was most concerned with the poor, the sick, the dying, and the outcast. His teaching included the story of the Good Samaritan who helped his enemy in time of need and distress. We also see the great story of the Last

Judgment in Matthew 25, where the People of God will be judged on how they cared for the most poor, weak, and vulnerable. This theme of Catholic social teaching addresses three issues of particular concern in our culture today.

The unborn and elderly

Human life is most vulnerable at both the dawn and dusk of our existence on earth. As we have clearly seen, abortion is an attack on the most weak and innocent of our society. An often neglected victim of abortion is the mother who receives the abortion. In most cases, these mothers are in desperate and vulnerable situations. By helping them in these difficult circumstances we can help save the life of the unborn child and also bring the light of Christ to a very dark moment in a woman's life.

On the other end of the spectrum of human life is the care and concern for the elderly of our society. How well does society meet the needs of our aged population who have already given so much of themselves to the benefit of the community and society? Issues such as Social Security, Medicare, dignified health care, and end of life issues are great social justice concerns that cannot be neglected.

The poor and homeless

This theme also calls us to be concerned with the poor, the homeless, and the outcasts of our society. Are our local communities and charities receiving enough resources to care for the poor and homeless? Are we helping them integrate back into society to become productive citizens, or allowing them to degenerate in an undignified and ineffective welfare system? These questions must be asked by us who are called by the example of Christ to concern ourselves with the poor and the outcast.

Immigrants

One of the most controversial issues of our present time is that of immigration. It is a very difficult problem with no clear-cut solutions. On one hand, our government and communities cannot ignore the dignity and rights of the human person. On the other hand, a country has the right to protect its borders and national security. This needs to be accomplished while preserving the human dignity of the person to the fullest extent possible. Many immigrants today are seeking the basic necessities of life and are often escaping horrible social and economic conditions in their home country. Our society must find just solutions to this growing problem.

5. The Dignity of Work and the Rights of Workers

The opportunity to work and be productive and creative is an important part of the dignity of the human person. The Book of Genesis gives witness to the dignity of work. God places Adam in the Garden of Eden and gives him the command to cultivate and care for it. Even in the original innocence of the human person, work was established as a fundamental good.

Work affects many aspects of a community and culture. The value of work within Catholic social teaching flows from the truth that human work is a good to be fostered and respected, and that the dignity of the worker is most important. The worker can never be considered a means but always an end. Through work, the person should experience personal growth and a supportive community.

This issue is so important that it was the subject of the first social encyclical issued on May 15, 1891 by Pope Leo XIII, *Rerum novarum* (On Capital and Labor). He defended the rights and dignity of workers in the face of the Industrial Revolution and the rising collectivist philosophies that would spark the communist revolutions of the twentieth century. On the occasion of the 90th anniversary of *Rerum novarum*, Pope John Paul II dedicated another social encyclical *Laborem exercens* (On Human Work) to the subject of the dignity of work. He said:

> Man is made to be in the visible universe and image and likeness of God himself (cf. *Gen* 1:26), and he is placed in it in order to subdue the earth (cf. *Gen* 1:28). From the beginning therefore he is *called to work. Work is one of the characteristics that distinguish* man from the rest of creatures, whose activity for sustaining their lives cannot be called work. Only man is capable of work, and only man works, at the same time by work occupying his existence on earth. Thus work bears a particular mark of man and of humanity, the mark of a person operating within a community of persons. And this mark decides its interior characteristics; in a sense it constitutes its very nature. (September 14, 1981, no. 1)

Catholic social teaching respects the rights of workers against both the state and unjust companies and corporations. Among these fundamental rights is the right to associate in unions in order to protect themselves from unjust practices and working conditions. Catholic social teaching also vigorously upholds the right of all men and women to work, and that all work, no matter how menial, contributes to the dignity of the human person and to the betterment of society. Pope John Paul II characterizes work as participation in a great process intended by God:

> As man, through his work, becomes more and more the master of the earth, and as he confirms his dominion over the visible world, again through his work, he nevertheless remains in every case and at every phase of this process within the Creator's original ordering. And this ordering remains necessarily and indissolubly linked with the fact that man was created, as male and female, "in the image of God." This *process is*, at the same time, *universal:* it embraces all human beings, every generation, every phase of economic and cultural development, and *at the same time* it is a process that takes place *within each human being,* in each conscious human being, in each conscious human subject. Each and every individual is at the same time embraced by it. Each and every individual, to the proper extent and in an incalculable number of ways, takes part in the giant process whereby man "subdues the earth" through his work. (*Laborem exercens*, no. 4)

6. Solidarity

The principle of solidarity, especially articulated by Pope John Paul II, confirms that the unity of the human family goes far beyond simply cultural, racial, and economic lines. It is the plan and vision of the Father to bring about the kingdom of justice, peace, and the complete unity of the human race in and through Jesus Christ:

> Solidarity is undoubtedly a Christian virtue. . . . Solidarity seeks to go beyond itself, to take on the specifically Christian dimension of total gratuity, forgiveness and reconciliation. One's neighbor is then not only a human being with his or her

> own rights and a fundamental equality with everyone else, but becomes the living image of God the Father, redeemed by the blood of Jesus Christ and placed under the permanent action of the Holy Spirit. (Pope John Paul II, Encyclical Letter On the Social Teaching of the Church *Sollicitudo rei socialis* [December 30, 1987], no. 40)

With this vision in mind the Church challenges us to be responsible for the needs of other people, communities, and nations. It seeks a more just social order and peace and harmony within the human family. The principle of solidarity is built around three essential elements that are indispensible to achieving true solidarity and unity in the human family.

Human solidarity

Human solidarity calls us to seek justice wherever there may be conflicts, injustice, or inequality in order to achieve a true unity within the human family (see CCC 1941). Human solidarity is the responsibility of all people, and no one is exempt from this important calling. Pope Benedict XVI beautifully summarizes this universal call to human solidarity:

> The family community, in order to prosper, needs the generous consent of all its members. This realization also needs to become a shared conviction on the part of all those called to form the common human family. We need to say our own "yes" to this vocation which God has inscribed in our very nature. We do not live alongside one another purely by chance; all of us are progressing along a common path as men and women, and thus as brothers and sisters. Consequently, it is essential that we should all be committed to living our lives in an attitude of responsibility before God, acknowledging him as the deepest source of our own existence and that of others. By going back to this supreme principle we are able to perceive the unconditional worth of each human being, and thus to lay the premises for building a humanity at peace. Without this transcendent foundation society is a mere aggregation of neighbors, not a community of brothers and sisters called to form one great family. (*Message for World Day of Peace*, January 1, 2008, 6)

Peace

Solidarity also calls upon governments and nations to find solutions to conflicts and tensions through peaceful means. As we have seen, the Church teaches that war is not always intrinsically evil, but must be avoided by all means possible and used only as a last resort. The Church also teaches that peace is not merely the absence of war. True peace requires justice and equality among all people, communities, and nations. In his 1972 letter for the World Day of Peace, Pope Paul VI said: "If you want peace, then work for justice." True peace will only be present if justice is established through a true effort to achieve human solidarity.

Conversion of heart

Pope John Paul II has said that solidarity is an eminently Christian virtue. Solidarity, justice, and peace can only be achieved through the conversion of hearts. Catholic social teaching calls everyone to a radical turning away from sin and toward God. It requires deep love of God and neighbor to the point that we see each person as another self, respecting their rights, dignity, and needs. True human solidarity (and thus true peace and justice) can only take place through the conversion of hearts and the grace of Jesus Christ.

7. Care for God's Creation

Creation is a great gift of God's love for us and has been entrusted to the human family as our home. Indeed, we are to be the stewards of this gift. Catholic social teaching calls us to have respect for God's gift of creation and to care for the environment.

Environmental concerns have become ever greater in recent years as we face such issues such as pollution, waning natural resources, and potential climate change. Catholic social teaching approaches these issues with concern and prudence, calling communities and nations to care for and preserve the natural environment.

However, ecology and concern for the environment must be considered within the whole of Catholic social teaching. Some radical environmentalists minimize human life and dignity, putting it on a par with the rest of creation. This fundamental and critical error, which has crept into some environmental circles, must be opposed and corrected. The human person is the pinnacle of

God's creation, and this world was given to humanity by God, who loves us. Creation is at the service of the human family. The fact that only human beings are created in the image and likeness of God sets man and woman far above the rest of creation in order and dignity. Environmental concerns and actions can never be at the expense of human dignity.

Human dignity must also govern the use and distribution of natural resources. In many cases the poor and the underprivileged are not given equal access to the world's resources. Countries rich in natural resources must ensure that they are not consuming an inordinate amount at the expense of poorer, third world countries. The dignity of the human person demands just and equitable use and management of natural resources.

God calls us to be accountable for the care of His creation. Catholic social teaching encourages collaboration between scientists, governments, and international bodies to ensure that environmental concerns are addressed justly and adequately, while respecting the legitimate needs of the human family. Prudent use of resources is required so that they benefit all, both now and in the future. Pope Benedict XVI summarizes these fundamental points of Catholic social teaching concerning the care of the environment:

> We need to care for the environment: it has been entrusted to men and women to be protected and cultivated with responsible freedom, with the good of all as a constant guiding criterion. Human beings, obviously, are of supreme worth vis-à-vis creation as a whole. Respecting the environment does not mean considering material or animal nature more important than man. Rather, it means not selfishly considering nature to be at the complete disposal of our own interests, for future generations also have the right to reap its benefits and to exhibit towards nature the same responsible freedom that we claim for ourselves. Nor must we overlook the poor, who are excluded in many cases from the goods of creation destined for all. Humanity today is rightly concerned about the ecological balance of tomorrow. It is important for assessments in this regard to be carried out prudently, in dialogue with experts and people of wisdom, uninhibited by ideological pressure to draw hasty conclusions, and above all with the aim of reaching agreement on a model of sustainable development capable of ensuring the well-being of all while respecting environmental

> balances. If the protection of the environment involves costs, they should be justly distributed, taking due account of the different levels of development of various countries and the need for solidarity with future generations. Prudence does not mean failing to accept responsibilities and postponing decisions; it means being committed to making joint decisions after pondering responsibly the road to be taken, decisions aimed at strengthening that covenant between human beings and the environment, which should mirror the creative love of God, from whom we come and towards whom we are journeying. (*Message for World Day of Peace*, January 1, 2008, 7)

These seven themes are not an exhaustive presentation of Catholic social teaching, but serve as an introduction to the main issues that affect us in our modern culture.

Above all, through our Baptism in Christ Catholic social teaching calls us to be His instruments in reaching out to the poor, the vulnerable, and the outcast of society, and to build up a true kingdom of justice and peace. All of us are called to pay particular attention to the pressing issues of justice in our culture. We are to be leaven in the world, always promoting and protecting the dignity of the human person. We are called to bring the light of Christ to all the important social concerns of our time.

From the Catechism: Key Words to Know

SOCIAL TEACHING: The teaching (social doctrine) of the Church on the truth of revelation about human dignity, human solidarity, and the principles of justice and peace; the moral judgments about economic and social matters required by such truth, and about the demands of justice and peace (2419–2422).

SOCIAL JUSTICE: The respect for the human person and the rights that flow from human dignity and guarantee it. Society must provide the conditions that allow people to obtain what is their due according to their nature and vocation (1928, 1931).

PRINCIPLE OF SUBSIDIARITY: Principle of Catholic social teaching according to which those in higher authority should respect the rights and appropriate autonomy of those with less authority. The term often comes into play when balancing the authority of a national government with the claims of individual families, local communities, and states, so as not to supplant the initiative, freedom, and responsibility of the latter (1883–1885).

COMMON GOOD: The conditions that facilitate the pursuit of happiness of everyone in the community. The principal components of the common good are respect for every human person, social development and well-being (e.g. health, education, family values, etc.), and peace (1905–1909).

Chapter 26

The Morality of Fertility and Biomedical Research

Reading the Catechism: Paragraphs 2373–2379; 2274–2275

> Human life is sacred and inviolable at every moment of existence, including the initial phase which precedes birth. All human beings, from their mothers' womb, belong to God who searches them and knows them, who forms them and knits them together with his own hands, who gazes on them when they are tiny shapeless embryos and already sees in them the adults of tomorrow whose days are numbered and whose vocation is even now written in the "book of life."
>
> —Pope John Paul II, Encyclical Letter on The Gospel of Life *Evangelium vitae* (March 25, 1995), no. 61

In our modern culture, much of the research and developments in the fields of fertility and biomedicine has become of great concern to the Church. It is the duty of the Church to defend the dignity and worth of the human person from the moment of conception to natural death. Procedures such as artificial insemination, in vitro fertilization, and human cloning present new and terrible threats to human life at its earliest and most vulnerable stages. The People of God must be aware of these emerging threats and be ready to defend the sacredness of human life at all stages with utmost urgency.

There are two important points of clarification before we explore the moral and ethical ramifications of fertility and biomedical research and procedures.

First, some people contend that the Church is anti-science. On the contrary, the Church loves, praises, and promotes science and scientific research that help to better our society and the human condition. God has blessed us with our reason to learn and discover marvelous things about the world and about human nature. Science, however, is not autonomous and must always respect the dignity of the human person from the moment of conception to natural death. In our modern culture science is moving forward without serious moral and ethical considerations, trampling on the dignity of the human person—it's a runaway train that is quickly outrunning moral principles. The Church's magisterium is vigorously addressing this serious problem.

Second, in the areas of infertility research and treatment, the Church understands and is sympathetic to those who are unable to conceive a child. The Church does not condemn the desire of the parents to receive that gift; it is the means by which that gift is achieved that is in question. Further, every child that comes into the world is a gift, regardless of the means through which that blessing was achieved. Children who have their existence through morally unacceptable medical procedures are still indeed gifts, and in no way is their intrinsic human dignity lessened.

With that said, it is my goal to give you insight into some of the more popular and controversial fertility and biomedical research techniques and procedures that are in use today. While there are many more that we could cover, I hope to give you the basic moral principles that will allow you to judge the morality of these procedures, and the increasing numbers of procedures and research techniques that are emerging each year. I will also give you a very basic insight into the biology and medicine involved. Although I am not an expert in biology or medicine, I hope to give you a better understanding on how these procedures are a threat to human life, and the moral principles you can use to help others to see this emerging threat.

Artificial Insemination (AIH) and In Vitro Fertilization (IVF)

Artificial Insemination

Artificial Insemination is the procedure in which sperm is taken from the husband, placed into a sterile container, and then injected into the woman through the vagina at the mouth of the cervix. This is usually done two to three times in a woman's cycle to bracket the time of ovulation.

Why is artificial insemination desired?

AIH is used when the man's semen is of poor quality due to an unusually small concentration of sperm or a very small volume of semen. It is also used when there is an insufficient number of sperm present in the cervical mucus, making it difficult or impossible for the sperm to travel to the ovum.

When the husband's sperm is found to be incapable of fertilization, donor sperm from another man is used to achieve pregnancy. There are now numerous sperm banks in the United States and around the world where sperm can be frozen for several years without damage or loss of potency.

The success rate of AIH has not been good when used by couples for reasons of poor semen quality. While the use of AIH with donor semen is much more successful, there are considerably more serious moral objections in these cases.

In Vitro Fertilization

"In vitro" means "in a glass," and this is where conception takes place. First, several eggs are removed from the ovaries of the woman. Usually at least three to five eggs are fertilized. The process of fertilization involves the injection of sperm into the egg because IVF is usually used when the sperm is incapable of penetrating the egg. Several eggs are fertilized so that the "best" can be implanted, and if one is unsuccessful there are spares on the side to use. Each of the new embryos is tested for quality, to see if it is worth implanting. If not, the embryo is discarded. The final step is to implant one or several of the embryos into the woman's uterus or fallopian tube, in a procedure called Embryo Transfer (ET). Several embryos are often implanted to ensure success.

Different Types of AIH and IVF

- ***Homologous AIH and IVF:*** This occurs when human conception is achieved using either method through the meeting of the gametes of spouses joined in marriage.
- ***Heterologous AIH and IVF:*** This occurs when human conception is achieved using either method through the meeting of gametes coming from at least one donor other than the spouses who are joined in marriage.

Moral and Ethical Objections to AIH and IVF

A Dual Sacredness

A dual sacredness must always and everywhere be upheld in infertility or biomedical research and procedures. These are the very foundation of fertility and biomedical ethics.

Sacredness of procreation and the conjugal act

God willed that human life be created through the love and mutual self-giving of spouses. Only within this context of life-giving love proper to the Sacrament of Marriage can procreation morally take place. Any procedure separating procreation from the conjugal act is always morally unacceptable because it subverts the plan of love instilled in our very nature by the Creator. We must always ask: Are we helping the marital act or replacing it?

Sacredness of human life

While science in itself is objectively good, it may never undermine the dignity of the human person. Once medical and biological procedures and research begin to degrade or destroy the dignity of the human person, they become morally illicit. In the areas of fertility and biomedical research, there are several threats to the human person. Pope John Paul II outlines these threats in *Evangelium vitae*:

> Unfortunately, this disturbing state of affairs, far from decreasing, is expanding: with the new prospects opened up by scientific and technological progress there arise new forms of attacks on the dignity of the human being. At the same time a new cultural climate is developing and taking hold, which gives crimes against life a *new and—if possible –even more sinister character,* giving rise to further grave concern: broad sectors of public opinion justify certain crimes against life in the name of the rights of individual freedom, and on this basis they claim not only exemption from punishment but even authorization by the State, so that these things can be done with total freedom and indeed with the free assistance of health-care systems.

All this is causing a profound change in the way in which life and relationships between people are considered. The fact that legislation in many countries, perhaps even departing from basic principles of their Constitutions, has determined not to punish these practices against life, and even to make them altogether legal, is both a disturbing symptom and a significant cause of grave moral decline. Choices once unanimously considered criminal and rejected by the common moral sense are gradually becoming socially acceptable. Even certain sectors of the medical profession, which by its calling is directed to the defense and care of human life, are increasingly willing to carry out these acts against the person. In this way the very nature of the medical profession is distorted and contradicted, and the dignity of those who practice it is degraded. In such a cultural and legislative situation, the serious demographic, social and family problems which weigh upon many of the world's peoples and which require responsible and effective attention from national and international bodies, are left open to false and deceptive solutions, opposed to the truth and the good of persons and nations.

The end result of this is tragic: not only is the fact of the destruction of so many human lives still to be born or in their final stage extremely grave and disturbing, but no less grave and disturbing is the fact that conscience itself, darkened as it were by such widespread conditioning, is finding it increasingly difficult to distinguish between good and evil in what concerns the basic value of human life. (no. 4)

Technical Domination over the Genesis of Human Beings

Modern fertility and biomedical procedures are transposing the generation of human life from the loving embrace of the marital act to the manipulative control of the laboratory bench.

Homologous IVF and ET is brought about outside the bodies of the couple through actions of third parties whose competence and technical activity determine the success of the procedure. Such fertilization entrusts the life and identity of the embryo

> into the power of doctors and biologists and establishes the domination of technology over the origin and destiny of the human person. Such a relationship of domination is in itself contrary to the dignity and equality that must be common to parents and children.(Congregation for the Doctrine of the Faith, Instruction on Respect for Human Life *Donum vitae* [February 22, 1987], II, B, 5)

The Exploitation of Human Beings in the Destruction of Embryos

Intrinsic to IVF and embryonic stem cell research and cloning is the destruction or "throwing away" of human life. This human reproductive technology is also becoming a huge and lucrative business. To make matters worse, this area is very unregulated at this time, and there are surprisingly very few serious moral and ethical questions being raised within the research community or by local or federal governments. Basically it is the "wild wild west" of biomedical research.

The "Moral Landslide" Regarding the Dignity of Human Life

Once contraception devalued human fertility, it became easy to devalue the fruit of that fertility in abortion. Once widespread abortion devalued human life, it became quite easy and convenient to manipulate and destroy human life at the embryonic stage. What is next?

Several Moral and Ethical Objections to AIH and IVF

Undermines the meaning of the sexual act

Both AIH and IVF undermine the meaning of the sexual act. Even if they are homologous (exclusive to spouses), they violate the sexual act because procreation is separated from the mutual love and self-gift of the marital act. Both procedures replace the marital act as the genesis of human life.

> The Church's teaching on marriage and human procreation affirms the "inseparable connection, willed by God and unable to be broken by man on his own initiative, between the two meanings of the conjugal act: the unitive meaning and the

> procreative meaning. Indeed, by its intimate structure, the conjugal act, while most closely uniting husband and wife, capacitates them for the generation of new lives, according to laws inscribed in the very being of man and of woman. (*Donum vitae,* II, B, 4)

Violates the marriage covenant and exclusivity of the marriage act

AIH and IVF also violate the couple's marriage covenant and the exclusivity of their marriage act by introducing a third party when the fertility specialist or laboratory technician becomes involved. Again, human life is being created apart from the exclusive and mutual self-giving of the marriage covenant that is most specifically and authentically realized in the marital act. In addition, heterologous AIH and IFV violate the marriage covenant because another person's gametes (sperm or egg) are being used. This is an even more serious violation of the couple's exclusivity.

> Respect for the unity of marriage and for conjugal fidelity demands that the child be conceived in marriage; the bond existing between husband and wife accords the spouses, in an objective and inalienable manner, the exclusive right to become father and mother solely through each other. Recourse to the gametes of a third person, in order to have sperm or ovum available, constitutes a violation of the reciprocal commitment of the spouses and a grave lack in regard to that essential property of marriage which is its unity. (*Donum vitae,* II, A, 2)

Requires masturbation

Both AIH and IVF require masturbation on the part of the man to retrieve sperm. That is always and everywhere a distorted act that violates the nature of the sexual relationship as the mutual self-gift between spouses (see CCC 2352).

Treats human beings as objects

IVF treats human beings as objects and relies on the expendability of embryos. Several are created so the best can be chosen, and the "spares" are on hand in case the initial procedure does not work. Those that are not used are either discarded or frozen. Here is part of the justification used: "What is wrong with throwing away embryos when so many fetuses are aborted?" This is clearly the moral slippery slope! Thousands of embryos are frozen to be used at a later time. Over 396,000 are frozen in the United States alone. These tiny human beings are seen as objects to be bought, sold, or manipulated to serve specific purposes.

Increases the risk of selective reduction (abortion)

IVF increases the risk of multiple-child pregnancies (four or more), and then selective "reduction" (abortion) is suggested and often carried out. The smallest of the babies are eliminated to help ensure the others survive. Note that the destruction of human life does not stop at the embryonic level.

Greater risk of birth defects

Children conceived by IVF suffer a much greater risk of birth defects (twice the rate). As mentioned previously, IVF is often done when the sperm is unable to penetrate the ovum. They are unable to penetrate the ovum because often there is some genetic problem with them. By force fertilizing the ovum in IVF, genetic problems are passed on to the child. An example of the greater risk of birth defects is that IVF babies are six times more likely to suffer cancer of the eye.

Violates the rights of the child

Heterologous IVF or AIH violates the dignity and rights of the child.

> Heterologous artificial fertilization violates the rights of the child; it deprives him of his filial relationship with his parental origins and can hinder the maturing of his personal identity. Furthermore, it offends the common vocation of the spouses who are called to fatherhood and motherhood: it objectively deprives conjugal fruitfulness of its unity and integrity; it brings about and manifests a rupture between genetic parenthood, gestational parenthood and responsibility for upbringing. Such damage to the personal relationships within the family has repercussions on civil society: what threatens the unity and stability of the family is a source of dissension, disorder and injustice in the whole of social life. (*Donum vitae,* II, A, 2)

Stem Cell Research

What Is Stem Cell Research?

A stem cell is a "blank" or unspecialized cell that is capable of becoming a specialized cell, with a cell function suited for a specific role in the body. Very early in embryonic life the embryo is filled with these stem cells that have not yet developed into the type of cell and tissue they will become. Behind stem cell research is the idea that if these stem cells are placed into other humans, the cells will become the kind of healthy cells that are needed.

The moral problem with stem cell research is how they are obtained. Retrieving stem cells from embryos results in the violent destruction of the embryo, and therefore the killing of a new human being. Embryonic stem cell research has yet to produce successful therapies, and embryos are not the only source of stem cells. In fact, the use of stem cells from adults creates no moral problem and has been proven to be quite successful.

Different Types and Sources of Stem Cells

Embryonic type

Embryonic stem cells are taken from an embryo conceived through IVF. To begin, a newly fertilized egg forms a cell called a zygote. The zygote cell divides, and through continued division becomes a blastocyst, which is filled with hundreds of stem cells. These cells would eventually become bone tissue, heart tissue, brain tissue, pancreas cells, or spinal cord tissue. There are 220 total cell/tissue types that these cells can become. Once they are retrieved they can continue to grow into what are called stem cell lines. Again, the ultimate goal is to place the cells into humans to grow new and healthy tissue that is needed to cure disease.

Embryonic germ stem cells

These are stem cells that are retrieved from the reproductive organs of aborted fetuses. These can also become all 220 cell/tissue types.

Adult stem cells

Adult stem cells are stem cells that are taken from an adult. Umbilical cords, placentas, and amniotic fluid can be saved after birth and adult stem cells can be retrieved from them. Adult stem cells can also be retrieved from bone marrow, from the hipbone, through liposuction, and from the nasal epithelium (neural stem cells) from cadavers within twenty hours of death (with full informed consent of family). However, adult stem cells cannot become all 220 cell/tissue types. They are more restrictive and not as flexible. This is why embryonic stem cells are so coveted.

Medical Difficulties with Embryonic Stem Cell Therapy

Embryonic stem cells are very powerful and can become all 220 cell/tissue types. However, because they grow so quickly they very often grow tumors when they are placed in the body. Embryonic stem cells are almost always rejected because they come from another person. This has led to experiments with therapeutic cloning. The idea is to create an embryo just like you from which to get stem cells so that your body will not reject them. To date, there has been no success in using embryonic stem cells in curing any disease.

Successful Use of Adult Stem Cells

There has been great success using adult stem cells to cure disease. Because these cells can be retrieved from your own body, they are much less likely to be rejected. The Family Research Council (FRC) issued three successive reports (2006–2008) on advances in human treatments and research with adult stem cells, which at the time were already being used to treat over seventy-three different conditions and were the subject of over fourteen hundred FDA approved trials. FRC continues to provide information on important advances with adult stem cells (www.frc.org). The Adult Stem-cell Foundation of Ireland (ASFI), established in 2012, also promotes awareness on the use and benefits of adult stem cells worldwide, providing up-to-date information on adult stem cell research, development, and therapies. Consider the following benefits:

> Adult stem cells have been used successfully for many years in treatments for leukemia and related blood cancers. They are being used to treat a number of human diseases. Umbilical

cord blood and Bone Marrow are currently the most successful stem cell treatments so far, mostly in the treatment of blood diseases such as Leukemia, Lymphoma, Sickle Cell disease, Thalassaemia, immune system deficiencies, and have been used to treat over 70 diseases routinely with Hematopoietic stem cells. However, in the last decade the discovery of other types of stem cells in umbilical cord blood and bone marrow has led to other "non-blood" disease treatments, such as bone and cartilage repair, heart repair, liver damage, inflammatory bowel disease, ALS (Lou Gehrig's disease), Diabetes Type 1, and many others. Currently there are over 600 clinical trials with Umbilical Cord Blood ongoing and over 3,000 with Bone Marrow in a wide range of conditions. (Available at www.asfi.ie)

Cloning

What Is Cloning?

Cloning is the process of copying DNA fragments, cells, or even organisms. Reproductive cloning is for the purpose of producing offspring. Therapeutic cloning is for the purpose of research and the curing of disease.

Overview of the Science of Reproductive Cloning

1. A cell is taken from a donor.
2. A woman donates her egg and the DNA is stripped from the egg.
3. The cell, with the donor's DNA, is fused with the egg and is chemically induced to begin dividing.
4. The developing embryo is placed into the uterus and the baby develops and is born.

Difficulties with Reproductive Cloning, Which Has Only Been Done on Animals

There is an extremely high rate of abnormalities during gestation and birth. Even the animals that have been born had many, many problems and did not live long. Cloning primates has never been done successfully. It is extremely more difficult to clone a primate than any other animal. How much more difficult will it be to clone humans?

Therapeutic Cloning for Stem Cell Retrieval

This type of cloning is the same as reproductive cloning except that after the cell divides and reaches the blastocyst stage, stem cells are removed to be used in therapy. The idea is that these stem cells will not be rejected since they contain the patient's own DNA.

Moral and Ethical Problems with Stem Cell Research and Cloning

The central issue is the destruction of human embryos. One can never destroy human life for therapeutic reasons, no matter how good the reason and no matter the benefit. Any form of stem cell research that results in the destruction of human life in the embryonic form is absolutely morally unacceptable.

In addition, the use of stem cells in medical research that have been obtained from the deliberate and violent destruction of human life is also absolutely morally unacceptable. Using stem cells from aborted fetuses and from already destroyed embryos is immoral.

Apart from the medical and biological difficulties, cloning human beings for the purpose of their destruction for medical research is gravely immoral. It is the purposeful creation of human life for its intentional and premeditated destruction. Pope John Paul II states:

> This evaluation of the morality of abortion is to be applied also to the recent forms of *intervention on human embryos* which, although carried out for purposes legitimate in themselves, inevitably involve the killing of those embryos. This is the case with *experimentation on embryos*, which is becoming increasingly widespread in the field of biomedical research and is legally permitted in some countries. Although "one must uphold as licit procedures carried out on the human embryo which respect the life and integrity of the embryo and do not involve disproportionate risks for it, but rather are directed to

> its healing, the improvement of its condition of health, or its individual survival," it must nonetheless be stated that the use of human embryos or fetuses as an object of experimentation constitutes a crime against their dignity as human beings who have a right to the same respect owed to a child once born, just as to every person.
>
> This moral condemnation also regards procedures that exploit living human embryos and fetuses—sometimes specifically "produced" for this purpose by *in vitro* fertilization—either to be used as "biological material" or as *providers of organs or tissue for transplants* in the treatment of certain diseases. The killing of innocent human creatures, even if carried out to help others, constitutes an absolutely unacceptable act. (*Evangelium vitae,* no. 63)

Immoral and Moral Sources of Stem Cells

There is no morally legitimate way to retrieve embryonic stem cells because that will always result in the killing of an innocent human being. Embryonic germ stem cells can be morally retrieved from babies who suffered miscarriage as long as parents give informed consent. It would be the same as organ donation. However, as we have stated, aborted babies can never be used. Adult stem cells can be morally retrieved from umbilical cords, placentas, and amniotic fluid. They can also be morally retrieved from a person's tissue as long as there is informed consent.

Common Arguments Used to Experiment on Embryos

"Embryos are merely cellular life."

The basis of this argument is that embryos are not human life but are just cellular life. However, human embryos are beings that are human—they cannot develop into cats, zebras, monkeys, or a plant. The embryo is a human being in an early stage of development, just as much as my two-year-old is in a different stage of human development than I am. The child is still human. The director of Education at The National Catholic Bioethics Center (NCBC), Father Tadeusz Pacholczyk, who earned his doctorate in neuroscience from Yale and did post-doctoral work at Harvard, puts it like this:

> What a human embryo actually is, even at its earliest and most undeveloped stage, already makes it the only kind of entity capable of receiving the gift of an immortal soul from the hand of God. No other animal or plant embryo can receive this gift; indeed, no other entity in the universe can receive this gift. Hence, the early human embryo is never merely biological tissue, like a group of liver cells in a petri dish; at a minimum, such an embryo, with all its internal structure and directionality, represents the privileged sanctuary of one meant to develop as a human person. (March 2008, available at http://www.ncbcenter.org/page.aspx?pid=305)

"In the womb vs. in the test tube."

A ridiculous argument is often put forth asserting that embryos used in the laboratory are not human until they have the "potential" of becoming human inside the womb. Just because we change their location does not mean we change their nature. Many frozen embryos that have been implanted in a woman successfully mature to birth. Putting human embryos in test tubes, or freezing them and stunting or stopping their development, does not change their being human but merely degrades it.

"Embryos are not persons yet."

Is a human embryo a person? Does the embryo have a soul? If not, is it morally acceptable to destroy the embryo for research? The National Catholic Bioethics Center offers this instructive lesson on the Church's perspective:

> People are sometimes surprised to hear that the wrongness of destroying a human embryo does not ultimately depend on when that embryo might become a person, or when he or she might receive a soul from God. They often suppose that the Catholic Church teaches that destroying human embryos is unacceptable because such embryos are persons (or are "ensouled"). While it is true that the Church teaches that the intentional and direct destruction of human embryos is always immoral, it would be incorrect to conclude that the Church teaches that zygotes (a single-cell embryo) or other early-stage

embryos are persons, or that they already have immortal, rational souls. The magisterium of the Church has never definitively stated when the ensoulment of the human embryo takes place. It remains an open question. The *Declaration on Procured Abortion* from the Congregation for the Doctrine of the Faith in 1974 phrases the matter with considerable precision:

> This declaration expressly leaves aside the question of the moment when the spiritual soul is infused. There is not a unanimous tradition on this point and authors are as yet in disagreement. For some it dates from the first instant; for others it could not at least precede nidation [implantation in the uterus]. It is not within the competence of science to decide between these views, because the existence of an immortal soul is not a question in its field. It is a philosophical problem from which our moral affirmation remains independent. (Congregation for the Doctrine of the Faith, Declaration on Procured Abortion [November 18, 1974], note 19. See 4 Origins 385–392 [December 12, 1974] at 392.) (NCBC, March 2008)

However—and this is a big however—the Church teaches that we must always treat a human embryo *as if* it were already ensouled, although it might not yet be so. We must treat the embryo *as if* it were a person from the moment of conception. That it might not be so remains only *a theoretical possibility*, and the precise timing of ensoulment/personhood of the human embryo is irrelevant to the rightness or wrongness of destroying embryos for research or other purposes. When the embryo is destroyed, that particular individual in a stage of development has perished.

The precise timing of *when* God infuses the soul into the human embryo is a fascinating but speculative theological question, and the mystery to that question does not lessen the truth that "human embryos are inviolable and deserving of unconditional respect at every stage of their existence" (NCBC, March 2008). Many would argue that it would be an even greater evil to destroy an embryo that had not yet received an immortal soul than to destroy an ensouled embryo. Why?

> Because the immortal soul is the principle by which that person could come to an eternal destiny with God in heaven, so the

> one who destroyed the embryo, in this scenario, would preclude that young human from ever receiving an immortal soul (or becoming a person) and making his or her way to God. This would be the gravest of evils, as the stem cell researcher would forcibly derail the entire eternal design of God over that unique and unrepeatable person, via an action that would be, in some sense, worse than murder. The human person, then, even in his or her most incipient form as an embryonic human being, must always be safeguarded in an absolute and unconditional way, and speculation about the timing of personhood cannot alter this fundamental truth. (NCBC, March 2008)

In conclusion, while science is a gift from God and can be used in many ways for the good of humanity, it must always serve the sacredness of human life and the conjugal act so as not to destroy life or the source of life and love. The Church will continuously defend the sacredness of all human life, from the moment of conception to natural death, and speak out against immoral practices in science and technology devoid of ethical guidelines. Catholics and all Christians should fight vigorously to bring the light of Christ into the area of fertility and biomedical research. We are all called to be the heralds of the culture of life in a world that increasingly embraces the culture of death.

Chapter 27

Prayer: Uniting Our Hearts with God

Reading the Catechism: Paragraphs 2558–2758

> For me, prayer is a surge of the heart; it is a simple look turned toward heaven, it is a cry of recognition and of love, embracing both trial and joy.
>
> —Saint Thérèse of Lisieux
> *Manuscrits autobiographiques*, C 25r.

Prayer is essential to faith and a natural extension of our faith. Through faith we submit our intellects and wills to God, while through prayer we lift up our hearts to Him. Through faith and prayer we offer our entire selves to Him. Our prayer may be through memorized words or spontaneous words, through song, or through silently raising our thoughts to Him. There are countless ways through different words and expressions to lift our heart and mind to Him. Through prayer our hearts our united to the heart of God.

What Is Prayer?

Prayer Is both a Human Act and an Act of God

Prayer is an expression of man's search for God. Our hearts were created to be one with Him, and they thirst for communion with Him. As Saint Augustine prays, "Our hearts will not rest until they rest in you." Prayer is also a fundamental and necessary response to the salvation offered by God through Christ. It opens our hearts to the grace and life that God desires to communicate to us. In prayer we surrender ourselves in love to the all-consuming love of our Creator, offering Him all of ourselves, our joys, sufferings, strengths, and weaknesses. It is the fulfillment of the deepest human longing—communion with the Almighty.

Prayer is also an act of God; it is the grace and gift of the Holy Spirit welling up within us. We cannot pray without the Holy Spirit, for it is He who prays in and with us. He is the source and initiator. We come to God in prayer because He calls and beckons us to Him. Our prayer is the "response of love to the thirst of the only Son of God" (CCC 2561). It is most profoundly through prayer that we experience the expression of the new and everlasting union between God and man. It is through prayer that the union of the hearts of man and the heart of God is expressed and realized.

Prayer as Covenant and Communion

Prayer is the gift of our hearts and very selves to God. When we speak of our "hearts" we speak of the deepest part of ourselves, the place where we encounter the sacred and true. It is the place where we experience communion with another. In order to give ourselves to God we must enter our hearts, the inner sanctuary of our very beings. We cannot give a true gift of ourselves unless we first possess ourselves, know ourselves, and ponder the deepest meanings of life and love. The only place in the whole universe that we can have a relationship with God is in our hearts.

Prayer very simply is the union of our hearts with God's heart. It can be expressed in many ways but it must be of the heart, a true giving of ourselves. He wants all that we have and all that we are, good and bad, so that in return He can give a complete gift of self to us. It is like a marriage, a covenant in which God and man give the mutual gift of self.

Prayer can be remarkably simple, and many of us make it much more difficult than it needs to be. As the true doctor of prayer, Saint Thérèse of Lisieux explains, "For me, prayer is a surge of the heart; it is a simple look turned toward heaven, it is a cry of recognition and of love, embracing both trial and joy." It is not how long, or how eloquent, or how powerful the words or expression of prayer are, as long as we pray from our hearts and with love. "If our heart is far from God, the words of prayer are in vain" (CCC 2562).

A problem with prayer in our culture today is that we are a people who find it difficult to enter our hearts, that deepest place of love and relationship within ourselves. We are constantly distracted and stimulated by media and business to such an extent that many of us do not ponder in our hearts the deepest meanings of life and love. This cultural climate makes it difficult to enter into and give our hearts in a human relationship, or more particularly a relationship with God. One of the challenges of being Catholic today is to resist the continual distractions of our society and be people of the heart, people of contemplation, so that we may have a deep and prayerful relationship with God.

The Different Types of Prayer

There are many different types and forms of prayer. It can be expressed through words, thoughts, and actions. It can be memorized or spontaneous. It can express a wide variety of emotions: joy, fear, anger, sadness, or anxiety. The Book of Psalms in the Old Testament is a remarkable collection of prayers that encompasses many emotions and situations. Prayer is lifting up to God our very lives and should reflect the many facets of our daily lives.

Prayer can be categorized into five basic types, but these are not exhaustive. They are, however, the most common types we encounter in the liturgy and forms that we express during our daily lives.

Blessing and Adoration

We bless God for having blessed us with His gifts, and we accept His gifts of grace and love. We give Him adoration when we exalt the greatness of the Lord and realize that we are creatures before Him. God deserves our blessing and adoration because of who He is and what He has done for us.

Prayer of Petition

We ask God for our daily needs according to His will. This is probably the most common type of prayer we pray. While we always have needs and we trust that He will take care of us, we must always be willing to surrender to His will. He knows what is best for us even if it is far different than how we see things. Prayers of petition also include prayers of reconciliation, in which we ask forgiveness when we fall into sin.

Prayer of Intercession

We participate in Christ's intercession before the Father when we pray and intercede for others' needs. A prayer of **intercession** is one of the most powerful forms of prayer. God is particularly moved when He sees someone praying for another out of love, and He powerfully showers His grace upon the one in need. He desires that we love one another and pray for each other. The intercessory prayers of the saints in heaven are particularly powerful because their prayer is perfect and God is especially moved by these holy souls.

Prayer of Thanksgiving

We should always be people of thanksgiving before the Father. The word *Eucharist* means giving thanks. We thank God continuously for His salvation and mercy. While we ask Him for our needs we must remember to thank Him for everything, for every gift and blessing comes from Him. Our entire lives should be lived constantly thanking Him for His gifts of life and redemption (see CCC 2637–2638).

Prayer of Praise

Praise "lauds God for his own sake and gives him glory, quite beyond what he does, but simply because HE IS" (CCC 2639). Prayers of praise simply tell Him how awesome He is. Praising God is a good way to start prayer, for it opens our hearts to His glory and presence. The *Gloria* in the Mass is a prayer of praise that opens our hearts and minds to receive the mysteries God desires to reveal to us.

Expressions of Prayer

As we have said, prayer can be expressed in many different ways. In the Christian Tradition, there are three basic expressions of prayer that are to lead us to communion with God and unfold the mysteries of His life.

Vocal Prayer

Vocal prayer is the expression of prayer most of us are familiar with and is the most common. It is simply the articulation of the interior prayer that is already welling up from our hearts. Even mental prayer when expressed through our unspoken words is a form of vocal prayer. It should always be an expression of what is in our hearts; it is never just a spoken set of words. "Whether our prayer is heard depends not on the number of words, but on the fervor of our souls" (CCC 2700). Through vocal prayer we are called to pray with our whole being. It leads to meditative and contemplative prayer.

Meditation

Meditation is a quest for understanding the mysteries of God and for communion with Him. It begins with silent or vocal prayer (often with the help of our imagination) and leads us to truth and to the source of truth, God Himself. Through meditation "the mind seeks to understand the why and how of the Christian life, in order to adhere and respond to what the Lord is asking" (CCC 2705). It deepens vocal prayer, lifting the mind and the heart to God to more deeply know and understand His ways and His plan of salvation. In the Catholic Tradition, the Rosary is a good example of meditation. The vocal recitation of the prayers enables one to ponder the mysteries of the life of Jesus. In the Rosary we imitate and pray with Mary, pondering the ways of the Lord and deepening our relationship with Christ.

Contemplation

Contemplation is the highest and most profound expression of prayer. Contemplative prayer is the complete abandonment of oneself to God, the true realization of the covenant of prayer, and the total unity of one's heart with God. It becomes a "fixed gaze" of love between God and His beloved. In contemplation one becomes so engrossed in prayer that they become completely united with the prayer of Christ and shares in His mystery. Contemplation is an intense time of prayer and is ultimately a gift of God. This high level of prayer and spirituality takes time and patience to develop and attain; however, it should be what all of us strive to achieve in our spiritual lives.

The Battle of Prayer

We will face many difficulties in prayer: distraction, temptation, laziness, and loneliness. However, we cannot become discouraged. Prayer is a relationship with another Person, Jesus, and like all relationships it will have great times and not so great times. We are to persevere in prayer with humility and trust. Remember, it is not so much how high you jump, but how far you walk.

Pray Always

A person can pray anytime, anywhere. You can pray while driving in the car, walking down the street, or cooking dinner. Don't fall into the perfect time, perfect place syndrome. You do not have to wait until everything is done, or until you are in a quiet place, or at the church. If we wait for the "perfect" situation, prayer will rarely happen in our busy lives.

It is not just the words, but it's the union of our hearts with God that is important. A sincere ten-second prayer said with all our heart is much more pleasing to Him than twenty minutes of "prayer" that is just lip service. Keep in mind Saint John Chrysostom's exhortation, "It is possible to offer fervent prayer even while walking in public or strolling alone, or seated in your shop, . . . while buying or selling, . . . or even while cooking" (Ecloga de oratione 2: PG 63, 585).

Are You Listening?

God always answers our prayers; it is not always yes or in the way we want or expect. He knows what is best for us, and His ways are not always our ways. When it appears to us that God is not answering, it may just be a different answer than we expect! When we are seeking the will of God, it is important to keep in mind that nothing in our lives happens without some meaning or purpose that in His providence is best for us. He can always bring good out of evil; look how the horrible fall of Adam and Eve gained us such a great Redeemer! The difficult task is to have faith and trust that God does have a plan, and to trust in His plan even through disappointment and suffering. That is all the more reason we need to go to Him in prayer and surrender ourselves to Him in trust.

Prayer Is a Vital Necessity

Prayer is a vital necessity. How can we have a healthy relationship with God if we do not have communion with Him in prayer? The more we pray, the more we are in communion with Him and share in His life. The more we pray, the harder it is to sin. When we pray, He showers us with grace, and the closer our hearts are to Him the more loyal, faithful, and in love with Him we will be. When prayer is dry or difficult, we are to open our hearts wider, and God will make us stronger and more faithful to Him.

Nothing is equal to prayer; for what is impossible it makes possible, what is difficult, easy. . . . For it is impossible, utterly impossible, for the man who prays eagerly and invokes God ceaselessly ever to sin. (St. John Chrysostom, *De Anna* 4, 5: PG 54, 666)

From the Catechism: Key Words to Know

PRAYER: The elevation of the mind and heart to God in praise of His glory; a petition made to God for some desired good, or in thanksgiving for a good received, or in intercession for others before God. Through prayer the Christian experiences a communion with God through Christ in the Church (2559–2565).

INTERCESSION: A form of prayer of petition on behalf of others. The prayer of intercession leads us to pray as Christ, our unique Intercessor, prayed (2634).

MEDITATION: An exercise and a form of prayer in which we try to understand God's revelation of the truths of faith and the purpose of the Christian life, and how it should be lived, in order to adhere and respond to what the Lord is asking (2705).

CONTEMPLATION: A form of wordless prayer in which mind and heart focus on God's greatness and goodness in effective, loving adoration; to look on Jesus and the mysteries of His life with faith and love (2628, 2715).

Chapter 28

The Role of the Laity in the Church and the World

Reading the Catechism: Paragraphs 897–913

> But the Lord wishes to spread his kingdom also by means of the laity, namely, a kingdom of truth and life, a kingdom of holiness and grace, a kingdom of justice, love and peace.
>
> —Second Vatican Council, Dogmatic Constitution on the Church, *Lumen gentium*, no. 36

One of the greatest contributions of the Second Vatican Council was the development of and emphasis on the role of the **laity** in the **mission of the Church**. Pope John XXIII and the council fathers envisioned an enormous opportunity for the enrichment of faith for all Church members. In the wake of a pervasive clericalism that had infected the Church for many years, the council brought to the forefront the importance of the laity and their share, by virtue of their baptism, in the threefold mission of Christ as priest, prophet, and king. The Council fathers stressed that Christ commissioned the laity to be His witnesses to the ends of the earth and in the most ordinary places and circumstances of the secular world. For the new evangelization of the third millennium, envisioned by Vatican II and Pope John Paul II, to truly take hold and set the world on fire, lay Catholics must have a deep understanding of their identity and mission in the Church.

In this chapter we will take a closer look at the role of the laity in the Church and their sharing in the priestly, prophetic, and kingly office of Christ. We will see this articulated especially by the teachings of Vatican II and Pope John Paul II.

Who Are the Laity?

The laity are the lay members of Christ's faithful people baptized in the Church who are not ordained through the Sacrament of Holy Orders and have not taken religious vows as a nun or brother. The laity make up a vast percentage of the Church's members and serve an important role in her life and mission. Like the entire People of God, through their baptism the lay members are given a share in the triple mission of Christ as priest, prophet, and king. They are called by Christ to be His witnesses and instruments in the world. The role of the laity is of such importance in the mission of the Church that Vatican II devoted an entire chapter to it in the Dogmatic Constitution on the Church, *Lumen gentium.*

What does the Church mean by "laity"?

> The term laity is here understood to mean all the faithful except those in holy orders and those in the state of religious life specially approved by the Church. These faithful are by baptism made one body with Christ and are constituted among the People of God; they are in their own way made sharers in the priestly, prophetical, and kingly functions of Christ; and they carry out for their own part the mission of the whole Christian people in the Church and in the world. (*Lumen gentium*, no. 31)

Because the laity live and work in the ordinary places and circumstances of the world, their role is of particular importance in the life and mission of the Church. They have the ability to bring the witness of the Good News of Christ to every corner of the world. Through their holiness and apostolate they act like a leaven within the very fabric of society. They have the ability to immerse the culture and various aspects of social and community life in the richness of the truth of Christ. Vatican II states:

> But the laity, by their very vocation, seek the kingdom of God by engaging in temporal affairs and by ordering them according to the plan of God. They live in the world, that is, in each and in all of the secular professions and occupations. They live in the ordinary circumstances of family and social life, from

> which the very web of their existence is woven. They are called there by God that by exercising their proper function and led by the spirit of the Gospel they may work for the sanctification of the world from within as a leaven. In this way they may make Christ known to others, especially by the testimony of a life resplendent in faith, hope and charity. Therefore, since they are tightly bound up in all types of temporal affairs it is their special task to order and to throw light upon these affairs in such a way that they may come into being and then continually increase according to Christ to the praise of the Creator and the Redeemer. (*Lumen gentium,* no. 31)

Thus, the role of the laity in building up the kingdom of God is an indispensable and crucial one, if the mission of the Church in bringing about the sanctification of the world is to be effective. There is a well-known story of a conversation between Pope John Paul II and a group of American bishops that so perfectly illustrates the importance of the laity. The bishops were meeting with the pope and telling him the many concerns they had about the cultural and moral decline in the United States. After patiently listening to the bishops, the pope paused for a moment and then asked them, "Are not the Catholics the largest religious denomination in the United Sates?" "Yes, Holy Father," the bishops replied. The pope then said, "Then why are not the Catholics setting the example and being more of an influence on the culture?" The pope was reiterating to the bishops the importance of the role of the laity in influencing and making incarnate the Gospel of Christ within the culture.

No matter what the pope, the bishops, or the parish priests do, the stark reality is that they are not going to reach the ordinary places of the world without the help of the laity. The laity are to be witnesses and instruments of Christ in the workplace, schools, soccer games, grocery stores, and especially in the family. We must be the leaven, which gives rise to a culture that is truly a reflection of the truth and saving power of Christ.

The Laity Receive the Triple Mission of Christ as Priest, Prophet, and King

Lumen gentium teaches that the laity receive the triple mission of Christ as priest, prophet, and king and are commissioned by Him to be His witnesses to the ends of the earth. This threefold mission is received at Baptism, strengthened and completed by the power of the Holy Spirit at Confirmation, and sustained and brought to fruition through the frequent reception of the Eucharist. These Sacraments of Initiation serve as a fountain of power, strength, and grace, enabling the laity to go forth to confirm and nourish the mission of building and promoting the kingdom of God in the world, carrying out in their lives the priestly, prophetic, and kingly functions of Christ.

The Priesthood of the Laity: A Living Sacrifice Pleasing to God

In chapter two of *Lumen gentium* (On the People of God), the council fathers develop this threefold mission of the faithful, beginning with priesthood. By virtue of their baptism, all members of the Church share in the priesthood of Christ:

> The baptized, by regeneration and the anointing of the Holy Spirit, are consecrated as a spiritual house and a holy priesthood, in order that through all these works which are those of the Christian man they may offer spiritual sacrifices and proclaim the power of Him who has called them out of darkness into His marvelous light. (*Lumen gentium,* no. 10)

The nature of the priesthood is to offer sacrifice to God. Therefore, as priests, the faithful are to offer "spiritual sacrifices" to Him. As sharers in the priestly office of Christ, the laity are called to offer their very selves to God, holy and pleasing in His sight. This priestly attitude of offering of self penetrates the whole of the Christian life, for it is in the very nature of man as created in the image and likeness of God to give a gift of self.

Mankind was created to know, love, and serve God. Man's very vocation is love of God and love of neighbor. This vocation of self-giving love is so central to the nature of man that the council's Dogmatic Constitution on the Church in the Modern World, *Gaudium et spes,* declares that "man can fully discover his true self only in a sincere giving of self" (24). Therefore, this priestly attitude is at the heart of Christian spirituality and the role of the laity. In the teaching of Vatican II and the pontificate of Pope John Paul II, the priestly mission of the faithful is enormously emphasized:

> The Conciliar teaching, which lays so much emphasis on this attitude, also shows its proper place in the inner life of every

> Christian and the life of every Christian community, in which the wealth of faith must be sought and developed. It can in a sense be said that the doctrine concerning Christ's priesthood and man's share in it is at the very center of the teaching of Vatican II and contains in a certain manner all that the Council wished to say about the Church, mankind, and the world. (Karol Wojtyla, before he was Pope John Paul II, *Sources of Renewal: The Implementation of Vatican II*, p. 225)

Through the priesthood of all the faithful the essence and foundation of faith is found. In *Dei Verbum,* the council fathers quote the Dogmatic Constitution on the Catholic Faith, which was drafted at the First Vatican Council:

> "The obedience of faith" (Rom. 16:26; see 1:5; 2 Cor. 10:5–6) "is to be given to God who reveals, an obedience by which man commits his whole self freely to God, offering the full submission of intellect and will to God who reveals," (First Vatican Council, Dogmatic Constitution on the Catholic Faith, Chap. 3) and freely assenting to the truth revealed by Him. (*Dei Verbum,* no. 5)

We respond to the revelation of God through the "obedience of faith." The nature of faith is to *offer up* our intellect and will to God. The "act of faith," the act of completely offering our intellect and will, is part of the office of priest shared through Christ by all the faithful. Therefore, this priestly attitude of offering of self is at the very source and center of the act of faith itself.

This attitude is particularly evident in our participation in the liturgy and the sacraments, which reaches its climax in the celebration of the Eucharist. The sacramental actions, especially participation in the liturgy, are a function of the priestly office of all the faithful. This is central to the teaching of the council:

> But the faithful, in virtue of their royal priesthood, join in the offering of the Eucharist. They likewise exercise that priesthood in receiving the sacraments, in prayer and thanksgiving, in the witness of a holy life, and by self-denial and active charity. (*Lumen gentium,* no. 10)

The council's emphasis on participation in the liturgy is crucial, because it is through the celebration of the Eucharist in particular that the priesthood of all the faithful reaches its spiritual climax. The Eucharistic sacrifice is not something the faithful simply witness and receive. As sharers in the royal priesthood of Christ, all the faithful offer themselves as a sacrifice to God *with Jesus* present in the Eucharist. This involves the same emptying of self, the complete and total abandonment to the Father as Christ exemplified on the Cross. Thus, the full meaning of the celebration of the Eucharist is seen only in the priestly attitude and participation of the lay faithful.

> By offering the Immaculate Victim, not only through the hands of the priest, but also with him, they should learn also to offer themselves; through Christ the Mediator, they should be drawn day by day into ever more perfect union with God and with each other, so that finally God may be all in all. (*Sacrosanctum concilium*, no. 48)

Lumen gentium develops another important aspect of the priesthood of the laity. There is an intimate link between priesthood and holiness. The laity exercise their priesthood "in the witness of a holy life, and by self-denial and active charity" (*Lumen gentium,* no. 10). This is another important teaching of the council that was often echoed by Pope John Paul II. As priests, Christians are called to holiness through offering of self to God through Christ. Christ, the Eternal High Priest, offered and emptied Himself on the Cross out of love for sinful man and brought about the salvation of the world. Through their sharing in this same priesthood, the lay faithful are called to share in this same salvific ministry with Him:

> The lay faithful are sharers in the priestly mission for which Jesus offered himself on the cross and continues to be offered in the celebration of the Eucharist for the glory of God and the salvation of humanity. Incorporated in Jesus Christ, the baptized are united to him and to his sacrifice in the offering they make of themselves and their daily activities. (*Christifideles laici,* no. 14)

Even the daily activities of every Christian become a means of the sanctification of the world. This is central to Christian spirituality, for all areas of human life and human existence become a means to holiness:

> For all their works, prayers and apostolic endeavors, their ordinary married and family life, their daily occupations, their physical and mental relaxation, if carried out in the Spirit, and even the hardships of life, if patiently borne-all these become spiritual sacrifices acceptable to God through Jesus Christ. (*Lumen gentium,* no. 34)

Thus, the priesthood of the laity encompasses all areas of human life and existence. It penetrates and impregnates with meaning every aspect of human existence when offered to the Father through Christ.

The Prophetic Mission of the Laity: Witnesses to the Ends of the Earth

Christ, the Great Prophet, came to reveal to the entire world the truth about God and man. Through their baptism the lay faithful share in His prophetic office. This office is closely linked to the office of priesthood. While priesthood involves a sacrifice of self in order to grow in holiness and charity, the prophetic office enjoins to priesthood a notion of mission and responsibility. As priests, the faithful offer their intellect and will to all that God reveals; as prophets, they bear testimony to that truth. All the faithful receive the responsibility of proclaiming the Word of God through word and deed:

> The holy people of God shares also in Christ's prophetic office; it spreads abroad a living witness to Him, especially by means of a life of faith and charity and by offering to God a sacrifice of praise, the tribute of lips which give praise to His name. (*Lumen gentium,* no. 12)

By virtue of the prophetic office of Christ shared by all the faithful, Christian spirituality involves witness. It is the responsibility and duty of all Christians, not only the members of the hierarchy and religious but also the lay faithful engaged in the daily activities of the world, to give testimony to the truth about Christ through charity and holiness of life. This witness involves responsibility for the truth as revealed by Christ. Karol Wojtyla (later Pope

John Paul II) explains that the prophetic office first requires responsibility for the Word of God:

> First and foremost here comes responsibility towards the word of God entrusted to the Church. The council too emphasizes this attitude above all. A prophet is one who speaks in the name of the Lord, who knows the truth contained in the word of God; he bears it in himself, imparts it to others and guards it as his dearest heritage. (*Sources of Renewal: The Implementation of Vatican II*, p. 244)

Before the Christian can bear testimony to the truth, he must first know and "bear it in himself." As prophets, the People of God are to testify to the entire world the truth about God *by means of their holiness and the proclamation of the Gospel.* Thus, what we have received as priests is shared and witnessed as prophets. The prophetic office involves an attitude of mission—a mission of responsibility and evangelization that cannot be separated from the life and mission of the laity.

The responsibility for truth does not end in merely hearing and accepting it. The Word of God is to be proclaimed to the entire world through words and deeds. All must be ready to proclaim Christ at any time or in any circumstance. Pope John Paul II especially develops this missionary attitude in his teachings concerning the role of the laity:

> [The laity] are also called to allow the newness and the power of the gospel to shine out every day in their family and social life, as well as to express patiently and courageously in the contradictions of the present age their hope of future glory even "through the framework of their secular life." (*Christifideles laici,* no. 14)

The prophetic attitude is indispensable to the Christian life. This is especially seen when the witness of the Gospel becomes a sign of contradiction in the times or circumstances at hand. The sharing of the faithful in the prophetic office of Christ requires that the truth be proclaimed even through hardship. Like Christ, the Prophet who was rejected by men, the laity too must bear responsibility for the truth and be prepared to proclaim it boldly, even in the midst of hardship or persecution. The secular world is in need of modern day prophets to proclaim the truth of Christ in a culture that has become increasingly anti-religion and skeptical toward religious truth. Today, more than ever, the laity need to witness this truth through their daily faithfulness to the Gospel, in their attitude and actions, and when necessary by their words.

The Kingly Mission of the Laity: Conquering through Conversion and Love

The laity also share in the kingly office of Christ. Through sharing in this kingly office the Christian comes to know true freedom from sin. The laity are to "reign" over themselves and over sin in order to experience the kingdom of Christ in their own lives. Vatican II states:

> Christ, becoming obedient even unto death and because of this exalted by the Father, entered into the glory of His kingdom. To Him all things are made subject until He subjects Himself and all created things to the Father that God may be all in all. Now Christ has communicated this royal power to His disciples that they might be constituted in royal freedom and that by true penance and a holy life they might conquer the reign of sin in themselves. (*Lumen gentium,* no. 36)

Through Baptism man shares in this kingly office and through it experiences conversion, turning away from sin and toward God so that the splendor of the truth of Christ may shine brightly through him.

This reigning over self and sin is proper to man as created in the image and likeness of God. In a sense, it is similar to the command of God to "fill the earth and subdue it" (Gen. 1:28). Reigning over the earth does not simply mean a temporal or material rule, but more importantly a moral one. For Christ, the New Adam, overcame the disobedience of Adam through perfect obedience to the Father, even unto death. The People of God are called to this same kingly rule over sin, and by doing so they come to know their true dignity and purpose. Pope John Paul II explains that we share in this royal office (*munus regale*) of Christ:

> Every Christian who conquers sin by imitating Christ achieves royal self-dominion that is proper to human beings; by doing so,

> he shares in the *munus regale* of Christ and helps to bring about Christ's kingdom. (*Sources of Renewal: The Implementation of Vatican II*, p. 263)

This reigning over sin is conversion, turning away from and conquering sin, and turning toward Christ who conquered sin and death on the Cross.

For Pope John Paul II, the Sacrament of Penance expresses in a special way the sharing in the kingly office of Christ. For it is in confessing our sin that Christians are restored to their full dignity. Then, like Christ, we reign over sin and manifests his kingly dignity, his "royal freedom."

> When a man goes down on his knees in the confessional because he has sinned, at that very moment he adds to his own dignity as a man. No matter how heavily his sins weigh on his conscience, no matter how seriously they have diminished his dignity, the very act of turning again to God is a manifestation of the special dignity of man, his spiritual grandeur. (*Sign of Contradiction*, p. 142)

The sharing in the kingly office of Christ restores to man his true dignity as created in the image and likeness of God.

This kingly attitude not only applies to conversion, but also to the apostolic nature of Christian spirituality. As sharers in the kingly office of Christ, the laity are to spread the kingdom of God as Christ did. "The Son of Man did not come to be served but to serve" (Mt. 20:28). Christ the King came to serve those He encountered. He freed them from sin, healed them of blindness and leprosy, and taught them about the kingdom. The lay faithful, too, are to share in this kingly attitude of service. Vatican II especially emphasizes the role of the laity "in the world" in this kingly spirituality:

> But the Lord wishes to spread his kingdom also by means of the laity, namely, a kingdom of truth and life, a kingdom of holiness and grace, a kingdom of justice, love and peace. (*Lumen gentium,* no. 36)

Through participation in the kingly office of Christ, the laity are to establish the kingdom of God through humility and patience, by pursuing justice and peace, through holiness of life, and in service to their fellow man.

Do not be afraid! Open Wide the Doors to Christ!

The role of the laity in the life and mission of the Church is one that is powerful and indispensable. Each and every lay person has been called by Christ to continue His mission as priest, prophet, and king. The new evangelization envisioned by Vatican II, Pope John Paul II, Pope Benedict XVI, and Pope Francis rests largely in the faith and witness of the laity. Now more than ever is the time to be courageous Catholics who proclaim through our lives the truth of Christ. As we go forth as the witnesses of Christ, may we be strengthened and emboldened by the great and powerful words of our great, late Pope John Paul II, "Do not be afraid, open wide the doors to Christ!"

From the Catechism: Key Words to Know

LAITY: Having been incorporated into Christ through Baptism, the faithful are made part of the People of God, the Church. The laity participate in their own way in the priestly, prophetic, and kingly functions of Christ. Laity are distinguished from clergy (who have received Holy Orders) and those in consecrated life (897).

MISSION OF THE CHURCH: The Church is missionary by its very nature, continuing the mission or work of Christ through the Holy Spirit, according to the plan of God. This apostolic mission of the Church is fulfilled according to the different states of life of the clergy, laity, and religious (849, 863, 913). Missionary activity is sometimes given in a more specific sense as the work of initial evangelization and establishment of the Church in non-Christian lands.